THE SCIENCE OF THE SOUL

THE
SCIENCE
OF THE
SOUL

On Consciousness and the Structure of Reality

Geoffrey D. Falk

Blue Dolphin Publishing

Published by Blue Dolphin Publishing, Inc.
P.O. Box 8, Nevada City, CA 95959
Orders: 1-800-643-0765
Web: www.bluedolphinpublishing.com

ISBN: 1-57733-131-1

Library of Congress Cataloging-in-Publication Data

Falk, Geoffrey D., 1966-
    The science of the soul : on consciousness and the structure of reality /
Geoffrey D. Falk.
        p. cm.
Includes bibliographical references and index.
    ISBN 1-57733-131-1 (pbk. : alk. paper)
    1. Consciousness. 2. Reality. 3. Physics—Philosophy. 4. Religion and
science. I. Title.

    B105.C477F35 2003
    191—dc22

                                                        2003024011

Printed in the United States of America

10   9   8   7   6   5   4   3   2   1

CONTENTS

	Introduction	vii
I	As Above, So Below	1
II	The Consciousness of Light	5
III	The Essence of Creation	10
IV	On Good and Evil	36
V	Freedom of Choice	45
VI	On the Nature of Om	49
VII	Holograms	64
VIII	Psychology and Motivations	77
IX	Symbolism and Structure in Mythology	102
X	Chaos, Light and Manifestation	170
XI	Wholeness and Fragmentation — I	183
XII	Wholeness and Fragmentation — II	206
XIII	Psychology and Transcendence	240
XIV	Summary	257
XV	Conclusions	267
	Bibliography	303
	Permissions	315
	Index	317

ACKNOWLEDGMENTS

I WOULD LIKE TO EXPRESS my sincere gratitude to Paul and Nancy Clemens at Blue Dolphin Publishing, for helping to make this publication dream a reality.

My heartfelt appreciation also goes out to James Fadiman and Huston Smith, for their valued words of support and encouragement.

INTRODUCTION

IT IS WELL KNOWN TO ALL who have undertaken a thorough investigation of the quantitative ideology underlying the practice of meditation as a means toward the attainment of expanded states of consciousness, that consciousness is the fundamental reality at the basis of all creation. The fact that the only difference between matter, energy and dualistic consciousness is in their respective rates of vibration has also been much emphasized.

Given, then, this nature of matter as a low rate of intelligent vibration or consciousness, and given also the validity of "As above, so below," we must find the behavior of consciousness reflected in the conduct of physical matter; the former qualities being ascertainable through meditation-born intuition or mystic insight, while the latter are measurable in the physicists' laboratories. However, the quantitative relations between the behavior of the physical world and the characteristics of its constituent consciousness have rarely been elucidated. What I have attempted to provide in this book is a non-reductionistic model of the behavior of consciousness as the basic stuff of the cosmos, to explain as many aspects as possible of the expanded or mystical states of awareness; as well as a concomitant demonstration that the principles upon which the operation of the physical world is based occur as a necessary consequence of the characteristics of the inner realms of consciousness.

Such a non-reductionistic model will, therefore, not attempt to explain mystical experiences in terms of Pribram's holographic model of the brain's storage of memory, for example. It might, however, embody a higher universal or archetypal structure, of which physical holograms are merely a lower reflection on the plane of matter.

Further, since all individualized finite consciousness is only a subset of the Infinite Ocean of Consciousness which has become all waves of matter, any valid explanation of the basic nature and behavior of mind and consciousness (such behavior being essentially the domain of psychology) must include within its scope the root of all physics and philosophy. Physics, for all particles are simply waves of certain rates of vibration of the Ocean of Consciousness; and philosophy, since freedom of choice, the fundamental question of philosophy, is a function of consciousness, not of anything at a reductionistic atomic or molecular level (e.g., the Heisenberg Uncertainty Principle):

> Quantum physics has nothing to do with the free will problem. If there is such a problem, it is not furthered a whit by the latest development in physics.
>
> —Erwin Schrödinger

Thus, the model we are seeking will necessarily bridge the disciplines of psychology, physics and philosophy. This cannot be avoided, nor should it be: once we acknowledge that consciousness is the basic stuff that has become all mind and matter—this, however, not at all implying a naïve idealism in which "I create reality through my perception of it"—we cannot inexorably compartmentalize psychology, philosophy and physics as separate from one another. As with any symbolic model, however, it is crucial that one remember that the map-model is not the territory of reality, but is merely a mental representation of that territory: it is the "menu," not the "meal." The "territory" of reality-in-itself can be known only through the direct experience *of* consciousness *by* consciousness in intuition, not through any sensory experiences or concepts of the intellect.

August, 2003   Geoffrey D. Falk
Toronto, Ontario   www.geoffreyfalk.com

CHAPTER I

AS ABOVE, SO BELOW

The world is illusory; Brahman alone is real; Brahman is the world.
—Ramana Maharshi

WE ARE INDIVIDUALIZED WAVES of consciousness on the Infinite Ocean of Spirit; so say the sages. But, although the Ocean has become the wave, and the wave, when it dissolves the illusion of ego-separation and limitation, realizes that it has always been one with the Infinite Ocean, the form-bound wave itself is not the Ocean. Nor is the Ocean merely the sum of its waves—the Ocean can exist without the waves, but the waves cannot exist without the Ocean. Everything you can see, hear, smell, touch, taste, and much more, is part of this Ocean. For all matter, energy and consciousness is merely waves of certain rates of vibration on the surface of the Ocean of Consciousness; Spirit has become, and is present in and as, every created thing. That is, consciousness is the "water" of the Infinite Ocean of Spirit, and all phenomena arise as modifications of this one stuff, or ripples on/of this Ocean of cosmic consciousness.

> When the wave rises, it is the water; and when it falls, it is the same water again. Tell me, Sir, where is the distinction?
> Because it has been named as wave, shall it no longer be considered as water?
> —Kabir

1

Though difference be none, I am of Thee,
Not Thou, O Lord, of me;
For of the sea is verily the Wave,
Not of the Wave the Sea.

—Shankara

The intellectually understandable characteristics of this rippling Ocean of Consciousness are in some measure articulated in the teachings of great spiritual personages such as Jesus Christ, the Buddha, Krishna, etc. While the individual emphases of these sages have varied, they have all acknowledged, implicitly or explicitly, the metaphorical basis of universal design expressed in the aphorism "As above, so below." The implication of this aphorism—expounded in scriptures as old as the Upanishads—is that the microcosm reflects the macrocosm. Thus, atoms (in the view of classical physics, at least) are miniature solar systems. Likewise, the human body mirrors the structure of the cosmos (the "body" of God)—so that humankind is created "in the image of God"—etc. In the words of the Buddha, "Verily, I tell you, the world is within this six feet high body!"

Also, "As above, so below" correspondences generally take the form of metaphors—e.g., "creation is waves on the Infinite Ocean." And, as Gregory Bateson noted, "metaphor is the language of Nature": creation is built on "As above, so below." As an alternative expression of this principle, consider that archetypes are said to be the first forms to emerge from Spirit in the creation of the cosmos, upon which all subsequent creation is patterned. These archetypes determine the form of every structure on every level of creation, from high to low. The lower structures (including myths) are not themselves the archetypes, but rather reflect a higher universal basis.

It is in imitation of the angelic works of art that any work of art such as a garment or chariot is made here.

—the Rig Veda

That which is below is like that which is above, and that which is above is like that which is below for the performance of the miracles of the One Substance.

—Hermetic saying

The Gnostics, the Greek philosophers Pythagoras, Plato, Heraclitus and Anaximenes of Miletus, as well as the twelfth-century Sufis (the esoteric branch of the Islam religion), the medieval Jewish philosopher Maimonides and the pre-Christian Jewish philosopher Philo Judaeus all accepted the idea that the microcosm is similar in structure to the macrocosm.

It follows from the truth of the above Hermetic maxim that the behavioral characteristics of all phenomena, in the physical sciences and in all other theorizing endeavors, must ultimately be derivable from metaphysical principles. If we know the archetypal characteristics of the manifesting Source, it must always be possible to derive the characteristics of its differentiated, interdependent aspects. This is demonstrable even in the context of currently understood scientific principles. As we will discover, the markings of both the inner and outer worlds follow directly from the characteristics that Divine Consciousness must adopt in its process of differentiation. Thus, the principles upon which the spiritual science of meditation is based are identical with those upholding the existence of created Nature.

Consider, for example, the behavior of physical light, the representative or clearest expression of consciousness on the physical plane. Any particle and its associated anti-particle can be created from light of sufficiently high frequency, by a natural process known as pair production. (An anti-particle has the same mass as its particle counterpart, but the opposite sign of electric charge. The anti-particle of the electron, for example, is the positron.) Light may therefore be rightly said to contain both matter and anti-matter in potential. An integrated state is one in which the two apparently opposite members of a duality (e.g., matter and anti-matter) are seen to be merely different aspects of the same source (e.g., light). More generally, to "integrate" means "to bring together into a unified, harmonious, or interrelated whole or system." Matter and anti-matter are therefore differentiated or derivative ("broken up") states of the integrated state of physical light. This form-in-potential of matter and anti-matter is thus different from their form-in-actuality: photons, being pure energy, do not consist of distinct particles of matter and of anti-matter, travelling together; light *includes* but *transcends* the matter/anti-matter duality.

When dualistic states (of matter and anti-matter, for example) recombine (in pair annihilation), returning to their integrated state, the result is not *nothing,* but rather a release of the energy which had become both of the dualistic pair. That is, two photons are produced, which then move away from the point of annihilation at the velocity of light. The simultaneous, spatially coincident annihilation of many particle/anti-particle pairs would produce a burst of photons moving outward in all directions from the point of annihilation, or an expanding sphere of light. If the matter/anti-matter pairs are of all possible energies, the expanding sphere will contain all possible frequencies, and so will be white light. The coinstantaneous realization of the underlying integrated unity behind all apparent dualities similarly results in the expansion of consciousness into omnipresence as a sphere of white Light. This is a concept of supreme importance, which will be explored in greater detail in the coming chapters.

CHAPTER II

THE CONSCIOUSNESS
OF LIGHT

WHEN ASKED TO GIVE A DEFINITION OF RELATIVITY, Albert Einstein volunteered: "When a man talks to a pretty girl for an hour, it seems to him only a minute, but let him sit on a hot stove for only a minute and it is longer than an hour. That is relativity." That is, the psychological sensation of the passage of time is dependent on one's state of mind/consciousness; as is the perception of the passage of objective or external clock time relative to subjective time. The former ("pretty girl") phenomenon includes the feeling of time "flying," as it does when we are wholly engrossed in an activity, and may look up from our work to find that hours had passed in what seemed like minutes. The latter aforementioned (objective/subjective time) phenomenon is the "dilation of subjective time," and occurs in higher states of consciousness such as the dream state, where we experience a large number of subjective events in a short period of objective time. It differs from the "flying" of time in that here we would "look up" from this activity to find that minutes had passed in what seemed like hours (rather than hours passing in what seemed like minutes).

Special relativity is concerned with an analogous "pliable" nature of time at high velocities of motion, as well as with how the measurements of length (or space) and mass made by one observer, differ from measurements of the same properties made by a second observer in motion with respect to the first. Such characteristics of the physical world as this are indeed relevant to our inquiry into the nature and behavior of consciousness, owing to the fact that both consciousness and matter are molded by the same universal archetypes. Thus, we find the behavior of consciousness reflected in the behavior of physical matter— as in the phenomena of pair production and pair annihilation. Some of these parallels may be easily demonstrated, if we proceed by noting that the perceptions of an observer identified with an expanding sphere of physical light can be obtained if we regard that observer as moving simultaneously in all directions at the velocity of light.

Consider first the behavior of measured distances with regard to such an observer. The distance between two arbitrary objects, measured by an observer travelling in any one direction, is always less than that measured by someone at rest with respect to the objects, and this measured distance decreases the faster the observer in question is moving. At the velocity of light, this measured distance will be equal to zero regardless of the "actual" separation of the objects.

For an ordinary observer, moving only in a single direction in a straight line, this length contraction occurs only along that one direction of motion—measurements made in directions perpendicular to that motion are unaffected. For an observer identified with an expanding sphere of light, however, all directions radially outward from its center are both "along its direction of motion" *and* perpendicular to the radial motions of other appropriately-chosen elements on its surface. Thus, all of its measurements of space are both contracted to zero *and* unaffected by its motion. This will then produce the experience, for that observer, of a point (containing the entire universe) at the center of a sphere of light expanding to fill the universe. As we shall see later, there is a precise mystical analog to this predicted physical experience.

We are familiar also with the colloquial expression of the relativistic time contraction: "Moving clocks run slower." What this experimen- tally-confirmed observation reflects is the variation in the measured passage of time in different coordinate systems or reference frames, moving with respect to one another. If I am in motion with respect to a clock, I will observe it to be ticking slower than my wristwatch. If I regard my wristwatch time as subjective, and the external clock time as objective, I will find that the faster I am moving with respect to the clock, the more subjective time I will have for each moment of objective time. In the limit of the velocity of light, I will have an infinite amount of subjective time for each moment of objective time: objective time will "stop." Of further significance is the fact that, regardless of his or her velocity, time can never appear to flow backward to such an observer in relative motion.

A similar dilation of subjective time is evident in human psychology, in the fact that we again have much more subjective time for each moment of objective time in the dream-state than in our ordinary waking state of consciousness. That is, to the dreamer, dreams seem to last longer than they actually do as measured by a physical clock: a large number of dream-events can take place in a relatively short period of objective time. (This can be—and has been—easily observed, by simply comparing R.E.M. durations with the dreamer's account of the duration and number of events occurring in the dream. R.E.M. or rapid-eye-movement sleep corresponds to our dreaming periods, in which the body is limp but the eyes seem to be following some lively action.) John Brodie, for many years a proficient NFL quarterback, described the same dilation of subjective time in waking consciousness this way (in Michael Murphy's *The Future of the Body*):

> Time seems to slow way down, as if everyone were moving in slow motion. It seems I have all the time in the world to watch the receivers run their patterns, and yet I know the defensive line is coming at me as fast as ever.

Further, the highest (omnipresent) state of consciousness—what is called herein the Consciousness of Light—is said to involve the experience of an infinite amount of subjective time for each moment of objective time. Generalizing then, the higher one's state of consciousness, the more subjective time there is available for each moment of objective time.

In the Consciousness of Light, as at the velocity of light, objective time stops relative to subjective time (i.e., one has an infinite amount of subjective time for each moment of objective time). This correspondence between higher states of consciousness and increasing relative velocities suggests that higher relative velocities of motion, as described by special relativity, mirror the characteristics of higher states of consciousness. The velocity of light is the highest attainable velocity at which matter may travel; and light is the representative, or clearest reflection, of consciousness on the physical plane. Thus, we may again reasonably refer to the highest state of consciousness (i.e., omnipresence) as the "Consciousness of Light."

In terms of states of consciousness, it obviously matters which of those are higher and which are lower. In special relativity, by contrast, it does not matter which of two or more entities in relative motion one is regarding as being at rest. For there, either one will observe a subjective time dilation and space contraction with respect to the other. That incongruity, however, is just as well set aside when considering this "As above, so below" reflection. For we are certainly not proposing that higher relative velocities or the constancy of the velocity of light *are* higher states of consciousness. Rather, higher relative velocities simply reflect, in certain *limited* ways, the behaviors of higher states of consciousness. That not all of those behaviors would be embodied in any particular physical theory is to be expected. Having said that, however, two individuals in higher states of consciousness observing each other would each, from his/her own perspective, experience a subjective time dilation relative to the objective time in which the other individual seemed to exist—just as special relativity would lead us to expect.

When faced with the question, "How much do you weigh?" most of us tend to give an answer related to the mass of the physical body, indicative of attachment to and identification with the physical form. But this narrow sense of identification is fairly arbitrary. In the literal expansion of consciousness beyond the narrow boundaries of the body, one's effective "mass," or region of conscious identification, increases. That is, there is an increase in conscious "mass" in higher states of consciousness. Comparatively, in special relativity too, measured mass increases with higher relative velocities. Further, no material object can ever actually attain the velocity of light: to reach this velocity, the object's mass would have to become infinite.

> The consciousness of a perfected yogi is effortlessly identified not with a narrow body but with the universal structure. [Thus, his mass is "infinite."]
> —Paramahansa Yogananda, *Autobiography of a Yogi*

A human being is part of the whole, called by us "Universe"; a part limited in time and space. He experiences himself, his thoughts and feelings as something separated from the rest—a kind of optical delusion of his consciousness. This delusion is a kind of prison for us, restricting us to our personal desires and to affection for a few persons nearest us. Our task must be to free ourselves from this prison by widening our circle of compassion to embrace all living creatures and the whole of nature in its beauty.

—Albert Einstein

If Spirit has created (and continues to create) the universe, It must also actively sustain its operation, and ultimately (and continuously) destroy or dissolve it. For creation, preservation and destruction are indissolubly related in the Oriental philosophies, as in the Dance of Shiva. That is, the universe is not simply a collection of energetic particles created once "at the beginning of time" and then left to interact according to the laws of physics. Rather, Spirit as the Sole Universal Substance and highest state of consciousness, is actively involved in the ongoing sustenance of creation, and the upholding of its observed regularities or laws. Indeed, that Spirit, when It takes on limitations, becomes all lower states of consciousness, and all energy and matter.

Consequently, any metaphysically tenable theory regarding the ultimate nature of creation, while necessarily including the subjective time and mass dilations reflected in special relativity, must also involve the truth that if the Cosmic Creative Will were withdrawn from creation for even a moment, the created worlds would cease to exist. This is just as, when the illuminating light of a movie projector is removed, there can be no more projected pictures.

Further, once we acknowledge that Spirit has created, and continues to create, the unisphere, we cannot avoid asking: How? How is it possible for formless Spirit to bring into being, sustain, and destroy the material forms of creation? How can It be active in creation, and yet be transcendent, untouched by these created relativities? Thus....

The heavens and the earth ... by the [word of God] are kept in store.

—2 Peter 3:7

CHAPTER III

THE ESSENCE OF CREATION

IT IS A VERY WIDELY STATED TENET of experience-based religion that creation consists of "ripples on the surface of the Absolute," and that we are "individualized waves of consciousness on the Infinite Ocean." Anyone who is at all familiar with Eastern philosophy will have encountered these phrases before: this idea is not specific to the teachings of any one sage, but is rather common to many independent paths and sources.

Such metaphors are again the "language of Nature." And when the mystics speak in such metaphors, there is often a strong literal or structural (i.e., reflected archetypal) truth accompanying the comparison. If, for example, they speak of the "sphere of creation," chances are that the totality of vibratory creation (that is, the finite cosmos) is actually spherical in shape. We may therefore reasonably hope to gain some insight into the manners of manifesting consciousness through consideration of the behavior of waves on an ocean. That is, it is natural for us to ask *how the rippling motion on the surface of the Infinite Ocean of Spirit is initiated,* and to expect to find an answer or analog in terms of the behavior of ordinary water waves.

In the case of our everyday "below" experience, one way in which waves may be created on a calm lake is through the effect of a strong wind passing over the water. However, lacking immediate control over the wind, an easier way by which we may produce such waves is through throwing a stone into the calm water. This will produce expanding circular wavefronts—or, in three dimensions, rippling spheres—with their center at the point where the pebble entered the water. Most likely, both of these structures (that is, of "wind" and of "stones") play fundamental roles in the construction of the cosmos, as we shall see.

Accordingly, consider the possibility that "stones thrown by God into the Infinite Ocean" may provide the points of impetus by which spheres of consciousness, on the surface of the Ocean of Spirit, are introduced. Given the truth that Spirit, and consciousness united with Spirit, is infinite, such spheres of consciousness must have the *potential* to expand to infinity from each such center. However, each such sphere will actually expand to infinity only if it is free of all limitations; else its expansion can be only to a finite radius.

Further, "tuning in" to higher states of consciousness is said to expand one's consciousness. Thus, an essential characteristic of the behavior of consciousness must be that it expands to a greater radius, the higher the level of reality to which it is "tuned in." That is to say, since the individualized consciousness of each one of us is simply a finite region of the boundless Ocean of Consciousness, an "expansion of consciousness" will correspond to a literal increase in the volume of this encompassed territory.

Now, in order for Spirit to have become all of the frequencies or "colors" of vibration present in creation, It must contain all of these frequencies in potential. Given this, the most natural manifestation of Spirit as vibratory consciousness must be in a "white" form. That is, it must manifest as consciousness containing all possible frequencies of vibration, from zero to infinity, all of equal amplitude. The simplest way in which such an unbiased whiteness may become manifest is in the form of a signal which is infinite in amplitude at a single point in time, having zero amplitude at all other times. Such a signal—known as an impulse— implicitly contains all possible frequencies of vibration, all of equal amplitude.

The potential for the expansion to infinity, or the manifestation of omnipresence, is exactly the characteristic expected of a primordial expression of Spirit. Such a *rhythmically* applied white light would then be seen to consist of a succession of such impulses separated in objective time, each having the potential to expand momentarily to infinity in spheres of consciousness, were it not limited. All finite radii of spheres of consciousness are then derived from limitations placed on this rhyth-mically omnipresent white light, present in potential in the conscious-ness of each one of us. (Such "light" is to be taken, of course, not as indicating physically observable photons, but rather as referring to the waves in spheres of consciousness.) Thus, each one of us is potentially omnipresent in consciousness; it is only through our limiting the mani-festation of this Light through ourselves that we find ourselves to be finite.

The infinity of possible levels to which consciousness may be attuned may be said to form a continuous spectrum of states of con-sciousness or levels of reality. These will then have resonant or "tuning in" frequencies from near zero (at the lowest mineral level) to infinity in cosmic consciousness. In the normal electromagnetic spectrum, the colors of visible light display only a small part or narrow band of the spectrum, which stretches (theoretically) from zero to infinite frequency. That is, visible light is bounded below by the infrared, and above by ultraviolet radiation. Such infrared light, then, is lower in frequency than visible light, while ultraviolet is higher in frequency, with many still-higher frequency bands of x-rays, gamma rays, etc., existing above the ultraviolet. Comparably, human waking consciousness expresses only a very small part of the infinite spectrum of consciousness. Indeed, human consciousness is bounded below by animal consciousness, while above the human waking state are astral realms of energy, and ideational levels of rarefied thought.

Thus, higher states of consciousness must involve higher resonant frequencies of consciousness, or the tuning-in of one's consciousness-"radio" to receive and interact with higher frequency "stations" or levels of reality. The resonant frequency is effectively a measure of how "close" one is to the realization of Spirit, or to perfection in conscious-ness. We would again characterize cosmic consciousness (and its asso-ciated omnipresence and transcendence) or complete identity with Real-ity as being attained to when one's resonant frequency of consciousness has become infinite.

Any system—and we may consider the human body and its con-sciousness to be a "system"—is said to be a "bandpass-filtering" one if it characteristically "tunes in" to a narrow range of frequencies of vibration (centered around its resonant frequency), while "filtering out" higher and lower frequencies. The related "bandwidth," then, is a measure of how wide the range of frequencies one is "tuned in" to is. And the astral and causal levels of reality, and their corresponding bodies, are again composed of higher and subtler frequencies of vibration than the physical, and so involve a higher level of consciousness, or higher resonant frequency, in our being attuned to (i.e., working through) them. When our attention is engrossed in sensory experiences, we are working primarily through the physical body. In visualizing or willing, or in dreamful sleep, we are utilizing the astral body (composed of life energy and mind; the seat of our mental and emotional processes). Further, in diving deep in introspection, or in deep dreamless sleep, we are working through the causal body (composed of ideas and consciousness).

Again, there is a rhythmic white light, or potential for the expansion to infinity in omnipresence, present at the basis of the consciousness of each one of us. However, owing to our being tuned in to only finite levels of reality, we "filter" this impulsive potential omnipresence. Thus, as long as we remain in the deluded identification with body and mind—thinking ourselves to be limited by these in time and space, when in truth we are (potentially) omnipresent in consciousness—we are creatures of only finite consciousness.

When analyzed mathematically, the characteristics of such a "band-pass-filtered impulse" can be very quantitatively expressed. Without going into the actual mathematics of the situation, we may convey these characteristics through the following imagery. First, let us visualize our spheres of consciousness as collapsed spherical balloons. When an impulse of potential omnipresence is "blown into" such a sphere, this balloon inflates very quickly to a large radius, then deflates back to a point in just as short a time. It then immediately inflates quickly again to a slightly smaller maximum radius than before, and once again contracts back to a point. (It will take exactly the same amount of time to inflate and deflate this second time as was required for the first, even though the second inflation is to a smaller maximum radius.) This rhythmic inflation and deflation (or "bouncing") continues at a constant rate—with each successive inflation being to a smaller maximum radius than the previous—until the next impulse is applied, at which time the cycle starts over again.

Now, the higher the level or resonant frequency of one's consciousness, the larger the maximum radius of expansion in the first inflation will be, and the less time will be taken for the balloon to inflate and deflate each time. Thus, higher states of consciousness will expand to encompass more space—they will be, literally, "expanded" states of consciousness. They will also contract to a point more frequently: higher states will "bounce" more times in the interval between successive impulses, than will lower states. The "limit" or highest extension of this behavior would then be for such a balloon to expand to an infinite radius, and contract back to a point, all within a single point in time. This is exactly what happens to consciousness when its resonant frequency becomes infinite. Thus, such perfected consciousness, expressing fully the inherent divinity hidden in everything, is literally *omnipresent.*

There are additional ways of arriving at the idea that consciousness has its basis in rhythmic impulses. The stimulated human nervous system operates in terms of electrical pulses or "spikes" uniformly separated in time, the frequency of these spikes being dependent on the strength of the applied stimulus. This has been characterized as a "Morse code of action and rest" (Figure 3.1). The human anatomy is a microcosmic representation of the universe. Thus, if the human body and nervous system operate in terms of "spikes" or semi-impulses evenly separated in objective time, the cosmos should have a similar structure, on some level. For that cosmos is exactly the body and consciousness of God.

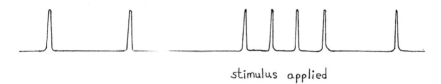

stimulus applied

Figure 3.1

Further, such a rhythmic series of impulses may be viewed as a Universal Breathing. In the mortal breathing process, the flow of *prana* (here, a specific subtle life current, or life energy, or life force, flowing in the astral body) in inhalation is held to have a spiritualizing effect on one's consciousness. The flow of an opposing *apana* current in exhalation is correspondingly identified as producing sensory awareness and restlessness. This alternating expansion and contraction (of one's lungs and one's consciousness) is then followed by a period of rest in which breath is neither inhaled nor exhaled. That is, an interval of temporary breathlessness. The corresponding period of rest in the Universal Breathing is, evidently, the period between successive impulses or Breaths applied to all spheres of consciousness. (The very word "spirit" derives from a Latin root meaning "to breathe.")

Spirit—and so mortal consciousness as a reflection of That—has both an immanent aspect in space and time, and a transcendent nature, "beyond" space and time; spaceless and timeless. We may say that we are bound by time and space whenever our consciousness is identified with the immanent aspect. Conversely, consciousness identified with the transcendent nature would not (so long as it remains in this identification) be constrained by relative time or space.

Now, there are symbolic (in some cases, explicit) indications in many of the world's scriptures that the ideal point is the "meeting ground between the manifest and the unmanifest." That is, the ideal point is the means of contact between immanent and transcendent God; the latter, by definition, being beyond time. (Transcendent God or Spirit is the unmanifested Absolute, which is ever-existent and ever-conscious, and in which the delusory material cosmos is non-existent.) The passage of one's sphere of consciousness through the individualized ideal point (of zero radius) at its center may thus be assumed to grant temporary contact with, or merging in, transcendent Spirit beyond relative time and space. Conversely, consciousness will be identified with the immanent, and time-bound, aspect of Spirit whenever the radius of its sphere is non-zero.

One corroboration of this view of the ideal point as being the "door" between transcendent God and immanent creation can be found in the Kabbalistic lore. For there, the symbol of the First Sephiroth, representing the unmanifested Absolute in its first step toward manifestation, is a point. Compare also A. K. Coomaraswamy:

> Moment without duration, point without extension—these are the ...
> Strait Way leading out of time into eternity, from death to immortality.

Consider also the following persuasive associations from Huston Smith's *Forgotten Truth:*

> The mathematical point is in everything. Kabbalists call it the Inward or Holy Palace; in Islam it is the Divine Station that combines contrasts

and antinomies. In China it is the Chung Yung, the Invariable Middle, the Taoist Void that unites the spokes and makes of them a wheel.

Likewise, in the symbolism of the cross, the horizontal and vertical lines, representing the finite and the Infinite, meet at a point.

Interestingly, in Roman mythology the two-faced god Janus is the patron of beginnings and endings, as well as the guardian of portals (i.e., gateways). Is this not reasonable, that the conditional beginnings and endings present everywhere within "two-faced" duality should be associated, both in mythology and in universal structure, with guardianship of, or the preventing of the passage through, a door between transcendent God and multifarious creation, the latter rooted always in polarities? For, as we shall see, it is only the varying-degreed inability of polarity-swayed consciousness to pass through the gateway between creation and transcendent Spirit that keeps it bound to beginnings and endings.

> Let us but transport ourselves in spirit outside this world of dimensions and localizations, and there will no longer be need to seek the abode of the Tao.
>
> —Chuang Tzu

The ideal point, of zero radius and no dimension, is the gateway out of the "world of dimensions." In passing through it, we have found the abode of the transcendent Tao. And, again according to Chuang Tzu, the viewpoint of the Simple Man, for whom contraries no longer exist,

> is one at which this and that, yes and no, appear still in a state of non-distinction. This **point** is the Pivot of the Law; it is the motionless center of a circumference on the rim of which all contingencies, distinctions and individualities revolve. From it only Infinity is to be seen, which is neither this nor that, nor yes nor no. To see all in the yet undifferentiated primordial unity, or from such a distance that all melts into one, this is true intelligence.

> The "this" is also "that." The "that" is also "this".... That the "that" and the "this" cease to be opposites is the very essence of Tao. Only this essence, an axis as it were, is the center of the circle responding to the endless changes.

In short, all opposites unify and dissolve in the ideal mathematical point. The problem, then, is this: how do we go about fitting our consciousness into such a point, and so attaining to identification with transcendent Spirit, beyond all dualities? And how to do this "more" in higher states of consciousness ... which are also expanded states. How can *expanding* a sphere/circle of consciousness result in it being more identified with the ideal point?

Higher states of consciousness expand to a greater maximum radius in response to each rhythmic impulse of potential omnipresence. They also exhibit a proportionately higher frequency of momentary point-contractions. This contraction of consciousness to a point is again equivalent to the temporary merging of consciousness in transcendent Spirit. Thus, the more one's consciousness is expanded, the more it transcends time and all other dualities, through its point-contractions. And, the state of infinite resonant frequency (i.e., the Consciousness of Light), "bouncing" at an infinite rate, is identified always with the transcendent "point without extension."

We may summarize the model developed thus far by invoking a motion picture analogy.

Movies are, of course, produced through the effect of a continuously shining bulb of white light, whose light is made "rhythmic" by placing a shutter between it and the film each time the film is advanced to its next frame. That is, white light is applied, at uniformly separated instants in time, to successive frames of a filtering film. Each small area of the frame in question then bandpass-filters the white light applied to it, according to that area's color or resonant frequency. That film thus allows only a limited range of the frequencies present in the underlying white light to become manifest through it.

> A cinema audience may look up and see that all screen images are appearing through the instrumentality of one imageless beam of light. The colorful universal drama is similarly issuing from the single white light of a Cosmic Source.
> —Paramahansa Yogananda, *Autobiography of a Yogi*

The potential impulse-movements of consciousness in the Infinite Ocean may thus be regarded as analogous to the rhythmic, shuttered, white light projector Beam, containing all possible frequencies of vibration. Frequency limitations placed on this light are the filtering film. The interval of rest following each Universal Breath is the "dark period" in between movie frames. And, the Ocean surface is the cinema screen, capable of reflecting within itself all possible colors or rates of conscious intelligent vibration.

We may further distinguish between a "Cosmic Projector" as the rhythmic, "shuttered," impulsive Light of consciousness, and its parent continuously shining Bulb. The Bulb (or Beam) is the state of continuous omnipresence which exists independent of, and prior to, vibratory manifestation. The Cosmic Projector—which is derived from the Bulb through its being "shuttered"—on the other hand, is the state of rhythmic potential omnipresence.

Regarding continuous omnipresence, we may note that, in responding to an input impulse, a system with a large bandwidth or range of frequencies that it can respond to will have its "bouncing" behavior decay rapidly toward a negligible amplitude. One with a narrow or focused bandwidth, however, will have a much more long-lived response. The limit of narrow or small bandwidth is zero—in which case the "bouncing" response will never decay at all. The limit of large bandwidth is infinity, producing an immediate and instantaneous decay to a zero amplitude of "bouncing."

Thus, a sphere of consciousness having infinite resonant frequency and infinite bandwidth will exactly follow the input rhythmic series of impulses in its instantaneous expansions and contractions, mirroring the Cosmic Projector. That is, it will be only momentarily omnipresent for each of those impulses, having zero radius (i.e., vibrating with infinite frequency but zero amplitude) at all other times. A sphere with infinite resonant frequency and any finite (not only zero) bandwidth, however, will still expand to infinity, but never decay in its amplitude of "bouncing." That is, it will vibrate with infinite amplitude and infinite frequency, thus being continuously omnipresent, as the Bulb/Beam.

Again, it is not only that the consciousness of sentient beings takes the form of regions of vibration in the Infinite Oceanic Consciousness of Spirit. Rather, the most basic mechanism of creation consists of fine created ripples on the Ocean surface, which add together or interact to produce all mind and matter, as lower and grosser rates of vibration than their underlying consciousness. The only difference between consciousness, mind and matter, is in their respective rates of vibration. Thus, mind is simply a subtler or finer vibration than is physical matter.

Accordingly, consider a number of waves meeting and interacting in a certain region of space. These waves may be produced by a wind blowing over the water, by stones thrown into it, or by any other means. In any of those cases, when the crests of one or more waves overlap, they will add to produce an even larger wave. Conversely, when the crest of one wave and the trough of another meet, they will cancel each other out, producing a region of temporary calm. If we producing these waves were very skilled, we could cause a number of such crests to meet to yield a localized disturbance or "island" (or condensed "iceberg"), surrounded by a region of calmness. We could, in short, create a "particle," or a differentiation of the continuum of the calm lake.

Given enough stones, and sufficient skill, we could bring into being and sustain the existence of many such particles simultaneously. And if we were, say, Supremely Intelligent, we could even cause the movements and interactions of these particles to appear to be governed by (e.g., Newton's) laws. But these laws, being of our own creation, could be circumscribed whenever we so chose. And, all particles would dissolve into serene unity if our will, in the form of stones tossed into the pond, were withdrawn. That is, this creation would have no existence independent of our guiding will.

This being the case, we can visualize the particles of the various levels of relative reality as arising from the interaction or addition of many colors or frequencies of ripples on the Ocean of Consciousness (again, whether such waves are produced by "stones" or by "wind"). These interacting wave-colors will produce an Ocean surface of constantly trembling excitation. Observable particles will then arise as regions of space in which the average disturbance of the Ocean surface is non-zero over a sufficiently long interval of time, this producing an apparent continuity in the existence of matter.

The waves issuing from these sources of vibration in the Ocean surface may thus be said to compose a universal interference pattern of light and shadow. That is, a pattern of ripples in consciousness, and calm, resulting from the destructive interference or cancellation of these waves. Or, non-zero-average particles, and the intervening zero-average "vacuum" state—the state of empty space in the absence of matter. This will produce matter as a "condensation," or lower rate (and larger amplitude) of vibration than/of consciousness: all matter is consciousness in various stages of evolution or spiritual unfoldment. The universe, again, is not merely a collection of moving objects, created once at the beginning of time by God or a big bang and then left to interact according to laws of physics. Rather, it is motion itself—indeed, motion of Spirit Itself—continuously sustained by the Cosmic Will.

Actually, the idea of particles being formed from a process analogous to "stones being tossed into a pond" can be found even in contemporary physics. Michael Talbot (in *Mysticism and the New Physics*) summarizes one view, in which

> the fabric of space-time or "superspace" is composed of a turbulent sea of bubbles. These bubbles are the warp and weft of empty space and comprise what [John] Wheeler calls the "quantum foam".... Various electromagnetic and gravitational forces can act on the quantum foam and set up vibrational patterns similar to the ripples created by a stone tossed into a still pond. It is these vibrational patterns or ripples in the quantum foam that we detect as subnuclear particles, both Wheeler and Sarfatti suggest. Some may be protons, others neutrons. The patterns interact to form atoms which interact to form molecules which interact to form the substance of the physical world.

Consider, now, Itzhak Bentov's injunctive portrait (from *A Cosmic Book*) of his own experiences in higher states of consciousness:

> Suppose you can expand your consciousness to encompass our sun. Once this is accomplished, keep inflating yourself until you contain many stars. Keep inflating yourself until you are encompassing our entire galaxy.... To do this properly, you have to feel your body as the Void, and the stars as pinpoints on your body. You can zero in on any star in your body and feel it, observe it, and love it.

Or the avowal of Lama Govinda (in his *Foundations of Tibetan Mysticism*) that

> to the enlightened man ... whose consciousness embraces the universe, to him the universe becomes his "body."

Self-evidently, the actual *experience* of "stars as pinpoints on your *r*" can arise only from the *literal* expansion of one's self-identity, not from any sensory experience. That is to say, it can come only from the expansion of one's consciousness to encompass the region in question. One would then be identified with the volume of space thus encompassed—a space inherently "filled with consciousness" as the water of the Infinite Ocean, even before the boundary of one's own consciousness has expanded to embrace it.

Alternatively, it is undeniable that our ordinary visual perceptions and visualizations are inherently two-dimensional. For the brain's superposition of the images from the left and right eyes, although producing a limited kind of depth in vision, does not allow us to see inside a solid object, for example. Thus, we cannot directly experience three-dimensional space merely through the two-dimensional mental objects of our visual sensory experience. Rather, the experience of one's consciousness being spread through space is of a different order (that is, literally, a higher dimension) than is sensory experience.

Note, then, that Bentov referred to the higher, subtly expandable aspect of ourselves as our "observers"—with these consisting of our astral and causal bodies. He actually showed this aspect graphically as consisting of overlapping, rippling *spheres* of vibratory information centered in each person's brain. He further proposed that those observers are expanding *even now* in response to the series of impulsive spikes driving them, but that this experience is registered only on the subconscious level. That is, his view was that, for the average person, no knowledge of this outing is communicated to the conscious mind and brain.

In any case, there can be no question that it is indeed possible for us to expand our region of conscious identification beyond the body to the solar system, galaxy and beyond. This voluminous identification, further, is realized only in high states of consciousness and interiorized attention, being no function of any sensory experiences of the two physical eyes. Such an expansion then "photographs" all vibrations, including those of other "observers," in a penetrating "flash" of contact, transcending linear thinking.

In Bentov's experiential view, further, intuition arises exactly from the effect of these interacting conscious "observers" or pulsating, expanded, overlapping, rippling subtle bodies of information of all living things, *from atoms to humans*. This interaction then gives us access, on

that rarefied level of pulsating consciousness, to the information contained in all similar rippling spheres overlapping with our own.

The amount of subjective time experienced for a given amount of
objective time increases as the level of consciousness is raised. Thus,
higher states of consciousness allow for a greater number (as judged
against our matter-identified standards) of mental images and therefore
experiences to be condensed into the same period of objective time. Such
objective time again passes the same for all states of consciousness.
However, we may propose that each successive inflation-deflation of
consciousness will allow for the experience of one element or fragment
of thought or visualization. That is, it allows for one frame in the
"subjective motion picture" seen by the transcendent, witnessing Self.
(Relative to this thought-less, memory-less, concept-less Self, the witnessed "World of Forms" of course contains the sensory impressions
arising from the normal external objects of our physical existence. But
that same World also contains the internal mental milieu of perceptions
and thoughts arising with or without those impressions, on all levels of
consciousness and mind.)

In this case, the increase in frequency of point-contractions as the
level of consciousness is raised will result in the expected proportional
dilation of subjective time in higher states of consciousness. Infinite
resonant frequency consciousness will then have an infinite amount of
subjective time per Universal Breath. That is, for such consciousness,
objective time will "stop" relative to subjective time.

Again, subjective time dilates in higher states of consciousness—
e.g., in the dream state, which is an altered state of consciousness in
which the dreamer is working primarily through his or her astral body.
However, we know also that "time flies when we're having fun." Such
"having fun" may involve concentration on bodily sensations, and so
relatively low states of consciousness. Time also flies, however, when
we are engaged in more elevated and subtle activities—in deep meditation, for example—so that this cannot be characteristic only of physical
states of consciousness. That is to say, we must again distinguish
between the "flying" of time and the dilation of subjective time in higher
states of consciousness, or actual progressive transcendence of relative
time and space. For in the former, we have not necessarily had an
increase in the rate of our conscious processes, or a raising of the level of

consciousness, but rather simply lack the psychological sensation of the passage of time.

Time tends to pass quickly, and we tend to breathe slower, whenever our attention is engrossed in intellectual or delicate physical pursuits. That is, our perception of "time flying" seems to be related more to depth and steadiness of attention than to specific state of consciousness. Indeed, whenever we concentrate deeply on an idea or activity, keeping the level of consciousness relatively constant and so calming the mind, time passes quickly. Thus, "clock-watching," by its very inattentive nature, will cause time to drag.

The company of Einstein's "pretty girl" will not, in general, raise one's level of consciousness, and so will produce no increase in subjective time. It will, however, in general favorably occupy one's attention, and so cause hours to pass like minutes. And, since we tend not to concentrate deeply on anything unpleasant, for obvious reasons, the placing of one's hand on a hot stove will cause minutes to pass like hours. And dreams, being the product, usually, of a restless mind, will again evidence a dilation of subjective time, but no corresponding temporal "flying."

This restlessness is also responsible for the arising of boredom when one's attention is not occupied by some form of entertainment. There is no activity that is intrinsically boring; it is only inattentiveness and unwillingness in the performance of our duties that causes time to drag. Indeed, experiments were done in the 1940s in which tuberculosis sufferers were placed in equalizing pressure chambers, enabling them to temporarily stop breathing. In the absence of the need for breath, the patients were able to rest comfortably for hours at a time without feeling the need to change position. Their minds were pacified as well, freed of worries, and none of the experimental subjects felt bored. ("Studies on muscle relaxation have shown that anxiety is not a feeling state produced by the psyche but a product of muscular tension. It is impossible to feel anxiety if your body is totally relaxed"—W. Brugh Joy, *Joy's Way.*) Yoga, in fact, explicitly states that there is a mathematical relationship between one's respiratory rate and the *variations* in one's state of consciousness.

One of Itzhak Bentov's primary suggestions, in his *Stalking the Wild Pendulum,* is that whenever any oscillating system—e.g., a pendulum —

reaches a point of maximum displacement, and so reverses its direction of motion, this momentary turnaround is accompanied by the consciousness underlying the oscillator expanding rapidly into space. That idea is, of course, very much in accord with the model we have developed herein. This correspondence should not be surprising, for Bentov considered that our consciousness is of a bandpass-filtering nature, and is "driven" by a rhythmic series of impulses. He also rightly recognized that higher resonant frequencies of consciousness carry a proportional dilation of subjective time, and allow one's balloon-like "observer" to expand to a greater radius in its response to this series of impulsive spikes, or positions of momentary reversal in the "direction of swing" of a Cosmic Pendulum:

> Frequency response may be described by the "agility" or speed with which a given system responds to a stimulus. We shall now take as the "stimulus" the very short period of time allowed us ... to expand into space and then to collapse back. The higher a person's level of consciousness, the higher his frequency response; the higher his frequency response, the farther away from his point of origin his [spherical] observer can penetrate ... he can expand into space with a higher velocity, and have more subjective time available for observation.

Further, Bentov's allowance that the highest state of consciousness, of infinite resonant frequency, is also omnipresent, carries with it the implication that the spikes driving the expansion of such a balloon of consciousness must themselves be infinite in amplitude. For, in order for such a balloon to be inflated to infinite radius in omnipresence, the signal driving it must likewise be infinite. However, he did not treat the bandpass-filtering nature of consciousness mathematically, and so did not note the "bouncing" of consciousness that must result whenever an impulse is bandpass-filtered by a system having a bandwidth less than double its resonant frequency. Nor did he connect this with the idea that the ideal point is the doorway between immanent creation and Spirit, so that a higher frequency of bouncing grants an increased transcendence of duality. Likewise, he did not make the association of impulses with true whiteness, or the equal presence of all possible rates of vibration. However, notwithstanding these significant additions, *if you accept Bentov's ideas, you cannot deny the filtered impulsive or motion picture-like character of consciousness.*

Again, the point-contractions of consciousness come only in proportion to the degree of expansion of that consciousness. That is, the more one's consciousness *expands,* the more it *contracts!* Now, any logician, when confronted with the assertion that "the more x expands, the more it contracts," would unhesitatingly dismiss such a statement as nonsense. But the universe is, to be sure, not based in nonsense: We would do well to not pass arrogant judgment too quickly on the seeming inequalities or illogicities of its clockwork mechanism. (There is good reason to say "clockwork": the Universal Breathing bears strong resemblance to, say, the rhythmic "ticking of a Cosmic Watch.")

Now, if Reality is infinite—and it is: for It to be finite would imply a dividing wall with an inside but no outside—and exists continuously (which it self-evidently must), full identification with It can come only from being continuously infinite in consciousness. That is, in the state of continuous omnipresence, wherein one's consciousness oscillates (i.e., inflates and deflates) with infinite amplitude and infinite frequency. Compare this state of omnipresent consciousness with St. Bonaventure's (and the ancient Greek Empedocles') characterization of the Divine as a "sphere, whose center is everywhere and whose circumference nowhere," and with the following direct perceptions:

> [The] all-pervasive ocean of existence ... seemed to be simultaneously unbounded, stretching out immeasurably in all directions, and yet no bigger than an infinitely small point. From this marvellous point the entire existence, of which my body and its surroundings were a part, poured out like radiation, as if a reflection as vast as my conception of the cosmos were thrown out upon infinity by a projector no bigger than a pinpoint, the entire intensely active and gigantic world picture dependent on the beams issuing from it.
>
> —Gopi Krishna,
> *Kundalini: The Evolutionary Energy in Man*

This microcosmic application of the idea of creation "pouring out" from a central point is symbolized in the cornucopia, for example, which is not so much a symbol of agricultural prosperity as it is an accurate emblem of metaphysics.

> I found myself spreading everywhere and identical with a kind of "Space" that embraced not merely the visible forms and worlds, but all modes and qualities of consciousness as well.... In one sense, I was, and

am, the primordial Self and co-terminus with an unlimited and abstract Space, while at the same time the subject-object and self-analyzing consciousness was a sort of point-presence within that Space. An illustration is afforded by thinking of the former as being of the nature of an original Light, in itself substantial, spreading throughout, but not derived from any center, while the latter is a point-centered and reflected light, such as that of a searchlight.

—Franklin Merrell-Wolff,
The Philosophy of Consciousness Without an Object

Note how this association of the "subject-object" or "self-analyzing consciousness" with a literal point seems to support our idea that the origin and dilation of subjective versus objective time would have to do with the same point. That is, with the "bouncing" of one's sphere of consciousness "chopping" the continuous awareness of the witnessing subject or Self up into discrete objective "frames." Compare also Sir John Woodroffe's statement (in *The Serpent Power*), on the basis of his study of tantra yoga, that "when Consciousness apprehends an object as different from Itself, It sees that object as extended in space. But when that object is completely subjectified, it is experienced as an unextended point."

My ordinary frontal vision was now changed to a vast spherical sight, simultaneously all-perceptive.... A swelling glory within me began to envelop towns, continents, the earth, solar and stellar systems, tenuous nebulae, and floating universes. The entire cosmos, gently luminous, glimmered within the infinitude of my being.... I cognized the center of the empyrean as a point of intuitive perception in my heart. Irradiating splendor issued from my nucleus to every part of the universal structure.

—Paramahansa Yogananda,
Autobiography of a Yogi

My sight had changed, sharpened to an infinitely small point which moved ceaselessly in paths totally free of the old accustomed ones, as if flowing from a new source.... It was as if some inner eye, some ancient center of awareness which extended equally and at once in all directions without limit and which had been there all along, had been restored. This inner vision seemed to be focused on infinity in a way that was detached from immediate sight and yet had a profound effect on sight.

—Flora Courtois,
An Experience of Enlightenment

Bentov similarly spoke of the sensation of his consciousness moving like a *dot* through the Void, without interference.

> When you leave your body [at death], you may feel yourself to be a point of gold light [on the causal level], but you will still feel yourself [i.e., your individuality].
>
> —Barbara Ann Brennan, *Hands of Light*

> Know the embodied soul to be a part of the hundredth part of the point of a hair divided a hundred times; and yet it is infinite.
>
> —Svetasvatara Upanishad

> The Supreme Soul is seen within the soul,
> The Point is seen within the Supreme Soul,
> And within the Point, the reflection is seen again.
>
> —Kabir

> The First Sephiroth is sometimes called the "primitive point" or simply the "point": "When the Unknown of Unknowns [the unmanifested Absolute] wished to manifest Himself, he first produced one point...." Sometimes they call it [the First Sephiroth] "white head" because in it are blended all colors, that is to say, all ideas, all definite aspects.
>
> —A. Franck, *The Kabbalah*

That is, the First Sephiroth or Crown/Kether/"I Am," is distinguished/derived from the unmanifested Absolute or "confused totality, without form or name, the mysterious unknown that preceded all things" (the "Ayn" or "Ayn Sof"), through the appearance of an (archetypal) point. This production of the first Point, with creation thus pouring out of it, is the macrocosmic referent of the cornucopia symbolism.

> Zen admits the existence of a circle that has no circumference nor center and, therefore, has an infinite number of centers ... a center everywhere. The universe is a circle without a circumference, and every one of us is the center of the universe.
>
> —D. T. Suzuki, *Studies in Zen*

Note that this is fully compatible with accepted laws of mathematics, and is in no way illogical or "beyond logic." Such infinite consciousness is not a state among other states, but a state which includes all lower states. For the Ocean of Reality is present in every wave, and so is the

Source and Suchness of all waves of consciousness. And in this highest state—which both moves with infinite velocity, and is present everywhere continuously in a state of complete rest—we have *become* the Ocean. Further, all lower states of consciousness are produced from limitations in frequency response placed on this omnipresent state.

Thus, continuous omnipresence both includes and transcends all finite states. For, although the Ocean has become all waves, it is no less the Ocean in vibrating as all phenomena, than it is when unruffled. This is just as a photon vibrating at one frequency can appear red, while the same particle vibrating at a higher frequency can appear as blue light, without the photon itself actually *becoming* red or blue. Or, it is as the sky-blue rippled ocean and its whitecaps are both formed of the same water.

Now, a paradox, we recall, occurs when two mutually-exclusive states are present simultaneously. For example, if it is both raining, and not raining, at the same place and at the same time, that is a genuine paradox. Omnipresent consciousness inflates to infinity, and then deflates back to a point in space, all within a single point in time. Thus, such perfected consciousness is both inflating and deflating, simultaneously. This is rightly paradoxical—nothing in our ordinary experience or logic can both inflate *and* deflate at the same time. It is thus proof that although the opposites of inflation and deflation are ordinarily mutually exclusive, the state in which they are reconciled is nevertheless mathematically expressible. This has an important impact on the prevailing ideas regarding the relation of paradox and of "mutually-exclusive concepts" to the nature of, and means toward, the transcendence of duality, as we shall see in later chapters.

Even if one has difficulties with the idea/interpretation that the ideal impulse is expanding and contracting simultaneously, it is still inarguable that a balloon or sphere driven by an unfiltered or unlimited ideal impulse would have an infinite radius for a single point in time—and so be spread through all space for that moment. That structure is true whether we regard the impulse as a true mathematical representation of paradox, or simply as being "as close as you can get" to that representation, before the concepts of instantaneous expansion and contraction cease to have any meaning. That is, where the paradox "dissolves" precisely at the infinitesimal moment where we thought we could express it.

For the expanded sphere of consciousness, the "inner space" of one's volume of consciousness or "subjective space," and the "outer space" of "objective space," coincide in a "space filled with consciousness." There, space is not merely experienced visually, but is *felt* in/as one's own consciousness. (Again, we cannot see "space" with our eyes. Visually, we experience only the presence of light-resisting objects; or, more accurately, the photons reflected from these objects. Neither those photons nor the objects, nor our eyes, have continuous or permanent existence, being constantly re-created waves in the Ocean of Consciousness. Similarly, although our binaural hearing affords us a means of localizing the origins of sounds within our auditory field, we cannot hear in "three dimensions." That is, the "inner sound" of all space can be experienced only in expanded voluminous consciousness.) In this state, "objects" are no longer illusorily seen as being "separated" by intervening space. Rather now, as always, form and space interpenetrate one another in a transparent dance of light and color; and our consciousness is aware not only of the surfaces of macroscopic forms, but penetrates them at their basis.

Now, the physical, astral and causal levels of Nature can be reduced/dissolved to vibrationless cosmic consciousness, but the reverse is not true, for the lower levels of reality condense or crystallize out of the higher: matter condenses out of astral-energy, which crystallizes out of causal-thought, which condenses out of vibrationless cosmic consciousness. In this way, then, the causal, astral and physical realities "interpenetrate," or coexist in the same space.

Finite Nature is thus not the *opposite* of the Infinite, but is rather simply a rippled subset of It. That is, transcendent Spirit has become, and is present in, all the waves of Nature, while yet being unchanged by its participation in this continuous creation. Note also that "Nature," as the word is used herein, is not merely our surrounding physical environment of leaves and trees. Rather, it is everything under the sway of *maya,* including mortal mental processes. Mother Earth's boundaries may end at the upper atmosphere, but Mother Nature or *Maya* includes planets, stars and all intervening space, in the physical and all higher realities.

Maya, in its most fundamental "application," is the power by which waves of causal, astral and physical-level matter are created on the otherwise-unruffled Ocean. It is, indeed, regularly spoken of as a wave-creating *wind.* That is, the wind which produces waves in the ocean is introducing measures where previously there was formlessness; and *maya* = "measurer," both etymologically and traditionally. *"Maya"* actually refers both to the wind producing the waves of manifestation, and to the waves themselves. That is, it is both the "measurer" and the "measures."

Microcosmically, *maya* is the veil of ignorance keeping each one of us unaware of our true nature as the unfettered soul, in our egoic experiences of the created physical, astral and causal aspects of Nature. This is as opposed to identification with the transcendent Self or soul, which is *individualized* Spirit. Thus, the mind/body split, properly speaking, is not a split between Spirit and Nature. Rather, it is simply a fissure between *two different aspects* of Nature.

The Oceanic cosmic consciousness of Spirit, through the taking on of limitations in its manifesting as the waves of creation, *becomes* the cosmos. Formlessness, then, is again not the *opposite* of form/Nature, but is rather the basis from which form is drawn. The two are in essence one (although formlessness is the more basic reality): "The Formless is in the midst of all forms"—Kabir.

> The Absolute is everywhere; it has to be seen and found everywhere. Every finite is an infinite and has to be known and sensed in its intrinsic infiniteness as well as in its surface finite appearance.
>
> —Aurobindo

Matter and anti-matter are again opposites. Mind and its associated astral body, however, are not the opposite of the physical body, but are rather the higher-frequency state out of which the physical body condenses. For the physical is a condensed subset of the astral, not the opposite of it. That is, condensed life energy (as physical-level matter) is not the opposite of "uncondensed" astral life energy (which itself is condensed ripples of consciousness), any more than ice is the opposite of liquid water, or water the opposite of steam. Unlike matter and anti-matter, these are merely different states of the same substance, not opposites which can annihilate each other.

Neither the physical nor the astral nor the causal body or level of reality has an "opposite," so that they cannot be balanced half-and-half with anything. For what substance is the "opposite" of water? or of ice or steam? and even if anti-hydrogen and anti-oxygen can in principle exist, neither ordinary ice nor steam are composed of them. And if the physical and astral bodies were to be balanced against each other, then what of the causal? Or would a being in the astral worlds after death—a soul clothed only in the causal and astral bodies—then be untenably viewed as inherently imbalanced, for having no physical component to balance against these?

We cannot collapse mind, consciousness and Spirit into a single entity, call it "mind," and then assert that this admittedly non-physical "mind" should be balanced against the physical body for our best benefit. To do so is comparable to viewing steam and liquid water as identical, and then asserting that this synthesized entity is the opposite of ice (since both steam and liquid water are "non-ice"), and should be balanced against ice to transcend all opposites in realization of their underlying unity as differing vibratory states of H_2O!

To repeat: although "physical" and "non-physical," as with "condensed" and "uncondensed," *sound* like opposites, in the present context they are not. The same is true of "form" and "formlessness," and of the "limited" or finite, and the "unlimited" or infinite. For, both the space surrounding any finite region, and the cosmic consciousness that has become both the enclosed region and the surrounding space, are infinite. This latter Tao-infinity has *become* all things finite, and so is in no way the opposite of the finite. Likewise, the non-physical realms are again not the opposite of the physical (any more than ultraviolet light and x-rays could be the opposite of the visible spectrum). They are rather the higher and subtler vibratory levels out of which the gross physical condenses.

Further, just because matter, too, is "spiritual," for being simply a rippled parcel of the Ocean of Consciousness, does *not* mean that sensory experiences of the physical level of reality are "as good as" higher states of consciousness, freed from the body. Even though all states of consciousness are simply modifications of the One Ocean, and witnessed by the transcendent Self, it is only in the *highest* state of consciousness that one expands to infinity, or *becomes* the Ocean. This highest state, in being unified with the Ocean, includes all lower states (which are simply modifications of that Ocean). No finite, lower state, however, contains all of the highest state.

All creational, Oceanic activity is nothing more than plays of light and shadow of the Creator. Neither villain nor hero, nor any of the other polarities of the cosmic drama are essentially real; it is only shadows and light producing the pictures of the cosmic movie. The "light" and "shadow" here refer, of course, not only to good and evil, but to the production of matter, just as a black and white slide, projected on a screen, is composed of areas of shadow, and areas of light. Both are necessary for the existence of the picture, but the regions of white and of black are not themselves "good" and "evil," as such. The shadow exists in contrast to the light, just as the zero-average regions of "empty" space exist in contrast to the areas of non-zero-average matter.

> Troubled or still, water is always water. What difference can embodiment or disembodiment make to the Liberated? Whether calm or in tempest, the sameness of the Ocean suffers no change.
> —*Yoga-Vasishtha*

> I am the Lord, and there is none else, there is no God beside me ... I form the light, and create the darkness: I make peace, and create evil: I the Lord do all these things.
> —Isaiah 45:5,7

> O Brother, what is good? What is bad? They are all reflections of the same Light! Life and death, union and separation, are all His plays of joy!
> —Kabir

This projected play is further a "seamless" coat of God, in that everything is interpenetrating waves of the same Sea. All objective manifestations arise as localized waves of disturbance in the Cosmic Ocean, and so are all made of the same stuff. They cannot be considered to exist independently of the Ocean or to be autonomous "things," "separated" by intervening space. Spirit-consciousness is not only the infinite limit of the spectrum of consciousness, it is the nature and source of each level of the spectrum.

God is in all things—all the world in truth is God—but all things together do not pantheistically constitute God. What every person and thing is, whether enlightened or not, is still only God, and is pervaded by the undivided omnipresence of God. Thus, when God is seen to be in the world, as the world, the world is radically divine. Each such person and thing, however, expresses that infinite omnipresence through itself in only a limited or finite way.

The Absolute is both the highest level of reality and the condition or real nature of *every* level of reality. It is not that the Absolute comes into existence only at that highest state. Rather, it existed all along, but could be *realized* only when consciousness itself evolved to its highest estate. Buddha-nature is both your real and present condition and your future potential or realization.

The realm of *maya* is "delusion" or "illusion," but it is also God's "creative play" or *lila*. Indeed, the Latin root *ludere,* common to both "illusion" and "delusion," means "to play." At its basis, creation is simply waves of light in an Ocean of Light. We react to these with emotion, however, thinking body and mind to be "what we are," and so imagine ourselves to be suffering. Our Self-awareness and causal-level consciousness, however, are so much more basic than that.

> I have freed myself from my body. I have discarded my reasoning powers. And by thus getting rid of my body and mind, I have become One with the Infinite.
>
> —Yen Huei

The drop slips into the shining sea ... or the sea slips into the shining drop: all boundaries disappear in the expansion to infinity. As the legend goes, it is as the salt idol who waded into the ocean to find himself dissolving in its waters, marvelling yet at the unplumbed boundless depths.

> The wide expanse of manifested Universe is lifted to absorption; and the [world] of forms and qualities merges in the vastness of the Void, with a splash like water on water falling. Then the ethereal Void dissolves and the Ineffable Supreme alone remains.
>
> —Lalleshwari

> The buildings with their different parts, the temple, and everything else vanished from my sight, leaving no trace whatsoever, and in their stead I saw a limitless, infinite, effulgent Ocean of Consciousness.
>
> —Ramakrishna

Such a perception of the Infinite as One Light again cannot, in any of its stages, be a mere sensory experience of any sort. For the physical eyes cannot see consciousness as such, much less could they register an infinite Ocean of Consciousness.

> Leap clear of all that is corporeal, and make yourself grow to a like expanse with that greatness which is beyond all measure; rise above all time, and become eternal; then you will apprehend God. Think that for you too nothing is impossible; deem that you too are immortal, and that you are able to grasp all things in your thought, to know every craft and every science; find your home in the haunts of every living creature; make yourself higher than all heights, and lower than all depths; bring together in yourself all opposites of quality, heat and cold, dryness and fluidity; think that you are everywhere at once, on land, at sea, in heaven.
>
> —the *Corpus Hermiticum*
> (from the late Greek-Egyptian body of Gnostic teachings)

> When I open my eyes to the outer world, I feel myself as a drop in the sea; but when I close my eyes and look within, I see the whole universe as a bubble raised in the ocean of my heart.
>
> —Inayat Khan, "Divine Symphony"

> O guiding night
> O night more lovely than the dawn!
> O night that has united
> The Lover with His beloved
> Transforming the beloved in her Lover
>
> —St. John of the Cross

> [The yogi in cosmic consciousness] feels that there is no such thing as blind force or dead matter, and that all is alive, vibrating and intelligent.... During illumination the flood-gate of joy breaks. [He] is inundated with waves of indescribable ecstasy. Bliss, immortality, eternity, truth and divine love become the core of his being, the essence of his life, the only possible reality. He realizes that the deep ever-lasting fountain of joy exists in every heart, that the immortal life underlies all beings, that this eternal, all-embracing, all-inclusive love envelops, supports and guides every particle, every atom of creation.
>
> —Swami Sivananda

Kabir ponders and says: "He who has neither caste nor country, who is formless and without quality, fills all space.

"They have sung of Him as infinite and unattainable: but I in my meditations have seen Him without sight.

"My heart is frenzied, and I disclose in my soul what is hidden. I am immersed in that one great bliss which transcends all pleasure and pain."

CHAPTER IV

ON GOOD AND EVIL

NUMEROUS REFERENCES ARE FOUND in Eastern spiritual teachings regarding the "relativities of creation." It is important that the meaning of this phrase be clarified.

First and foremost, it must be understood that the above expression has nothing in common with the proclamations of neo-relativistic philosophers to the effect that "everything is relative." This erroneous point of view presumably has taken a large degree of impetus from a misunderstanding and subsequent distortion of Einstein's relativistic postulate that the laws of physics are the same for all observers.

That postulate may be alternatively expressed as: The observations in any one reference frame are not preferred above those in any other. It would take only a slight deterioration in the meaning of this phrase to arrive at the fallacy that "all points of view are equally valid," and that therefore the judgment as to which of all possible actions would produce the greatest good is subjective. That is, that "there is no absolute right or wrong, no objective good or evil; it's all in what you choose." The inconsistency of this philosophy with the actual character of creation is easily demonstrated, as follows.

God is present everywhere within and beyond His creation: He has become it all, and yet is transcendent, untouched by its relativities. An expansion (or raising of the level) of one's consciousness takes one closer to omnipresence—omnipresence being granted when one's consciousness has expanded to infinity, to include all finite creation and more. If we acknowledge that the purpose of existence is exactly this evolution of consciousness from initial finitude and ego-identification to final emancipation through the dissolution of self in the omnipresence of God, we must then regard good as being related to an expansion of consciousness. That is, to a raising of the level or resonant frequency of consciousness with the passage of time.

Further, since the contraction of one's consciousness (that is, the lowering of its level) reduces the degree of one's conscious identity with immanent-transcendent Spirit and so goes contrary to the highest hope of every heart or purpose of creation, such a contraction must be regarded as evil. And, that thought or action which results in the greatest expansion of consciousness among the creatures of Nature is to be recognized as producing the greatest good. It will be readily seen that this greatest good must correspond to the action advocated by the Divine Will in any circumstance. For the Creator can have in mind no lesser goal for His creation than the eventual, inevitable, unlimited expansion of imagined mortal consciousness into reunion with its Divine Source.

> Know that all creatures pursue and act, by nature, to the end to become like God.
>
> —Meister Eckhart

> God became man, that man might become God.
>
> —St. Augustine

> God, the Ocean of Mercy, who ever blesses the world, pours out His grace at all times. It is incumbent on man to consider everything that happens to be for the best: "for the best" denoting what is most helpful towards the realization of the Divine, the realization of the fullness of Bliss.
>
> —Ananda Moyi Ma

> The winds of grace are blowing all the time, you have only to raise your sail.
>
> —Ramakrishna

As good is intimately related to the expansion of consciousness, and evil then concomitant with contraction of consciousness, we must next ask: If consciousness is rightly cognized as expanding by an observer in one state of consciousness, will it be seen to be expanding by observers in all states of consciousness? For, if this is the case, then good and evil are absolutely distinguishable.

It is easy to see that only a reversal in the flow of time could result in an expansion being observed as a contraction. For if we were to take a motion picture of a balloon expanding, and then play this film through the projector backward—effectively reversing the direction of the flow of time—we would see the balloon contracting. (Likewise, the roots of many Hebrew verbs can be read in either direction—from right to left, or from left to right—producing opposite meanings. This is consistent with the idea that good and evil are time-reversals of one another.) But the Universal Breathing does not reverse itself. And there is again no relative velocity, and likewise no state of consciousness, for which time flows backward. (The claimed ability of clairvoyants to consciously travel into the past is different from time itself flowing backward.) Also, the entropy or amount of disorder in the universe is constantly increasing on an overall scale; this is the traditional scientific basis for the argument that time cannot be reversed. Therefore, good and evil, as the raising and lowering of the level of consciousness, are absolutely distinguishable.

If your goal is to be "whole" rather than "good," feel free to make that substitution. It is nevertheless true here also that progress *toward* wholeness is the time-reversal of regression *away from* wholeness. It is equally true that undivided wholeness can be realized only in the state in which there are no boundaries circumscribing one's circle of compassion, which is exactly what is meant by becoming unconditionally good. Good actions are the natural expression of the expansion of consciousness or realization of wholeness, while actions of evil or selfishness arise from, and contribute to, the contraction of consciousness.

> Evil makes things fragmentary, as good makes them whole; good dilates whereas evil contracts.
> —Frithjof Schuon

> Good is what is constructive and facilitating to the whole.
> —David Bohm, *Unfolding Meaning*

Interestingly, Einstein held that the only difference between God and the devil was that one had a plus sign in front of it, and the other a minus sign. That statement is not fully correct, of course, since God has become both good and evil. These latter two terms, however, are indeed negatives or time-reversals of one another, having opposing pulls.

> Whatever exerts a pull toward God is "good." Whatever pulls beings away from God is "evil."
> 						—Paramahansa Yogananda, *Journey to Self-Realization*

Whatever conception of God one accepts, and whether or not one accepts the validity of visions and other higher-state-of-consciousness experiences—the existence of which logically implies a *highest* (infinite) state of consciousness—it must be acknowledged that doing good makes one more Godlike, or brings one closer to God or Spirit over a period of time. Likewise, the performance of evil takes one further away from God. This is so by any reasonable definition of good and of evil. And "going closer to" as time passes is again absolutely distinguishable from "going away from" if we can ascertain the direction of the flow of time—which we can.

Thus, in any God- or Perfection-based view of the universe, good and evil are absolutely distinguishable. And, as soon as one rightly acknowledges that consciousness can be expanded, and that the consciousness of God is omnipresent throughout and beyond creation, it cannot be denied that the expansion of one's consciousness must take one closer to God, just as the contraction of one's consciousness takes one further away from conscious union with Him (or wholeness).

Now, there have been two primary "theories" of beauty expounded in the history of philosophy. The first of these is that "beauty is the proper conformity of the parts to one another and to the whole." This view begins with the school of Pythagoras, who is credited with the discovery that vibrating strings under equal tension sound together in harmony if their lengths are in a simple numerical ratio. The consonance of two strings yields a beautiful sound while, owing to the discomfort caused by beat-effects among frequencies not related to one another in the appropriate ratio, the human ear finds dissonance disturbing. Thus the mathematical relation was also the source of beauty. In the case of music, the parts are the individual notes, while the whole is the harmonious sound.

The second definition of the concept of beauty stems from Plotinus. That is, that "beauty is the translucence, through the material phenomenon, of the eternal splendor of the 'One.'" This idea has, at various times in history, yielded magnificent religious art.

There is, of course, nothing at all irreconcilable in these two seemingly-disparate views. For, any waves on the Infinite Ocean are going to be mathematically describable, and so will have numerical relationships to one another. And the "eternal splendor of the 'One'" underlies all such vibratory manifestations, and shines through in proportion to their harmony and fineness.

As is the case with good and evil, then, relative beauty and ugliness are also non-subjective. Personal judgments of relative physical beauty made in ignorance of the consciousness that has become the external manifestation have no necessary validity. That is, it is not metaphysically sensible to speak of beautiful faces or paintings without consideration of the consciousness underlying the outward physical manifestation. (Matter is again merely a low rate of vibration of consciousness—with consciousness being the "water" of the Infinite Ocean. All phenomena, then, arise as modifications of this one stuff, or ripples on/of the Infinite Ocean. Thus, in order to make fully valid judgments regarding the attributes of matter, we need first to be aware of the vibratory characteristics of the exterior energy, interior feeling and consciousness that have become it.)

Further, the full recognition of the contributions of all consciousness to any outward expression can be had only through being aware-in-oneness of all of the frequencies of vibration underlying the given material manifestation. And this full and unbiased sensitivity obtains only in the state of continuous omnipresence, where one *is* all vibrations of the Ocean of Light.

We can, however, make approximate judgments of relative beauty based on partially developed intuitional feeling. Such judgments will be valid to the extent that such feeling is unclouded by personal tastes and desires, with the extent of this clarity of feeling being proportional to one's inner calmness and so to the height of one's state of consciousness and stage of psychological development. And in this light, vases and visages, music, poetry and prose will be seen to be beautiful to the extent that they reflect and encourage the unconditional expansion of consciousness that is the melting of self in Spirit.

The nature of beauty as a characteristic of the vibrations underlying any given material manifestation does not mean that beauty is quantifiable on the basis of physical empirical measurements. Nevertheless, the feelings and emotions—i.e., the literal "vibrations"—of the artist are undoubtedly captured in the work of art. Indeed, these would be enfolded in the subtle rhythms of rippling consciousness and energy underlying the sensorially-perceivable matter, just as they are claimed to be enfolded by a cook in the food which he or she prepares.

In thus treating beauty as an attribute based in consciousness, we are not reducing it to "mere vibrations." Rather, we are acknowledging that all "mere vibrations" are movements *of* the Ocean of God, and so are based in Intelligence-Beauty-Truth. A particular rate of objective, "exterior" rippling vibration simply allows a characteristic degree or quality of this Ocean to express itself as the "interior" of that consciousness—e.g., as subjective feelings of hope, fear or joy. Indeed, given that everything is ripples of the Ocean of Spirit, what possible essential objective difference could there be between the phenomena of all levels of reality, other than the rate of vibration of their constituent God-ripples?

> It was suddenly revealed to me that everything is Pure Spirit. The utensils of worship, the altar, the door-frame—all Pure Spirit. Men, animals and other living beings—all Pure Spirit.
> —Ramakrishna

Just because an object is true to sensory impressions does not mean that it is what it appears to be. For example, if we were to take a large orange, dye and flavor it appropriately so that to the five senses it appears as a grapefruit, will it actually have become a grapefruit? No—the DNA structure, for example, of the pseudo-grapefruit would differ from that of a real grapefruit. This would be detectable through the application of x-ray technology, which reacts to higher frequencies of vibration than do our bodily senses.

We cannot validly know the real nature of anything without first being aware of its entire spectrum of frequencies of vibration; which again necessitates awareness, on our part, of all possible frequencies, through to infinity. No physical extension of our senses can grant this awareness, owing to the fact that anything physical can, by definition, react only to a very limited range of vibrations. This full awareness can be gained only through the unconditional expansion of consciousness.

Now, truth may be reasonably defined as "that which is in harmony with, or reflects accurately the state of, all levels of reality." It is not merely the statement of observed facts, as the behavior or external appearances from which such facts are generally drawn, from sensory data, reflects the status of only one level of reality—the physical. Consequently, just as with relative beauty and good, truths regarding creation can be stated unequivocally only in conscious knowledge of the status of all levels of reality—in the omnipresence of God-consciousness.

Further, relative truth must reflect some measure of the perfect, limitless consciousness of Spirit—in that the highest state of Being is ever-perfect, and is the Goal and Ground of all phenomena and evolution. And this perfect highest state must be taken into account in considering *all* levels of reality. Thus, the unconditional adherence to the full harmony of truth must be intimately related to the greatest expansion of consciousness, and so to the most profound wisdom and everlasting beauty.

Given the absolute nature of all qualities normally regarded as subjective opinions, the artist's "model of reality" must be as valid as is the mathematician's. That is, valid so long as it is recognized that one's opinions, tastes, and beliefs do not constitute "personal truth." Opinions change daily and are dependent on one's state of consciousness and stage of psychological development. But good is absolutely distinguishable from evil, for all states of consciousness. And the unconditional adherence to truth in all facets of life must be intimately related to the production of the greatest possible amount of good. Thus, truth, love, wisdom and beauty—the corollaries of, and manifested proportionally with, good—are in their undistorted absolute essence not at all "subjective," or merely "in the eye of the beholder."

> "Beauty is truth, truth beauty,"—
>   that is all
> Ye know on earth, and all ye
>   need to know.
>
>   —John Keats

> If then beauty is the cause of good ... we devote ourselves to the pursuit of wisdom and of all other beautiful things for the reason that their

product and offspring—the good—is worthy of devotion, and from our explorations it looks as though beauty is metaphorically a kind of father of good.

—Plato

The ideals which have lighted me on my way and time after time given me new courage to face life cheerfully, have been Truth, Goodness, and Beauty.

—Albert Einstein, *The World As I See It*

To a true artist only that face is beautiful which, quite apart from its exterior, shines with the Truth within the soul. There is ... no Beauty apart from Truth. On the other hand, Truth may manifest in forms which may not be outwardly beautiful at all....

I see and find Beauty in Truth or through Truth. All Truth, not merely true ideas but truthful faces, truthful pictures, or songs are highly beautiful. People generally fail to see Beauty in Truth, the ordinary man runs away from and becomes blind to the Beauty in it. Whenever men begin to see Beauty in Truth, then true art will arise.

—Mahatma Gandhi

From the Divine comes all the Beauty and all the Good in beings.

The Primal Good and the Primal Beauty have the one dwelling-place and thus, always, Beauty's seat is There.

—Plotinus

Plato is right; beyond the beauty that is predicated of various forms and relationships, there is a pure Transcendent Beauty, and this is a mode of the very Being of the Self. That Beauty is not *something* that is beautiful. It is Self-existent and casts Its luster upon all things for Him who has found Himself identical with that Beauty.... Ecstasy is pure Beauty, as well as pure Joy and Knowledge. Beauty is one of the many facets of That which is the Fullness appearing as Emptiness.

—Franklin Merrell-Wolff,
Pathways Through to Space

Thus, although in both art and science what we measure or see depends on our frame of reference or state of consciousness, there is again an all-encompassing level of consciousness in which absolute values are defined in all of interrelated aesthetics, morality, and external measurement.

The idea that "beauty (or good) is relative" fails, not merely when considering the cosmic structural basis of all thought and matter, but even if one takes ideas such as those presented at www.beautyanalysis.com seriously. For there, our perceptions of beauty are regarded as being rooted in a structure which exists independent of human cultures and sociologies. That is, of course, an eminently satisfying idea, whether or not one agrees with the particular geometric basis, in the Golden Mean, proposed there. The effect of beauty, poetry and rhythm on the human psyche, after all, is so profound that it could never be totally subjective, without reference to cosmic absolutes. Rather, those expressions of artistry clearly tap into the vibrational structure of the cosmos in ways well beyond any attempt to reduce them to mere culture-specific conceptualizations.

With or without such particular and quantitative standards, however, it is obvious that whenever we pass judgment on the relative beauty of earthly vases and visages, poetry and music, the structures which we are evaluating are mathematically and geometrically describable. That is so regardless of how long it may take us as a species to abstract the specific characteristics or patterns (whether visual, auditory, or otherwise) which are widely regarded as beautiful/harmonious or ugly/inharmonious, etc. And that is obviously true even if those evaluations come simply in the form of "internally" rating them on a scale of one to ten, for example, and then pretending that that could remove them from having an objectively measurable validity.

CHAPTER V

FREEDOM OF CHOICE

FAMILIARITY WITH THE CHARACTERISTICS of consciousness developed in the previous chapters also facilitates a discussion of the free choice problem, as will now be explored.

The inquiry as to whether free choice exists is the most fundamental question of existence. For, if we have no choice in the actions we perform—that is, if our "choices" are either random or completely predetermined—we cannot be held ultimately responsible for our actions. Thus, it is only if we have some freedom of choice that it really "matters" whether good and evil are distinguishable or not, whether God, heaven, or hell exists, etc.

The orthodox philosophical argument against the existence of such free choice runs as follows: Mental and physical processes are all either deterministic or indeterministic, or some combination of the two. Every mental choice or event that is deterministic has, by definition, a cause or series of causes, and is therefore not free of past influences. Further, any mental event that is indeterministic is, by definition, purely random, and so cannot be considered as a conscious "choice." Therefore, free choice cannot exist.

The logic of this argument is valid; its conclusion can be circumvented only if we can find some flaw with the premises. We thus ask: Is it true that all mental processes are either deterministic or indeterministic? Or is there a third alternative?

45

Both determinism and indeterminism relate only to circumstances in which there are temporal distinctions of "before" and "after." However, *beyond* time there can be no divisions of before or after, past or future, so no past causes. Thus, consciousness that is beyond time is neither deterministic nor indeterministic: it is truly free. That is, we can have free choice if and only if it is possible for our consciousness to go beyond time—to go beyond both cause-effect and indeterminism—in some way.

Because transcendent Spirit is entirely free of cause-effect constraints, the impulse response contractions of consciousness toward a point, which allow for conscious identification with Its timeless nature, must confer the ability to make choices unconditioned by past causes. However, in all finite states of consciousness, one's mergings of consciousness in timeless Spirit occur at a non-infinite frequency, and so cannot be considered as complete (i.e., continuous) identification with It. Nor can they be regarded as granting the unlimited freedom of choice characteristic of perfect transcendent intuitional knowledge of Spirit. The higher one's state of consciousness, the higher the frequency of these point-contractions of consciousness will be, hence the greater the degree of transcendent Spirit-identification and free choice.

Thus, while it is of course true that our choices are influenced by habit, as well as by our judgment as to the desirability of the probable effects that any particular decision may have, in the actual *choice* between alternatives, we can just as freely choose one side as the other. The next time you are lazying in bed on a weekend morning "trying to get up," try to be aware of the internal process in choosing between the alternatives, and especially be aware of how you can just as easily follow one course of action as the other. Likewise, do the same when meditating and considering whether to "cut it short" and do something else, or watching television and contemplating just getting up and turning it off to go do something productive, or eating and being tempted to have a "second helping" when your actual hunger has already been satisfied.

It is only by considering the probable effects of our choices and potential actions that they become conditioned by our desires and habits, including the wish or desire to win the approval of others. Consider how much easier it is to get up on a weekday morning, when the alternative is to be late for work and suffer the consequences of that, than on a weekend, when there is "no reason" to get up ... unless one has enjoyable activities planned for the latter, in which case it may well be easier to get up than on a weekday.

This does not mean that we should not consider the probable consequences of our actions. On the contrary, what is called for is an unbiased and impartial use of our reason and developing intuition in order to discern which of our potential behaviors will produce the greatest spiritual, moral and physical benefit for ourselves and others, which right behaviors may then be enacted, in spite of the biasing effect of our likes and dislikes.

The principles upon which the spiritual science of meditation is based are again the selfsame as those which uphold the existence of all Nature. That is, were it not for the validity of higher and highest levels of consciousness and thought, physical creation—and free choice—could not exist. Further, since matter reflects the behavior of consciousness, we must find some aspects of the behavior of consciousness reflected in any theory that is at all successful in describing the phenomena of the physical level of reality. The more comprehensive and true the theory is, the more clearly its predictions will mirror the manners of consciousness.

The order implicit in mathematical regularity is the very hallmark of intelligence, not its gainsay. For it is only through the omnipresent influence of the Great Coordinating Intelligence underlying all creation that there can be any order and regularity to the workings of the universe. Without this Intelligence, the material forms produced from the interactions of the various aspects of differentiated consciousness could have no sustained order. By analogy, in working with a computer, pressing a specific combination of keys will cause a certain predictable, mnemonically-related response. However, this response is not intrinsic to the keys pressed, but is effected only through much "behind the scenes" electronic activity.

In a like manner, if the objects of our daily experience behave according to predictable and sensible laws, this is no fundamental or inexorable characteristic, but arises only from much hidden activity on the part of the Great Programmer. (One might grant varying degrees of freedom of choice, or creativity, to every sphere of consciousness in the cosmos, taking all observed regularities in the behavior of the particles condensed from those spheres as being simply cosmic "habits." Even

there, however, the rhythmic series of impulses of potential omnipresence driving those spheres, and the kept-in-store archetypal laws of
mathematics governing the "bouncing" response to those impulses, must
arise from a more fundamental level than the spheres themselves.) Seen
in this light, the teleological argument—the argument from design, or the
idea that the clockworklike regularity of the universe infers the existence
of a Cosmic Watchmaker—becomes one of the most convincing arguments of philosophy. *In any metaphysically tenable view of the universe,
we cannot talk about the basic structure and behavior of creation
without necessary recognition and active inclusion of the existence of
consciousness, God, free choice, and the absolute distinguishability of
good and evil.*

CHAPTER VI

ON THE NATURE OF OM

The eye by which I see God is the same eye by which God sees me.
—Meister Eckhart

TO THE MEDITATOR VERSED IN THE ART of deep concentration, a light will appear at the point between the eyebrows—the place of the ajna chakra. A dark spot or area will form in the center of this light, surrounded by luminous rays. As concentration deepens, the golden luster of the surrounding luminous halo increases manyfold, and the dark central area becomes resolved into a sphere of opal blue, centered with a white five-pointed star. As the meditator is counseled always to face toward the East in his or her practice of the universal methods of yoga meditation, this spiritual diadem, being seen most often in the East, is called in the Biblical idiom the star of the East. (East is simply the direction from which subtle spiritual currents are averred to be constantly flowing.) In the yogic lore it is named *Kutastha Chaitanya*—the Christ consciousness center, or spiritual eye.

The three forms and colors (the white pentagonal star, blue sphere, and golden ring) of this single eye of light are said to represent, microcosmically and respectively

(i) the cosmic consciousness of Spirit existing continuously in the infinite space surrounding the sphere of vibratory creation;

49

(ii) the universal intelligence of God underlying all vibration within the sphere of the cosmos, which is Christ consciousness. This is the sole reflection of the continuously omnipresent cosmic consciousness present in an undisturbed state within the finite vibratory sphere of the cosmos: vibration or coherent motion implies guiding intelligence. Christ consciousness is the awareness of Spirit as immanent in all vibratory creation; of the ever-unchanged blissful consciousness therein. It is the unmodified "anvil" upon which all matter is hammered out—the "mirror" within which all of creation is reflected, but which itself remains unchanged. *Christ* and *Krishna (Christna)* are titles; they denote one who is united with this universal consciousness. Krishna is thus often shown *blue*-skinned in East Indian religious art. That blue color is sometimes explained in terms of Krishna's association with water or the ocean. This too is reasonable, in that the ocean, if it were to rise and cover all earth, would form a blue sphere; and

(iii) the vibratory realm of creation—Om, or the Holy (sacred) Ghost (invisible intelligent vibration). The sound of Om is omnipresent throughout the vibratory sphere of creation, and is said to be the root of all other sounds—that is, the basis of all matter and all vibrations. It may thus be rightly spoken of as the sole causative force within creation; the only Doer of all creational activities.

> Aeons ago in the land of Eternity, when God was alone as the ever-existing, ever-new Joy, He mused: "I am alone, with nobody to enjoy Me." He breathed a wish, and the Holy Ghost (symbolized in the Virgin Mary) was born. The Holy Ghost or Mary carries within its "womb" the Christ Consciousness (symbolized in the Son)—the reflection of the Cosmic Consciousness (God the Father) in and beyond all creation.
>
> —Paramahansa Yogananda,
> "The Inner Celebration of Christmas,"
> in *Self-Realization* magazine, Winter 1995

In Hinduism and yoga, the Father, Son and Mother are termed *Sat, Tat* and *Om,* respectively. The following verses, then, all refer to the Christ *consciousness,* to which we all may attain, not merely to the historical personage of Jesus.

> God ... created all things by Jesus Christ.
>
> —Ephesians 3:9

Before Abraham was, I am.

—John 8:58

I am the Light that is above them all,
I am the All.
The All came forth from Me and the All attained to Me.
Cleave a piece of wood, I am there:
Lift up the stone, you will find me there.

—Jesus, in the Gnostic Gospel of St. Thomas

Likewise, in the Mahayana Buddhist view, the entire world, as seen by us, is delusory—its substance, in actuality, being the Buddha-Christ. Interestingly, in Christian symbolism, a star with five points, centered in a circle, represents the Epiphany or manifestation of Christ to the Gentiles in the persons of the Magi or three Wise Men (who followed the Star of the East to the Christ child). The astral components of the same figure come up in witchcraft, as the pentagram. The fact that contemporary spiritually-advanced persons almost invariably fail to understand these full meanings shows that there are indeed ways in which isolated members, at least, of past cultures, have seen farther into the cosmos than have all but a handful of today's figures.

The Holy Ghost of Om is again synonymous, cosmically speaking, with the Virgin Mary—the womb of matter within which the Son of God is born. This Christ consciousness is the sole reflection of the Uncreated Infinite within the sphere of creation. That is, it is the only Son of the Father, born within the womb of the Mother. In Buddhist mythology too, the virgin Queen Maya gives birth to the Christ-like Buddha—he enters her womb as she rests in a golden palace with her head toward the East. Given these cosmic or archetypal associations, it should come as no surprise that "mother," "matter"—etymologically derived from "mother"—"measure," *"maya,"* its Buddhist equivalent of *"mara"*— the "tempter" or "ruling spirit of evil"—and "Mary" are so closely related.

The "measuring" nature of *maya* or cosmic delusion is fundamentally necessary in order for matter, as the body of the Cosmic Mother, to be drawn from the Ocean of cosmic consciousness, in the production of the illusion of limitation and separation within the Indivisible Infinite. (The Latin *matrix,* meaning "womb," is similarly derived from *mater,* "mother.") And this Great Mother of all creation—pervading, nurturing and sustaining all Nature—is no mere vestige of pre-patriarchal Earth-goddesses, for even pantheism goes well beyond the celebration of Mother Earth, or the presiding deity/consciousness of our one small planet.

The Hindu religion, too, goes further than this, in terms of the roles of Shiva and Shakti:

> The Sanskrit word *Shiva* means literally "tranquil" [cf. unruffled Ocean]. In tantra yoga it refers to the static (Masculine) pole or aspect of the ultimate Reality, whereas the word *Shakti* designates the dynamic (Feminine) pole. Shiva stands for pure, object-transcending and self-transcending Consciousness, and Shakti stands for the world-creating Power of Consciousness [e.g., the wind producing waves on the other-wise-tranquil Ocean].
>
> —Lee Sannella, *The Kundalini Experience*

Without Shakti, Shiva is as a corpse, unable to move—without power. However, if "all is Brahman," there must be no essential difference between Shiva as the possessor of power, and Power as It is in Itself: the power of Consciousness is Consciousness in its active aspect. That is, Shiva is the static or changeless aspect of Consciousness, while Shakti is the active or kinetic aspect of the same Consciousness. *Maya,* then, is the particular power by which the dualistic world is brought into being, seemingly making the Whole into not-whole, the Infinite into the finite, the Ocean into apparently autonomously-existing waves, etc. Since Shakti and *maya negate* the natural, tranquil state of the Ocean, She is regarded as the *negative* pole of the Shiva-Shakti pair, with the Masculine conversely being held as *positive.*

Further, according to tantra yoga and the Sanskrit language, Shakti is denoted by the letter "i"—as is found in the middle of "Shiva." This very word then denotes the union of Shiva and Shakti. That is, Shakti, so long as She remains inactive, is united with Shiva. When this "i" or Shakti is removed from "Shiva"—that is, when Shakti takes on "a life of Her own," in her active role in manifestation—He becomes "Shava," meaning "a corpse." In hatha yoga, too, the inert "sleeping" position is known as the Shava or "corpse" posture—an *asana* consisting of being stretched out straight on one's back, with the arms relaxed alongside the body.

This idea of manifestation having arisen from the Inactive Transcendent is encountered regularly in the world's mythologies. It is represented in burial sites by either symbolic figures or actual burial positions of a woman lying on top of a man; or of an active Kali, and a reclining Shiva figure atop a dead, eyes-closed Shiva. For the same reason, the female form is represented in sexual union as being above the male.

The transcendent state of Spirit beyond and prior to all manifestation may again be characterized as one in which Shiva and Shakti—Consciousness and Power—are united. Manifestation then springs from that state through their "separation," or through that Power rising from its latent form and acting on Consciousness to produce the finite forms of relative reality as modifications of that same hitherto-tranquil Consciousness. Thus, the Commentary to the *Sat-Chakra-Nirupana* records that

> from the unmanifested Paramesvara [Supreme Lord], *the united Shiva and Shakti,* emanated the first Devi Bhagavati, who is Tripura-sundari, the Shakti from whom came *Nada,* and thence came *Bindu* [the Point].

Nada is the "integrated [chaotic] state of vibration from which all possible kinds of vibration can be derived by a process of differentiation."

> Pure Consciousness is Shiva, and His Power (Shakti) ... in Her formless self is one with Him. She is the great Devi, the Mother of the Universe who as the Life-Force resides in man's body in its lowest centre at the base of the spine, just as Shiva is realized in the highest brain centre, the cerebrum or sahasrara.
> —Sir John Woodroffe, *The Serpent Power*

Now, the Holy Ghost or Holy Spirit is experienced as an archetypal Divine Feminine Consciousness—or as the figure of the Divine Mother in visions of a personal God—irrespective of one's own gender, sociological surroundings or beliefs. And the Father, Mother and Son of creation are all aspects of Shakti, or the cosmic creative Power, acting on Shiva. How this is so will be explained in greater detail in later chapters. Briefly, it has to do with the fact that the Infinite Ocean surrounding *and suffusing* the sphere of creation is actually chaotically vibratory, through space and time. That is, that Ocean surface has an *average* value of zero displacement, and so appears as a "Void" to all lower states of consciousness, but is not actually vibrationless or tranquil.

Such a turbulently agitated state is obviously the product of the action of Shakti, or Power, on the Ocean of Consciousness or Shiva—for chaos is a kinetic, not a static state. This chaotic state is *relatively* transcendent and unmanifest, and is beyond the power of *maya,* but is nevertheless not the *ultimate* Unmanifest State. This is a vital distinction to make and understand. Further, a detailed mathematical analysis shows that, like the impulses we have considered earlier, such a chaotic state will be "white," or contain equal amounts of all frequencies, from zero to infinity.

The traditional association of the Father with transcendence, and of the Mother with vibratory immanence, has nothing to do with "splitting" God and creation apart. Nor does the existence of Divine Father and Mother figures originate in the projection of human characteristics onto an attributeless God. Rather, *it is exactly the other way around,* for these archetypal consciousnesses predate and form the basis of *all* masculine and feminine traits, not only in their application to human beings.

In Nature, the female of (nearly) every species gestates the child—with rare exceptions such as seahorses, where the female of course produces the eggs, by definition, but then deposits them in the male's pouch, wherein they gestate. This is true in terms of cosmic archetypes also, in terms of the Cosmic Feminine being associated with the womb of all creation, within which the Son of God, or Christ Consciousness, is born as the sole reflection of the Father within creation.

Prior to creation, neither the Father nor the Mother exist, only Spirit exists: *"Maya* creates the [non-zero-average] waves on the Ocean, but who created the Ocean of Light?" the answer being the ever-existent, causeless Spirit. "Men" and "women" are not the be-all and end-all of the cosmic creation. Rather, the principles of male and female, of masculine and feminine, are much, much broader than our little species. Even a cursory observation of Nature on this small earth must disclose that. The sagely originators of the Bible, too, were fully and undeniably aware of the existence of the immanent Feminine aspect of God. They were equally well apprised, however, of the transcendent nature complementary to this immanence; although it is nevertheless true that many persons *validly* regarded as sages yet lack the experience of these states and of the structure underlying them.

To summarize, then, we have the (chaotic) Infinite Ocean surrounding the sphere of creation as God the Father or the transcendent Cosmic Masculine; the chaotic Ocean within the vibratory region as the Christ consciousness; and Om or the immanent Cosmic Feminine as the (non-zero-average) waves of that finite vibrating region, manifesting as all created things. That is, the (chaotic) Christ consciousness is *spatially* immanent, but *vibrationally* transcendent of relative creation.

In all of the following Biblical verses, then, the Father refers to the chaotic Infinite Ocean surrounding the sphere of vibration—active in creation only indirectly—while the Son refers exactly to the Christ *consciousness:*

> I am the way, the truth, and the life: no man cometh unto the Father, but by me.
>
> —John 14:6

> No man [with consciousness under the sway of *maya*] hath seen God [i.e., Unmanifested Spirit] at any time; the only begotten Son, which is in the bosom of the Father, he hath declared [subjected to form via cosmic "speech," i.e., the Word of Om] him.
>
> —John 1:18

> For the Father judgeth no man, but hath committed all judgment unto the Son.
>
> —John 5:22

> The words that I speak unto you I speak not of myself: but the Father that dwelleth in me, he doeth the works.
>
> Believe me, that I am in the Father, and the Father in me.
>
> —John 14:10-1

> The Monad is a monarchy with nothing above it. It is He who exists as God and Father of everything, the invisible one who is above everything, who is imperishability, existing as pure light which no eye can behold.

> I am the Father, I am the Mother, I am the Son. I am the unpolluted and incorruptible one.
>
> —Jesus, in the Gnostic gospels
> (Apocryphon of John)

Given this latter statement, no one should be so unadventurous as to wishfully or misleadingly assert that the Gnostic gospels demonstrate a Christ who presented himself, not as the Son of God, but simply as an ordinary man. That is, as a mere moral teacher, rather than as one fully identified with the Christ consciousness.

Consistent with its representation in the spiritual eye, finite vibratory creation in its entirety is said to take the form of a luminous blue sphere. The sky, too, forms a blue sphere from the earth's point of view; so that all created forms may be viewed as "frozen" sky, or condensed vibrations of consciousness within the opal sphere. Each of our spheres of consciousness is thus a "drop," or small sphere, of the "vast blue ocean of sky." Conversely, in metaphysical terms the sky is blue because, from the earth's point of view, it forms a spherical region studded with stars— as with the third eye. In order for us to reach the *star* of cosmic consciousness, then, we first have to pierce through, or expand our consciousness beyond, the finite blue *sky* of the (spherical blue) cosmos. Further,

> the sage Jan-hsiang achieved perfection by attaining the center of the ring. Along with all things, he was free from endings, beginnings, moments, or time.
>
> —Chuang Tzu

Penetrating the (also Janus-guarded) star at the center of the golden ring of the spiritual eye indeed grants the transcendence of relative space and time, in cosmic consciousness.

The sphere of vibratory creation is again surrounded by infinite space. Put another way: God, to be perfect and without limitation, must be literally infinite; vibratory creation, being a delusory, dualistic, limited phenomenon, must be finite. And in order for creation to not be separate from God, it must exist as a subset of the Infinite, not as something "in addition" to it. Thus, it must consist of some region, however shaped, of vibration, necessarily surrounded by a non-vibratory (yet chaotic) Infinitude—a small region of which *has become* the cosmos. The Infinitude surrounding the region of vibration is perfectly transcendent of manifestation—a God "apart" from His creation, just as the Bible says. In/as the vibratory sphere, however, the Void-Ocean is spatially and vibrationally immanent: "Having pervaded this whole universe with one fragment of Myself, I remain"—the Bhagavad Gita. Thus, we see that this attribute of perfect transcendence is not only valid, but is *absolutely necessary*. Nor does it deny the immanent aspect, which is also absolutely necessary.

> That which unseen is and will not be felt,
> Which hath no creed, no source, no attribute,
> Nor sees, nor hears, nor moves with hand or foot,
> Eternal, limitless, immeasurable, pervading all;
> That subtle Spirit and unchangeable Truth which is everywhere
> The wise perceive as vast creation's Source.
>
> —Mundaka Upanishad

> Do not ask whether the Tao is in this or in that; it is in all beings. It has ordained that all things should be limited, but is Itself unlimited, infinite.
>
> —Chuang Tzu

The maternal structural link between the finite and the Infinite is again universally held to be the "Unstruck Sound" of Om—the Word or Name of God.

> By the word of the Lord were the heavens made; and all of them by the breath of his mouth.
>
> —Psalms 33:5

> Listen to the Word, the Truth, which is your essence. He speaks the Word to Himself; and He Himself is the Creator.
>
> The Creator brought into being the Game of Joy: and from the word Om the Creation sprang.
>
> All things are created by the Om; The love-form is His body.
>
> Receive that Word from which the Universe springeth!
>
> —Kabir

Om is recognized as the *"mother* sound of the universe" in the Sikh religion, too, whose name for the Absolute Reality is *Omkar.*

> The Lord is indestructible; He permeates the universe entire.

From the Lord's sole Word the endless stretch of creation arose; and millions of rivers of life came gushing.

By the will of God alone is all life provided. Everything in the entire creation is with God's Name renewed;

The Name of God is sung by all beings of all worlds.

Hearing His Name, the devotee plunges into His vast ocean of virtues.
—Guru Nanak (S. P. Kaur's translation)

Om is the rhythm by which the Dance of Shiva—the continuous creation, preservation, and destruction of matter at the basis of manifestation—is performed. It is indeed regularly referred as the "sound of the Cosmic Drum," where drumming is always periodic. Significantly, artwork depicting Shiva in this cosmic dance—as Heinrich Zimmer notes in *Myths and Symbols in Indian Art and Civilization*—shows him holding a drum "for the beating of the rhythm. This [drum] connotes Sound, the vehicle of speech, the conveyer of revelation ... and divine truth." Further, Shiva's consort (or *shakti)* Kali continually gives birth to all things as Mother Nature. Similarly, in *The Tibetan Book of the Dead,* the "Lord of Dance"—i.e., the lord of all that moves and is moved—is regarded as the agency of creative sound and the sacred word, and is characterized by the qualities of air, wind and breath. Guru Nanak, founder of the Sikh faith, likewise refers to the "Lord of Cosmic Dance."

In the beginning was the Word, and the Word was with God, and the Word was God.... All things were made by him, and without him was not anything made which was made.
—John 1:1-3

In the beginning was Prajapati, the Brahman, with whom was the Word and the Word was verily the Supreme Brahman.
—the Rig Veda

The sacred word Om is one with God and indeed is God.
—the *Srimad Bhagavatam*

The "Word of God" is the very basis of all created things (cf. "And God *said*...") and is the linguistic means by which God introduces distinctions in (the vibratory rate of the waves on the surface of) the

Ocean of Reality. This then gives rise to localized wave-disturbances or particles, and thence to sensorially-experienced apparently independently-existing objects, seemingly divorced from the Ocean of Light which permeates and surrounds, and *is,* they and I.

His form is infinite and fathomless,
He dances in rapture, and waves of form arise from His dance.
—Kabir

Om!—This imperishable sound is the whole of this visible universe....
What has become, what is becoming, what will become—verily, all of this is the sound Om.
—Mandukya Upanishad

Every revealed Divine Name when ritually pronounced, is mysteriously identified with the Divinity. It is in the Divine Name that there takes place the mysterious meeting of the created and the Uncreate, the contingent and the Absolute, the finite and the Infinite. The Divine Name is thus a manifestation of the Supreme Principle, or to speak still more plainly, it is the Supreme Principle manifesting Itself.
—Frithjof Schuon,
The Transcendent Unity of Religions

Thus, we see that Om is not merely a word or name—although it is the Word and Name of God—but is rather an objectively-existing sound, audible to one's inner consciousness: an "intuitively audible illumination." Being related to the ripples on the surface of the Infinite Ocean, Om is also referred to as the "noise of many waters" (Ezekiel 43:1-2). AUM is the philosophically preferred spelling of this Name; however, the proper pronunciation is "Ommm," not "Aauuummm." In the spelling and chanting of *Aum,* "A" is said to represent and refer to the waking state, "U" to the dream state and "M" to the deep sleep state. Each inner repetition of *Aum*/Om thus works to take us upward in consciousness from the waking state, through the astral stages of dreamful sleep and the causal state of deep, dreamless sleep. The silence that follows each recitation of the word Aum then suggests the state of *turiya* or the Absolute beyond the physical, astral and causal realms, which is the Source and End of everything.

It is interesting to note that, technically speaking, the bandpass-filtered impulse consists of a sinusoidal oscillation —producing the periodic wavyness or "bouncing" behavior. This is then modulated or multiplied by a decaying exponential, causing the decrease in amplitude of oscillation (i.e., the "decay" of the signal) with the passage of time. In such a filtered impulse, the pitch or rate of oscillation is (for narrow bandwidths) roughly proportional to the resonant frequency. Larger bandwidths, however, cause a greater rate of attenuation of the radii of expansion in successive inflations. This monotonic decrease in amplitude may be compared to the effect, in human speech, of a mouth, initially fully open, but then closing as time passes—"modulating" the vocal vibrations being passed through it.

In chanting Om audibly, then—which is generally done *once* per *breath*—we observe that the first step is for one's vocal cords to produce a sound of a certain pitch or rate of oscillation. Then, in modulating this sound, one's mouth is initially open and circular, in producing the vowel "o" sound, and closes (i.e., the circle contracts slowly to a point) to vocalize the "mmm" aspect. Understandably, then, the human voice is considered, in India, to be the finest musical instrument. For, of all means of musical expression, singing most closely emulates and so expresses the basic structure of consciousness.

Further, if one takes a conch shell and divides it in half vertically, one finds that it has a spiral form inside. The form of this curve—called a "logarithmic spiral"—is repeated frequently in Nature, in elements as diverse as the arrangement of seeds in a sunflower head, the design of spider webs, and the structure of galaxies. Fascinatingly, the same mathematical curve is also created when ocean waves break on the shore. Equally fascinating is the fact that we can hear "the ocean's roar" in seashells. Both of these sounds are then viewed as physical approximations of the seed sound of creation, Om—as expressing a fundamental mathematical order to creation.

The white light of a movie projector contains all pictures in potential, but does not produce any until it has been filtered by the film. Likewise, it is only when the Void-Breath of God is modulated or made vibratory that it gives rise to waves of finitude on the surface of the Infinite Ocean, or an intuitively audible sound of the Cosmic Drum in Om. Full union with the sound of Om then consists of feeling oneself as this sound of all waves of light, in every unit of space within the finite spherical cosmos, for it is present everywhere within the vibratory sphere. Consider also that this rhythmic sound could be characterized not only as arising from the beating of a Cosmic Drum, but also from the rhythmic clapping of Divine Hands—the structure is identical—or, more accurately, from the clapping of One Hand. That is, *Om is the sound of one hand clapping.*

> Sounds heard by the outer ear are produced by "two things striking together," whereas the sound of Brahman is "the sound which comes without the striking of any two things together." This sound is Om.
> —H. Zimmer, *Philosophies of India*

Alternatively: What is the sound of one hand clapping? It is everything and nothing. For the rarefied sound of Om produced by this clapping is the root of all manifest creation. And yet, being the basis of all vibrations, this sound itself is utterly unmeasurable and undetectable, except in conscious oneness.

Such koans as the above are further said to each have a unique, recognizable solution. As such, they cannot be merely "nonsense riddles," allegedly having the sole function of working to suspend the conceptualizing activity of the intellect via their unsolvability. For one "nonsense riddle" would surely have the same "solution" as any other such riddle. Significantly, then, the contemporary healer Barbara Ann Brennan notes, in her remarkable *Hands of Light,* that

> my reaction to this well-known koan is to find myself stretching out into the universe on a pattern of unheard sound that seems to flow on forever.

This, indeed, is the unique solution to the koan in question.

The human body, being made "in the image of God," is again a microcosmic representation of the body of God in the cosmos. And human speech is made possible through the effect of air being exhaled from the lungs, thus being intrinsically associated with the breathing process. We would thus expect that the process of Divine speech, in the production of the sound of Om, should be inherently associated with a cosmic breathing process.

"These things saith the Amen [Om], the faithful and true witness, the beginning of the creation of God.... Behold, I stand at the door and knock:

if any man hear my voice, and open the door, I will come into him, and will sup with him, and he with me" (Revelation 3:14, 20). Knocking, as with drumming, etc., consists of a rhythmic series of impulsive sounds.

Further note the association of this knocking with a voice. Normally, we do not knock with our voices, but rather with our closed hands or knuckles. Such a melding of voice and hands would thus be an unnatural alliance, were this knocking not to be inherently associated with a mouth (of God, i.e., the medullary chakra, connected by polarity with the spiritual eye) and a Word (and with breath). The translation of the Biblical "Logos" as "Word of God" is thus eminently perceptive, offering much insight, via the invoked metaphors, into the basic cosmic structure.

The mythologies of many peoples consider creation (or creative power, i.e., free will) as being based in the power of words (thought-forms uttered/broadcast with deep concentration) spoken by God. This apparently simplistic view is, in fact, very significant and profound. For what is a word? It is a certain pattern of vibration. What, then, is the Word (Vibration) that contains all other words (rates/patterns of vibration)? And does the presence of such a Word infer the existence of a mouth or mouths (of God)? And what is the function of the human mouth? humans being created "in the image of God." Mouths are simply means of speaking, and of eating or drawing energy of differing vibratory forms into one's body. And what is blood, but a means of distributing this energy within one's body?

Any body must further have a presiding intelligence. In the case of the cosmos—the body of God, or *body of Christ*—this is exactly the Christ intelligence/consciousness. That Christ consciousness, being present everywhere within the (blue) sphere of the cosmos, may again be said to be spherical—and so is represented by a blue sphere in the spiritual eye. Human consciousness likewise takes the form of a sphere of intelligence, as a "bubble" or small sphere in the big blue sphere of the Cosmic Sea. And, existing as it does within the blue sphere of the cosmos, the Christ consciousness is the "spirit in the *sky.*"

The principle of "As above, so below" again implies that objectively measurable behavior (the physical manifestation of archetypal symbols) is a reflection of the behaviors of mind and consciousness (based in the subtle and causal manifestation of the same symbols). By that precept, any metaphysically valid myth will embody strong structural truths. The most important and interesting aspects of human religious mythology and ritual are thus not merely arbitrarily assumed superstitions having a shared pagan ancestry, but are rather imitative of higher levels of reality than are generally subjected to rational analysis. Consequently, the archetypal themes which appear and reappear as valid mythological elements—those based not merely in superstition but in higher truth—of the earth's many cultures must be understood not only as having a psychological manifestation, demonstrating the collective subconscious desire for return to the lost state of Perfection, but as having a *structural* manifestation also. The metaphorical nature of creation straightforward implies this.

CHAPTER VII

HOLOGRAMS

HOLOGRAMS ARE A MEANS OF visual information storage, similar in some ways to photographs. The two means of storage differ in that every piece of a hologram film contains information about the entire three-dimensional scene being holographed—and can be made to project a light-formed "duplicate" of its objects in three dimensions when illuminated with a proper source of light, usually a laser. Photography, on the other hand, "collapses" this information irretrievably into a two-dimensional planar view of the objects, so that a slide transparency can project only a two-dimensional view of its contained scene.

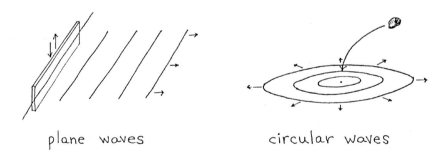

plane waves   circular waves

Figure 7.1

The means by which holograms are made may be easily described. The light emitted by a laser is said to be "coherent"; that is, its light waves are all in step with one another, giving rise to what are called plane waves. (The waves produced when a pebble is dropped into a pond are circular/spherical, while plane or straight waves could be produced by rhythmically raising and lowering a long stick in the water; see Figure 7.1.) Such planar wavefronts have the desirable property that, since they are all of the same frequency and all "going in the same direction," they do not spread out much as they travel farther from their source.

If ever such a plane wave tries to "squeeze through" an aperture of width much smaller than the waves' wavelength—where the wavelength is the distance between crests of the wave—a source of circular or spherical waves, having the same wavelength as the incident waves, is effectively produced. Imagine a barrier with a small vertical slit placed in a shallow tank of water: any plane waves incident on the barrier that pass through the slit will emerge on the other side as circular waves, as in Figure 7.2.

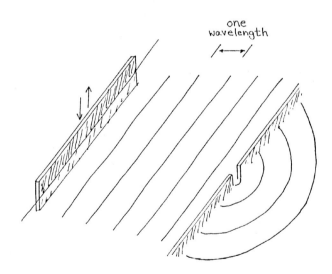

Figure 7.2

Now, any physical object is made visible through its ability to reflect visible light. And any ray of light, when allowed to reflect off of an object, is effectively converted by this reflection into a point source of spherical light waves (as if it were squeezing through a very small aperture). These reflected waves then spread outward from the object; the spherical waves having their center at the point where the particular ray met the object, with their intensity being determined by the color and reflectivity of the object at that point. If and when some of these light waves impinge on an eye, the sensation of sight of that part of the object is produced. That is, when you "see" any object, you are not experiencing the object itself, but are rather cognizing a sphere-of-(physical)-light representation of it. The information from these expanding spheres of light is carried from the sense organs to your brain by means of impulsive spikes of electricity, which are then decoded to produce the idea of the object within your own mind (Figure 7.3). That is, visual perception is based in spheres of light and impulsive spikes. And holograms are made by allowing the reflected spherical waves of the aforementioned setup to interact with the reference or unreflected plane waves, and recording the interaction on a piece of film, which plays the part of an "eye" (Figure 7.4).

Figure 7.3

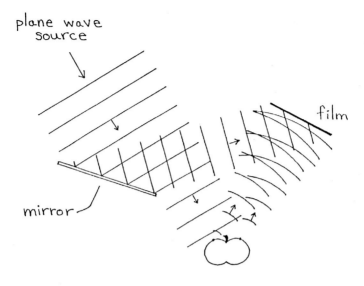

Figure 7.4

Because the waves, after having been reflected by the object, travel as expanding spherical wavefronts, they diverge rapidly as they leave the object.They thus spread out to interfere with each other and with the reference beam across large areas of the photographic plate (or film). This large-surface-interaction will occur for every sphere of light reflected from the scene, so that every small area of the holographic plate will contain information about large areas of the object/scene.

Interestingly, there are indications in neurological research that there is not a one-to-one correspondence between the areas of the brain and the places where our past thoughts or memories are stored. That is, it has been suggested that our memories are stored in holographic, rather than photographic, form by the brain.

Now, if we illuminate a hologram with a reproduced reference beam of coherent light, as these plane waves pass through the hologram film they will be diffracted by the recorded interference patterns on the film into myriad spherical waves. These will continue on through the film and interfere with one another, effectively reversing or undoing the procedure through which the hologram was encoded. In this way, the illuminated holographic film reproduces the same pattern of centers and intensities of expanding light-spheres as was generated by the original object, producing a three-dimensional light-formed image of the object, suspended in space (Figure 7.5).

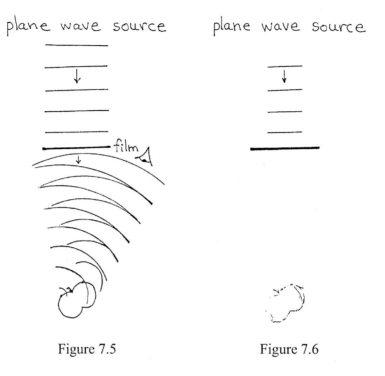

Figure 7.5   Figure 7.6

In illuminating the entire developed plate (with a reproduced reference beam), we will recover a very sharp and clear picture of the object. However, if we illuminate only a small area of the photographic plate, although we will still be able to recover the three-dimensional picture, the sharpness of the image will depend on how much of the plate we have illuminated.

In illuminating only a small area of the plate with the same intensity of laser beam, less total light energy is incident on the plate—the small area of which further contains less precise information as to how that light should be diffracted. Thus, less light can be diffracted by the hologram. Consequently the image produced, although still being three-dimensional and of the same size as the original object, will appear dimmer and fuzzier than the original object (Figure 7.6).

The only way to shrink or enlarge the three-dimensional image produced from a holographic plate is to use a different frequency of light in projecting it than was used to make it. Illuminating only a small piece of the holographic plate will display the scene at its original size, but from a restricted number of viewing angles. That is, choosing an element close to the top of the holographic plate will project a more "overhead" view of the scene, while illuminating a lower portion will show a more "horizontal" perspective. Thus, it is incorrect to say that every piece of a holographic plate contains *all* of the information about the entire scene.

Holograms thus reduce to the interaction or interference of point-source spheres of light, with plane light waves of the same frequency. But plane waves are simply special cases of spherical waves: any plane wave may be regarded as arising from a spherical wave *of infinite radius* (and so having zero curvature). That is, *holograms are formed through the interaction of finite spheres of light with infinite spheres of light!* It looks suspiciously, then, as if consciousness is cosmically structured as a universal hologram, where the perfected Consciousness of the Absolute contains all frequencies, and so can serve as an absolute reference for all possible relative vibrations in finite spheres of consciousness. Bentov's view of consciousness as being "driven" by the impulsive swinging of a Cosmic Pendulum similarly recognizes the holographic nature of interacting rippling "observers" or spheres of consciousness, again as the basis for intuition. That is, an expanded sphere of consciousness "illuminates" a larger region of the hologram of creation, and thus has a greater and clearer access to the information contained in the myriad other spheres overlapping with itself.

> For light everywhere meets with light, since everything contains all things in itself and sees all things in another, so that all things are everywhere and all is all.
>
> —Mystic saying

> Each person, each object in the world, is not merely itself, but involves every other person and object and, in fact, on one level *is* every other person and object.
>
> —Buddhist Avatamsaka Sutra

> From a non-understandable pattern of random light, [the inwardly-perceived lights] snapped into an understandable, fixed, holographic pattern of large, luminous balls.... My body-sense, with which my self had associated all my life, had changed into a "luminous-ball-sense," in which the new environment of luminous spheres was my new body.
> —W. Thomas Wolfe, *And the Sun Is Up*

Indeed, again according to Brennan in *Hands of Light*—this book being a fascinating elucidation of the principles underlying higher-body healing—many persons, when undergoing psychodynamic (i.e., "laying-on of hands") healing of their bodies' energy fields or aura at the hands of a *highly proficient* healer,

> begin to have a beautiful golden-silvery point of light in the center of the head that grows into a brilliant ball of light. As the person develops, this ball grows larger and extends beyond the body.... The location of this light seems to be in the root area of the crown and third eye chakras, where the pituitary and pineal glands are located.

The pituitary is the master endocrine gland in the body, affecting all of its hormonal functions, while the pineal regulates biorhythms on the basis of the amount of light received by the retina, and of daily variations in the earth's magnetic field. (The seven major cerebrospinal chakras are located in the coccygeal, sacral, solar plexus, heart, throat, medullary/forehead and crown regions. Each of these is correlated with the activity of a specific endocrine gland in the physical body: the adrenals, gonads, pancreas, thymus, thyroid, pituitary and pineal, respectively.)

René Descartes, among others, regarded the pineal gland as the "seat of the soul," i.e., as the point of connection between consciousness and body. Further, the idea of the soul being a diamond-like, immaterial, indestructible point is found frequently in archaic and medieval philosophical writings. Compare also the Western alchemical idea of the "rotundum"—the "round" vessel in the skull that is the place of the final alchemical transmutation, of union of the created with the Eternal Ground of Being. That is, the creation of the cosmic, whole, or "round" Man; a transmutation into *golden* light, no less. The metaphor of gold in the context of the divine spark in humans—of the "real self," as distinguished from the personality—is a common one in the world's mythologies.

Now, any localized island-particle is produced only through the interaction of many overlapping subtle ripples. Thus, these impermanent islands—formed in the whole flowing movement of the Ocean, and shortly to dissolve back into that movement—are not "ordinary [i.e., autonomous and continuously-existing] objects." Thought, energy and matter are all ultimately illusory—they are all transitory, rising-falling waves on the Ocean of cosmic consciousness, having no permanent or autonomous existence. They are not, however, all *equally* illusory, in the sense that the fine ripples of thought are a higher state, closer to the basic reality of the Ocean, than is physical matter.

Moreover, since the Ocean *is* Consciousness, and since thought is merely a fine vibration of that Ocean, clearly consciousness, in its purest form, is more basic than thought. We have the feeling of self-awareness with or without thought; we do not need to think in order to know that we exist. Conversely, with regard to Descartes' dictum, "I think, therefore I am": the ability to think does indeed assure us that we exist—we must exist in order to think; "I think, therefore I exist." However, thinking does not itself give us self-awareness, i.e., consciousness and existence, or the feeling that *"I am"*—that is, existence, plus consciousness of that existence, or the intuitive feeling that "I exist consciously."

In the same way, whatever important role which the use of language may play in the development of the psychologically-defined ego or the definition of one's separate self-sense, it does *not* give us self-awareness. Likewise, the hope is sometimes advanced that if a computer or machine were to become advanced enough in its operations, it would spontaneously develop self-awareness. Again, however, neither language nor the ability to think are what give us the intuitive feeling that "I exist consciously," so that particular science fiction-like hope is almost certainly wildly misplaced.

Again, whenever a plane wave tries to "squeeze through" an aperture of width much smaller than its wavelength, a source of spherical waves, having the same wavelength as the incident waves, is effectively produced. Similarly, in the universal structure, finite spheres of consciousness are produced in the Infinite Ocean wherever the infinite undivided ("planar") omnipresence of Spirit tries to "squeeze into" creation. The finite spheres there have the same rhythmic frequency of *recurrence* as does the incident planar signal of the Universal Breathing (Figure 7.7). With regard to this picturesque "squeezing in from outside," however, recognize that each impulse of the Cosmic Projector is merely a potential movement of the Ocean; it is not something separate from those waters.

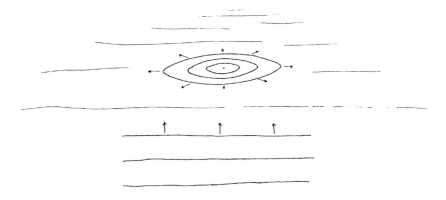

Figure 7.7

Physical holograms, in being derived from the interaction of finite spheres of light with infinite spheres of light (i.e., plane waves), again reflect the basic structure of consciousness. Creation is not a hologram, as such; it does, however, have exactly the same *structure* as do physical holograms. The hologram-like archetypal structure of consciousness proposed here, however, is not merely pantheistic. For pantheism recognizes only the immanent aspect of God, or considers Brahman to be only the "sum of all created things," ignoring the fact that the Ocean exists with or without the waves, as well as beyond the finite waving region. Rather, this view or model includes inherent reference to the transcendent nature of God.

God is not one thing among many, nor is He the sum-total of all things. Rather, God is One without a Second, is the Source and Suchness of every created thing, and yet exists also beyond all things. It is therefore of great importance that we keep in mind that just because a certain (archetypal) structure is repeated or reflected on many different levels of creation does not license us to attempt to derive the higher levels from the lower. We can at best find some of the behaviors of consciousness reflected in the behavior of matter, but never validly derive the characteristics of consciousness from those of matter. That is to say, since matter reflects the behavior of consciousness, we must again find some aspects of the behavior of consciousness reflected in any theory that is at all successful in describing the phenomena of the physical level of reality. The more comprehensive and true the theory, the more clearly its predictions will mirror the manners of consciousness.

Thus, in the sense already discussed, we may rightly say that creation *is* (structured as) a universal time-varying hologram, or holomovement. The latter term was coined by David Bohm in connection with his concepts of the implicate and explicate orders. Bohm has also been a major contributor to the development of the ontological formulation of quantum mechanics, which is able to derive subatomic Nature's apparently irreducible randomness from a non-random (but still chaotic) basis. In Bohm's holomovement, a particle "moving" from A to B is not the same particle at B as it was at A. Rather, each intermediate position of the particle as it moves from A to B—that is, each discrete re-creation (or projected "frame") of the particle in the "holomovie"—is actually a "different" particle than it was in its previous position:

> [Imagine] a wave that comes to focus in a small region of space and then disperses. This is followed by another similar wave that focuses in a slightly different position, then by another and another and so on indefinitely until a "track" is formed that resembles the path of a particle. Indeed the particles of physics are more like these dynamic structures, which are always grounded in the whole from which they unfold and into which they enfold, than like little billiard balls that are grounded only in their own localized forms.
> —David Bohm and F. David Peat,
> *Science, Order, and Creativity*

That is, in the holomovement, matter has no continuous existence independent of whatever may be "projecting" this time-varying hologram. This obviously compares favorably with the discontinuous nature of matter implied by a universal rhythmic basis, where all matter is being constantly re-created, or kept in store, as waves in the Ocean of God, by the Word of God.

Additionally, the ontological formulation of quantum mechanics has very sensible ideas regarding the nature of the "vacuum state"—the state of empty space in the absence of matter. In it, the quantum vacuum state is viewed as a randomly fluctuating background, having an average level of fluctuation equal to zero. Physically observable particles then correspond to regions of space where the level of fluctuation is non-zero over a sufficiently long period of time. (Such a turbulently fluctuating or "random" background, however, is not to be confused with the inherent causelessness at the basis of creation asserted by modern physics.)

All such "objects" or particles are abstractions of relatively invariant forms of waves on the Ocean of Light. That is, they are, as the Tibetan Buddhists note, patterns of movement, as opposed to autonomously-existing "things" or "ordinary objects" in motion, interacting with one another. Thus, any "forces" seeming to act between such abstracted-from-the-flowing-oceanic-movement particles are likewise only abstractions "projected" from the Oceanic Intelligence of God (as we have noted earlier in the case of the "Newtonian laws" governing ripple-produced islands).

It is not just that everything is changing, or in flux: all *is* change, all *is* flux. As Bohm noted, the process of becoming is *what is* (in terms of the waving, finite levels of reality: these exist only as change or motion in the Ocean of the Absolute, which itself exists with or without the vibratory process of Becoming).

Ultimately, it is of no use or sense to talk of cause-effect laws in physics or genetics—although it does have a relative and pragmatic usefulness. For all such "inexorable laws" can hold sway only in so far as they are continually upheld by the uncaused Will of God, by whose Hand all matter is continuously created, preserved and destroyed. (For particles to exist at all—whether "running down" in the increase of entropy or otherwise—bespeaks the existence of an underlying inconceivable Intelligence and order. This order is present in "inanimate" matter as much as in living things.)

Again, then, if you place an object in a drawer, and take it out hours or years later, it is not the "same" object as it was previously (nor are you or the drawer the same). Rather, its atomic islands—as well as your body, mind and memories—are being constantly re-created by the Divine Intelligence immanent in all matter, and exist only as waving modifications of this One Great Consciousness. If God were not continually active in creation, it would dissolve at once. Conversely, it is true that there is no birth or death, only change: all differences emerge and submerge in the same Being.

As the web springs from the spider and is again withdrawn, as the plant springs from the soil, hairs from the body of man [i.e., from point-like pores], so springs the world from (and is reabsorbed into) the Everlasting.

—Mundaka Upanishad

There are no objects "in movements," it is the movement which constitutes the objects which appear to us: they are nothing but movement. This movement is a continued and infinitely rapid succession of flashes of energy.... All phenomena of whatever kind and whatever aspect they may assume, are constituted by a rapid succession of instantaneous events. [Impulses are literally, and mathematically, instantaneous events.]

One [theory] states that the course of this movement (which creates phenomena) is continuous ... the other declares that the movement is intermittent and advances by **separate flashes of energy which follow each other at such small intervals that these intervals are almost non-existent.**

—Alexandra David-Neel and Lama Yongden,
The Secret Oral Teachings in Tibetan Buddhist Sects

We are deceived if we allow ourselves to believe that there is ever a pause in the flow of becoming, a resting place where positive existence is attained for even the briefest duration of time. It is only by shutting our eyes to the succession of events that we come to speak of things rather than processes.

—A. K. Coomaraswamy,
Buddha and the Gospel of Buddhism

This is true not only of the normal application of this idea to our sensory gestalt and internal mental milieu, but more importantly and profoundly of the basic, quantitative structure of the cosmos. We thus find here the solution to the age-old philosophers' question as to whether reality is Non-Being, static Being or flowing Becoming, for Becoming bears the same relation to Non-Being as the waves do to the ocean. That is, the Substance from which all creation is drawn is Non-Being—the "water" of the Infinite Ocean—but wherever there is manifestation, this is inherently a flowing and inherently constantly-changing process of Becoming, rooted in that Non-Being. Being then arises as the relatively stable aspects of the process of Becoming, as apparently continuously-existing matter of all degrees of subtlety. Such Being may appear to be static, but is rather highly dynamic. (One can, however, reverse this ontological order of Becoming and Being if, instead of a process-based view in which Becoming gives rise to a Being which is Many, one takes either the chaotic Ocean of Being or the Point as the One source of polarity and multitudinous Becoming.)

CHAPTER VIII

PSYCHOLOGY AND MOTIVATIONS

REASON IS WHAT GIVES US our faculty to discriminate, while feeling gives us the ability to enjoy. That is, reason tells you that a certain pattern of sensory impressions is a flower rather than a tree or a house, a rose rather than a lily. Feeling, then, allows you to enjoy the rose for its beauty—you do not enjoy it more for having dissected it and weighed its petals. Validly-recognized-by-feeling harmonious and inharmonious (to the welfare of the body or mind) sensations, however, regularly become polarized into arbitrary likes and dislikes. And after that has occurred, emotional attraction and repulsion, and thus attachment (to objects or environments which we have developed a "liking" for) will generally follow.

> Attachment is that which dwells upon pleasure. Aversion is that which dwells upon sorrow.
>
> —Patanjali, *Yoga Sutras*

That is to say, since we have to like something before we can desire to have more of it—or dislike something else before we would wish to avoid it—it is obvious that likes and dislikes give rise to desires, not the other way around.

The emotions involved in attachment include anger toward, and hatred and fear of, that which threatens, or seems to threaten, our continued enjoyment of liked objects; volatile love of that which produces such enjoyment; jealousy/envy of those who possess attributes which, if we only had or could gain them, would produce happiness in us; short-term, conditioned happiness when these desires are satisfied, greed for more objects of attachment, frustration at the thwarting of desire, and sorrow when these objects are taken away; and the willingness, then, to harm others in order to secure our own egoic happiness. Dissolving the emotional reactions to the egoic likes and dislikes then in no way leaves one bereft of feeling, but rather clarifies and enhances it, removing the generally discoloring and clouding effect of biased personal tastes.

> Inwardly always renouncing everything, devoid of desires within and performing externally what is to be done, the yogi remains perfectly equable.
>
> —*Yoga-Vasishtha*

In a related vein, conceptualization—of one's sensory experiences, or otherwise—does not by itself result in attachment. For, just because one must necessarily first conceptualize "things" out of one's sensory gestalt before one can be attached to them, does not mean that the simple act of conceptualization produces attachment. Equivalently, it is not *intellect* that reacts *emotionally* to the events of one's life.

Likewise, it is not the simple continued visualization and expectation of "the best" happening in one's life that produces disappointment if and when that hoped-for result fails to materialize, but rather our emotional attachment to that outcome. Conversely, being "nonattached" to the fruits of our actions does *not* mean that we should not have and visualize specific goals in our lives! Rather, it means that at every setback one regroups and works with renewed enthusiasm toward the goal, while simultaneously keeping in mind the sincere attitude that if that goal is actually, unbeknown to oneself, against the will of God, it would be better if circumstances or even the end of one's life prevent it from ever being realized. In the same way, following one's intuition does *not* mean that "if at first you don't succeed," it must be because you're working against God's will! As the saying goes, it is all about having the courage to change the things we can, the patience to accept the things we can't change, and the wisdom to know the difference.

Just because one's actions may be motivated more by feeling than by reason does not in any way necessarily contribute to them being irrational, any more than does being motivated primarily by reason make one cruel or unfeeling. Pure feeling gives rise to the most reasonable behavior, indistinguishable from that arrived at through undistorted reasoning based in correct postulates. For both of those, when pure and undiscolored by desire or preconceived prejudice, are guided by the higher source of partially-illuminated intuition, and in that proportional measure are valid. That is, when one's heart is undistorted by fear, selfishness, hatred, jealousy or anger—in short, uncolored by attachment—its feelings are intuitive.

Although both intuition and instinct appear as simply "knowing," their basis is fundamentally different. Instinct is programmed into us as part and parcel of our material nature, and present just as well in the animals as in human beings. Intuition, however, has nothing to do with our personalities or heredity, but rather derives from contact with our higher selves, transcending our animal natures and personalities.

It can be very beneficial to guide and compare one's reasoned conclusions with the feelings of the *pure* heart. However, this "checking with the heart" does little good if the heart's feelings are discolored by the same prejudices and desires which influence one's processes of reasoning. Generally speaking, the flawed use of logic will not be corrected, but will rather be reinforced, by an appeal to the (impure) heart; and vice versa.

Thus, basing one's decisions in feeling rather than in reason, while equally valid, will not prevent self-destructive behavior, so long as the same short-sightedness that sways the use of logic is still present. After all, humans are as likely to act selfishly based on short-term emotion-discolored feelings, as on short-sighted reasoning.

Further, in the dichotomy of thinking/reason and feeling, the "feeling" here has nothing to do with sensory awareness, but refers rather to the function of the heart in love and compassion, for example, or at least to the emotionally-discolored and self-centered versions of these, when biased by one's arbitrary likes and dislikes. When we ask someone how they feel, we are inquiring (primarily) as to their emotional state, not their current sensory impressions, such as whether their clothes "feel" too tight. Even when we talk of having a bad feeling about a person or situation—i.e., an intuitive sense of "bad vibes"—that information is picked up through our subtle bodies, not our physical senses. That is, it is no identification of intuition with the physical body.

Now, each of the body's seven cerebrospinal chakras is associated with a level of structure of our selves. Thus, the coccygeal chakra at the base of the spine is related to the physical body (that is, to the etheric template underlying the purely physical). The next two centers are associated with the sexual and with the mental-rational aspects of our earthly selves—i.e., with the subtle body in which our conscious reasoning processes occur—respectively. The fourth subtle bodily level (the astral), corresponding to the heart chakra, is then regarded as the seat of human emotions—of our desires, moods, longings, sensual appetites and fears, etc. It thus contains the energies of our emotional relationships with others. The fifth is, according to Brennan, a cobalt blue "negative" blueprint of everything manifested on the levels below it. The sixth chakra and sixth level of the auric field correspond to the faculty of conceptual understanding and the experience of a celestial love that encompasses all life as manifestations of God; it is through this body that we experience spiritual ecstasy or Bliss. The seventh layer and its allied "thousand-petaled lotus" or "Golden Flower" are associated with the experience of direct knowing or the level of Divine Mind, the integration of personality with spirituality, and the ability to "clearly understand broad overall concepts about existence, the world, and its nature"—that is, with wisdom. The only "emotion" allowed at levels above the astral is the energy of love.

The third auric level is sometimes called the "lower astral"; while the fifth is on occasion designated the "lower mental" body, but is also often included, along with the sixth and seventh, as constituting the causal or ideational body. (Thus, while the fifth or "mental" level is *higher* than the astral, the third or "linear mental-rational" body is *lower* than the astral. This can obviously give rise to some amount of confusion.) The causal body may thus be said to be formed of wisdom, love and Bliss— the first of these arising from the seventh level, with the latter two attributes being characteristics of the sixth level. The causal level is the "intuitive" level also, owing to the penetrating activities of the expanding sphere at that level being the basis of intuition, in its contact with the Universal Mind. That is, in having access to the information contained in all spheres overlapping with its own. This intuition takes the form of profound intuitive flashes of understanding, comprehending broad principles all at once, the details of which can be abstracted later into linear form, if need be.

Each of the seven major chakras—as well as the more numerous minor chakras, acupuncture points, and the subtle counterparts to our physical organs—actually exist on each of the seven layers of the auric field. Thus, although the crown chakra, for example, is associated with or has the greatest influence on, or relation to, the seventh or "golden egg"-shaped level of the aura, it exists not only on that plane, but has grosser spatially coincident counterparts on each of the lower six levels also. Each of these bodies, from the physical to the seventh or ketheric, has a successively higher and finer frequency of vibration. Thus, for us to work through or be attuned to them requires an increasingly high resonant frequency of consciousness.

In addition to the characteristics stated above, the first chakra is also associated with our "will to live," while the third or solar plexus center is regarded as being "tied in to the higher astral and lower mental forces," i.e., the fourth and fifth levels.

> Thus, the [third level] lower mind is considered to be the objective, material mind which is affected by various emotional influences.... The upper three chakras are closely connected with the spiritual nature of human beings. They mediate the integration of higher spiritual forces into the physical personality, while the lower three chakras regulate more of an individual's physical nature.
> —R. Gerber, *Vibrational Medicine*

Gerber goes on to summarize the traditional esoteric ideas regarding the attributes of our subtle bodies:

> Whereas the [fifth level] mental body is more concerned with the creation and transmission of concrete thoughts and ideas to the brain, for their expression and manifestation upon the physical plane, the causal body [levels six and seven] is involved with the area of abstract ideas and concepts. Causal consciousness deals with the essence of a subject while the mental level studies the subject's details. The lower

mental [i.e., third level] body dwells upon mental images obtained from
sensations, and analytically reasons about purely concrete objects. The
causal body deals with the essence of substance and the true causes
behind the illusion of appearances.... On this plane we no longer deal
with emotions, ideas, or conceptions, but with the essence and underlying nature of the thing in question.

On the levels above the physical, we *are* what we *think*. That is, the
energy flows corresponding to our thoughts and feelings are recognized
as having as real an existence as physical matter does on the earthly
plane. Further, we note that in our dreams, in which we are identified
with the fourth-level astral body, we are the same person as in the waking
state—our personality does not change, much less is it transcended. The
rational mind, however, is inactive there. That is, we are quite content to
put up with "illogical" turns of events in our dreams, reacting to them
emotionally rather than reasoning that "this can't be happening." We are
thus led to associate our everyday personality or "lower self" with levels
two through four of the auric field. (But not level five, since mental
processes uninfluenced by emotional biases are impersonal, i.e., are not
part of one's "personality.") This grouping thus contains the emotional
and rational energies of ourselves.

Our "higher self" or spiritual component, which we are normally
largely unconscious of, then coincides with the remaining levels beyond
this, especially with levels six and seven. Of course, we are largely
unconscious even of our astral body in our waking lives—it is, indeed,
the level of our *subconscious*. (Repressed/suppressed physical, emotional and intellectual energies and thoughts, however, are also held in
the lower three levels of the auric field, as stagnant energy blockages and
muscular tensions.) If one wanted to define the "psyche," that would then
be bodies four through seven. The more traditional name for everything
from the fourth (astral) body up is, of course, the soul. For reasons
primarily related to maintaining a consistency with other sources quoted
herein, however, in this book "soul" is used as synonymous with the
transcendent Self.

There are differences in the degree of refinement of the subtle selves
of each one of us, just as there are mental, emotional and physical
differences between us. The lowest three of those seven subtle bodies
disintegrate at death, but the higher four continue to exist beyond that

transition. Persons with developed higher clairvoyant faculties have delineated the existence of an additional two perceptible levels above these seven. First, that of our intentionality, with the primacy of this Intentionality level being the structural reason for the fact that intentions are ultimately more important than actions. Then, above that, our Star-Self, a limitlessly expandable 360-degree sphere of white light at the highest ninth level, of self-awareness. This is the witnessing soul or Self—the "Holy of Holies"—underlying all of our states of consciousness. Finally, within the tips of the funnel-shaped chakric vortices are seals which control energy exchange between the layers of the auric field, and which knit together or unite the causal, astral and physical bodies.

The levels of the aura become clearer and more distinct from one another as we begin to understand them and learn to use the different aspects of our mind and consciousness. However, that does not mean that we are "creating those levels [from a unified auric field] just by thinking about them." That is, it does not mean that their form is just a product of our own expectations. Rather, that differentiation—e.g., the ability to introspectively distinguish between intellect and emotion, or the workings of the subtle bodies associated with the third and fourth chakras—occurs in the same way as the development of our muscles causes their distinct shapes and functions to emerge, thus making them "more distinct" from one another. The distinctions between various muscle groups and levels of the aura may be accentuated and clarified by appropriate exercise, but they are not *created* simply by that exercise. After all, we were not "one large muscle" prior to working to develop any particular bodily muscle.

If the first level of the auric field is low on energy, we will be physically lethargic. A subpar third level will show as mental listlessness, e.g., a disinterest in intellectual pursuits. A poorly charged second level will manifest as depression—i.e., a shortage of self-related "emotional energy." Since such shortages result from energy flows which we have ourselves blocked—cf. "hard feelings"—we have here the basis for the classic viewing of depression as resulting from repressed anger, for example. That is, psychological repression is an attempt to stop the flow of the subtle energies carrying hurtful sensations or thoughts—which are the same flows which carry pleasurable ones—creating energy blockages and imbalances in one's psyche. After all, nothing is ever repressed but with the hope of avoidance of physical or psychological pain. Interestingly, even simple exercise and stretching are said to have the effect of loosening such psychic energy blockages.

Our thoughts and memories are spatially distributed throughout our subtle bodies, which "overlap" or fully penetrate and extend beyond the physical body. It is precisely *and only* because of this that hatha yoga, massage, rolfing, acupuncture and other therapies affect not only our bodies but our minds also. The right half of the body is likewise traditionally and validly considered as masculine, and the left half as feminine. It is thus only because of this underlying structure that integrating the masculine and feminine aspects of one's psychology into conscious awareness, and so balancing the associated subtle energy flows, can have any relation to progress toward cosmic consciousness. Clearly, without the existence of this structure and of its energy flows, nothing in the realm of one's psychology could aid or hinder realization of the Point from which only Infinity is seen.

Now, it is true that our most deeply-rooted behaviors arise, either directly or indirectly, from protecting/indulging our individual psychological "original wounds." Brennan explains that the primary psychic wound for each one of us is indicative of the period of psychological development (from the time in the womb through latency) during which we first experienced life so traumatically that we wished to block its incited psychological pain, and began distorting our auric fields appropriately to suppress that discomfort. These patterns learned in childhood are then repeated in our relationships throughout our lives as our habitual psychological self-defenses—automatically reverted to in times of stress.

Needless to say, such involuntary tensions can have a great effect on our freedom of choice, causing us to behave in certain ways even against our conscious will. The examples given in Chapter V of the freedom to choose between alternative courses of action all involved activities which, for most people, are not emotionally charged. Obviously, however, a person who eats compulsively to fill an emotional "emptiness" inside, for instance, is going to have a much more difficult time saying "no" to a second helping than will one who overeats only for enjoying it on a sensory level.

The action of endeavoring to stop the relevant energy flows, in the attempt to avoid physical or psychological pain, again gives rise to energy blockages and so to a deficiency of energy in the relevant region of the corresponding subtle body. Such behavior thus yields not only repression but also sets the stage for disease in that domain.

> Before the beginning of this century, Freud and Josef Breuer had recognized that neurotic symptoms—hysteria, certain types of pain, and abnormal behavior—are in fact symbolically meaningful. They are one way in which the unconscious mind expresses itself, just as it may in dreams; and they are equally symbolic. A patient, for instance, who is confronted with an intolerable situation may develop a spasm whenever he tries to swallow: He "can't swallow it." Under similar conditions of psychological stress, another patient has an attack of asthma: He "can't breathe [or is being suffocated by] the atmosphere at home." A third suffers from a peculiar paralysis of the legs: He can't walk, i.e., "he can't go on any more." A fourth, who vomits when he eats, "cannot digest" some unpleasant fact.
>
> —Carl Jung, *Man and His Symbols*

Sufficient energy flow on the lower levels of the auric field, then, will not only clear out the stagnant painful psychic energy blockages which manifest as neuroses and/or physical illness, but will equally allow the energies of our astral, causal and transcendent selves to flow into our daily lives. That being the case, such clearing—or the reconnecting with one's "inner child," which has been obscured by those blockages—does indeed have a relation, albeit indirect, to the experience of the witnessing Self. After all, if resting in the Witness and realizing the dream-texture of the cosmos frees one from timidity to radically play in life, and if getting in touch with one's "inner child" has the same playful effect, can the two approaches really be so far apart? Are they not both ways of allowing higher energies to emerge or flow into one's daily awareness? even if, in actual childhood, one lacks the mature psychological structures in waking consciousness to "take the role of other," etc., which in any case certainly does not mean that such playfulness itself has merely a selfish or "impulsive" basis, even if it does *manifest* in selfish joy at that early age. Not that the infant was in any way "identified with his transcendent Self" or "one with the whole world in love and bliss." Rather, the early absence of suppression of energy flows in its waking consciousness simply allowed for the energies of the astral and causal bodies to flow more readily into his or her daily awareness— i.e., to be *grounded*—even if they were there translated into the infantile stages of psychological development in the waking frontal personality.

Intense energy flow in any of the seven levels of the aura will induce similar flows in the levels adjacent to it—akin to an induced current in electromagnetics—this potentially having an effect all the way down to the physical level. Conversely, energy blockages on any level have a similar retarding effect on adjacent levels, e.g., second-level emotional energy blockages are said to manifest as physical tensions, and as disruptions to the free flow of linear thought. For all of those reasons, "getting in touch with one's inner child" is *not* simply "recontacting an infantile/repressed psychological state." For again, the re-integration of those early repressions, etc., does not merely steady the foundations upon which subsequent psychological growth has been built, but equally allows for higher energies to be grounded into one's daily life and awareness. Thus, it is much more than what one would typically think of in terms of a "regression in service of the ego."

Our most noble impulses originate from the core of our beings as creative energy flows, which must then be allowed to flow unimpeded through oneself—i.e., through one's higher self and personality—to become manifest. The free flow of this energy in the absence of stagnant energy blockages or malfunctioning chakras certainly also has the effect of expanding one's consciousness. Thus, the seeking of this kind of "creative, positive pleasure" is not at all detrimental. Indeed, those creative, intuitive promptings of the blissful soul and higher self originate at a level which is in constant and instantaneous contact with all other Selves. Thus, they implicitly take into account the needs of beings other than oneself, so that following them results not only in one's own greatest good, but in good for all.

Even in the relaxation and temporary undefendedness felt upon awakening from a sound sleep, we may find a foretaste of the happiness that is our birthright. For the feelings of peace and contentment that come when we are deeply relaxed are not themselves generated by that relaxation, or even by the release of emotional energy blockages as neuroses or repressions. Rather, that muscular relaxation and stagnant energy release simply allows the peace that is already latent within us, but which is normally covered or masked with restlessness and by our habitual psychological defenses, to "peek through" when the energy blockages and tensions in our waking consciousness—i.e., in our lower three bodies—are temporarily relaxed. Conversely, even when meditation "silences the chattering mind" and takes us into a similar state of relaxation, that feeling of peace does not itself derive simply from the absence of the activity of the rational mind, i.e., the two are not at all mutually exclusive.

Our Self and causal body are constantly generating energies of peace, wisdom and Bliss, whether or not we can feel these in our daily lives, and even if there be differences in the degree of production of these energies based on the spiritual evolution of the individual. That is, differences again exist in the degree of refinement of our subtle bodies, not only on the extent to which we can get in conscious contact with them in meditation and retain the effect of that contact in daily life. These positive energies, however, are easily eclipsed in our waking consciousness when we live according to the personality and its various kinks—as opposed to relaxing and receiving all events in our lives as gifts from God. For it is exactly our inner cringing and habitual tension in defensiveness that mask the peace and Bliss already within us.

Interesting experiments have been done with animals, in which dogs were taught, first, to distinguish between circles and ellipses, via a system of reward and punishment. Then, the circles were gradually "flattened," while the ellipses were slowly made more circular, until it was not possible for the dogs to distinguish between them, i.e., to give the correct response. The effect on the experimental subjects was that, if they were "happy and excitable" dogs beforehand, they began biting the experimenters. On the other hand, if they were "carefree and relaxed" dogs before the experiment began, they became lethargic, not caring about anything.

Exactly the same thing happens to human beings when faced with the many mutually-contradictory demands placed upon us by our peers and parents—and which we in turn place on them and on our children. Thus, we may become uptight and "tie ourselves into knots," trying to please everyone and thus avoid the pain of rejection—constantly tensed both against the possibility of being hurt, and from frustration at the impossibility of satisfying the many mutually-contradictory demands placed on us. Or, we may "be relaxed about it" and not try at all, ignoring the effects that our chronic tardiness or unreliability in the performance of our duties has on others—believing that they should simply "relax more," to not be bothered by this. These two poles of human behavior, however, are equally ways of avoiding pain; one is not better than the other. In particular, there is nothing spiritual about the latter "relaxation."

Further, the former "uptight" approach leads readily to the attempt to avoid pain by "getting all the details perfect," while the aforementioned apparent "relaxation" avoids pain by glossing over details, or "not worrying about them" *even in situations where they definitely need to be attended to.* For, details of which one is not consciously aware cannot result in psychological pain for being done "wrongly," even if, by default, they are rather not done at all. Nor need one feel guilty at being inconsiderate of the negative effects of one's actions on others, if one chooses rather to simply be unaware of those effects.

Thus, albeit as a gross oversimplification of the many factors involved in each individual case, we may say that the former "uptight" approach will tend to produce artists, philosophers and theory-oriented scientists—for whom every detail is important, and precision is revelled in, down to the last decimal place or brush stroke. The latter "relaxed" defense, conversely, can be easily incorporated by business people, for example. Of course, even when we do not choose our professions to fit in with our deeply-rooted psychological defenses, we will certainly bring those defenses to bear on the way in which we do our jobs.

Gregory Bateson tells a story which sheds much light on both human and animal behavior. It seems that he arrived home one day feeling very fatigued from his work and wanting just to be left alone for the evening. His dog, however, was in a very frisky and playful mood, and kept trying to involve his master in various "games" they regularly played together. After several increasingly-annoyed admonitions to the animal, Gregory shouted very harshly at it, whereupon the dog finally caught on, and slunk away feeling very hurt. Seeing this, Bateson apologized and petted the animal, and "explained" again to it that he just wasn't "in the mood" at that time. Their relationship, however, was permanently affected by that incident—there was always a "distance" between them after it, or a defendedness on the part of the dog, where previously there had been complete and unconditional openness and friendship.

Through analogous experiences we have each learned, like Bateson's dog, to be guarded and to keep a "safe emotional distance" away from one another. (Such experiences include having our early spontaneous displays of affection rebuffed; or being made to feel that questions we have asked are "stupid" ones to which anyone should know the answer; or that our highest and most noble ideals are naïve and foolish; or that in asking for help from others we are intruding on their limited "precious time" and energy, etc.) The emotional and energetic armor goes up and becomes habitual, simply because the pain hurts so much more, in the short term, when we are not defended against it.

Very few people "outgrow" the need for approval from others, one aspect of which is certainly to have them value one's advice. Rather, what human beings do is to populate their immediate environment with others who will fulfill that need—e.g., children and subordinates/disciples, who *have* to show respect, whether or not it has been earned—and then pretend to have outgrown the need for approval by, for example, spiritual practice. Of course, emotional atrophy—where the need still exists but simply isn't felt—will equally well deal with such needs.

We all want and need recognition for our work, whether or not we are able to admit that to ourselves. It is only the insecure and mediocre ones, however, who want to receive bowing *respect*—for position, age, etc.—on top of that, and inflate their (monastic or secular) egos by giving unsolicited advice or management, on spiritual and/or secular topics. Even if every compliment is welcomed and accepted graciously, persons who consistently do a high caliber of work don't need to be told that their work is valuable in order to feel psychologically secure. Likewise, persons who are genuinely unselfish—as opposed to helping others so that God or Man will notice them—don't need to keep a mental list of "how much effort they're making" on behalf of others. Nor do they need to make others feel that the latter are "intruding on their precious time" when asking for favors.

In terms of reincarnation, now, consider a character from a play, re-used in a sequel, but having forgotten all of the lines from the previous play. The personality of the character at the beginning of the present play or life is identical to his/her personality at the end of the previous play—all of the character attributes are the same. But the specific scenes previously enacted (i.e., the bare facts of the prior incarnations, including the environments in which they were performed) are forgotten; only the character changes wrought by those scenes remain. This is true whether the reincarnation is into a body of the same gender as in the previous play, or into a different-gendered (or different-raced) body. The personality, ideals, goals, and virtuous or vicious means of attaining those goals remain the same.

Given a comparable set of circumstances, then, without radical character transformation by the end of the previous play, such a character would behave in the next play or life in substantially the same way as before. That is, the character would make all of the same mistakes over again, simply from "the other side of the fence" if the reincarnation is into a body of a different gender or skin color. We do not shift from selfishness and the willingness to mistreat others in the pursuit of power and happiness, to unbiased concern for "justice for all," simply for having our gender, skin color or environment altered. Conversely, "the ambition of the downtrodden is always to become middle-class imperialists themselves"—Gregory Bateson.

> In life, people change in very small increments. They don't make those big massive leaps that people love to make in "television land." Most of us tend to make the same mistakes over and over again. And what we do is we trick ourselves into thinking they are different mistakes ... by disguising the circumstances of the error. But the truth is that we screw up the same way almost always. And what that means is that when we change, we change in the smallest increments over a pretty long period of time.
>
> —Steven Bochco, in Wolff and Cox's
> *Successful Scriptwriting*

The same holds true of the process of death and rebirth: as they say, we will not become angels at death, if we have been devils during our lifetimes! In this slow process of change also lies the danger in the willingness to dismiss aspects of Truth that one finds uncomfortable. For when this one life ends, and the specific reasons for the discomfort are forgotten, the willingness to play lightly with Truth, or reject uncomfortable aspects of it, remains. And devotion to the psychological comfort of the ego, rather than to Truth, is unlikely to produce any good effect for oneself or for others. ("He who trifles with truth cuts at the root of *ahimsa* [i.e., non-violence]. He who is angry is guilty of *himsa* [i.e., violence]"—Mahatma Gandhi.) We demonstrate, in our reincarnated childhoods, not only the natural interests, talents and proclivities developed in our previous lives (witness Mozart, for example), but also the basic character traits evolved through the same period. The ability to think independently or one's contentedness in spending time alone similarly do not mysteriously "vanish" at death. Rather, they form the basis for the childhood behaviors of the next incarnation.

Fascinatingly, now, the ideas of being "green with envy," "blue with unhappiness," "red with anger," "white with fear," of carrying around a "gray cloud of sadness," of being "beside oneself" and of shooting angry "daggers" (of destructive energy) through narrowed eyes are all claimed to be visible to clairvoyants as exactly these colors/forms in our higher bodies, when we are charged with these emotions. The same is true of the rose-colored light of love—the color of the heart chakra on the fourth, astral level, is pink; so that, whenever we are feeling love for others, our aura will be charged with rose light. Such a pink hue "combines white unconditional spiritual love (from the higher chakras) with red emotion (from the lower chakras)"—Ric A. Weinman, *Your Hands Can Heal.*

The visibility of colors/emotions in the aura is also true of rich brown being a "grounded," earthy color (with other sickly browns indicating disease, however); as well as of scarlet or red-orange being associated with sexual passion, as in Revelation's "Scarlet Woman." One would guess that cowardice corresponding to having a "yellow streak down one's back" or a "yellow belly," and inharmonious interactions with others leaving a "bad [or bitter] taste in one's mouth" are likewise objectively true; as with the idea of getting "cold feet." (Regarding yellow, though: high spirituality also shows as a brilliant yellow [cf. gold] in the aura, this perhaps being the origin of the "Yellow Castle" and "Yellow Emperor" of the Taoists.)

Further, according to the same tangible perceptions, psychological "projection" literally involves the flow of subtle energy from one's wrongly-functioning chakras into the surrounding environment. The forming of relationships similarly shows the actual growing of subtle "strings" of attachment from heart to heart—i.e., "heartstrings." Likewise, inharmonious thoughts may be felt as pinpricks by persons sufficiently sensitive to this, as in "By the pricking of my thumbs, something wicked this way comes." Further, the auras of two people in love, when in close proximity to one another, combine to form the heart-shape traditionally associated with romance; while pregnant women who "glow" do so because of an actual increase in life energy in their auras.

The same "literal" nature, according to Brennan, can be true of back problems developing from one's "backing out" of challenges, or not following one's intentions through. Poor energy flows through the legs and a resulting weakness there likewise frequently derive from not "standing up" for oneself. Or alternatively, we may add, from not wanting to "stand on one's own two feet," i.e., to accept responsibility for one's actions and life circumstances. (Of course, this is not to be confused with the sudden and radical upward pull of one's energies in the face of intense or other-worldly beauty, as causing one to feel faint or "weak in the knees.") Likewise, one finds pancreatic difficulties indicating an inability to absorb "sweetness" not only from edible foods but in one's relationships also; and persons having "vacuum-cleaner eyes" that literally suck energy out of the people around them. Plus, chakric "cords" or strings of energy in our relationships moving from the front to the rear of the body when we put elements of our past "behind us."

A clairvoyantly-visible shaft of light is further said to be visibly present in the body of one who has been "shafted" by a lover. With comparably predictable structure, when a person is having difficulty understanding something, his auric field becomes foggy; and when we feel "butterflies" in our stomachs, it is because the third chakra situated there is wobbling (cf. "not having the *stomach*" for the situation). Likewise, we instinctively focus at the spiritual eye when "gazing heavenward," from which comes the idea of heaven being "above" us.

Similarly, when we feel "centered" in our core Star-Self—located in the belly—or inner divinity, or when we straighten our Intentionality line at the eighth level of subtle bodily structure in *"aligning* ourselves [i.e., our intentions] with a higher will," these are accurate statements about objectively-existing microcosmic bodily structure. One cannot help but wonder if "learning things by heart" in memorization, having words "on the tips of our tongues" and giving ideas "off the tops of our heads" might equally refer to clairvoyantly visible/audible literal structures and energy flows. Likewise for seeing the world through "rose-colored lenses" and having recognized memories "ring a bell."

Cosmic structure, both macrocosmically and microcosmically, is invariably based in metaphors. This is only natural, in that the frequencies composing our higher bodies—where our mental processes of thoughts and emotions take place—and the corresponding higher levels of reality, are "higher harmonics" (i.e., higher octaves) of those found on the physical level of reality. The physical is then the "end product," not the origin, of the higher "life fields" and mental processes. That is, when a certain pattern is established in our thoughts or emotions, it will eventually "work its way down" into the lower harmonics of the physical *in a similar form*. Whether we describe creation in terms of metaphors, "as above, so below," higher/lower harmonics, or similarity in patterns, the meaning is the same.

> Metaphor, far from being a decoration that is added to language, purifies it and restores it to its original nature.
> —Claude Levi-Strauss

> Water "symbolizes" Universal Substance, and thus, in a certain way, "is" Universal Substance.
> —Frithjof Schuon

> It is the greatest thing by far to be the master of metaphor.
> —Aristotle

Undoubtedly, many more of our "superstitions" are based, like the above, in truthful observations of reality, meant to be taken fully literally, not "interpreted" or explained away as fanciful subconscious projections. Certainly this is also claimed to be true of the existence of feminine winged angels and Nature spirits; of the form of the sphinx and of the personification of evil in the form of a black cat; and of soft pastel colors in the aura being associated with femininity. It is also claimed to apply to the colors and number of "petals" or energy vortices traditionally associated with each chakra—with each vortex metabolizing energy of a specific frequency, characteristic of its rate of spin. Likewise for the shapes of the cross, ankh, triangle, Star of David and swastika (this being an archetypal symbol representing cosmic energy, according to Bentov) when used in spiritual contexts.

Every one of those forms has been independently perceived by numerous sages, in meditation or through higher senses than the physical. Although figures such as these are indeed "symbolic"—for *everything* in creation is symbolic in its structure, from atoms to universes, being based in "As above, so below"—there is nothing arbitrary about them. That is, they are not merely human-created or in any way culturally-influenced, but are rather basic to the structure of the cosmos, and of the microcosmos in the human body.

Emotional states and the recognized stages of psychological development exist not merely in amorphous, abstract terms, for every mental characteristic, every thought, has a corresponding objective vibratory structure and flow of subtle energy. This must be the case, for such attributes are functions of our higher bodies, thus having definite location in space. Indeed, "thought bubbles" of subconsciously-formed ideas are said to be clairvoyantly visible in the aura, these having exactly the same "pictures" inside them as when one would visualize the same objects. (Interestingly, comic strips commonly portray their characters' thoughts as rising in comparable bubbles.) For instance, psychics have recorded "silver spoons, silver plates, and similar objects," circling around the head of a man who imported and exported those very items. They have likewise reported subtle wispy layers of mud clinging to the hands and arms of a sculptor; and clairvoyantly-visible images of potatoes whirling around the head of a woman whose job involved them.

In a more dramatic example, Michael Talbot has related, in *The Holographic Universe,* his experience of having the translucent, ghostly image of a werewolf's body form around his own—complete with visible individual hairs in his "fur," and canine nails in his wolfish hand—while deep in thought about a novel regarding that subject. As he was sheathed in that phantomlike werewolf body, another psychic house guest of his happened to walk into his room, immediately remarking on his having "become a werewolf." They compared notes, and found that they were each observing the same features.

Indira Devi, in *Pilgrims of the Stars,* describes a related experience she had while meditating in her guru's temple hall in Poona, India, with a group of friends. She could see (clairvoyantly) very clearly that most of them had an aura of tension around them; not one person in the group was completely relaxed, the first necessary condition for meditation.

Suddenly she *saw* a sex thought floating in from without and touching one person who accepted it. He became restless, but the thought developed in his mind in the form of jealousy.... He played with the thought and was soon carried away on the wave of a grievance and anger against the guru, the world and God.

The thought touched two other people but as they did not give it a fireside seat, it quickly turned away from them. Another friend accepted the thought as his own and felt terribly anxious about his health.

Devi thus concluded that "many of the thoughts we take to be our own actually float in from the atmosphere and that it is our own free choice whether to accept or reject them."

In vain you believe, oh artist,
You are the creator of things.
For ages they rove in the air
Invisible for our eyes.

—A. K. Tolstoy

Now, what we tend to do in our lives as human beings is to concentrate on the most prominent "pain" currently afflicting us, ignoring for the moment our lesser discomforts. We then pretend that, if only that largest trouble would go away, we would be happy and have nothing to complain about or react angrily to. It is like the person who has an itch, and complains about it—for misery, like a good secret, cries out to be shared; it is a very difficult thing to keep to oneself, as it loves company and recognition. He then bangs his funny bone and forgets about the itch; then stubs his toe. Temporarily, such a person forgets about the funny bone's disagreeable sensation and the itch, believing that "as soon as my toe stops hurting, I will be comfortable." But, of course, when the toe recovers, he simply goes back to complaining about the funny bone, and then about the itch.

Additionally, we tend to look at the people around us, and feel unfairly treated and deprived if they possess things we lack, although rarely feeling comparably grateful for our own unique good fortunes. If everyone had the same "itch," we would much more willingly bear ours. Indeed, consider how we generally "get along quite well" without a developed sixth sense of intuition, and do not feel "mistreated by the universe" in lacking that sense, but how damage to any one of our normal five senses would be considered as a great loss (for there we "know what we are missing"). But if we have an itch, however mild, that most others lack, we focus on this minor misfortune, while ignoring our many blessings and the significantly greater misfortunes of others around the world.

We tend, in that way, to be insensitive to others' suffering, while being keenly aware of our own. We would do better, however, to be insensitive to our own misfortunes and intolerant of our own complaining, but tireless in the compassionate effort to alleviate the suffering of others. Shared, extended or projected self-pity is not the same thing as compassion, even though it regularly masquerades as such. Rather, it simply trades lamentations of "poor little me" for the collective "poor little *us*," encouraging that commiseration.

Sympathy in general depends on *identification* with the person suffering. That is, it depends on the evocation of the memory of one's own distress in similar situations, and a converse intolerance for suffering elicited in others by circumstances which one would not find distressful oneself. This attitude sometimes presents itself as non-attachment, but is actually callousness. Compassion, however, requires no such identification as the above. Rather, it seeks to ease suffering even in situations where people are overreacting to their loss, i.e., in circumstances through which one could easily pass without distress oneself. Thus, without encouraging others' lamentations or miring them deeper in self-pity, compassion recognizes that *self-pity and anger are themselves kinds of suffering,* or a stunting of one's spiritual growth, deserving thus of alleviation, not of contempt.

Compassion is indeed defined as "a feeling of deep sympathy and sorrow for someone struck by misfortune, *accompanied by a desire to alleviate the suffering.*" In the common confusion of extended self-pity with compassion, however, we sympathize with others largely *in order to justify our own feelings of sorrow* or of being "picked on" by the universe in comparable situations. These other "innocent victims," by virtue of their having suffered the same type or degree of real or perceived mistreatment as we have, become members of our "group," thus being eligible for sympathy.

Now, the following of intuition in one's life requires not only the development and use of one's higher spiritual bodies, but an equal absence of biases and prejudices in one's everyday personality, that one's inner promptings may be received clearly and without distortion.

Undoubtedly this is a large part of the reason why yoga maintains that any person who *reasons clearly* will sooner or later develop a keen *intuition*. And this clarity entails a willingness to consider equally all possible sides to every story, without projecting one's own psychological kinks onto it—this is what it *means* to be unbiased, after all. The recognition then quickly and inevitably follows that both the liberal and conservative elements of society regularly dismally fail to do this, each seeing only their own side but presenting it as the full and unbiased truth. There is no point of view, no matter how blinkered and biased, that cannot be given an apparently inarguable basis in logic, simply by ignoring what one doesn't want to see, and thinking only so far—and no farther—as to get the answers which one wanted to hear from the beginning.

Needless to say, although the astral-level expansion underlying Nature mysticism indeed qualifies as one type of "intuition"—as does even rudimentary clairvoyance—it is of a vastly inferior grade to that gotten through the refinement of one's causal body and the literal expansion of one's causal-level sphere of consciousness. One can get shamanic-type knowledge—e.g., of knowing the location of every woodland animal within one's vicinity, without having to look at them— and fitful emotive artistic inspiration or other guidance from the afore-mentioned astral expansion and clairvoyance. Thoughts of genius, how-ever, require the development of, and contact with, one's causal body. That is to say, not all "intuition" is created equal. In particular, something like the "physicists' intuition" as to which of all possible paths to pursue to the solution of a problem, is of a much higher grade than is common clairvoyance, such as knowing who is on the other end of the line when the phone rings before having picked the receiver up, for example.

Actually, a person who can see auras on the causal level can discern whether someone is highly intuitive simply by observing the latter's sixth and seventh subtle bodies. If an individual's causal body is highly refined, and in particular if he has a large amount of clairvoyantly-visible pure light flowing into his crown, it is certain that a good amount of intuition will percolate down into his daily consciousness, even without his having practiced any explicit spiritual discipline in this one life. (With regard to "pure light flowing into the crown," consider that intuitive, "aha!" moments are commonly represented in the form of a light bulb going on above one's head.)

Owing to the development of the higher spiritual bodies in past lives and past after-lives, the causal-level intuition underlying all genius may be likened to a brilliant lamp covered with a thick veil (of unopened chakras and restlessness). By contrast, much astral-level shamanism, clairvoyance and contemporary spirituality arise from a relatively dim "lamp," but one having a very thin and transparent veil (of opened chakras). The weak and easily-visible lamp may actually give off more light in its daily use than the heavily-covered bright bulb. That pragmatic characteristic, however, is no certain indication that the former is of a higher spiritual grade than the latter, for very often exactly the opposite is true. Conversely, much if not most "spiritual advancement" derives from simply becoming attuned to aspects of our higher selves which existed well prior to this one incarnation, and which need simply to be "uncovered" and brought down into our daily lives. And none of that real advancement or attunement ever comes simply from being able to "silence the linear conceptualizing mind," or from isolated visionary experiences.

Generally speaking, "spiritually advanced" persons have simply opened "doors and windows" into higher levels of being that exist, *with varying degrees of refinement,* for all of us. These are levels to which we will all return at death, and which do not necessarily increase in refinement simply for our having opened those doors. That is, such persons have "let the sunshine in" to the rooms of their daily lives—or at least into temporary meditative experiences. That, however, does not at all imply that the sun (of their astral and causal selves) shines brighter, or that their intuition will be keener, than for someone who has yet to effect those openings.

Thus, while no one should diminish the value of "spiritual awakenings," it is nevertheless very easy to exaggerate their importance. In particular, one could easily wrongly assume that they would grant a level of wisdom, intuition, compassion, tolerance or forgiveness which in reality extremely few "spiritually awakened" persons possess. Indeed, the common idea that spirituality needs to be "manufactured" or created by meditation and spiritual discipline/ascetism/celibacy leads in practice to an inflated reverence for the degree of wisdom *and spirituality* possessed by persons who have undergone "spiritual awakenings," especially kundalini-related ones. For rarely is it admitted that such spirituality exists to varying degrees for each one of us right now, not merely on the level of Self *but even on the astral and causal levels,* and is largely merely "unveiled" by spiritual effort. After all, we are not merely higher animals, in our physical bodies, but fallen angels as well, in our spiritual natures; we do not need to create that higher nature through any form of discipline.

The undue reverence for "manufactured" spirituality further breeds a dangerous readiness to regard the questionable actions and opinions of such "advanced" persons as being God-guided "working in mysterious ways." In reality, however, those actions are much more often the product of the same ignorance, ego and garden-variety neuroses and other personality quirks—not to mention power issues—that existed before the awakening, thus having *nothing* to do with intuition. After all, ignorance suffused with Bliss is still ignorance, for the two are not in any way mutually exclusive. Indeed, anyone who does believe that they cannot co-exist is probably more blissed-out than wise.

Of course, no conscionable person would accept or encourage adulation for his own "spiritual advancement," if that was unmerited. But the degree of conscience and self-honesty needed to discourage that following—i.e., to be uncomfortable with having others view one as being radically more infallible than one actually is—are, sadly, no prerequisite for spiritual awakening. Indeed, that following is much more likely to be *welcomed,* as a way of helping others to become "as spiritually advanced as oneself." That is, the same situation leads too often to a degree of arrogance on the part of such "awakened ones," a substantial number of whom are given to the comfortable and ready (but wrong) assumption that anyone not so explicitly "awakened" as they are must have a lower degree of wisdom and intuition and, ironically, a larger ego than themselves!

Personally, I would far rather do without any "spiritual path" filled with leaders and followers drastically lacking in integrity, honesty, reliability, tolerance and the basic ability to keep their promises. Any decent person does not need to be practicing spiritual discipline, in meditation or otherwise, to be *more* "spiritually advanced" than the bulk of the spiritual seekers *and leaders* in this world. Conversely, the idea that leaving an ashram or stopping one's practice of meditation, etc., equates to "leaving the spiritual path," is utterly self-serving nonsense, enforced primarily to make the persons still practicing that discipline feel important ... and superior. And whether or not one believes in God, karma, or higher levels of reality, etc., while on or off any of those "paths," makes no difference at all in qualifying one's degree of "spirituality"—it's utterly unimportant and irrelevant.

It has been rightly observed that the term "mystic" should really be reserved for persons having some actual degree of explicit higher-state-of-consciousness experience. That is, a person's intellectual beliefs or vague feelings about a wholeness to the universe, however sincere, do not qualify him as a mystic (nor do *wrong* intellectual conceptions disqualify him). Thus, the founders of quantum physics were definitely *not* mystics, regardless of their sincere sympathies toward Eastern philosophy. (David Bohm, however, had at least one significant personal mystical experience, of light and wholeness.) Having said that, however, it is undeniably obvious that the depth of insight, self-honesty, concentration, compassion and consideration of the feelings and needs of others, along with the height of moral character, loyalty and commitment to truth, and the degree of causal body refinement of a "non-mystic" (and non-meditator) such as Einstein were definitely inestimably greater than the comparable attributes in all but a small percentage of genuine mystics. Even a minimal contact with contemporary advanced meditators, healers, shamans and psychics will disclose and confirm this.

Deep spirituality, compassion, integrity, and an intrinsic sense of morality and responsibility (i.e., conscience) again come much more from the past-lives' development of one's causal body, than from any astral-level experiences in this life, in meditation or otherwise. One's conscience is a mixture of causal-level intuitive promptings as to what is the "right" thing to do, clouded by astral-level emotions and by internalized or subconscious parental and societal rules regarding how one is allowed to think and behave and yet still remain a "good person."

Of course, in practice it is not necessarily easy to separate those different levels of influence. Indeed, one can feel guilty and "know" that one has done wrong for violating any of these bases, but only the former has any metaphysical or moral validity as a guide for one's behavior. In any case, it is obvious that the subtle inner voice of conscience arises from the causal level, not the astral, for conscience is a *superconscious* faculty, not a *subconscious* one. Our subconscious mind may sway our decisions, but it most certainly is not the high voice of conscience.

One's inner conscientious sensing of higher or universal principles of morality is again a function not only of causal-level development but also of attunement to that level. That is, it arises from a combination of the brightness of one's inner "lamp," and the thickness of the shade covering it. When properly developed, this results in that high inner voice speaking so loudly that one cannot ignore it. This advanced moral sense is of course *correlated* with the highly abstract thought of the causal bodily level and the ability to consider perspectives other than one's own. It is not, however, *caused* simply by that broadly-synthesizing thought, i.e., by mentally seeing, from multiple perspectives in waking awareness, how "all things are connected," and behaving accordingly.

Thus, as is the case with "spiritual advancement" in general, much of our progress through the higher stages of conscious psychological growth is simply a process of integrating or grounding attributes of ourselves which already exist in our higher bodies from past-lives development (that is, in lives both on the physical level and in higher realities), and which we need merely to become attuned to or unfold in our waking consciousness. Conversely, if those higher bodies/levels are thus highly developed to begin with, it is certain that their attributes will shine through in one's daily life, whether or not one follows any "spiritual path" or discipline in this one life.

CHAPTER IX

SYMBOLISM AND STRUCTURE IN MYTHOLOGY

WE HAVE NOTED EARLIER that the underlying auric structure of the human body contains seven major chakras, located along the spine and in the brain. These cerebrospinal chakric vortices form, symbolically, the serpent—the kundalini energy coiled three and a half times at the base of the spine—with seven "heads" found in many of the world's mythologies. The Kabbalistic Tree of Life, too, has seven such levels. (The raising of the kundalini energy into the brain produces ecstatic spiritual realization, or the union of the Feminine and Masculine principles of Shakti and Shiva in the individual.) Of the highest of these bodies, the Mundaka Upanishad states:

> In a beautiful golden sheath hides the stainless, indivisible, luminous Spirit.

> Partless, limitless and sinless, Brahma stays inside the supreme golden case. He is pure and white; He is the light of all lights. Those who know Soul, also know Him.

Compare also Snow White and the Seven Dwarfs: She, the most beautiful in the land—poisoned but not killed by the jealous wicked Queen, *Maya,* in the latter's hope of being regarded as "the most

102

beautiful"—and brought back to life by the actions of her handsome Prince.

The serpent of the kundalini energy, however, should not be confused with the symbolism of the two snakes entwined around a pole. This structure is seen in the winged caduceus adopted as the symbol of healing by the Western medical profession, and found regularly in mythologies throughout the world. These latter two serpents represent two of the primary life currents in the body, criss-crossing the spine in exactly the "figure-eight" manner of the snakes of the caduceus. That is, these have their tails meeting at the lowest spinal chakra in the coccygeal region, and their heads at the spiritual eye, in between the eyebrows.

In mythological symbolism, poles, sticks, staffs and the like invariably represent the *sushumna*. This is the astral spine, coincident with the axis of the physical spinal column, and intertwined by the aforementioned serpent-shaped breath-current passageways, called in Sanskrit the *ida* and *pingala nadis*. (The same structure is referenced by "Trees" which, in mythology, stand for the human body's nervous system, with its "roots" of hair, "trunk" of the spine and "branches" of afferent [sensory] and efferent [motor] nerves bearing the "fruits" of various sensations. Thus, this nature of the nervous system as an "upturned tree" accounts for the Inverted Tree motif found in mythology.) *Nadis* are the "astral nerve-tubes" or channels for subtle energy flow in the body, this flow being akin to the circulation of blood through the veins and arteries of the physical circulatory system. These energy conduits are "nerves" too, in that they are said to carry sensations from the body surface and interior to the spine and brain.

The astral nervous system is empowered by the *prana* and *apana* currents—which flow with the ingoing and outgoing of breath, respectively—working through the astral *nadis* that correspond to the physical sympathetic or involuntary nervous system. (Consider that we tend to inhale deeply, smile and have good posture when invigorated—on the first day of spring, for example—and to sigh and walk with slouched shoulders when depressed. This is claimed to be due simply to the predominance of the upward-flowing *prana,* and the downward *apana,* respectively.) The primary *nadis* of that astral sympathetic nervous system are the *ida* and *pingala* nerves.

When the *prana* and *apana* currents are neutralized and the breath thus stopped through meditative practice, the life force normally expended in maintaining the body and producing awareness of it withdraws from the *ida, pingala* and subsidiary astral nerves—i.e., from the internal organs and involuntary nervous system, causing a temporary bodily "death"—into the spine and brain. That is, the spine becomes spiritually magnetized—the positive pole being in the brain and the negative pole at the base of the spine. This magnetization is then claimed to draw the life energy from the muscles and organs into and up the spine, into the brain. This produces a condition of suspended animation, in which the crown of the head has been described as becoming hot "like a stove element," while the rest of the body goes cold. Such a condition of suspended animation obviously cannot be lumped in with other states of unresponsiveness to external stimuli as a mere "trance" state, however, any more than death could be viewed as such a "trance." During this "conscious death" of *samadhi,* the bodily cells are sustained directly by subtle energy from the medulla, without the intermediary of breath or blood circulation. Finally, *ida* and *pingala* are sometimes viewed, not as crisscrossing the spine, but simply as running alongside of it—corresponding to the chains of sympathetic nerve ganglia on either side of the spinal cord—from the coccyx to the spiritual eye.

The kundalini energy rises upward along the *sushumna* when awakened, and has been inwardly seen as a "golden-like white fire" ascending into the brain, with some of the flames spreading outside either side of the head into a "winged radiance." In mythology, the holy river of life energy in the spine is also represented as the sacred river Ganges in India—Jordan in the Christian faith—with the Yamuna and Saraswati symbolizing the *ida* and *pingala* nerves. The *Popul Vuh*—the scripture of the Mayan Indian Zunis—likewise speaks of an "air-tube," a "twofold air-tube," and "Hurakan" or lightning. These clearly represent the *sushumna,* the two-fold *ida* and *pingala* nerves, and the kundalini energy, respectively. The American Indian "peace pipe," too, is said to represent the spine, with the ornamentations along its length symbolizing the various chakras. It is claimed that the smoke drawn along these hollow pipes was not inhaled, but was rather gathered in one's cupped hands and then spread over the head and shoulders as an auric cleanser.

Yogic treatises speak of a second subtle channel called *vajra* inside the *sushumna,* and of another of *chitrini* or *chitra*—from *chit:* consciousness or intelligence—inside that second passage. The interior channel of the astral *chitra* is called the *Brahmanadi*—this being the causal spine—which leads into the *Brahmarandhra* or "cavity of Brahma" in the crown chakra. The *vajra* channel begins at the second or sacral chakra, while the opening of the *Brahmanadi* is at the third or lumbar center. Traditionally, as the kundalini energy rises from the base of the spine it is said to pierce the seals of each of the spinal chakras in turn in its ascent. However, in Aurobindo's system, the upper chakras opened first when the kundalini energy rose. Also, it is sometimes suggested that the gold, blue and white of the spiritual eye correspond to actual currents of the same colors, in the subtle spine. Finally, each of the seals in the chakras actually exists on all seven levels of subtle bodily structure—there is thus not merely "one" seal to open in each center.

The two objectively-existing life currents symbolized in the intertwined snakes of the caduceus are, predictably, one masculine or solar *(pingala),* and the other feminine or lunar *(ida).* (The light-giving sun is traditionally a masculine symbol, while the moon, shining by reflected light, is taken as feminine.) The Kabbalistic Tree, likewise, has its positive right and negative left sides—representing, as in Taoism, the light and active masculine, and the dark and passive feminine aspects. Compare this with the fortune of Tiresias in Greek mythology who, in accidentally striking a pair of mating snakes with his *stick,* was changed from male into female for *seven* years; and then back to male again, when striking the snakes a second time. After these encounters, Tiresias was made blind to the outer world, but given the gift of prophecy, i.e., had his inner eye opened. The supreme Norse god Odin—who could see into the future—likewise sacrificed an eye (i.e., leaving him with only a single eye) in return for being allowed to drink from a secret *stream* of wisdom and poetry.

The Cyclops, of course, with its single eye, represents the same subtle eye of intuition, pierced with a "hot stick" by Odysseus in Homer's epic. Odysseus' guide on his journey was Hermes, the god associated with the caduceus—the guide of souls to the underworld, the patron of rebirth and lord of the knowledges beyond death, which may be known to initiates even in life, via the "conscious death" of *samadhi.* We find in the same peoples' mythology the virgin-born, resurrected god of wine, Dionysus. This is akin to the presence of Christ in the bread and wine of the Mass; where bread and wine, in scriptural contexts, typically refer to life energy and to the intoxicating joy of God-communion, respectively. (The swell of Bliss in high states of consciousness can actually cause one to sway as if "drunk with new wine.")

The "calabash gourd"—a well-known creation symbol—as with the cosmos, similarly consists of an (animal) *skin, filled with wine.* Likewise, we find in Roman mythology that Vulcan made a mirror for Bacchus, "into which the god looking, and beholding the image of himself, proceeded into the whole of a divisible fabrication." (Bacchus was the immaculately-conceived and twice-born god of wine, Son of the Zeus-Father.) That is, Bacchus or the spiritually intoxicating Christ consciousness is the mirror which reflects all the images of creation, but which itself remains unchanged. A mirror is, of course, also found in the Snow White tale. There, however, it informs the wicked queen or *Maya,* gazing at her own reflection, that not She but the snow-white soul or Self is the "fairest of them all."

Any sphere (or disk) of light is inevitably going to be compared to the sun, for their undeniably similar appearances—the discus was a sun-symbol in ancient Greece, for example. Likewise, any inner perception of the life currents of *ida* and *pingala* criss-crossing the astral spine is going to give rise to the symbolism of two snakes intertwining a pole/tree/stick. Nor is it absolutely necessary for one to have practiced techniques of meditation working specifically with these currents in order to see them. Indeed, Gopi Krishna perceived the actual *ida* current and precipitated the rise of the kundalini energy simply through concentration on the golden lotus of the crown center, without specifically trying to raise the kundalini. Similarly, the existence of the spiritual eye in the center of the forehead, and its claimed ability to see inside solid objects with "x-ray vision" of varying resolutions—it being, quite literally, a "third eye"—could give rise to any number of variations on the Cyclops myth. The actual sphere of light centered in the midbrain, likewise, is inevitably and validly going to produce an association of that center with the sun.

Now, in tantra and kundalini yoga philosophy, the seat of the soul in every human being is designated by a point or *Bindu*—the dwelling-place of Shiva (e.g., the masculine sun)—in the crown of the head, atop the *sushumna.* The kundalini energy coiled at the base of the spine is conversely the microcosmic seat of Shakti (or the feminine moon, or serpent). Given the presence of this highly important and objectively-existing point at the top of the spinal "Tree of Life," it need not surprise us that trees and staffs are regarded as symbolic of the *axis mundi*. That is, they are symbols of the World Axis, and its associated World Center or "still point of the turning world," in T. S. Eliot's words.

The esoteric and primary meaning of this axis and point concerns, not merely the ubiquitous center of Divine influence in the world, but rather the *sushumna* and inner spiritual sun at its pinnacle. That is, they refer to the spinal axis of the *inner* world, through which the omnipresent Divinity is realized for oneself, as we shall see shortly. These "symbolic"—i.e., structural—trees and points are well-known images. Indeed, in his analysis of the common themes and symbolisms of folktales from around the world (in *Cinderella's Gold Slipper*), Samuel Denis Fohr notes that in these stories

> the spiritual aspirant is often pictured as one who must climb a pole or tree which symbolizes the *axis mundi* or Divine Spirit. At the top is the Spiritual Sun, which is at once Heavenly Paradise and Being.... The aspirant must actually go through the Sundoor to what is beyond the cosmos.... The climb up "the heavenly ladder" begins at the Earthly Paradise [i.e., a balanced life].... The Divine Spirit is the Way to break out of the universe, the "single track" and the "strait way" which penetrates the "cardinal point" where all contraries coincide.

Similarly, the Kabbalistic Zohar confirms:

> In the center of [the whole of the heavens] there is an opening facing the opening of the supernal Palace on high and forming the gateway through which the souls soar up from the Lower Paradise unto the Higher Paradise by way of a pillar that is fixed in the Lower Paradise reaching up to the door on high.... The garments [i.e., bodies] of the Lower Paradise are made of men's actions [i.e., karma]; those of the Celestial Paradise of the devotion and earnestness of his spirit.

Fohr provides compelling interpretations of many of the well- and lesser-known "fairy tales," based in the timeless philosophy underlying yoga and all true religions. That is, he gives readings based in the perennial philosophy rather than the standard interpretive fare in which the stories are reduced to either sex or sexism, neither of which exist there except in the minds of those misled analysts. After all, if we look in a mirror, and do not like what we see, we should not blame the mirror or its manufacturer! for it is just showing us what is in ourselves first. Only by clearing out our biases or freeing ourselves from the psychological problem of "seeing only what we want to see" can we perceive what is really present in these tales and in the world's scriptures.

The insights provided by Fohr, however, are greatly enhanced by an appreciation of the microcosmic structure to which so many of these folk stories clearly refer. If Snow White goes to live in a house (i.e., a body) in the woods (of duality), for example, with seven spiritually-helpful dwarfs (chakras) who mine gold ore—mining being "digging for the hidden treasure" of God "buried" in us—the consonance of this with the clairvoyantly-visible subtle structure of the human body can hardly be accidental.

> If you want your children to be intelligent, read them fairy tales. If you want them to be more intelligent, read them more fairy tales.
> —Albert Einstein

There can be no question that folk and fairy tales were originally told, not for their entertainment value, nor for simply "finding a moral" in them. Nor were they relegated to mere "children's stories," any more than should the tales in the Bible have been so denigrated. Rather, these were all told for precise and profound instruction on the spiritual path.

Indeed, the spiritual journey of the "solar hero" mentioned by Fohr above, in the ascent of the "tree" or "ladder" of the spine in the raising of the kundalini energy, begins at the first chakra, and reaches an actual microcosmic sun or sphere of golden light at the root area of the sixth and seventh cerebral chakras. (Also, there is "an energy center [or chakra, which] exists eighteen inches to two feet above the head. Although this energy center is outside the body, it is still within your aura and is very much a part of you. It looks like a white sun"—Ric A. Weinman, *Your Hands Can Heal.*) This sphere is regarded as the seed kernel which brings energy into the sixth-level or "celestial" body.

When meditators feel themselves to be "egg-shaped," "spherical" or "ten feet tall," then, it is because through deep meditation they have become temporarily identified with their appropriate subtle bodies. The same obviously applies when they feel the self-contraction into ego as being "localized behind the eyes."

World's End is not to be found *by walking,* but it is within this very
fathom-long body that the pilgrimage must be made.
—*Samyutta-Nikaya (The Book of the Kindred Sayings)*

Now, we find in mythology and folklore many tales in which the
solar hero must pass through either clashing rocks or mountains, or
between lions, lion-birds or other sun-symbols, in his journey. That hero
then sometimes secures a "Water of Life" from a guarded palace after
striking on the castle entrance gates with an iron *rod.* (That palace is the
golden cerebral abode of the regal soul, in the crown center.) The pair of
cherubim stationed at the Eastward entrance to the Garden of Eden
following Adam and Eve's Fall and exile fulfill the same "guardian"
function, preventing them from getting back into the Paradise of the
spiritual eye.

> Cherubs were not the angelic little winged infants of popular imagina-
> tion—they were sphinx-like mythological monsters, part lion, part bird
> and part man, which are familiar to us now from the art and religious
> symbolism of the ancient Middle East, and which the Israelites bor-
> rowed and adapted for their own religious iconography.
> —Magnus Magnusson,
> *BC: The Archaeology of the Bible Lands*

The four rivers mentioned in Genesis 2:10—"And a river went out of
Eden to water the garden; and from thence it was parted, and became into
four heads"—are presumably the four currents of life energy in the
spine: the *sushumna, vajra, chitra* and *Brahmanadi.* In support of this,
we note that "the esoteric tradition of Islam teaches that [the] four rivers
of Paradise refer as well to subtle nerve channels in the human body,
which the practitioner is instructed ... to activate in various ways"—Lex
Hixon, *Heart of the Koran.*
    The Water of Life mentioned above is an actual fluidic energy
current flowing in the body and brain in high states of consciousness.
(Other names for that Water include ambrosia, *amrita,* soma or the
Nectar of Immortality.) Water is the standard metaphor for the flow of
currents of life energy simply because "the actual sensation of transmit-
ting energy is like flowing water, like a force moving through the
healer's body"—Rosalyn Bruyere, *Wheels of Light.* ("The Greek word
energeia from which our word 'energy' is derived was also the New

Testament word for 'spiritual'"—Allegra Taylor, *Healing Hands.*)
Likewise, the "iron rod" is one of the standard symbols for the spiritual-
ized spine simply for reasons such as Tara Mata notes in *A Forerunner
of the New Race:*

> Another important change [during the time following my first experi-
> ence of illumination] was felt in [my] spinal column. The whole spine
> seemed turned into iron for several weeks, so that, when [I] sat to
> meditate on God, [I] felt anchored forever, able to sit in one place
> eternally without motion or consciousness of any bodily function.

Now, in his essay "Symplegades," A. K. Coomaraswamy notes that
the themes of guardian clashing rocks, and heroes passing through doors
but leaving a small part of themselves behind, are found world-over.
(That "small part" symbolizes the ego/personality.) Indeed, we can
recognize these themes in cultures ranging from the Grecian and East
Indian to the Greenland Eskimos, the North American Indians and the
Polynesians. The Mexican dead, too, "had to pass clashing mountains."
Likewise, in the Grecian saga of the Quest of the Golden Fleece, after
Athena drives between the clashing rocks in a winged ship, the rocks
remain in close contact afterwards, barring the way to other mortal
voyagers. And tellingly, in the Rig Veda, "rolling mountains" corresponding to the clashing rocks are associated with light and darkness, or
day and night, i.e., with *solar* and *lunar* principles.

The *Sarada-Tilaka* likewise speaks of the kundalini energy making
its way through the "mass of sounds issuing from the clashing and the
dashing of the two winds in the midst of *sushumna.*" In between the
"clashing rocks" and the Sundoor are varying degrees of enlightenment,
carrying potentially-distracting psychic powers, and the possibility of
much "backsliding." Since the breath is intrinsically linked with the flow
of "watery" life currents, it is reasonable that an alternative mythological
symbolism of "the passage between" these into breathless *samadhi* Bliss
should be of passing safely between two walls of water

Such a passage can be found, for example, in the Israelites' journey
through the Red Sea toward the Promised Land. At the Red Sea, a strong
East wind parts the waters, after Moses had lifted up his *rod* (i.e.,
kundalini energy) in response to the Lord's command. (The various
experiential portraits in Chapter III of the literal expansion of conscious-

ness and of being "point-like and yet infinite" are all descriptions of high states of *samadhi.*)

The accepted interpretation of the "clashing rocks" or their many variants is that these refer merely to conceptualized "pairs of opposites"—e.g., hot and cold, pleasure and pain, good and evil, heaven and earth. One must then "pass between" these contraries, as does Homer's Odysseus, in order to transcend such conceptualized dualities in reaching the sun. And it is true, of course, that we do indeed transcend the operation of the linear intellect in any one-pointed concentration. That is, we transcend even when focusing on a visualized image or audibilized sound, even though these are inherently based in memory, i.e., in concepts. We also go beyond all of that in identification with our sphere of consciousness or "causal eye of intuition."

Likewise, Merrell-Wolff described his experience of a state in which to conceive of any particular (archetypal) idea was to automatically conceive of its opposite. Tellingly, however, although the aforementioned two clashing "winds in the midst of *sushumna"* would in general be taken unhesitatingly as referring only to dualistic, conceptualized opposites, these two winds explicitly refer to specific life currents in the text considered. That is, they refer to the subtle structure of the human body and its relation to ascending the spinal Tree of Life to reach the Sundoor, not to mere figurative "clashing opposites in the midst of the World Axis"! And these oppositional currents keep us body-bound and enthralled by *maya whether or not we conceptualize them.* Only when one's environment is perceived through one's being consciously spread through it is this knowledge non-dual, i.e., *intuitive.*

We pass between the clashing, dualistic opposites of inhalation and exhalation when these are stopped, leaving the personality behind and reaching the Sundoor (i.e., the spiritual sun or golden-silvery sphere of consciousness) in the breathless state of *samadhi.* It is, of course, only on levels of experience below this sphere that the conceptualization (i.e., the "concrete thoughts and ideas") of the fifth and third-level bodies is present. That is to say, concrete conceptualization is only present at the fifth-level mental body or below, where *each of the chakras corresponding to those lower bodies is associated with one of the five senses.* Nevertheless, we do not get to that high and intuitive level in any way merely by removing conceptualization from our sensory experiences!

Now, in the *Katha Sarit Sagara,* too, a sun-bright wheel—"wheel" being the literal translation of "chakra"—guards the Water of Life from soma-"thieves." This wheel is situated atop five others: a lowest "earth" center (the chakra at the base of the spine) and four intervening centers of water, fire, air and ether. These astral elements, traditionally corresponding to the five lower spinal chakras, are of course not the physical mud, H_2O, flame and oxygen. Rather, they are the elemental *ideas* underlying the solid, liquid, igneous and gaseous states of matter. Atop these five centers, at the literal center of the wheel of the potentially x-ray visioned sixth chakra in the forehead, is again found the microcosmic bodily sun, or limitlessly-expandable spherical eye of intuition. (That sixth chakra itself is the "third eye" or "spiritual eye," the central tip of whose energy vortex seats into the midbrain, as does the tip of the seventh "thousand-petaled lotus" center.) Identification with this inner sun grants conscious presence throughout that expandable sphere of consciousness, penetrating the grosser matter within its circumference.

Kundalini and tantra yoga, too, traditionally place the third eye in the proximity of the pineal gland; while Shiva is everywhere spoken of as having three eyes. The cone-shaped pineal gland "atop" the spinal column (i.e., in the midbrain) is also represented, for example, by the thyrsus, a wand associated with Bacchus and made from a pine-cone fixed to a fennel stalk. "In lower animals such as reptiles the pineal gland is still associated with a rudimentary third eye, complete with lens and retina-like photoreceptor"—R. Gerber, *Vibrational Medicine.*

Given the aforementioned close association between "suns" and "eyes," it is understandable that the Maitri Upanishad likewise associates the Sundoor with an "Eye," and regards the *sushumna* as a path for ascent toward the *sun.* Further, given the close relationship of this inner sun with the medullary chakra, which is regarded as the seat of Om in the human body, we cannot be surprised at the Chandogya Upanishad's statement that "the Sun is Om, for he is ever sounding forth 'Om.'"

If we were to voice the subtle bodily structure in terms of a three-level (rather than seven-level) cartography, we would speak only of body, mind and spirit; or the physical, astral and causal bodies. That is, we would focus on the first, fourth and sixth/seventh levels. Yoga has traditionally recognized that the pull of *maya* is especially strong at exactly the coccygeal, heart and forehead chakras, and has thus emphasized the three-body system, while yet fully honoring the existence of all seven cerebrospinal chakras and of the transcendent Self beyond these. In religious symbolism, these three primary centers are often represented by three beads, strung on a common string—the latter representing the threadlike *sushumna.*

Additionally, just as lightning is a stream of light and electricity, joining sky (or heaven) and earth, *ida* and *pingala* may be viewed as "lightnings" joining together the forehead and coccygeal chakras; as may the risen kundalini energy. (The forehead and coccygeal chakras are the seats of Heaven and Earth in the human body.) Thus, just as with paired serpents, paired lightnings differ in their meaning from single ones.

In Indian iconography, lightnings are commonly represented in the form of golden snakes. Further, in some East Indian texts, two lightnings (or snakes, or dragons, or reeds) are pictured as soma-wardens, while a solar-symbol *eagle* (i.e., winged bird) plays the part of soma-thief, flying between these two guardians to obtain the precious nectar. (Taoist symbology likewise contains *yin* and *yang*—or feminine and masculine—dragons, in appearance like unto serpents.) Similarly, Zeus kept a flock of doves to fetch ambrosia for him. And, in the Chandogya Upanishad, the Tree of Life itself in the Brahma world is described as "soma-dripping."

Finally, just as the Mayan Indians envisioned the kundalini energy too as a kind of "lightning," practitioners of the Samaya School of yoga will actually perceive the roused kundalini energy as a momentary sharp flash of lightning. (The risen kundalini is described as lightning in all of the Tantras as well, being accompanied by the thundering sound of Om, or a waterfall-like "noise of many waters," as described by Gopi Krishna.) Indeed, the word *"vajra"* refers not only to the inner channel of the *sushumna,* but can mean "sword" as well (cf. King Arthur's Excalibur). And Coomaraswamy, in Part II of his "Symbolism of the Dome," argues that the sword-symbolism is derived worldwide from a "root" *lightning* symbolism. Likewise, as W. Y. Evans-Wentz notes in *Tibet's Great Yogi Milarepa,* the celestial first Buddha has the name Dorje-Chang, which in Sanskrit is Vajra-Dhara—meaning literally "Holder of the Vajra," or the Spiritual Thunderbolt of the Gods, symbolized by the scepter. Lightning is thus a "weapon" only in the sense that it destroys the enemy Ignorance. Lightning gods are "war gods" for the same reason.

Investigating the aforementioned Tree of Life idea in greater depth now, we note that Gopi Krishna inwardly perceived subtle "tongues of flame" leaping from his spine into other areas and organs of his body after his kundalini energy was awakened. That subtle fire then worked to "rewrite/refine the cellular circuitry of his body," as he and other persons with similar experiences have explained. Thus, the spinal Tree of Life may also be characterized as a *burning* tree. That is, it may be symbolized as a tree or bush (or *pillar,* separating and yet uniting heaven/sky and earth, or the sun/eagle and the moon/serpent) that burns but is never consumed. This bush may indeed literally "speak" to one so enlightened, for the same reason that the Biblical sages frequently heard voices *behind* them (i.e., from the medullary chakra region), "as the sound of a trumpet." For, such modulations of the life currents in the spine and the characteristic sounds of the chakras do indeed allow for scriptures to be "directly heard," as is said to be the origin of the Vedas. The bodhi tree under which Buddha became enlightened is likewise, literally, a tree of *light,* for bodhi = light (e.g., enlightenment).

The presence of the coiled "serpent" of the kundalini energy at the base of the spinal tree, as well as the two other "serpents" coiled around and up the spine, account precisely for the connection of serpents with trees in world mythologies. In addition, in the rising of the serpent-like kundalini energy, the feeling of the circulation of a current of life energy from the base of the spine, over the top of the head, and then down the front of the body to the coccygeal region again is often reported. This has for ages been symbolized in the *uroboros*—the *snake* swallowing its own tail, representing the union of Heaven and Earth, and the continuity or great principle of life. (It is probable that this current of energy exists in all of us from infancy or earlier, but only becomes intense enough to be felt after significant spiritual awakening.) The spiritual eye with its central white star, further, as the esoteric gateway through which we may "shed our skin" or consciously exit the body to fly through space unhindered in blissful *samadhi,* accounts for the eagles and other birds often found living in the boughs of the aforementioned mythological trees.

Yoga regards the spiritual eye as the "pearly gate" or white "dove of light, descending from heaven." While the blue sphere and golden ring are regarded as the "wings" of that dove, when this center is imperfectly seen—i.e., in the "early stages"—its light may actually show in the form of two arcs, i.e., as "wings." When we speak colloquially of knowing something because "a little bird told me," we are, however unintentionally, making reference to the same third eye or eye of intuition. This is exactly the origin of "Wish-Fulfilling Trees" such as Cinderella's, in which a little *white* bird would throw down to her whatever she had wished for. Needles—rodlike, with an "eye" at the top—can symbolize the same esoteric passageway, topped by the spiritual eye:

> The loop of Death's lasso is still another aspect of the Gate [i.e., Sundoor], and [to] slip through the noose without its tightening upon you is the same as to have passed through the jaws of Death without their closing upon you, just as the "threading of the needle" is the passage of the Sundoor in the symbolism of embroidery.
> —A. K. Coomaraswamy, "Some Pali Words"

Related to all this, chimneys and descents down into wells are symbols of birth. That is, they are symbolic not merely of the birth canal, as the Freudians would have it, but of descent from the (astral) heavens to earth through a "tunnel with a [serpent] fire at the bottom of it." Conversely, we have the reverse ascent through a tunnel with a sun-like light at its end, as is frequently reported in near-death experiences, when the consciousness withdraws from the body via the spine, exiting as a "luminous ray" out the crown chakra.

Wells are tunnels filled with water, just as the tunnel of the spine is filled with "watery" life energy. Thus, "inside the head, there is an inverted well with an opening behind the eyes. A current of nectar [*amrita* or the Water of Life] issuing forth from the well is coming into the body"—Kirpal Singh, *Naam or Word*.

> I beheld in the firmament an inverted well and was filled with the resplendence of the Light within.

> In the resplendence of brilliant Light, I had a glimpse within the flame;

> All was suffused with brightness, and I had a peep into my Self.

> The path leading to the shores of the Lake of Nectar was revealed unto me.

In the Sukhmana *(sushumna)* I went into a trance and then crossed to the other side. Whosoever hath thus experienced, O Tulsi, hath got the pledge of union from the Lord.

—Tulsi Sahib of Hathras

The rumbling or other sounds heard when passing voluntarily or involuntarily through this tunnel are simply the sounds produced by the life currents in the spine and its chakras. The ability to enter *samadhi* at will is exactly the ability to "die daily," or exit the body in this way, "just as a blade of grass is pulled from its sheath." And this, of course, is also the process of being spiritually "born again," or baptized in the river of life energy flowing in the spine.

The Om sound manifested in the first chakra is heard inwardly as the sound of bees. It takes the form of the tinkling of bells, the sound of a flute, the continuous peal of a gong, and the noise of rushing waters or of a waterfall in the higher chakras, in that order. Normally these sounds are only inwardly audible to the meditator. However, there have been contemporary cases, involving extremely highly spiritually advanced individuals, where the "buzzing bee" sound of the coccygeal chakra, for example, was so loud as to be audible to the physical hearing of other persons in the vicinity.

The lower five chakras are again associated with the astral elements of earth, water, fire, air and ether. And these same elements are also said to be symbolized in the fingers of each hand. That is, the thumb, being the "grossest," represents earth; the middle finger, as the longest, symbolizes the darting flames of fire; the ring finger is affiliated with the fourth (astral, heart) chakra, and thus with the circular golden ring of Om in the astral spiritual eye; and the little finger, being the finest, signifies ether. These elements and sounds are all differentiations of the Om sound (which has both causal and astral aspects), and are further represented in the fingers of each hand. This therefore provides one more reason why we may view Om as the sound of one *Hand*—composed of five fingers/ elements—clapping.

The aforementioned "flying" in *samadhi* is of course not to be regarded simply in terms of astral travelling, in which we are identified with the astral body. Rather, it is to be taken in terms of Bentov's sensation of his consciousness moving like a dot through the Void, without interference and independent of the body, i.e., in being identified with the sphere of consciousness at the seventh bodily level. This literal expansion on the causal level, however, is superseded by the experience of the Self beyond the astral and causal bodies. That Star-Self, as a limitlessly-expandable sphere of white light, also qualifies as an inner spiritual "sun," but one which is not spatially centered atop the Tree of Life.

Yoga records that persons for whom the worship of God takes an impersonal direction will often experience the Divine in the form of an expanding sphere of light. Visions of a personal God occur at the same level as this, however. That is, they are not "lower" than the structural experience of the expanding light-sphere, whether this latter occurs on the causal or the transcendent Self level.

Of course, the idea of the seventh-level crown chakra being "the seat of the Self" is not incompatible with that Self actually being spatially located in the belly on the ninth level. The throne is where the King sits when he is in his castle, but the King is not *confined* to the castle. Nevertheless, when ruling His kingdom, that is where He gives his orders from.

The Self or soul has descended from beyond duality successively into the causal, astral and physical bodies. In reversing this path of descent, we progressively transcend identification with the physical, astral and causal forms to realize the Self as an individualized spark of Spirit. That is, just as a person who drops his physical body at death must automatically become identified with the astral, and as one who drops the astral body would necessarily attain to immediate identification with the causal, *a person who can at will get out of the causal body the same way he got in must necessarily realize the Self.*

By analogy, a person (Self) wearing an undershirt (causal body), sweater (astral body) and overcoat (physical body), may erroneously come to identify himself with his clothes—e.g., believing that "the clothes make the man." If he removes the overcoat, however, he can no longer be identified with it, or erroneously believe that "I am my overcoat." He may then further take off the sweater and undershirt *by reversing the series of actions by which he put them on*—thus realizing through experience that "I am not my sweater or undershirt." His sense of identification must then necessarily shift from those discarded garments to his own denuded Self.

We have all descended from the cosmic consciousness of the Self into the garments of the three bodies, but have become so used to wearing them that we have forgotten how to take them off. The accomplished yogi, however, puts on and removes his "clothes" at will. Further, it is precisely because techniques of life-force control, visualizations of the spinal energies, and the raising of the kundalini energy work exactly and explicitly toward retracing the path of descent of the Self into duality that they are concerned with nothing less than Self-realization, and are indeed a highly efficient means of effecting this realization.

Thus, the reason why the snake is regarded as a symbol of immortality is not merely because it sheds its skin to "live again" in a new skin. Rather, it is thus regarded simply because there are yogic techniques involving the breath-currents and the raising of the serpent-like kundalini energy which, when mastered, enable the person practicing them to similarly regularly "shed his skin," or leave and re-enter the body at will. This, again, has nothing to do with mere astral travel, but rather denotes the ability to drop one's gross and subtle bodies at will, toward the goal of identification with the immortal Self—having climbed the *"Tree* of Immortality," and taken flight into omnipresence.

There are many degrees and stages of *samadhi,* culminating in Self-realization. It would perhaps be a bit much at this early stage of understanding to expect to be able to explain or derive *all* of them from our rudimentary understanding of subtle microcosmic structure! We may gain some confidence in the validity of the ideas given thus far, however, by noting that Bentov explicitly described his literal "ballooning" expansion into space as occurring well prior to his own permanent realization of the Self—so that this expansion must occur on a level below that of the Self. He further again showed these inflating/deflating spheres as being centered in the midbrain of each one of us. And we correspondingly note that Gopi Krishna, although he experienced the "point-like and yet infinite" (causal) *samadhi* state regularly, made no claim to be Self-realized. If we then locate Bentov's expanding sphere at the causal level, it again meshes with Brennan's clairvoyant perceptions. It also connects with Hiroshi Motoyama's statement that "a causal being appears disembodied to an astral being—the astral individual perceives the causal one as a dazzling sphere of light or as a shining halo."

Brennan further locates the illuminative Star-Self or transcendent soul in the belly of each one of us, at a position in the region of the navel, and regards it as placing each one of us *experientially* "at the center of creation." (Some sages, such as Ramana Maharshi, however, regard the transcendent Witness or Self as being physically located in the "right hand heart." That is, they would place it at a point above the heart on the right hand side of the chest, which we indeed normally point to when identifying ourselves.) That is to say, the testimony of sages with regard to their feeling, in high states of consciousness, of being at the center of the cosmos, is not a mere poetic description or esoteric point of philosophy. Rather, it is obviously an accurate and literal reporting of the experience of that level. Yoga too, like Brennan, considers the Self/soul to be a "reactionless vibration," of a white effulgence which neither gives off heat nor casts a shadow, being all-pervading and infinite in oneness with Brahman.

Our locating of Bentov's expanding sphere at the causal level further provides a precise and holographic basis for intuition at exactly the level at which this inner sight is traditionally placed. That is, in terms of the causal body being the "intuitive" body. (Actually, yoga speaks not only of a spherical causal eye centered in the midbrain, but of a spherical *astral* eye located there as well. This statement is qualified, however, to mean that the causal eye of intuition is inherent in an astral eye of light and life force.) And Bentov himself allowed for the expansion of this sphere to infinity. He also again described his own experience of being consciously beyond the sphere of manifestation, and moving like a dot through that "cold, black" Void or Absolute, even before realization of the Self, explicitly relating this to an intuitive state:

> You assumed that once you reached the Absolute, the thinking processes would stop automatically. But here you go, romping around in the Void and apparently thinking. This present thinking process is not the kind of linear, deductive thinking that people normally do, but rather an intuitive knowing, where very complex ideas are imprinted on the mind instantaneously.
>
> —Itzhak Bentov, *A Cosmic Book*

Now, the astral body is attached to the physical by a silver cord of light. This cord is regularly seen by persons who have developed the ability to do conscious astral travel, where one merely has to "wish" or visualize being at a certain destination in order to travel there. It is said that the vast majority of people do this travelling unconsciously during sleep, without being able to remember it upon waking. It is also claimed that feelings of rising into the air, or of falling as if from a cliff as one awakens, come from being on the verge of remembering these travels.

By the same token, we must all have much unremembered contact with spiritual guides, astral libraries of knowledge and institutes of learning, astral friends, and the higher selves of other presently-incarnated human beings in sleep. Indeed, much of the direction of our lives, i.e., of our "karma," would be planned out by our higher selves in that state. Probably many or most "synchronicities" would fall into the same "planned" category. And where else does "love at first sight" come from, regardless of any basis in physical attraction, if not from the same planning, in meeting friends and lovers from past lives?

Healers have actually observed that most of us experience higher levels of reality during our sleep, without remembering those experiences upon awakening. Conversely, they have also found that persons undergoing healing sessions will frequently "go to sleep" as the session progresses, then conversing in their astral bodies with the guides surrounding them. Upon awakening, the subjects have no memory of that; with a higher degree of spiritual awakening, however, they would indeed remember those experiences. Likewise, persons nearing death from terminal illness have been observed to spend much of the time near the end of their lives in a similar state, "out of their bodies," preparing for that transition to life in the astral. For exactly this reason, spiritual experiences of God/Peace and/or Guru in the last days of one's life are not a "sign" or "reward" for loyalty or having otherwise "lived a good and spiritual life," but are rather an artifact of that same transition process.

Interestingly, according to contemporarily channeled information, it takes approximately the equivalent of half a year, measured according to our physical standards of time, for the astral and causal bodies of persons who have recently died to fully regenerate from the effects—or rather, the higher causes—of the illness or accident. (Brennan notes, for example, that she has seen tears in the chakras, even up to the seventh auric level, of persons suffering in the latter stages of cancer. These higher levels do not immediately return to their "mended" state simply for our having dropped the physical body in death. Rather, it takes some time for that healing to occur. On the other hand, though, blind persons who have had out-of-the-body experiences—i.e., in working through their astral bodies—have repeatedly claimed that they were able to "see" in that state.) There is reported to be no pain during that after-life healing time, unless the entity chooses to temporarily inhabit a physical body, e.g., in channeling through a medium. In that latter scenario, the ordinarily disembodied being would feel the same location and type of pain as was suffered at the end of the physical incarnation.

In any case, the aforementioned silver cord between the astral and the physical bodies forms a kind of umbilicus, which is severed at death:

> Or ever the silver cord be loosed, or the golden bowl [the clairvoyantly-visible glow of light around the crown chakra, which is extinguished at death] be broken, or the pitcher be broken at the fountain [and cease pouring its life energy—its *"Water* of *Life"*—from the well/fountain of the spine into the body], or the wheel [chakra, by which water is hauled] broken at the cistern [water reservoir].
>
> Then shall the dust [i.e., the physical body] return to the earth as it was: and the spirit shall return unto God who gave it.
>
> —Ecclesiastes 12:5-6

Now, when we as human beings dream, our unconscious thoughts and desires are transformed from literal into metaphorical or symbolic language. This is in the same way as our physical ailments are symbolic expressions of our psychological patterns, e.g., asthma often indicating both a physical and a psychological "suffocation." Thus if, for example, we have been brooding over being spoken to with harsh or "biting" speech, we might well dream of actually being bitten by some animal or insect. Now, creation is regularly spoken of as being the "dream" of God. And when the Lord dreams the universe, condensing His thought into energy and matter, the underlying ideas are similarly expressed meta-phorically. The same metaphorical style of expression is true for us when we participate in our own generally small way in this ability to create by the power of thought.

We tend to view our "subconscious" as a lower level of conscious-ness than our daily, waking awareness. However, the subconscious is not merely something which needs to be psychologically integrated into waking awareness—so that the motivating influence of repressed thoughts/emotions no longer involuntarily sways our behaviors, for example. Rather, it is a level which we must learn to go through consciously in order to get to the superconscious faculties of the soul, i.e., to consciously tap into *those* faculties, in the causal and Star-Self realms. We can easily understand that the astral level of reality is a higher one than the physical. But note that dreams—the product of the *subconscious* mind—occur exactly on that astral level, i.e., the dreamer is working largely through his astral body. (The increased powers of visualization in the dream state derive from the retiring of the life energy from the muscles, to be used by the brain. The same withdrawal of energy into the spine and brain occurs whenever we are deep in concentration on any thought or visualization in the waking state, and is invariably accompanied by a calming of the breath and a stilling of the body.)

It may not be obvious that dreams can thus be considered to be a higher state of consciousness than our waking awareness. However, it is certainly obvious that astral travel, involving the same astral body as do dreams, is indeed such a higher state. And very significantly, in Carlos Castaneda's books he speaks of "dreaming" himself into the astral body, and then working through it; exactly as is done in astral travel. Astral-level dreams, then, are a higher state than is our waking, third-chakra "mental-rational" awareness ... but are lower than the fifth-chakra "mental" body.

In our physical bodies and daily activities, we create and work out primarily physical-level karma. On the astral level after death, however, we work out our astral karma, particular involving emotional growth. (Regarding the common nature of dreams, astral travel, and the after-death existence on the astral level of reality, it is significant to note that the Australian aborigines refer to the afterlife as the "dreamtime.") Of course, we certainly deal with emotions in our physical daily lives as well. The biases and fears which give rise to them, however, are generally "hidden" from us, in the subconscious, and are thus not generally directly addressed or worked on (aside from our astral-level dreams, in which the subconscious is given more of a free reign). In the astral worlds, however, we cannot help but meet our emotions and fears "head on"—there is no avoiding them behind the screen of subconscious repression there. Thus, our emotional problems do not end at death, but rather become stronger.

> The feelings, emotions, and thoughts which make up the unconscious ... are the minds we take with us to the astral dimension when we die.
> —Hiroshi Motoyama, *Karma and Reincarnation*

The fact that the astral reality is the level of the subconscious mind, however, does *not* mean that our decisions in the astral worlds are "motivated predominantly by our subconscious habits," and thus might be supposed to be *less* free than our conscious choices in our physical daily lives. Rather, we are so much closer to the superconscious intuition of the causal body and Self when freed from the physical body that our choices are *more* free in the astral than on the physical level. That would be so even were the astral level not replete with the ability to immediately condense objects into being via deep concentration/visualization, just as we do nightly in our dreams.

Or course, it need hardly be repeated that our conscious "choices" in our daily lives are *in practice* far less free than we generally suppose, for they are weighted heavily by those same subconscious biases. It is again the intuition of the soul, not the logical thought and reflection of the rational mind—valuable though that is when used in concert with real intuition—that confers free choice on us. Besides, the whole mechanism by which free choice is possible in the first place necessitates that the higher state/resonant frequency of consciousness entailed in working through the astral body is going to grant to the individual a greater degree of free choice.

The reason why Eastern sages regard incarnation in a human body as a "precious gift" thus has nothing to do with our sensory-based decisions in that state allegedly being freer from subconscious influences than they would be in the astral realities. For our simply being unaware of those influences certainly does not mean that they affect us less than if we were fully aware of them—exactly the opposite is true! Rather, human incarnation is so regarded simply because the typical person in the astral worlds after physical death, enjoying the great beauty and freedom to creatively play in those realms, neglects to make any deep spiritual effort to go beyond that level. By contrast, in life on the physical plane, we are regularly brought out of any paradisical "daydreaming" by the hungers and pains of the fleshy body, by our worldly duties, etc. And that "rude disturbance," if used properly, can be very conducive toward one's making a concerted spiritual effort in meditation: "pain is a prod to remembrance." Human incarnation is precious in another way as well, in that lower animals do not have intuition, the full ability to reason, or the ability to know God.

All of that, however, is still only a part of the reason why we keep returning to the physical plane of reality, when the higher levels of existence are so much freer of pain and of limitations. Yoga emphasizes that if a person dies with the craving for apple pie, for example, he or she will need to reincarnate on the physical level of reality in order to satisfy that desire. However, each one of us knows, from our nightly dreams, that the astral-level dream of eating an apple pie seems as real, during the dream, as when the food is actually consumed in physical reality. The same is true of all of our other sensations, including sexual ones.

Why, then, if these experiences can be had in imagination as well as in physical daily life, is there any need to incarnate on the physical level at all? (Or, if everything that can be done in imagination can also be done at a subtler level in causal-level thought, why should there be any need to incarnate on the astral level?) The answer can only be that the physical experience of those sensations has a degree of reality, or force, or grossness, which is quite literally missing on higher levels of existence.

Descriptions by astral-level entities given through reliable contemporary mediums have confirmed this. That is, the astral level after death can be as much like daily physical life as one wants it to be, even to the point of farmers reaping seasonal harvests and people holding "9 to 5" jobs. Nevertheless, while alcoholics, for example, can still make and drink alcohol on the astral level, they lament that it "isn't the same" as on the physical. That is, it doesn't have quite the same effect on them, lacking the low-frequency vibratory component which makes it "more real" on this low level. (By analogy, consider a popular song with its bass drum and bass guitar tracks removed from the mix. It would still be the same song, but it wouldn't pack the same "punch"; something would be "missing" from one's enjoyment of it.) It is that fact, plus the linear nature of time and space on this level, not the wrong idea that food, wine or money (or even sex) cannot exist on levels higher than the physical, which drives people to reincarnate on the physical level in particular.

Indeed, as far as those interests being present beyond the physical goes, all of those exist perfectly well in our imaginations, and yoga itself acknowledges that anything which a physical-bodied being can do in imagination, an astral-bodied one can do in reality.

In terms of "working out our karma" then, via illness or otherwise, there is no reason why the "wise avoidance" of the indulgence in detrimental desires could not extend to resisting the desire to physically incarnate. That is, in simply refusing to come down to this level, despite the pull of one's "karma." No one "forces" us to come down to incarnation on the physical level. Rather, we do it completely of our own volition, in some combination of desire for the gross tangibility of experiences on this level of reality, coupled with the learning-value of experiences in *linear space and time,* and a wish to improve things and ease the suffering of others on the physical level, i.e., to bring a "gift" to this level. And of those three influences, surely the (linear) second is the most relevant for any refined soul—even if gross tangibility may be more relevant for the average human being. For one can bring "gifts" to any level of reality, while any physical experience is not so far removed from the same experience in astral-level imagination.

With regard to "sex and spirituality," Rosalyn Bruyere, in Chapter Eight of her *Wheels of Light,* gives by far the most insightful and balanced view that I have encountered:

> The exchange of energy in lovemaking is an aspect of the first chakra, the true purpose of which has long been misunderstood. Orgasm is a trancelike state; the purpose of sexuality is the expansion and empowerment of one's partner through an exchange of energy....
>
> The quality of this mergence is dependent upon how much energy we can accumulate and hold in our system. The Oriental sexual practice of *kamasutra* is designed to access this greater energy. In the union of *kamasutra,* the partners open the feeder systems in the legs, arms, the jaws, and above the ears, and if the *kamasutra* technique is mastered, the hundred or so secondary chakras in the body are also opened. This makes an enormous amount of energy available to the couple.
>
> For orgasm to occur, one must first learn to master the undulating movement of the kundalini energy. One must know when to move or push the energy and when to surrender, when to release and pull the partner's energy.... Furthermore, this must be a reciprocal process. Besides the obligation to give, there is an obligation to surrender.

The mergence or oneness of sexuality is intended to be a heightened awareness, not a deadening, a numbing, or a sleep state. Besides empowerment and mergence, the goal of sexuality is to center and maintain a simultaneous state of deep relaxation and expanded consciousness.

The mutual letting go into deep communion through giving and receiving in sexual intercourse is one of the main ways humanity has of deeply letting go of the ego "separateness" and experiencing unity. When done with love and respect for the uniqueness of your mate, it is a holy experience culminating from the deep primordial evolutionary urges of mating on the physical level and the deep spiritual yearnings of uniting with Divinity. It is a wedding of both the spiritual and physical aspects of the two human beings.
            —Barbara Ann Brennan, *Hands of Light*

Undoubtedly, the same energy balancing via sexual touching—and the same pleasure and satisfaction which this activity produces—can be done on the purely astral level as well, without need for recourse to a physical body, or for penetration of the male organ into the female in order to produce the bodily bath of life energy accompanying orgasm. For the latter is, after all, a temporary stimulation of the kundalini energy. Conversely, persons undergoing kundalini awakenings have at times reported feelings of intense sexual desire. Indeed, Brennan notes that, in order for full-body orgasm to occur, all of one's chakras must be open. This is obviously a highly spiritual state, not merely a "wallowing in primal lust."

In any case, given that male and female bodies exist on the astral level as certainly as they do on the physical, the idea that any intimate interaction between them could only occur on the physical level is evident nonsense. On the contrary, whatever sharing would occur on the astral or higher levels could only be *more* intensely intimate than the physical act of sex. In fact, Ken Wilber, in *Grace and Grit,* describes exactly such a commingling of hearts, in a spontaneous dissolution of the separation between them, upon first meeting his future wife Treya; with her experiencing the same thing simultaneously.

Now, our astral and causal bodies, which underlie the conscious waking personality, are again coarse or refined in their vibrations depending directly on the spiritual effort we have made in past lives and past after-lives in the astral and causal worlds. Consequently, it is fully possible for a person to have a high degree of spiritual development and even of unconscious astral/causal functioning—such as being highly intuitive, in terms of being able to distinguish which ideas or actions "feel right"—without having made any explicit spiritual effort in this life. Of course, one is unlikely to effect any significant further refinement in those higher bodies until one gets into conscious contact with them through meditative practice. Nevertheless, in the interim, many of the fruits of past effort can remain fully present on a largely unconscious level prior to their conscious emergence in this life. These are unconscious but not repressed, and are simply "lying around waiting to emerge," or to be brought into one's waking consciousness. To the extent to which they have been developed through the prior evolution of the individual, then, they need not to be developed but merely to be uncovered. In that sense, meditation is indeed an "uncovering" (or rather, an "emerging") technique; but not merely of uncovering the repressed unconscious from this one life. Rather, that uncovering simply allows those higher levels of one's being, which pre-exist this one life, to emerge into one's meditative/daily awareness.

Even aside from a significant refinement on the astral and causal levels, however, the fact is that *most* young children (according to clairvoyants) are able to see auras, but later "outgrow" (or subconsciously filter out) this ability when they discover that other people do not see them. (Those early auric experiences include having "invisible" astral "spirit playmates." That is, beings whom they knew before this one incarnation, and are still strongly tied to emotionally, even after having been "born.") Conversely, most of our wishes for perfection—in love, health, eternal youth, etc.—come from subconscious remembrances of life in the astral worlds, not from the level of Self or the idea that "perfection is possible only in God."

One could view the youthful belief that one will "live forever" as deriving from the same subconscious knowing—in which case it is to be admired, not cynically scoffed at as one ages and commonly feels the need to burst other people's idealistic bubbles. Likewise, we could take impatience with the slow terrestrial pace of knowledge acquisition, and the length of time that it takes to bring one's ideas into manifestation, as a product of the higher knowledge and experience, between physical lives, of the relative ease and rapid pace of those in higher levels of reality.

Perhaps even some of the childhood belief in the "magical" power of words to "create things" comes from the same subconscious source, even aside from the pre-rational stage of psychological development which gives rise to the same belief. Conversely, the fact that young children tend to produce similar "religious" symbols as do archaic cultures could just as well derive from the former being subconsciously attuned to the astral, as from the latter being in collectively pre-rational stages of psychological development. Most likely, though, *both* of those sides contribute to the full story.

In any case, it is not merely through the subconscious that we dwell on higher planes of reality in early childhood. For it is reasonable to assume that not only most adults but children also regularly astral travel in their sleep, without remembering it upon waking. Brennan further records her higher-sensory perception of infants emerging as "twelve-foot tall [astral] spirits" when they leave their small physical bodies. (Significantly, children undergoing near-death experiences frequently see themselves as adults, i.e., after their astral bodies have temporarily left the physical. Compare Itzhak Bentov's experiential testimony that, if one could penetrate the consciousness of a seed, he would find that it sees itself as a fully-grown plant.) Even those few facts alone show that our (astral-level) minds predate their expression in the psychological stages—especially in terms of the waking expression of one's "frontal" personality through the lower three chakras/bodies—of this one lifetime.

Actually, since the lower three chakras and bodies generally regulate and express one's waking personality, but since none of those on any of their seven levels, from etheric to causal, are *physical,* it is not really correct to associate that frontal personality with the physical brain. As Bentov noted, the brain is a thought *amplifier,* not the *source* of even our daily thoughts. After all, if our thoughts and memories were stored merely in our physical brains, there could be no such thing as validly remembering our past lives, nor could there be any survival of individual knowledge beyond death.

Compassion and devotion again come from the prior-life evolution of our astral and causal bodies. Further, given the present-life "emergence" of hitherto-unconscious but past-lives-developed refinements in those bodies, we must admit that the subconscious is not merely what has been either repressed or simply forgotten from our previous stages of psychological development in this one life, but that much of it exists even prior to this incarnation.

Brennan actually describes specific changes which take place in the chakras and auric structure as we advance through our childhood stages of psychological development. One may thus very reasonably conjecture that comparably definite changes in the aura occur when we enter the higher (e.g., post-conventional) stages of conscious psychological development. Definite and unmistakable structural changes have likewise been observed (by John Pierrakos in *Core Energetics,* for one) to underlie the development of psychoses and mental retardation. A comparably insightful explanation as to the nature of clairvoyance, mediumship, and expanded states of consciousness—given from the basis of the activities of the chakric structure underlying these varied states—can be found in Valerie Hunt's *Infinite Mind.*

We are again substantially the same persons, emotionally speaking, in our astral-level dreams (and travels) as we are in waking consciousness. In being identified with one's individual sphere of consciousness and the dimensionless point at its center, however, the personality is wholly transcended so long as this mystical experience lasts. Since this spherical level is the holographic basis of intuition also, this *conscious* contact with the Universal Mind, or potential access to the information contained in all spheres overlapping with our own, is a profoundly intuitive and creative one. (The same contact occurs to varying degrees for all of us on an *unconscious/superconscious* level.) And since the personality again dies in identification with the golden-silvery sphere of consciousness or "sun," and the ego is likewise annihilated in realization of the sun-like transcendent Self, in both cases we have the association of the sun with death. That is, we have Death as "the Person in the Solar Orb." This further provides the idea of emancipation by passage through the center of the sun: it is "through the hub of the wheel, the midst of the Sun, the cleft in heaven, that is all covered over by rays, that one is altogether liberated"—Jaiminiya Upanisad Brahmana.

Now, Cinderella's "Wish-Fulfilling Tree" is rightly held as symbolic of the World Axis, i.e., the *sushumna.* (In the Disney version, this tree is replaced by a fairy godmother with a *magic wand.* That is, a *rod* having a *star* at its tip; just as we "wish upon a star," of royal beauty bright.) And genies such as in the Aladdin tale serve a similar wish-granting role. Such genies are non-physical *spirits* trapped in physical bottles, as are our astral and causal selves. It would be interesting, then, to examine the spiritual truths hidden in the genie symbolism.

"Genie" is derived etymologically from the Latin "genius," meaning the guardian deity of a person, accessed through intuition. Any attempt to interpret its meaning must then begin from and inherently incorporate that root.

> In ancient Roman religion, the genius was the protective spirit which inhabits all living things. By the time of Augustus, the genius was defined as the guardian spirit of man. Each Roman male was thought to have his own *genius tutelae*. Each woman was believed to have a similar guardian, known as the *juno*. The genius and the *juno* accompanied the individual throughout life, and, in anticipation of the Christian doctrine of personal immortality, they were considered to maintain their separate identities throughout eternity.
>
> —the *Encyclopedia Americana*

Again, then, genies and geniuses appear to fit the description of our astral and causal bodies, from which our intuitions and profound insights or "thoughts of genius" come, "trickled down" into the waking personality. (Genius again doesn't come from one's genes—it's not gene-ius. Rather, it comes from causal-level development, most of which predates this one life, and which in any case has precisely nothing to do with one's heredity.) Note further that, in folktale, genies have the power to grant the fulfillment of one's wishes. This being the case, such a genius or "guardian deity" ultimately cannot refer merely to a spirit guide or guardian angel, as these, helpful though they may be, would be as unable as is desire, to grant all of one's noble wishes. Nor are guardian angels trapped in physical bottles, requiring release.

Now, there is an *Arabian Nights* tale in which a poor fisherman casts his net into the sea four times, hauling up nothing of value on the first three attempts, but bringing up a copper jar on the fourth. Opening the jar, a giant genie emerges and threatens to kill the fisherman, who saves himself by doubting aloud that such a huge genie could ever have fit into such a small jar, whereupon the genie returns to the jar to prove him wrong, and the fisherman throws the jar back into the sea. Alternatively, there is a Grimm fairy tale, "The Spirit in the Bottle," in which a voice from within a bottle at the base of a great old *tree* calls to a passing youth, "Let me out." Opening the bottle releases a spirit which threatens his life, but he tricks it back into the bottle. The genie then offers to provide for the poor student if freed again, whereupon the boy releases it a second time, and the spirit lives up to its word, giving him a magic cloth with the capacity to heal and to change iron or steel into silver. (Silver has long been renowned for its healing properties, both in its colloidal form, and more recently when woven into a kind of space-age cloth. The latter has been known to heal infected wounds which would not respond to any other treatment.) Through the silver and healing abilities, the poor student returns to university, and eventually becomes "the most famous doctor in the world."

When initially released from its imprisonment, the spirit in both of these cases threatens to kill the person that released it—it must be tricked to return to narrow confinement in its bottle. Likewise, in the deathlike bodily immobility of *samadhi,* the gigantic "genie" trapped in the small bodily jar of each one of us is released, and the ego/personality that had worked in spiritual discipline for its release temporarily "dies." (That is so whether that genie is read in terms of the transcendent Self, the higher self of the causal body, or even just in terms of our astral selves.) Only when this genie is returned to its bodily "bottle" does the ego/personality come back into functioning.

Contact with that genie, further, bestows also the ability to heal through the means of subtle energy flows; thus, the caduceus is very reasonably a symbol of *healing.* The poor fisherman in the earlier story above may then be taken as having obtained nothing valuable in his first attempts at "diving into the ocean of meditation"—a common Eastern image—but having then succeeded in releasing his "genie," which naturally threatens to kill him. As this is the genie's first release, it is equally natural that the body-bound ego wins and the genie ends up back in the bottle after a short time.

An actual sound like a cork popping is said to be clairvoyantly audible when one's Intentionality line is straightened and reinserted into its individuation point in the Godhead. (That line again represents one's intentions, at a level above the seven layers of the auric field, and exists as an actual laser-like vertical line of light, grounding into the earth, running up through one's body, and terminating above the head.) Most probably this provides part of the structural basis for the metaphor of the soul being imprisoned in three bodily "bottles"—the causal, astral and physical—and being released when these are "uncorked." In any case, this yogic metaphor strongly anticipates the genie idea, concerning the release of the imprisoned spirit from these bottles. The Buddhists, too, compare the body to a jar; while Bentov shows one component of the psyche graphically as an elongated hot air balloon-like shape, extending above the body and tapering down to where it meets the cranium. That is, he shows the psyche as being similar to the shape of genies, where these meet the mouths of their confining bottles or lamps.

The magic lamp which fulfills its owner's wishes occurs in the folklore of nearly all of Europe, as well as that of India and China; and lamps inherently have to do with light, which is one of the primary indicators of spiritual experience. Further, prior to the advent of electricity, lamps were constructed by burning oil or wax on a wick—the latter here evoking the *sushumna,* "burning" on the fuel of life energy withdrawn from the senses. Supporting this interpretation, the Bible refers more than once to seven lamps burning on a golden candlestick (e.g., Zechariah 4:2), and to "seven lamps of fire burning before the throne" of God (Revelation 4:15). Aladdin actually ascends a *ladder* to get his magic lamp, after passing through a garden full of *trees* filled with *birds* "glorifying with loud voices their Great Creator," these trees bearing precious jewels instead of edible fruits.

In the *Arabian Nights* story, Aladdin amasses great wealth and is made a sultan through the help of the genie—sultans being the sovereign rulers of their respective Islamic counties, or local monarchs. Again we note, then, that our selfish personal *desires* do not make *kings* of us. That is, they do not lead us to conscious realization of that inner aspect of ourselves which already is King of the Universe. Rather, they lead in exactly the opposite direction. Thus, in the example of Aladdin, the "wealth" obtained cannot be earthly riches, but must rather be symbolic of the divine wealth of God-realization.

If the *magician* in the Aladdin tale had gained control of the lamp, it would have been used for selfish, worldly purposes, as indeed happens later in the story. (Symbolically, this is simply *maya* influencing the use of one's astral and causal energies toward selfish ends.) However, throughout the narrative, Aladdin's own uses of the genie are always noble, never grossly selfish. In fact, the most extravagant manifestations of the genie are done explicitly toward setting the stage for a *royal wedding* between Aladdin and a virgin princess! That is, the genie's powers are used most for proving Aladdin worthy to the King, against the court Grand Wazir's envious objections. (Mythological royal weddings, as we shall see shortly, are events having a great degree of spiritual significance.)

Prior to pursuing the Sultan's daughter, although he possessed the magical lamp to grant his every desire, Aladdin and his mother "ceased not to live after their olden fashion as middle class folk without spending on diet overmuch or squandering money." Then, after the wedding, Aladdin becomes known for his benefactions, among them regularly distributing alms to the poor by his own hand, "and all the world, stranger and neighbour, far and near, were fulfilled of his love for the excess of his liberality and generosity." Further, it is exactly this genie that provides him with his magic carpet, or the ability to *fly* (i.e., in *samadhi*). Interestingly, Moslem/Islamic prayer rugs and Persian carpets are frequently decorated with woven images of *sacred/magic lamps.* Of course, the "flying" on these carpets could also refer, on a lower level, to simple astral travel. Given their affiliation with magic lamps, however, that can hardly be the highest reference.

As with the function of sacred lamps, the genie in the fisherman story likewise ends up bestowing riches on the one who freed him, and was prevented from escaping from his bottle by a cap or stopper marked with "Solomon's *seal.* " That is, the six-pointed Star of David, which yoga has traditionally associated with the heart chakra. The fisherman *opened this seal,* releasing the entrapped spirit. Note, then, that opening the seal at the heart chakra—or at least becoming centered there—is basic to the early (i.e., astral) stages of *samadhi.*

Now, when the Jaiminiya Upanisad Brahmana states "As one would keep climbing up a tree by steps ... he keeps ascending these worlds," this ascent up the Tree is explicitly toward a marriage. Further, in both human marriage and the aptly named "mystical marriage" of God-communion, wherein one's consciousness penetrates the spiritual eye, passage through a golden ring plays a significant role. That is, the veil of *maya* is lifted, and the union in "wedded bliss" of lover and pristine Beloved is sealed with a "kiss" as the devotee's lips touch the "mouth of God" (medullary chakra). Equally, we have there the union of clothed black and white, together forever, their love constant even in the midst of the dualities of "sickness and health, richer and poorer." Again, there is nothing arbitrary in these images.

> Mystics speak of a "mystic marriage" that takes place at the time of enlightenment. Hindus speak of the female, *Shakti,* meeting and merging with the male, *Shiva,* to consummate a mystic union in the brain.
> —W. Thomas Wolfe, *And the Sun Is Up*

Likewise, the symbolism in the loss of one's "maiden name" or prior egoic identity in this ecstatic union has not to do with becoming the *possession* or property of the Beloved. Rather, it has to do with becoming *unified* with Him. And just as marriage provides the social sanction for the indulgence in sexual relations, *mystical* marriage involves the activity of the same "sex energy" of the kundalini force, but directed up the spine rather than being used to stimulate the sex nerves. (Of course there is, by itself, nothing magical or sacred about a marriage license or ceremony. Conversely, sex or common-law relationships without that piece of paper or ritual are by no means "sinful" or a "bad example to set for others," in spite of the wonky and judgmental perspectives of both organized and disorganized religions in that regard.)

Indeed, the archaic and Biblical meaning of "to know" is conjugal, with the import "to have [sexual] union with." The "union" with God, by which we "know" Him, again involves simply a higher and *inner* application of the energy normally expended outwardly in sexual activities. In fact, the word "gnosis" derives etymologically from a Greek word meaning "to know"; and gnosis, in spiritual terms, is always intuitive, never sensory knowledge.

The dual nature of the procreative energy is surely the prime reason for the "phallus worship" met throughout the world, particularly in the "Shiva *lingam*" found in India. For an erect column of stone—as with turrets, steeples and obelisks—need not be viewed as merely a phallic symbol, but can equally be seen as a *pillar* reaching from earth toward heaven; *"linga"* means not only "phallus" but also "astral." (The Sanskrit name for the astral body is the *linga sarira.* The Shiva *lingam* is also said to represent infinite space, i.e., the Ayn Sof, or Shiva as the perfectly transcendent and undifferentiated Space-Consciousness.) The *yoni* like-wise—a circular stone with a hollow center, into which the *lingam* slides—represents far less the female generative organs (although its literal translation is indeed "womb") than it does the point at the center of one's sphere of consciousness, atop the *sushumna*—and the Point from which all creation is born. Indeed, the *Sat-Chakra-Nirupana* explicitly associates the yoni with the pericarp of the crown center. (Note the androgyny here: the snake-like, "phallic" kundalini energy coiled round the Shiva *lingam* is a *feminine* or Shakti principle. Likewise, the point or *yoni*-receptacle into which this risen energy fits, after having ascended the spine, is the seat of the *masculine* principle of Shiva. Thus, both masculine and feminine principles are present at each of these poles.)

It is precisely because of the mystical marriage of Shiva and Shakti in the spine, coupled with the lightning-like nature of the awakened kundalini energy, that thunderstorms are regarded in "primitive" thought as the *marriage* of Heaven and Earth. That is, as a bolt of *electricity* and *light* connecting these two poles, accompanied by the thundering sound of Om. Exactly the same basis underlies the mythological marriage of the sun with a serpent or dragon, or with the moon. (We may perhaps view Tiresias' "seven years" of living as a woman, as corresponding as well to the ascent of the feminine kundalini through the seven levels of the Feminine *mayic* reality. His return to life as a man would then relate to the transcendence of those relative levels of being.)

Further, just as, in the human case, this covenant is made in a church "in the sight of God," the divine counterpart on which this ceremony is based centers on the ajna/medullary chakra or "church," site of the "third eye." The "seven churches" of St. John in Revelation, for example, are said to refer to the seven major chakras, or holy places in the spine and brain. Not surprisingly, then, we find that a great many of the words used in East Indian (i.e., Sanskrit) scriptures with respect to the unification of the Many in the One imply both *death* and *marriage*—*samadhi* being both "conscious death" and "mystical marriage." Hence also the archaic idea that the bride and groom should be virgin. For just as we are mundane virgins before the outwardly-directed activity of the kundalini energy in the physical sex act, we are all "spiritual virgins" prior to the raising of the same energy up the spine in mystical marriage.

Thus, in Navaho society, virgin girls are referred to as "non-sun-light-struck," i.e., having not been touched by the rays of the *spiritual* sun. Comparably, in many cultures, an *unmarried* woman is considered a *virgin,* even if she's a prostitute! It is only after *marriage* that she loses her virginity. Further, the idea of "disenchantment through *marriage"* is a regular theme in folktales—mermaids, for example, lose their fishy tails in favor of legs only upon marriage to a human, with the fishlike aspect symbolizing their lower or animal natures.

We find, further, stories in which spellbound-by-a-*wicked-witch* frogs retrieve *golden balls* (spheres) which princesses have dropped into *wells.* Such frogs are beset by the incarnational curse of being confined as amphibians—equally at home in the water of earth as in the air of heaven—to a well in a "great, dark forest" of *maya.* They are then freed to return to their true, handsome-prince form, by the princess's (Cosmic Beloved's) *kiss.* Or, freed by being thrown against the princess's *castle bedroom* (seventh chakra, cf. royal nuptial chamber) wall, in the original Brothers Grimm version.

The varying roles of male and female in these tales becomes totally understandable when one considers that, on the one hand, all of creation can be viewed as a passive feminine *Maya* with respect to God the Father, the sole Masculine—and is so viewed in the Catholic religion, for example. On the other hand, when considering the "Redemptive Cosmic Mother" aspect of the same *maya,* one would naturally, by polarity and its hoped-for resolution, represent the duality-bound suitor as male. (That Cosmic Mother aspect frequently shows up in the spiritual context of pagan "folk tales." *The Frog Prince* tale mentioned just above, for example, dates from thirteenth-century Germany.)

Maya and Shakti are again regarded as negative, not as a denigration of Feminine qualities, but rather simply because they *negate* (i.e., "negate-ive") the natural, tranquil state of the Ocean, creating duality where previously there was transcendence. More broadly, principles which act in opposition to transcendence in any given situation are generally regarded as negative, while those which encourage transcendence are taken as positive. It is for exactly this reason that Taoism can assert that salvation comes from a return to the original unity of negative *yin* and positive *yang,* while yet placing *yang* ahead of *yin,* at times verging on identifying the primordial Tao with the *yang* power. (Note that if it were only the human conceptualization of reality into positives and negatives that blinded us to the omnipresent Tao, the idea of positives leading toward It and negatives away from It could not be sustained: they would be equally "part of the problem.")

Further, this regard of principles encouraging spiritual realization as positive, and those opposing it as negative, seems to be constant in the structure of creation. That is, these poles apparently never interchange their functions. However, the regard of the masculine principle as positive, and the feminine as negative, is not similarly consistent. For example, the masculine life current flowing in *pingala* is a negative one, while the feminine *ida* is positive.

In Taoism, too, although popular accounts invariably make the association of *yang* with masculine and positive, and *yin* with feminine and negative, "it is accepted that the negative and positive powers can, and do, change places on different levels, such as the emotional plane in which the feminine aspect assumes the positive and the masculine becomes negative"—J. C. Cooper, *Yin and Yang: The Taoist Harmony of Opposites.* That point, of course, is completely missed by superficial popularizers of Eastern religions in general.

The association of Shakti with the kinetic aspect and Shiva with the static is opposite to the standard Taoist pairing of active with "masculine" and passive with "feminine." Nevertheless, in the human body the right *(pingala)* half is indeed traditionally held as masculine and having more active or aggressive tendencies, while the left half is regarded as feminine and more passive. These are not arbitrary designations: if a person's intentions are overly aggressive—e.g., going "full steam ahead" even in situations where receptivity is called for—his or her Intentionality line will be distorted or bent exactly toward the right half of the body. Conversely, in one who is overly passive—holding back even when action is called for—the Intentionality line will be bent toward the left.

The subtle "relationship cords" grown between us and our families, friends and lovers are similarly said to issue from the right side of our chakras when the relationships in question are with men, and from the left side for our relationships with women. Also, it has been found in rolfing sessions that both men and women report images of men when the right leg is rolfed, while experiences with women are recalled when the muscles and nerves of the left leg are stimulated.

Further, it is said of both men and women that the positive right side of the body generally contains a stronger flow of divine life current than the left. It is exactly because of this that there is a traditional scriptural association of the "right hand" with goodness and that, conversely, the tantra yoga which makes use of sex and raw meat in its spiritual practices is referred to as "left hand tantra." This same characteristic is responsible for the fact that, as Brennan notes, when persons hold hands in a circle and send energy around that ring, it will generally flow naturally from left to right (or counterclockwise when viewed from above). That is, it will flow from the higher energy level of each person's right hand, to the lower level of the next person's left hand being held in that grip. (It is considered bad luck to pass drinks around a table clockwise, i.e., against this natural energy flow.) For the same reason, there are healing techniques which involve sending healing energy into a person's head with one's *right* hand, and feeling it come out of a lower chakra with the left hand.

Comparably, "sinister" is a Latin word meaning "left handed" and also "unlucky," from a superstition that omens seen on the left boded ill. ("Sinister" also means "morally wrong, malevolent, bad, evil"; these are all traditionally regarded as *yin* characteristics.) It likewise used to be considered unlucky to put your left foot on the floor first when getting out of bed. The common Islamic legend-based depiction of a devil residing on one's left shoulder, and an angel on the right—keeping track of one's good deeds—has the same origin. Indeed, spilled salt is thrown over one's left shoulder for exactly this reason, i.e., as a "salaried" payment to placate the devil and avoid the otherwise-ensuing bad luck. Similarly, wedding rings are worn on the left hand to ward against evil, i.e., against *maya*.

The *structural* (i.e., not human-created) association of the left half of the body with both the feminine and with a weaker flow of divine life current than the masculine or right side, however, is no reflection on the respective potentials or spiritual propensities of men and women. It could, of course, be easily and detrimentally misunderstood along those lines, but that is a function of human psychology, not of truth. The same points are obviously relevant to *maya* or the redemptive Cosmic Mother as being also the source of all duality and delusion.

Now, it should be obvious that the Tao does not *consist* of the opposites of *yin* and *yang*—of dark/light, passive/active, cold/hot, moist/dry, malignant/beneficent, negative/positive, etc.—any more than the Ocean *consists* of a vast number of independently-existing waves. The Tao-Ocean, which *becomes* all the waves of *yin* and *yang,* exists with or without the waves; the primal reality is the Ocean, not the waves. And the raising/lowering of the state of consciousness with the passage of time, which increases/decreases the maximum radius of expansion, affects the level of reality to which one is attuned, with conscious omnipresence again being gained only through the raising to infinity of the level of consciousness.

Obviously, then, we must exercise caution when grouping pairs of apparent opposites as *yin* and *yang.* There are opposites which can be validly balanced—e.g., hot and cold, passive and active. There are also, however, pairs which appear to be opposites, but where the higher includes and has become, but transcends, the lower. In the latter category, we find the Infinite Ocean and its finite dualistic waves; and intuition versus reason/feeling. We also find there the wrongly-considered "opposites" of mind—which is not to be confused with Self or causal-level spirit—and body.

We thus cannot afford to take any two seeming opposites—or even valid opposites, such as good and evil—associate them without due consideration with *yin* and *yang,* and then assert that these states must be "dynamically balanced" in order for us to reach the Tao. In the case of good and evil, for example, this leads quickly to the obviously mistaken idea that to be always good would be an "imbalanced" or undesirable state! The same mistake leads further to the absurd suggestion that the best possible state would consist of one's actions of good and evil being "dynamically balanced"!

The untenability of that blindly "balancing" position is particularly evident in the face of the *I Ching's* statement that "good people stop evil and promote good, obeying Heaven and accepting its order." It would take a great deal of wishful thinking, then—if not outright denial—to assert that Taoism regards "too much good" as *bad!* Any "dynamic balance" between the expansion and contraction of consciousness (i.e., its raising and lowering with the passage of time), for example, is obviously not the same as the integrated state which implies omnipresence and the full genuine transcendence of duality in timeless Spirit.

The fact that not all pairs of opposites can be validly grouped as *yin/yang* is obvious even on the most simple level. For, no sensible person would ever attempt to beneficially balance wisdom and ignorance, love and hatred, altruism and selfishness, honesty and dishonesty, or truth and untruth. Self-evidently, the former member of each of these pairs results in an expansion of consciousness, and so is to be maximized. Thus, although the alternating inflations and deflations of consciousness are a very exercise in balance—the inflation of this sphere, when it reaches its maximum, gives way in transition to deflation—spiritual realization, when it reaches its maximum of transcendence, does *not* give way to its opposite of ignorance!

Likewise, no one should be impressed or fooled by facile arguments such as "Too much of a good thing—be it food, exercise, etc.—is bad; therefore, good and bad are relative." Indeed, if *all* polarities were meant to be dynamically balanced, then the opposites of "balance" and "imbalance" too would need to be balanced (at least half the time!) and we would spend our lives in quest of a dynamic balance between balance and imbalance. Comparatively, it has actually been suggested by some scholars that the opposites of *yin* and *yang* are both unified and *not unified* in the Tao! Of course, if it were only the "dualistic nature of all concepts" that prevented us from seeing reality as it is, we would have no choice but to agree ... and to disagree! Thankfully, however, there is much more to the cosmos than such inadequate understandings can disclose.

The golden ring plays a significant role in both secular and mystical marriage. In the Aladdin story too, the genie is initially released from its lamp by the rubbing of a *ring,* given to Aladdin by a lying magician—i.e., *maya,* the Cosmic Magician—in the latter's hope of gaining mastery over the genie in the lamp. In the same way, in the Quest for the Holy Grail, the task of the solar hero Lancelot is the liberation of the fair Guénévere, who is imprisoned by a *magician* in a castle that lies beyond a *river* that can be crossed only by the "straight and narrow" *sword* bridge, guarded at the castle entrance by two solar-symbol lions.

As Brennan experienced for herself, the idea of a lion-bodied sphinx guarding the "Holy of Holies" has its basis in actual mystical perceptions. (That "Holy of Holies" is the "sun" or "star" of white light which is the transcendent, witnessing Self.) Thus, the regard of lions as sun-symbols, whatever its deep metaphysical reason may be, is no mere human invention, arbitrary symbol or superstition. Rather, it is again simply an accurate transcription of actual inner experience.

Doubtless the wizard's high regard for rings and bracelets as potent objects of magic derives from their higher root in the golden ring of Om as the source of all power in creation. Similarly, the threadlike *sushumna* provides the basis for the talismanic significance of tied threads, "sacred threads" and of lassoing in folktales, as well as the metaphysical meaning of the rosary and the necklace. (The seals in the chakras are also referred to as "knots" along the thread of the *sushumna*. Compare the protective "seven-knotted bamboo rod" carried by fakirs in India.) That same *sushumna* also provides the symbolism of fishing with a line—consider the previously-related genie-fishing episode, although there involving not simply a single line but rather a net or network of strings. That is, symbolizing a nervous system, in which the spine is only one component, albeit the most important among the ropes by which the net is hauled up.

Interestingly, the "Liege Lady" of all the genies in the Aladdin narrative is an egg laid by a Great Bird found in Mount Kaf. Aladdin requests that this egg be hung from the dome-crown of his pavilion, whereupon the offended genie threatens to kill him. The center of any such architectural dome symbolizes, according to Coomaraswamy, not only the progression from diversity into unity but, especially when left with a circular opening at that crown, the means by which the consciousness of an advanced yogi exits the body. Frequently, a tree or pillar grows through this opening in the roof. Mountains likewise taper from variety to unity at the summit; as do triangles, cones and pyramids—whose shape mountains closely approximate. There, the single point of the triangle's apex descends into duality, dividing to become the two points of the base.

The upright triangle has long been one of the symbols of Shiva, with its inverted counterpart being associated with Shakti; superimposed, these form the Star of David. And just as the upright and inverted triangles are associated with the crown and coccygeal chakras, respectively, the Star of David is again associated with the heart chakra. The same shape, though, is also sometimes linked with the pineal gland and

---

ajna chakra, i.e., the place of the union of the inverted and upright triangles of Shakti and Shiva.

> Hindu temples have a dome-like shape with a big saucer-shaped bell hanging from the center of the dome, and whoever goes in for worship first clangs the bell. In the temple of the human body also, in the dome-like structure of the head, the pilgrim soul, as it enters the astral region [i.e., the "third eye" of the astral body], hears a sound that resembles that of a gong or a conch. Similarly, the Christian cathedrals are either in the formation of a big dome resembling the human head or are steeple-shaped, reminiscent of the ascending human nose, over which, as the soul concentrates at the still-point behind and between the two eyebrows, a bell-like sound is heard.
>
> —Kirpal Singh, *Naam or Word*

In Grecian architecture, too, we find pillars used to symbolize the World Axis. Likewise, in the Erechtheion temple, there is an opening *purposely* left in the roof immediately above the *trident*-mark of Poseidon. There, the outer two tines of the trident obviously represent the *ida* and *pingala* channels, and the central prong, coincident with the handle, the *sushumna*. (Shiva, too, carried a trident.) Compare Revelation 3:12: "Him that overcometh [i.e., who transcends *maya*] will I make a *pillar* in the temple of my God, and he shall go no more out [i.e., be compelled to physically incarnate no more]." We find also that "in shaman tree-shrines, the top of the Tree projects through an opening in the roof, through which it is possible to [symbolically] pass from one world to another"—Coomaraswamy, "The Inverted Tree." Similarly, in the Bible, Jacob

> dreamed, and behold a ladder set up on the earth, and the top of it reached to heaven: and behold the angels of God ascending and descending on it.... And he was afraid, and said, "How dreadful is this place: this is none other but the house of God, and this is the gate of heaven." And Jacob rose up early in the morning, and took the stone ... and set it up for a pillar.
>
> —Genesis 28:12, 17-8

There are (or were) likewise American Indian tribes who would not enter their houses except by the smoke-hole, descending via a stepped ladder. Among other peoples and folktales featuring heroes who ride on eagles or thunder-birds, a matching hole in the roof is identified with the Pole Star. (The "thundering" sound of Om again accompanies the "lightning" of the risen, "winged" kundalini energy; thus, "thunder-birds.") Further, in the saga of King Volsung, a similar tree to the shamanic is given the name "Branstock"—which literally means "burning bush"! Architecture and religion have traditionally gone hand in hand, with one's dwelling being an outer representation, in its essential attributes, of the bodily "house." The priest in early societies was often an architect as well; the Freemasons are only one instance of this.

Now, mountains such as Aladdin's Kaf are commonly and rightly taken as representing the World Axis. These formations reach up from earth to touch the sky, with the clouds in between mythologically forming the barrier between heaven and earth. Thus, in India, Meru is both the spinal column and a sacred "mountain of the gods," the ascent of which leads to the snowcapped summit, corresponding to the crown chakra. The same ascent leads to the snow-white light of the star of the East, or the cosmic consciousness at the spiritual eye; and to the "sun center" above one's head. "Having fully awakened [kundalini], let the wise one lead Her to *Bhanu* [the Sun] at the summit of the Meru"—*Sat-Chakra-Nirupana*.

In Grecian tradition, the mythical abode of the gods and the place of Zeus' *palace* and *throne* was the summit of Mount Olympus. Likewise, in Hindu mythology Shiva dwells on the summit of Mount Kailasa. Homer, then, wrote that "a white splendor spreads its radiance round" the luminous and self-splendid god-abode of Mount Olympus. The same white-light Star-Self hidden within the seventh-level golden egg is the white *"Bird* of Paradise," held within the "supreme golden case" or cage of the ketheric body. And the "door" of that cage, then, by which the bird escapes from its accustomed confinement, is the crown chakra.

The same principle is relevant to the ziggurats of the Mesopotamian civilizations, with the tops of these stepped pyramidal structures representing "the pivotal point in the center of the sacred circle of space, where the earthly and heavenly powers join." Those powers also join at the point atop the *sushumna,* in the marriage of the Earth-Mother and Sky-Father. (The idea of a Sky-Father, associated with sun and thunder, and having as his consort an Earth-Mother, is found world-over.) The four sides of these temples faced North, South, East and West. That is, they faced toward and away from the Pole Star—i.e., in line with the earth's rotational axis, or perpendicular to the apparent yearly motion of the sun from solstice to solstice—toward the rising sun, and toward the setting sun.

We find also in the Buddhist tradition the World Mountain Sumeru, which "rose from the mid-point of the earth as the *vertical axis of the egg-shaped universe.*" Comparably, for the Tibetan Buddhists Meru is explicitly a gold mountain at the center of the universe. In China, the "Mountain Men" or "Immortals" are pictured as feathered, like birds, or as floating through the air on soaring beasts; while the Apaches per-formed rituals in the attempt to make the World Mountain grow and carry them to the world of light. Likewise, in the *Mahabharata,* there is a White Mountain, Svetaparvata, situated in the regions beyond the darkness of this world. Equally, a Mountain of Lights—i.e., chakras—is found in the Zoroastrian, Gnostic and Mandaean traditions. The Ba-linese, too, have a sacred mountain at the center of their island; many more examples of this phenomenon could be given from cultures around the world. Additionally, almost every country in Europe contains folk-lore in which mountains are regarded as the natural abode of souls. Consider further that the Chinese holy mountain, K'un-lun,

> has two tiers: an upright cone matched with a reversed cone. [Compare the upright and inverted triangles of Hinduism: other cultures explicitly associate such upright and reversed mountains with Heaven and Earth.] K'un-lun is also in the human head. There are in its most secret parts a "chamber like a grotto" *(tung-fang,* a term which also designates the nuptial chamber! [i.e., the place of the "sexual" union of Shiva and Shakti in mystical marriage]) and "nirvana" *(ni-wan).*
> —N. J. Girardot, *Myth and Meaning in Early Taoism*

It is exactly because principles leading toward the Tao are regarded as positive that mountains—as symbols of the *axis mundi* or the inner means toward transcendence—are regarded as *yang* phenomena. That is so even though many of the steps toward this transcendence have to do with *balancing yin* and *yang* (e.g., the masculine and feminine energy flows in the right and left halves of one's body). Indeed, it is said that the original meaning of *yin* and *yang* referred to the shaded and sunny sides of a mountain, respectively. And since mountains represent the spine, this may be taken with complete reasonableness as indicating the feminine ("shaded," negative) and masculine ("sunny"—i.e., containing a stronger flow of divine life current or *light*—or positive) sides of the body. Of course, one must keep in mind that this particular application of "masculine" and "feminine" characteristics, like the association of good with *yang* and evil with *yin,* has nothing to do with men versus women.

Yang is actually also sometimes associated with the *North* side of the mountain. Compare the Pole Star being the North Star (at least for cultures in the northern hemisphere). Compare also the regard of the top of the *sushumna* as being the North or *masculine* (and transcendent) pole of the spinal magnet, and seat of the microcosmic spiritual sun, or Star of the East. The ancient Egyptians likewise aligned their pyramids and temples to the North because they believed that their pharaohs became *stars* in the *Northern* sky after they died.

The relation of eggs or of winged birds to mountains may not be as immediately obvious as is the association of birds with trees, for example. However, their kinship readily shows when we realize the inherent relation of birds, wings and eggs, and that trees and mountains are equivalent symbols of the spinal axis, the "center of spiritual influence" of one's *inner* world. (With regard to birds, the flames of the risen kundalini energy again spread outside either side of the head into a "winged radiance"—this accounting for the "feathered serpent" symbolism—while *samadhi* grants the ability to fly through space in consciousness.) This inner, esoteric symbolism—based as always on objective microcosmic bodily structure—may well be projected outwardly or given an exoteric reading after having been clothed in mythological language. In this case, the "World Axis" will invariably be taken as corresponding to one specific local physical mountain, with appropriate rituals being performed at that particular site.

One might, for example, symbolically re-enact the marriage of Heaven and Earth on the summit of the holy mountain or its ziggurat counterpart, outwardly mimicking the corresponding inner mystical marriage of the Zeus-Father and Earth-Mother at the summit of the *sushumna.* In the same way, one may stoop to viewing heaven as being situated above the clouds, and hell as literally below us. But the primary, esoteric and most important meaning of such symbols and rituals has *always* to do with the subtle bodily structure underlying spiritual evolution.

Thus, birds are not symbols of heaven merely because they fly through the sky, any more than serpents are associated with water and the ocean only for being quasi-amphibious, or considered as symbols of immortality simply for shedding their skin. Nor is gold held as a symbol of spiritual attainment and purity simply because it does not rust. In the same way, raising kundalini to the sun at the summit of the Meru is not about mountain climbing, and the "razor's edge" separating and linking Sky and Earth is not the horizon but the *sushumna:*

> Verily he who without wings [i.e., without a risen kundalini energy] goes up to the top of the Tree [the crown chakra, atop the spinal Tree of Life], he falls down from it [or returns soon to bodily awareness]. But if one having wings sits at the top of the Tree, or on the edge of a sword, or on the edge of a razor, he does not fall down from it. For he sits supported by his wings ... sits without fear in the heavenly world, and likewise moves about.
>
> —Jaiminiya Upanisad Brahmana

Similarly, the "still point of the turning world" does not refer merely to the North Pole, or to the Pole Star in line with the earth's rotational axis—where this axis, of course, passes through the poles, by definition. That star holds a constant position in the sky, and so may be taken as a symbol of the point "around which our world or 'universe' rotates." That is, it may be regarded as a symbol of the spiritual sun atop the Axis of the Universe or World Axis, through which duality is transcended by "climbing out of" the finite cosmos, placing us mystically and *experientially* at the center of creation. (The spinning of the earth, which of course causes the sun to appear to rise and set, is the same mechanism responsible for the starry heavens seeming to circle around the North or Pole Star.) Here, the North and South poles are magnetically positive and negative poles, akin to Shiva and Shakti.

The sun atop the World Axis again corresponds to the white light of the five-pointed star at the center of the spiritual eye. It also corresponds to the ideal point and potentially-infinite sphere of consciousness—"in line" with the spinal axis just as the Pole Star is in line with the axis of the earth/world. That center is the individualized expression of the "sphere of center everywhere, circumference nowhere" and "still point of the *inner* turning world," and places each one of us at "the center of the universe." It does not at all derive merely from a superstitious regard for the North Star, seemingly stationary in the heavens. Rather, the esoteric and primary referent of the symbolism is to the sun or star atop the microcosmic spinal axis. We have seen the same relation earlier in the aforementioned "hole in the roof," corresponding to the crown chakra, being identified with the Pole Star. (In India and elsewhere, the Pole Star is regarded as being fixed to the summit of the Cosmic Mountain.)

The transcendence of duality in the marriage of Heaven and Earth, or Shiva and Shakti, at the "still point" or "center of the universe" at the summit of the spinal axis, is again re-enacted at the peak of the external World Mountain. This, then, is what allows us to view mountains (as well as ziggurats and pyramids) as symbols of the *axis* of the world. For these are otherwise not in line with the earth's rotational axis, nor do they have a similar shape. The progression from duality to unity as one ascends to the peak of a mountain also contributes to this view; as does the fact that, just as the top part of the cerebrum is the highest place in the human body, the peak of the holy mountain is the highest point in that geographic locality. Likewise, the "climbing" up a pole or tree is no mere metaphorical device to reenact the progress or ascent toward a God and heaven naïvely conceived as existing above the earthly clouds, *but rather refers to the actual raising of consciousness up the spine, to pass through the spiritual sun.*

In the same way, if the Buddhist World Mountain referred esoterically to the axis of rotation of our planet, it would make no sense for it to coincide with the "vertical axis of the egg-shaped universe." Nor, for that matter, would it be logical to place the *sun* mythologically atop the World Axis—or at the summit of the Meru. For, unlike the Pole Star, *the sun is never in line with that axis, i.e., with the North Pole, regardless of one's latitude.* And to regard this placing of suns atop axes as merely an "inseparable mixture of polar and solar symbolisms" is to have stopped short of penetrating to the core esoteric meaning, which requires no such generous allowances. Only in the absence of an appropriately detailed understanding of subtle bodily structure does one need to appeal to such "fudging" to "make things fit."

If, on the other hand, these "mountains" and "axes" refer, as with the Indian Meru, to the subtle structure of the human body, with the spinal column coinciding with the vertical axis of the seventh-level golden egg, the correspondence is exact. (Living creature eggs too have a flow of electromagnetic energy along the axis where the spine eventually develops.) Similarly, in the Buddhist *Dhammapada Commentary,* Moggallana ascends to speak with the Buddha by climbing up the *center* of Mt. Meru, this being *"in appearance like a thread of a yellow blanket strung through a gem."* That description can hardly be made to fit an actual mountain, but it again makes complete sense when referred to the thread of the *sushumna,* strung through the bodily gem and jewels of the chakric lotuses to form a chain of lights.

Every symbol of the "World Axis" can be sensibly read as applying to the *sushumna,* but the converse is not true, yielding instead combinations of symbols which do not quite fit the external physical facts. It is this actuality which indicates that the inward and microcosmic structural interpretation is intended as the primary one. That is, it indicates that these symbolisms are not meant to be taken merely figuratively or poetically, or regarded only as human-devised aids for visualization in meditation, but are rather intended to be received as referring to objective subtle structures. For, if this were not the case, one would find that the outward readings fit, whereas the attempt to apply them inwardly produced discrepancies. It is true, of course, that since the structure of the microcosmic bodily universe is highly similar to that of the macrocosm, most spiritual symbolisms can be given both inward and valid outward readings. But the fact remains that the *meaningful* marriage of Heaven and Earth, for example, is definitely internal.

All of this demonstrates quite clearly that the caduceus, holy mountain, Burning Bush, pillar, the *soma-dripping* Tree of Life and of Immortality, and all other verticals leading to a *Sundoor* at their apex, refer in every case first to the *sushumna,* and only secondarily or symbolically to any other literal or figurative center or axis of rotation. ("Figurative" in that since the Divine Spirit or "center of spiritual influence in the world" has no specific location, being present everywhere, the "World Axis" representing it could be taken only symbolically, not as corresponding to a literal axis in the external universe.)

Indeed, if the subtle microcosmic structure of creation exists at all, the structural interpretation of myth *must* be the primarily *intended* meaning. It is inconceivable that symbols such as the "World Axis,"

"Tree of Life" and the "still point of the turning world," which mesh exactly with the meditatively-experienced subtle structure of the human body, could have been conceived *independently* of it, as merely a figurative representation of the path toward the transcendence of duality. It is completely reasonable, however, for us to allow that the structural understanding *degenerated* into figurative interpretations *after the knowledge of that structure was lost.*

Now, it is highly interesting to note that the North Pole is the traditional residence of Santa Claus, who not only descends to earth and reascends via a chimney, but is sometimes shown holding a *staff.* Recall also the many associations of bells with this figure and the Christmas season, and Kirpal Singh's aforementioned comment on the spiritual connotations thereof. Also compare "wedding bells": the mystical marriage of Shiva and Shakti again takes place in the nuptial chamber of the cerebrum, at the literal still-point behind and between the eyebrows.

It is well known, of course, that "Santa Claus" derives from "Saint Nicholas," traditionally honored on December 6, whose robe enabled him to travel from place to place instantaneously, and whose custom it was to give presents in secret during the night, in legend dropping them down chimneys on the eve of his festival day. Santa Claus's "flying," use of reindeer and descent down chimneys were first introduced in Clement Moore's poem "A Visit From Saint Nicholas," published in *The New York Times* in 1823. Moore was a professor of Oriental languages, and from that gained a scholar's knowledge of the activities of Siberian shamans. The latter worshipped a "great reindeer spirit," and "flew" to the realm of astral spirits through the smoke holes in the roofs of their huts.

The name "Christmas" further derives from the medieval *Christes Masse*—the Mass of Christ. Christmas as such was not celebrated until the fourth century, owing to the Christian custom, at that time, of celebrating the *deaths* rather than the births of important spiritual personages. As no certain knowledge of the date of Christ's birth existed, the Church ordered the feast to be celebrated on the day of the Mithraic rites of the birth of the sun—Mithra being the ancient Persian god of light and truth, and later of the sun—and the close of the Saturnalia festival, the Roman celebration of the winter solstice. (The solstice fell on December 25 in those centuries.)

Yule, too, was a winter solstice festival—of German and Celtic pagans. Thus, the common factor here is the rebirth of the *sun* following the winter solstice, when the days begin to grow longer again. Consequently, while Saturn was the Roman god of agriculture, an activity which does indeed depend on the strength of the sun in its growing season, the important meaning here is esoteric, referring to the increased shining of the microcosmic *spiritual* sun, so closely associated with the Christ consciousness center—the "Sun of God." Correspondingly, we have the Christmas tree of the cerebrospinal nervous system, decked with spherical globes and lights, and crowned with a five-pointed star.

Now, in the yogic view, the Masculine principle of Shiva is represented by the syllable "Ham"; with the Feminine principle of Shakti taking the sound "Sah." These combine to form *"hamsa,"* meaning literally "I am He" (i.e., "God and I are one"), and also the word for "goose" or "swan," a symbol of high spiritual realization associated with the crown chakra and its "golden egg" level. Hence, we have the association of golden eggs with geese and swans; as is found even in the "Jack and the Beanstalk" tale, where Jack climbs a beanstalk from earth to the heavens, returning after one of those ascents with a bird that lays golden eggs, and afterward marrying a princess. "Ham" and "Sah" are also associated with the twelve-petaled lotus in the pericarp of the golden-egg-level crown chakra—from which it becomes very easy to accept the fact that one of the alternative meanings of *"hamsa"* is *sun!*

Lama Govinda has suggested that Elijah's "chariot of fire," in which he was "taken up to heaven," refers to the axis or axle of the spine—with spinning circular "wheels" of chakras along it. In coupling that with the traditional placing of a point atop the *sushumna,* we cannot help but feel that Chuang Tzu's "axis ... the center of the circle responding to the endless changes" refers to the same staff. Chakras, in general, are regarded as sun-symbols; and we note again that the sun, as with all stars, is a sphere of light. In any case, the "solar chariot" is widely recognized in mythological studies as having a profound and precise meaning. That is, of the two wheels connected by the axle passing through their centers symbolizing Heaven and Earth, or the crown and coccygeal chakras. These wheels are then joined through their centers by the axis of the spine, representing further the penetration through the center of the *sun* by the Universal Axis or Tree of Life.

In the symbolism of archery, the piercing of the bull's eye by the arrow-axis is regarded as representing the same structure as that of the chariot wheels. Indeed, the cow is traditionally a lunar or feminine symbol—along with the serpent and dove (of the Holy Ghost) which, significantly, were often the sacred animals of early Mother-Goddesses. Thus, such a lunar symbol's consort would logically be a *solar* symbol. Shiva's animal, in fact, is indeed the sun-associated bull.

According to yoga, the straight spine and correspondingly arched front of the body in the meditation posture form the "bow" from which the "arrow" of the kundalini energy is shot to pierce the eye of its target. Even Cupid—*flying* on cherubic *wings*—is regularly shown piercing hearts with his arrows. The "Valentine's heart" symbol traditionally associated with him again derives from the clairvoyant perception of the auras of persons in love—whose heart chakras are thus stimulated— forming exactly that shape.

The same reference to the spine is made by "lances that pierce the vault of the sky and thus make an ascent to heaven possible" and by "arrows that form a chain reaching to heaven." That is, contrary to the accepted interpretation, these are far from being mere elaborations of the superstitious animistic worship of the spirits of primitive tools! And tellingly, the Rig Veda mentions a *seven*-wheeled chariot, as well as a three-wheeled one, i.e., focusing on the coccygeal, heart and ajna chakras.

Thus, when the same scripture speaks of Indra—the conqueror of the senses or *indriyas*—drawing Apala through the naves of the three-wheeled cosmic chariot, causing Apala's scaly skins to be shed, so that she is made "sunskinned," this refers of course to the drawing of consciousness through the *sushumna* to the spiritual sun, via the rise of kundalini. Indeed, the Sanskrit word for "axis" and "axle-tree" is distinguished only by an accent mark from *aksa,* the word for "eye," and from which the English "eye" is indeed ultimately derived.

The center of a chariot wheel, into which the axle fits, is known as its "nave"; the word "navel," referring to any central part or point, is etymologically related to this. Further, the navel on the human body is the vestige of our umbilical connection with our biological mother. Similarly, the "vestige" of our latent connection with our Divine Mother is at the base of the axis or axle of the spine; and at the top of the same axis—where that axle seats into the crown chakra—when this Shakti is awakened. Thus, we have the origin of the mythological "Tree at the Navel of the world." This Tree, as with the "Tree of the knowledge of good and evil," or dualistic experiences, is no different from the "Tree of Immortality," by the climbing of which we transcend duality. Likewise, the Inverted Tree and the Upright Tree or Tree of Life both refer to this same spinal axis.

The English "eye" has meanings including "center of revolution" (e.g., eye of the storm), "place of exit or ingress," "socket" (for insertion of another object), "fountain" (well-eye) and "brightest spot or center." These refer metaphysically to the rotation of the central star in the ajna chakra or third eye and to the rotation of the "universe" around the "still point" at the center of one's sphere of consciousness; to the exiting and entering of consciousness from the body via the medullary and crown chakras, which meet at a common point at the root of that eye; to the joining of the astral/causal spine to the same receptive "socket" point (i.e., its seating into the twelve-petaled lotus in the pericarp of the seventh center); to the top of the watery fountain of *amrita* flowing in spiritual awakening; and to the point itself, at the center of one's sun-like sphere of consciousness. The Arabic and Persian languages likewise have words simultaneously meaning all of "eye," "sun" and "well-spring."

Prana is generally seen as either yellow or red by clairvoyants. Presumably this accounts for the East Indian tradition of women placing dots of *red* sandalwood paste on their foreheads in between the eyebrows, i.e., representing the gathering of life force there in spiritual awakening. In any case, red—as in the color of blood, the physical distributor/counterpart of life force—is recognized in yoga as being a "transformation" of gold. And this latter color is intimately associated with the area between the eyebrows, of course, in terms of the golden ring of the astral spiritual eye.

Now, the "kingdom" made frequent reference to by both Chuang Tzu and Lao Tzu is standard scriptural metaphor for King Soul—whose dwelling place is, of course, the Inward or Holy *Palace*—and his throng of obedient mental and physical bodily faculties or subjects.

Gross man seldom or never realizes that his body is a kingdom, governed by Emperor Soul on the throne of the cranium, with subsidiary regents in the six spinal centers or spheres of consciousness.

—Paramahansa Yogananda,
Autobiography of a Yogi

The "scepter" of the *sushumna* extends from the hand of King Soul (or the usurping King Ego) seated in the "throne" of the thousand-petaled lotus in the brain. The spiritual eye is the "revolving door" gateway to this royal castle—i.e., the star within it is literally seen as turning about its center. Thus, when folktales speak of a hero entering a revolving castle, or one with a revolving door, this refers not to the apparent revolution of the stars in the sky around the Pole Star. Rather, it points instead to the rotation of one specific star in the blue sphere of the ajna chakra (or to the "still point" at the center of one's sphere of consciousness).

As in the quote above, the ancient Greeks likewise considered the incarnating soul to pass downward through seven spheres to its life on earth, and to retrace this path in the reverse, ascending order at death. This idea is more often encountered in its application to their physical theory of cosmology, where the earth was considered to be a stationary, solid sphere in the center of seven transparent, concentric, revolving spheres. Each of these spheres was believed to hold a visible planet on its surface, thus defining its orbit—the moon, Mercury, Venus, the sun, Mars, Jupiter, and Saturn, in that order outward.

The same planets are often associated with the chakras from the coccygeal to the crown. The "still point" of each of these "turning worlds" or planets may then be regarded, in one sense, as the tip of the respective chakric funnel, where it seats into the axis of the *sushumna*. There were likewise ziggurats having seven terraced stories, corresponding to "the seven heavens of the planets," with a "Water of Immortality" to be found in the sky-realm of the gods. Further, many esoteric religions associate a genie or minor god with each of these seven planets. Since each of the major chakras is also associated with the same planets, and has its corresponding subtle body, the existence of a microcosmic genie corresponding to one's higher bodies is very natural and substantiated by this. (These "worlds" are thus connected to the sun "by a thread of spiritual light," i.e., the current in the *sushumna.)*

In any case, the aforementioned seven celestial bodies are the same ones after which our days of the week are named. Thus, Sunday is the day of the sun, Monday the day of the moon, and Tuesday the day of Tiw (the Anglo-Saxon counterpart of the Roman god of war, Mars). Wednesday, then, is Wotan's day (a corrupted form of the day of Mercury), while Thursday is Thor's day. (Thor was the Norse god of thunder and the sky, akin to the Roman god of the sky and of rain, Jupiter. In German, Thursday is "Donnerstag," or "Thunder Day.") Friday is the day of Freya (she being the Norse goddess of love, cf. Venus), and Saturday, finally, is Saturn's day. The sounding tones of these seven planets in the Greek cosmology were believed to produce the "music of the spheres"—heard microcosmically as the characteristic sounds of the cerebrospinal chakras.

On the second or emotional bodily level, the chakras take the seven colors of the rainbow in the expected order, from red at the coccyx, through orange, yellow, green, blue and indigo at the spiritual eye. (Scarlet is again red-orange, or the combination of the first two chakras, relating to sexuality.) The crown center is then violet, violet-white or white. The spine is thus also the "rainbow bridge" leading to the "pot of gold," with rainbows then being symbols of the *axis mundi.* The diffraction of white light into a spectrum of seven colors thus evidently parallels the differentiation of the white light of cosmic consciousness into its component spectrum of consciousness or levels of reality. For those latter are most often listed as seven in number, corresponding to the seven cerebrospinal chakras.

The fact that each of the chakras is clairvoyantly seen to have a specific color means that even though sunlight is indeed a continuous spectrum, the conceptualization of its prism-diffracted light as being into the "seven colors of the rainbow" is not merely arbitrary, but is rather an accurate mirroring of cosmic structure. Further, each of those chakras has a specific function(s) on each of the various levels of reality. Thus, each of those colors has a range of *intrinsic meanings* associated with it, regardless of any additional meanings which human beings may attach to them. This is obvious even just in terms of emotions showing up as specific colors in the aura.

Fascinatingly, "Leonardo da Vinci maintained that the power of meditation could be enhanced tenfold if carried out under the influence of violet rays passing through the stained glass windows of a quiet church"—R. Gerber, *Vibrational Medicine*. Further, Isaac Newton's wish to find seven colors in his prism-diffracted sunlight—many people can detect only six distinct ones—was based in the attempt to relate these colors, and their respective frequencies, to the seven musical tones of the aforementioned Western musical scale.

Presumably the association of the crown chakra with the seventh or "golden egg" level of our subtle bodily structure, and seated into the location of the golden-silvery expandable sphere of light, is the reason for its designation as a *"golden* lotus" flower. The "thousand petals" then derive from the approximate number of clairvoyantly-visible sub-vortices composing the main funnel. All energy patterns and vortices at the seventh level are themselves said to be composed of threads of golden light. This constitution of Nature at its basis, as structural "threads" forming the "garment" or body of God, then reinforces the idea of *maya* as a macrocosmic woven *veil*.

The gold crowns worn by kings are symbolic of the same golden chakra—of the "kingdom of the soul"—while their scepters again represent the *sushumna*. Such golden crowns equally well represent the spiritual sun, but precisely and only because the objectively existing golden-silvery sphere or sun of consciousness of each one of us has its center located exactly at the root of that chakra. Likewise, any orb atop such a scepter represents the sun not merely in imitation of the "spheri-cal" shape of one's head atop the rod-like spinal column, but rather for the actual sphere of light centered there.

Interestingly, Hermes—the allegorical founder of the Hermetic tradition of higher knowledge—carried a staff (his caduceus) with the power to change anything it touched to gold. That is, that staff conferred the spiritual advancement of the seventh (causal) level, and the experien-tial view of all Nature as being composed of threads of golden light on that plane of its structure. Further, as the messenger/guide of intuition, Hermes flew on winged sandals; representing, for one, the ability of consciousness to exit the body through the spiritual eye to fly through space. Hence, we have the association of gold, of winged birds, and the sun, from whence come figures such as Horus, the golden falcon sun-god of the Egyptians. The same basis gives us Ra, the winged sun-god, whose symbol was the post—representing, as always, the *sushumna,* by which the spiritual sun is reached. The sun is typically winged in Vedic and Upanishadic representation also. Even in the aforementioned caduceus, the pole around which the serpents entwine is topped by a sun-symbol winged sphere.

The winged disk occurs in Egyptian mythology too, surmounting a closed Sundoor. Their mythology also contained a serpent with seven necks, a Tree of Life, an afterlife which was reached by climbing a ladder, and four genii (i.e., subtle bodies) of the dead—the four Khu of the Book of the Dead. ("Khu" = "shining or translucent, intangible casing or covering of the body," which is exactly the appearance of the aura. Scholars regard this "casing or covering" as referring to the sarcophagus in which the mummified body was interred, but that stone case is hardly *translucent,* much less *intangible,* and "shines" only from being highly polished!) Further, the Egyptians used to place a winged solar disk flanked by two *uraeus*-snakes over the gateway of every temple-court, for the banishing of evil, while the pharaoh's crown had a serpent placed over the third eye. (Gateways and doorways are, of course, standard metaphors for the spiritual eye.)

The Tibetans, too, had a *Book of the Dead,* which was read to dying persons to help them understand their experiences as consciousness withdrew from the physical body into the spine during the death process. (The seven- or nine-branched candlestick or Menorah is a symbol of the journey the soul makes after death—i.e., through the spine and its chakras—for exactly this structural reason.) Their Book was explicitly for the benefit of persons who had not practiced the "ejection of consciousness," by which the yogi "learns how to shoot his consciousness up through the crown of his head into a visualized image, and at death he is able to direct it" to the realm of Buddha-nature.

> When your body and mind separate, the Dharmata [i.e., the totality of the basic elements, the essence of reality] will appear, pure and clear yet hard to discern, luminous and brilliant [i.e., the Clear Light of the Void].... A great roar of thunder will come from within the light, the natural sound of Dharmata, like a thousand thunderclaps simultaneously.

This Book was *read* to dying persons because *hearing* is the last of the senses to cease functioning in the process of death. It is used as a daily spiritual text as well, simply because *samadhi* is "conscious death." That is, the process is the same whether the exit from the body is daily and voluntary, or terminal and involuntary.

Hearing, further, is sometimes viewed as a "feminine" characteristic. This is not simply for the reputation of women as being "good listeners," but rather because the Cosmic Feminine sound of Om is inwardly *heard.* (That same sound is symbolized in the blowing of the conch shell, for example.) Similarly, sight is regarded as a "masculine" sense owing to its dependence on the light produced by the *sun.*

The "unique solutions" to koans such as "What is the sound of one hand clapping?" again fit perfectly with the yogic exposition of cosmic structure. This indicates that the structure *underlies* the "paradoxical" koan, and further, that koans cannot be designed simply to "frustrate the activity of the rational mind," that we might differentiate from the conceptualizing intellect in a higher state of awareness in which, by "watching" or operating upon the mind, we realize ourselves to be *more than* it. Koans do indeed have the effect of halting the rational mind's activity. But the fact that, for example, the solution to "What is the sound of one hand clapping?" is the feeling of "stretching out into the universe on a pattern of unheard sound that seems to flow on forever"—while other koans have other *experiential solutions*—shows inarguably that there is much more to the situation than that.

Indeed, it is again possible to develop the ability to shed all three bodies at will through techniques of life-force control—i.e., in taking one's consciousness into the spine, without explicit reference to "silencing/frustrating the mind." Thus, that silencing must be a symptom, not the cause, of transcendence. A comparable situation likewise occurs, according to Brennan, with regard to the various "complexes" in psychology, since these all have to do with subtle energy blockages, which can be seen and moved directly by an "energy therapist" with sufficient skill.

The astral spine or *sushumna* again contains within it the astral *vajra* and *chitrini* channels, and the causal *Brahmanadi,* which leads into the *Brahmarandhra* or "cavity of Brahma" in the crown chakra, through which the accomplished yogi may shed all three bodies at will to realize the Self. The *sushumna,* however, itself enters the astral brain. We might then allow that the kundalini energy can be raised up the *sushumna* into the brain, without that energy being refined enough at that point to traverse the *Brahmanadi*—or perhaps even the *vajra* or *chitrini* channels—for example. In that case, we have an inherent gradation in the levels of spiritual experience produced by the raising of kundalini.

There could even be additional causal-level chakras in the brain between the third eye and the crown center; the kundalini energy would still need to ascend the causal spine *after having ascended the astral spine* in order to get to and activate them. Thus, we can allow that the shamanic trance state is not the same thing as the transcendent enlightenment attained by the Buddha and Christ, etc. We can further do that *without denigrating the raising of the kundalini energy (or dissing structural techniques of meditation in general) as being allegedly inherently able to produce only astral-level experiences of subtle phenomena.* Conversely, we can make the same allowances without committing the error of assuming that everyone with an active kundalini energy is equally enlightened, which is certainly not the case.

> First, life and consciousness move upward through the physical spine and brain, freeing the yogi from the physical body [in astral *samadhi*]; then transition through the three astral spines of light *(sushumna, vajra, chitra),* freeing the yogi from the astral body [i.e., in causal *samadhi*]; and, lastly, ascension through the causal "spine" of consciousness *(Brahmanadi),* whereby the soul is liberated in Spirit [i.e., in cosmic consciousness, freed from all three bodies].
> —Paramahansa Yogananda, *God Talks with Arjuna*

Thus, we must climb the spine "three times," in order to realize the Self. Given that we get out of the physical and into the astral body on the "first" of these ascents, and that witchcraft and shamanism both have much to do with astral travelling and the like, we may perhaps relate the notion of witches flying on broomsticks to this idea. T. Lobsang Rampa actually does exactly this in terms of the flight, without accounting for the broomstick motif as being another reasonable symbol for the spine.

> Shamanism [is] associated with the idea of the tree in its various forms—the World Tree, or the Cosmic Axis—that stands at the center

of the earth and forms a ladder or pathway between earth and sky. The roots of the tree penetrate to the underworld [i.e., the physical body], its branches rise to the sky, a serpent lies at its base, and a bird perches at its crown. It is the ladder that allows the shaman to travel and conduct traffic between the two worlds [i.e., the astral—not the transcendent Self—and the physical], or realities.

—F. David Peat, *Lighting the Seventh Fire*

Significantly, but not surprisingly, the Yakut shamans of Siberia, in their mystical journeys, climbed a mountain having seven storeys, i.e., chakras.

Consider now that the name "Zeus" is derived from a root meaning "to shine"; Zeus thus means "the Bright One." Zeus was the Sky-Father god of the Grecians, frequently associated with the *sun,* and is at times shown standing on a *pillar.* (Mythologically, the cornucopia was held to be one of the horns of the goat who suckled the Sun-Father Zeus. The point at the end of such a horn is again the Point from which the entire universe proceeds; or, microcosmically, the point atop the sushumna.) Further, Zeus is said to have climbed the sky (i.e., as the sun) wearing a golden fleece; that is, to have ascended the sky in the coat of a golden ram. Commonly, this is regarded as merely a pre-rational attempt to explain the ascension of the sun in the sky—rams being rightly recognized as traditional *solar* symbols. However, consider that in Vedic, Christian and Grecian religion, wool—as with gold—was associated with purity. And wool comes from sheep, of course; rams being the *male* of that species. When such wool or fleece is carded and spun, it forms thread, out of which garments were regularly made before the advent of synthetic fibers. This specific use was presumably a prime reason why sheep in particular were domesticated. Thus, the association of sheep with garments and thread must have been obvious to even the most unlettered members of these early cultures.

Golden threads, then, would be derived from a *golden* sheep, i.e., golden fleece. (Such threads are again found at the seventh level of cosmic structure, forming the basis of all lower matter and mind.) Or, rather, such threads would derive from a golden *ram,* owing to the fact that the point at the top of the *sushumna,* at the center of the microcosmic spiritual *sun* (so that rams are *solar* symbols), is everywhere regarded as *masculine* or the seat of Shiva in the human body. Conversely, as we have seen, the base of the spine, being the site of the coiled kundalini energy, is held as feminine.

As the keepers of wool-bearing sheep, shepherds generally carried a crook or hook-shaped staff—a tradition and symbolism carried on by Catholic bishops and abbots in their crosiers. The hooked top end of that staff of course evokes the shape of the astral spine as it curves forward into the spiritual eye, between the eyebrows. Understandably, then, the staffs carried by Mayan priests were *serpent* crosiers.

Lambs, of course, are simply the innocent offspring/Sons of that same woolen, thread-bearing, solar/ram/Father species. Thus, we have the "Lamb of God, which taketh away the sins of the world," as the pure white, stainless, transcendent Christ consciousness, in which all duality dissolves and salvation from *mayic* delusion is obtained.

The Quest for the Golden Fleece, then, is the hunt for the spiritual advancement and divine wisdom of that seventh, "ketheric" level. Recall that Athena's *winged* ship passed through clashing rocks on this Quest. Odysseus, too, escaped in the guise of a ram, after grinding out the Cyclops' eye with a hot stick. The Cyclops were possessed of a single *round* eye in the center of the forehead. Indeed, the very word derives from "cyclo," meaning circle or ring—akin to Sanskrit "chakra" = "wheel"!—plus "ops," meaning "eye."

Interestingly, in the Jack and the Beanstalk tale, the Giant's wife, who protected Jack from her husband's carnivorous appetites, was cyclopean. Jack's trading of the family cow for five magic beans, which grew to become the beanstalk, may perhaps refer to the relinquishing of the body-animal, and the withdrawal into the spine of the five differentiations of life current normally expended outwardly in the five senses. The Rapunzel folk tale—wherein the fair Rapunzel, sequestered in a turret, lowers her long braided hair to enable her prince to climb up it to meet her—must likewise be a spiritual allegory, referring again to the spine.

Beans are actually regarded as fertility symbols in many of the world's mythologies. It has been suggested that this is because they resemble testicles in their shape. That reading, while somewhat Freudian, may actually well be valid, given the claimed possibility of transmuting the "sexual fluids" into life energy and raising them up the spine for the effecting of spiritual evolution. Comparably, chocolate was considered to be a holy food by many cultures, and is produced from roasted and ground beans, i.e., those of the cacao plant. Such roasting is effected by applying *fire*—cf. the kundalini fire—to the bean/seed; just as the alchemists heated base metals in the hope of purifying them into (seventh-level) gold.

> The "food" the body uses to nourish the nervous system during [spiritual] transformation comes from the sex organs—the "essence" of seminal fluid in men and what Gopi Krishna called "the erotic fluids" in women. Thus, the reproductive organs increase their activity dramatically, producing many times more copiously than usual. This, incidentally, explains why ancient statuary and paintings show men, even a pharaoh and an Egyptian god, in meditation with an erect phallus. This is not meant by the artist to be erotic at all, Gopi Krishna said, but rather is a frank and literal depiction of a biological fact about kundalini.
> —John White, *The Meeting of Science and Spirit*

Chocolate is, of course, traditionally closely associated with Easter and its fertility-symbol bunny rabbits, and with holidays (i.e., "holy days") in general. And Easter itself is "named after the Saxon springtime festival honoring the goddess Eostre, or Ostara"—www.philomuse.com. Rabbits and hares, further, living both underground and above, are generally associated not only with fertility but also with the resurrection gods and goddesses who return from the underworld in spring; among them, Inanna, Persephone and Attis.

Grapes are essentially the same testicle-like shape as are beans, being connected to the "vines" of the subtle nervous system. Their mundane "fluids" are transformed into wine, as into the "new wine" of spiritual bliss. Understandably, then, the wine god Bacchus again carried a "phallic-symbol" thyrsus staff. The pine-cone atop that staff, as we know, represents the pineal gland—"pineal" derives directly from the Latin for "pine." Aside from that metaphysical reference, however, pine resin was also involved in more practical ways in Greek viniculture, both in terms of producing particular varieties of wine itself (e.g., retsina), and for sealing its clay containers.

Just as we find significant spiritual truths embodied in the shapes of beans and grapes, we can find comparable truths in other structures also:

> [The standard Near East temple is] recognizable as a microcosm of the womb. It was divided into three parts; the Porch, representing the lower end of the vagina up to the hymen, or Veil, the Hall, or vagina itself; and

> the inner sanctum, or Holy of Holies, the uterus. The priest, dressed as
> a penis, anointed with various saps and resins as representing the divine
> semen, enters through the doors of the Porch, the "labia" of the womb,
> past the Veil or "hymen" and so into the Hall.
>
> —John Allegro, *The Sacred Mushroom and the Cross*

If one cares to look a little bit deeper than those one-dimensional readings, however, he may find that (i) the (bridal chamber) Holy of Holies represents the Self; (ii) the Hall is the *sushumna,* the entrance to which is indeed spoken of in yogic texts (cf. Woodroffe's translations) as being covered by a hymen-like membrane; (iii) saps and resins (differentiations of life force) come from *trees* (cf. the tree of the spine); (iv) semen = life force, transmuted for spiritual use; (v) the "penis" is the risen ("erect") kundalini, piercing that membrane/veil. Or, piercing the veil of *maya* in holy communion, particularly in other cases (such as Solomon's Temple) where that curtain is not at the entrance to the Hall, but rather separates the Holy of Holies chamber—its walls lined with pure *gold*—from the temple proper. When such temples are oriented North-South (with the Holy of Holies to the North), that is with obvious regard for the averred North-South polarity of the spine. When aligned East-West, that can only be for the Star of the East being the gateway to that Self. (When one stands facing North, the West is to one's *left,* and the East to one's right. For these and other reasons, "wicked witches" come from the West/South, and good ones from the East/North.)

Interestingly, bees are still called *hymenoptera*—i.e., "veil-winged"—after the hymen or veil of these temples. (Cf. the "buzzing bee" sound of the lowest chakra, so closely associated both with sexuality and with the early stages of spiritual awakening. Bees' honeycomb is made in hexagonal cells; the six-pointed Star of David—Solomon's seal—can be inscribed inside any hexagon.) This *mayic* temple veil was split in two by Jesus, the only righteous priest—in Christ consciousness—allowing Him into the Holy of Holies. The Hindus, too, have a special regard for bees, spreading honey on the bride to symbolize the consummation of her wedding night. Indeed, the couple's celebratory time together was supposed to last one moon in duration, or a "honeymoon" of about 28 days. This lunar cycle is, of course, also a woman's cycle of menstruation and reproductivity/fertility.

The almond-shaped "double-pointed oval" or "vessel of the fish" is reasonably claimed to have been a world-wide symbol of the Great Mother Goddess. (That shape is as of two cupped hands joined in prayer.) That is, it is regarded as representing the shape of the external female genitalia when viewed from the dilated "giving birth" (or magical "creation of new life") perspective. This is argued to be the origin of the "Jesus fish" symbol as well—with the "fishy" aspect referring to the smell of that region. The related primitive baptismal ceremonies often involved the recipient being drawn bodily through a large vagina-symbol, to be "born again."

There is, further, a well-established relationship between fish and pagan goddesses. The Chinese Great Mother, Kwan-yin, for example, often appeared as a fish goddess; as did the Egyptian Isis and the Hindu Kali, both of whom became fish-like after swallowing their respective consort's (Osiris/Shiva) penises.

> In Greek, the word for fish and the word for womb were the same: *delphos*. The original delphic oracle belonged to the Fish-Goddess of the Abyss. The fish goddess (vagina) would devour the father (penis) and resurrect the son (birth) in a cycle which found its way into religious systems of symbolism [e.g., in the Bible's tale of Jonah]. The fish goddess Aphrodite (Goddess of Love) was said to bring sexual prowess if you ate a lot of fish on her sacred day, Friday. The Catholic Church inherited the pagan custom of Friday fish eating and pretended it was a holy fast. Friday was *dies veneris* in Latin, "the Day of Venus" (Aphrodite) or love-making. The notion that fish are aphrodisiac food is still widespread even today.
>
> —www.minitru.org

All of that may well be true and relevant. Fish, however, are also the most obvious forms living within any body of water. And "abyss" derives from the Greek for "bottom of the sea," but also refers to the "primal Chaos before creation." On the other hand, Mary in Hebrew means both "sea" = water, and "mother" = matter. (The blue robe and white pearls of both Mary [the "Star of the Sea"] and Aphrodite Marina—who "brought forth all the fish in the oceans"—are indeed "classic symbols of the sea." They are also obviously much more than that, however, as the colors of the spiritual eye.) So we can have "water" referring either to the chaotic Void within which *mayic* manifestation swims, or to that *mayic* manifestation itself (as the sound of Om, or the "noise of many waters").

Taking it here as the former Void, fish are tangible differentiations of form or matter, swimming within the oceanic, watery, zero-average chaotic Void. (That Chaotic state itself again consists of subtle, rippling vibrations of Spirit, only appearing "empty" or void or *without structure* when viewed from within *mayic* reality.) And the manifestation of form from the Void (e.g., the Mother "swallowing" or being fertilized by the Father, becoming fish-like in the manifestation of form) effectively "devours" that formless Chaos, while simultaneously allowing it to be born as the Son. Further, baptism by raising one's "phallic" (yet feminine) Kundalini-Goddess up the "birth canal" (or inverted well) of the spine, between the "labia" of *ida* and *pingala*, frees one's consciousness to first hear and "swim within the ocean of Om," and ultimately to "slip into the witnessing Self" at the level of Chaos/Void.

Significantly, early Christians saw the double-pointed oval (formed as the intersection of two partially-overlapping circles) as a bridge between Heaven and Earth. That is, it served the same role as any *pillar* connecting the same two "places"/states, where this latter pillar symbol undeniably refers to the *sushumna*. And for all the myriad different symbols used to represent that "bridge," there is only one concrete structure in astral/causal reality to which they all refer.

Any association of the fish symbol with the Son then comes only indirectly, via his affiliation with the Mother. Vishnu—as the setting sun—and Neptune both have "fishy" associations as well, though, so even aside from its necessary inclusion in the mermaid's figure, we should not attempt to reduce the use of the fish symbolism to only the ideas discussed above. Nevertheless, to this day, the official "miter" headdress of Catholic bishops and abbots resembles a fish head with its mouth open—just as carvings of earlier Assyrian priests show them with fish-head hats on their heads, as a symbol of their worship to Dagon, the sun-fish god.

It has likewise recently been suggested that Stonehenge's inner bluestone circle may represent the labia minora, with the giant outer sarsen stone circle corresponding to the labia majora. The altar stone would then be the clitoris, and the open center the birth canal, according to researchers. One would, of course, then equally wish to read each of those structures metaphysically, as above, with the addition now of the clitoris.

The clitoris is regarded biologically as the female equivalent of the penis, in sensitivity and structure. (The seam or raphe along the underside of the penis conversely arises from the growing together, in the womb, of tissues which would otherwise form the labia minora in a female child.) Thus, we would, again after noting the androgyny there, relate that biological structure to the "phallic" kundalini.

Through all of this, then, it is not a question of a Freudian "seeing sex everywhere"—fun though that may be. Nor is it a question of reducing even primitive religions to nothing more than an uncomprehending worship of female sexuality in the Great Mother. Rather, it is just a matter of recognizing that human sexuality is simply a low form of spirituality, embodying an "As above, so below" reflection of spiritual principles and structure which is active throughout all levels of the cosmos.

How much of that wisdom was actually known to even the most advanced members of any primitive culture can, of course, be debated endlessly. Within that debate, however, if one grants any validity at all to clairvoyance/clairaudience and life-after-death, or even to the reality of deeply-penetrating intuition, the attempt to account for the existence of world-wide symbols and religious ideas only on the restricted basis of "cross-cultural assimilation" cannot be sustained. Nor can one demand that religion and spiritual understanding must inherently slowly "evolve" over generations, rather than being given relatively "all at once" to any individual or culture.

Note also that, in relating religious symbolisms to the structure of human physical sexuality, etc., contemporary mythological scholarship is already practicing a structural analysis of those symbols. That same method simply needs to be extended beyond the physical, not merely via interpretations as to "what the symbols might mean" in terms of psychological dynamics, but rather into literally-existing astral and causal geometric structures, in order to disclose a much fuller meaning. After all, any explanation of religion which does not reach beyond the physical is no "metaphysics" at all.

It need hardly be said, after all this, that myths are not simply superstitious or anthropomorphized attempts to explain natural phenomena—e.g., the sun's daily course through the sky—in supernatural terms.

Nor, for that matter, are they merely "the pattern to which growth may aspire." For, properly understood, they have little *if anything* to do, in their esoteric sense, with defining/reflecting the social roles of men and women, or with providing "role models" for boys and girls to emulate. (Notwithstanding that it cannot be denied that they do have that latter exoteric and often detrimental effect.) Rather, "what we have been viewing as quaint folklore and charming but naïve mythology are actually sophisticated accounts of the cartography of the subtler levels of reality"—Michael Talbot, *The Holographic Universe.* For example,

> to use the terminology of ancient Greece, Unconditional Love is most closely equated with Philos, or brotherly love, and is beautifully poised between Eros, which is sexual-emotional love, and Agape, which is purely spiritual love. While Agape tends to exclude the form nature, Eros tends to exclude the spiritual aspects. Unconditional Love synthesizes Agape and Eros.
>
> —W. Brugh Joy, *Joy's Way*

Consider, also, the following interpretations of Roman mythology, proposed by Joscelyn Godwin in *Mystery Religions in the Ancient World:*

> Persephone is the power of fertility which disappears underground in winter and returns with the spring. [Esoterically, however,] the stolen goddess represents the soul [i.e., psyche], alternately descending at birth for "half a year" in the "underworld" of bodily existence, and returning at death to the familiar and fruitful fields of her true home.... Dionysus' fascination by a looking-glass, followed by his temporary death, represents the fate of the human soul which, according to Platonic doctrine, looks down from its home in the heavens and sees its reflection in the deceptive surface of the material world. Allured like Narcissus by the beauty of its own image, it tries to grasp or follow the evanescent vision, and in the effort tumbles down into the miry toils of a life that is death to the soul.

Gnostic literature similarly describes a prince who "goes down into Egypt [or delusion]" to recover a lost pearl, having to remove an article of clothing at each of seven stations along the way. That is, losing awareness of the states of consciousness above the physical. Joseph likewise lost his "coat of many colors," and was thrown into a pit. And the Sumerian Innana, in travelling down to the underworld, took off some of her jewelry at each of seven gates she passed through.

If Prometheus, then, brought fire down to earth in a *hollow tube* he had touched to the *sun,* while the phrase "fiery *sushumna"* occurs more than once in the *Sat-Chakra-Nirupana,* for example, this can hardly be viewed as mere coincidence, much less should it be dismissed as merely a primitive attempt to explain the origin of fire! (Ancient Persian religious texts likewise assert that if one looks at the sun, he will see a tube hanging down from it, and that the movement of the tube from side to side—cf. *ida* and *pingala*—causes the wind—or breath—to blow.)

Equally, the symbolic significance of fires—particularly of *speaking* ones!—and of burning objects in general does not derive merely from the fact that the smoke from a household fire will rise out of the hole in the roof of a physical house, thus forming a symbol of the World Axis or the *figurative* means for the conscious transcendence of the dualistic universe. Rather, it again refers to the inner, clairvoyantly-perceptible *literal structure* of the human body. That is, there is nothing arbitrary or "made up" in these symbols, which is exactly why they are constant (even if potentially misunderstood) across diverse cultures and exoteric systems of belief.

Similarly, the fact that Taoism, Christianity, Hinduism and Buddhism all recognize the presence of a "heavenly light between the eyes" in no way proves the influence of cross-cultural exchange of religious ideas or the existence of a "collective unconscious" from which this hardly-obscure symbolism is supposedly "unknowingly" borrowed. Rather, it simply demonstrates the fact that all religions necessarily deal with the same subtle psychophysical bodily structure! In any case, there can be no doubt whatsoever that Taoism, too, has long concerned itself with the raising of the kundalini energy in opening the "Golden Flower" (or *golden* Palace) or thousand-petaled lotus chakra in the brain, through the emphasis on the circulation of life energy and on the "mid-point between the two eyes."

> Now if you have a big tree and are at a loss what to do with it, why not plant it in the domain of non-Existence, whither you might betake yourself to inaction by its side, to blissful repose beneath its shade?
> —Chuang Tzu

In the absence of an understanding of subtle bodily structure and the mythological symbolism arising from that structure, one might well take this as nothing more than an invitation to partake in an afternoon siesta beneath a shady tree! But in reality something quite beyond that is being encouraged by the rarely-comprehended and wryly-humored Taoist sage!

Now, in the death-like immobility of *samadhi,* the consciousness and life force having been withdrawn from the muscles, sense-organs and internal organs into the spine, the formerly confining house of the body is again left "dead"—inanimate, untenanted.

> As long as you do not know
> How to die and come to life again,
> You are but a sorry traveler
> On this dark earth.
>
> —Goethe

> The Kingdom of God is for none but the thoroughly dead.
> —Meister Eckhart

> I protest by our rejoicing which I have in Christ [consciousness], I die daily.
> —St. Paul, I Corinthians 15:31

> If thou wishest to have everlasting life,
> Learn thou to die in the body, before death overtakes thee.
> —Maulana Rumi

> In the square inch field [the space between the eyebrows] of the square foot house [the face], life can be regulated.
> —the Book of the Yellow Castle

> Learn to die while alive, for in the end death overtakes all.
> —Baba Farid

Thus, the withdrawal into bodily immobility in *samadhi* is not merely a trance-like temporary absorption of the ego-idea in deeply concentrated attention, to the exclusion of the "Universal Field of Existence" surrounding and permeating one's body and mind. Rather, it involves the freeing of the life force or consciousness from the body via the same internal pathway traversed at final physical death. The senses being then inactive, yet with the consciousness spread through space, the sage "sees all without looking."

In more straightforward terms, the most obvious symptoms of "death" are obviously the absence of breath and of brain activity. Thus:

> "I can tell when you start to meditate," Marci said this morning. "How's that?" "Your breathing changes, becoming very regular but very subtle, sometimes stopping."

> The video starts with me hooked up to the [EEG] machine; I am in normal waking consciousness, so you can see a lot of alpha and beta activity in both hemispheres. But you can also see a large amount of delta waves; in both hemispheres the delta indicators are at maximum, presumably because of constant or stable witnessing. I then attempt to go into a type of *nirvikalpa samadhi*—or complete mental cessation— and within four or five seconds, all of the machine's indicators go completely to zero. It looks like whoever this is, is totally brain-dead. There is no alpha, no beta, no theta—but there is still maximum delta.
> —Ken Wilber, *One Taste*

Compare also Ramana Maharshi's description of *samadhi* as "sleep in the waking state." This is no "unsolvable paradox" or product of limitations in dualistic logic or language, but refers rather to the subtle processes or underlying structure by which we enter the sleep state. It also refers to the maintaining of a "continuous witnessing consciousness" through waking, dreaming and deep sleep; *samadhi,* in this sense, is "conscious sleep." The goal of yogic techniques of life-force control, then, is to withdraw the "sap" or life energy from the nerve-branches into the trunk of the spinal Tree of Life, and raise it up the core of the trunk to pass through the five-pointed star at the top, into omnipresence.

CHAPTER X

CHAOS, LIGHT AND
MANIFESTATION

LET US AGAIN CONSIDER the idea of matter being motion picture-like, rhythmically re-created particles, which arise as relatively conserved and temporarily stable oscillations "on top of" a randomly-fluctuating cosmic Ocean surface.

"Randomness" here refers to unpredictable "order of an infinite degree," not to the absence of a cause of this behavior. In such infinite-degreed order, the motion in any one infinitesimal region of space is uncorrelated with the motion anywhere else. Further, a random state with a maximum displacement of one hundred units, say, differs from one having a maximum value of ten units or from one with a maximum of one thousand units. Likewise, a "flat" or "uniform" distribution of random numbers, for instance, differs in its content from a "bell curve" distribution, even though both may be chosen to have an average value of zero.

The simplest example of a uniform distribution is in the rolling of a single die, in which the chance of rolling a "one" is the same as the chance of getting a "six," for example. If we roll a pair of dice, however, and add them together, the repeated results of this addition will approximate a "bell curve" statistical distribution of numbers. That is, since there are, for instance, many different ways of rolling a sum of "seven," but only one way of rolling a "twelve," seven will come up much more often than twelve.

One may obtain a slightly more interesting uniform distribution than that gotten via rolling a single die, by using a computer random number generator. For both the die and the computer, each successively-generated number is (ideally) completely uncorrelated with all previously-generated numbers. If we use these numbers to represent, for example, the time-varying amplitude of a sound wave, we can mathematically examine the frequency content of this wave using a technique known as Fourier analysis. We will then find that this wave, like white light, contains equal amounts of all frequencies. Thus, a sound signal which varies in this completely uncorrelated random way is called "white noise." If we have an Ocean surface which is randomly disturbed in a similar and most chaotic way, it will still have an *average* value of zero in all regions of space. It too will then contain equal amounts of all frequencies, and so will be "white."

Further, in physics, "white noise" is different from "white *Gaussian* noise." Both of those are random, but the former begins from a uniform distribution of random numbers, while the latter originates in a Gaussian or "bell curve" one, which is "bunched up" near its mid-point or average value. That average value is zero here, but in the case of two dice would be seven. Nevertheless, even if the amplitudes of the disturbance begin to "cluster" around the quiescent zero-level—with the average value of disturbance still being zero—as they do in white Gaussian noise, so long as they remain completely uncorrelated or independent of the values of their neighbors, the frequency distribution will still be "flat" or completely "white." This is owing to the fact that any uncorrelated signal can, by definition, have no periodicity to it. Thus, no frequency component can predominate over any other, for such a predominance would introduce exactly such a periodic behavior. It then follows that all frequency components must have equal strength, regardless of the specific characteristics of the probability distribution underlying the uncorrelated signal. (The *phases* of the components will be different for differing resultant waveforms, however. In fact, if all of the frequency components of a "white" signal are in phase or have their maximum value simultaneously, one ends up with an impulse.)

This zero-average "white" randomness thus nevertheless allows for the turbulent vibration of the Ocean of Spirit to be *concentrated* in various regions, via an increase in its local amplitude there. (If we take a series of random numbers having an average value of zero, and double the value of every number, for example, the resulting series will still be random, and will still have an average value of zero.) That is, such randomness allows for inhomogeneities to be present at that basic level, even though the average value of disturbance is always zero in all regions of space (at that chaotic level).

Such a Void, then, can be both "velvet black"—i.e., of zero average displacement—and "white," i.e., having a random or chaotic motion. That "whiteness," further, can then be concentrated around various centers or *transcendent Selves*. Such a randomly-agitated chaotic state would be experienced as a zero-average "empty" Void, "free from distinguishing characteristics," on all levels below this, however. Thus, we have the equating of "Chaos" and "Void." Hence also the idea that the Void is simultaneously a Plenum, for this zero-average state underlies and suffuses the production of all matter.

This structure also accounts for the yogic statement that the Self is "of a white effulgence, which neither gives off heat nor casts a shadow," being "all-pervading and infinite" in oneness with Brahman. Yet that individualized Self is at the same time "invisible by nature, and distinguished only by the presence of one or more bodies."

Normally, if something is "white," it is not simultaneously "invisible." However, mathematics readily shows that an appropriate truly white state, having equal amounts of all frequency components, will have an average value of zero. It will thus be "invisible" to all lower states, as a "reactionless vibration."

Note further how this regard of the Self as a reactionless *vibration* implies the applicability of mathematics to its description. For vibration inherently has a mathematically-expressible component. The fact that this "white, effulgent" vibration is *reactionless* then means that it must be a qualitatively different type of vibration from that forming the matter of *mayic* reality. That is, it must be not merely a subtler or finer version of the particles of the causal region of reality—for none of those are *reactionless*—but rather a different *type* of vibration altogether.

Brennan's pictorial description of her experience of the Star-Self level of a group of people is exactly that of a network of stars, or radiating centers of light. She further states that the light of these transcendent Stars can expand infinitely, and that the experience of the Self "has a very familiar feeling of unhindered self within it." That is, it has the feeling of being the "you" that exists beyond relative time and space, prior to and through all incarnations in bodies of matter, energy and thought.

Although this level is "white" or chaotic everywhere, then, the *intensity* or magnitude of its turbulence will be greater exactly when concentrated to form transcendent Stars or individualized Selves. This is just as a light bulb on a dimmer switch can be varied from "off" or black, to its maximum intensity, giving off white light of varying intensities in all of its intermediate positions.

Being a product of the most primary manifestation of Spirit, these Selves are one with Spirit, as the wave is one with the Ocean. Matter, by contrast, although ultimately a product of the same Ocean's rippling, is at least one more step removed, existing "on top of" the chaotic state. This is just as, we may picturesquely say, the ripple feels its unity with the ocean, but the tidal wave, for being so much more gross and disruptive, does not.

Thus, we are indeed, and quite literally, "waves on the bosom of Spirit," even at the level of transcendent Self. Conversely, however, although the wave of Self may rightly say "the Ocean of Spirit has become me," it is both wrong and arrogant for anyone, even having realized the Self, to say "I am God." For Spirit or *Paramatman* is greater than the individual *Atman* or Self.

Further, since such Selves exist on the chaotic level of flux of the Star-Self, the *Atman* is an eternal and timeless individualized wave on the bosom of Supreme Spirit. It is not, however, a permanent *static* object, separate from other souls. Rather, it is a dynamic individuality continuously sustained by Spirit, and interpenetrating all other Selves. None of this, of course, is the least bit genuinely paradoxical, much less is it logically or mathematically inexpressible.

Both the quiescent, fully unmanifested and tranquil Spirit, and that same Ocean, when fluctuating with random agitations, have an average value of zero disturbance. Thus, they cannot, at that point, give rise to any non-zero-average "particles." Further, these are two fundamentally different states. The former is completely formless and transcendent of manifestation, and preserves the union of Shiva and Shakti, while the latter is the mythological chaotic state. That Shakti is still "formless," but no longer fully beyond vibration. That is, in the chaotic state the Power of Shakti has obviously already been differentiated or separated from the Consciousness of Shiva. For without that Power acting the Ocean surface absolutely could not be agitated. (Mythological "chaos" is normally regarded as "the infinity of space or formless matter supposed to have preceded the creation of the cosmos." This "formless matter" must be sensibly read as referring to a turbulently-agitated but zero-average state, however, rather than to a quiescent one. Chaos, after all, even if it contains all forms in potential, is not a *static* state.)

> The Kabbalists postulated the Ayn or No-Thing as the Zero from which, in a mysterious manner, the Universe arose. Next, they say, the Ayn Sof, or Limitless Space, became the Nature of the Ayn, and this conception was followed by that of Ayn Sof Aur or the **Limitless Light of Chaos.**
>
> It was not until this Limitless Light had concentrated Itself to a Centre [the Point] that the First Positive Idea arose, and this was called Kether and attributed to the Number One.
>
> From this One there arose in succession the other Numerical Emanations or Sephiroth from Two to Ten.
>
> —Frater Achad, *The Anatomy of the Body of God*

> Envision the universe in its original state as an expanse of Light without borders or limits, which the Source of Power gradually shapes into life-bearing worlds.... Gazing at this process, how can anyone fail to see manifest Being as one vast demonstration of love.
>
> —the Koran, v. 21:30-3

> The Inner Light is beyond praise and blame;
> Like space it knows no boundaries,
> Yet it is even here, within us, ever retaining its serenity and fullness.
>
> —Yung-chia Ta-shih

> The things of this world come from Being,
> And Being comes from Non-Being [i.e., the Ayn or No-Thing].
>
> —Lao Tzu

> When the Many have been reduced to the One, to what shall the One be reduced?
>
> —Zen koan

From that which has no origin, everything that is has taken its origin;
Yet in so having taken its origin, it remains that which has no origin.
—Buddhist hymn

Between noumenon and phenomena there is no boundary.
—Buddhist Avatamsaka Sutra

Before the Unconditioned, the Conditioned dances:
"Thou and I are one!" this trumpet [of Om] proclaims.
—Kabir

Note that the Kabbalists refer to the First Sephiroth or Point not only
as *"white* head," but also as the "I Am" level. The feeling that "I Am" or
"I exist consciously" is again a product of both consciousness and
existence. That is, existence plus consciousness of that existence yields
the intuitive feeling that "I Am." And Shankara again characterized
Spirit as Existence-Consciousness-Bliss, so that it is exactly from this
Star-Self level that the feeling that "I exist"—that is, *self-awareness*—
must arise.

The same First Sephiroth is referred to as the "Kether" or "Crown,"
with the "ketheric" bodily level being the seventh or high causal one,
corresponding to the crown chakra or thousand-petaled lotus. This is not
for any identification of self-awareness with the causal body, but simply/
presumably because, along with the presence of a literal point at the
center of one's sphere of consciousness in the crown, the white light of
the cosmic consciousness of the embodied soul or Star-Self is manifested
in the five-pointed star at the spiritual eye. In consciously penetrating
this star, we enter (at least temporarily) cosmic consciousness. This
implicitly has to do with "going out through the *crown* of the head" or
Brahmarandhra to drop the three bodies and realize the Self. (That
crown, as the causal chakra having the highest frequency of vibration, is
the "closest" to transcendence of those subtle centers.)

Evidently, then, the "Clear Light of the Void" is no mere metaphor
intended to indicate "clear spiritual realization of the Self in the absence
of superimposed concepts" or the like. Rather, as usual, it is meant to be
taken completely literally, as referring to an objectively-existing and
mathematically-describable aspect of cosmic structure. That is, as referring to the chaotic white light of the Self in cosmic consciousness. (If one

is merely considering the *symptoms* of spiritual awakening and the realization of the Witnessing state, the analogy of consciousness being "a wave of the Infinite Ocean" may be regarded as an overused and even a "boring" one. When one is considering the detailed *structure* underlying that awakening, however, it becomes *much more* than a mere analogy, even providing a basis for the understanding of what metaphysical Chaos is.) Indeed, in *Coming Home,* Lex Hixon records his own experience of having

> stepped into a realm of golden light. My body was of the same color and nature as this light. I was not floating, but fully aware of this golden [i.e., seventh-level] body, which responded just like my ordinary body.... My body blended with the light, and soon there was no body, only golden intensity. I was still aware of myself as an individual center [i.e., point] of consciousness....

After passing through a "membrane" between this state and the Ultimate One to reach the latter, i.e., the Clear Light, Hixon temporarily experienced a

> clear brightness, natural and buoyant. This brightness was so total that there was no room for an *I;* yet even in the absence of a particular *I,* awareness was fully present. This intense, consuming presence or brightness was not substance but simply clarity of awareness. The clarity appeared white, or faintly opaque, because there was nothing to be seen through this clarity that would make it appear transparent. And because there was nothing to be seen, there was no sense of distance or vastness—only a sense of completeness.

John White describes his own similar spontaneous (and temporary) experience of the transcendent Self:

> Time stopped. "I" [i.e., the ego] ceased to exist. Limitation and boundary dissolved into infinite consciousness of unity. All was light, unending light, and love the foundation of the cosmos.

Brennan again described her own experience of a network of such Star-Selves, regarding each such white-light Star as being an individualized but impersonal "you," existing beyond relative time and space, prior to and through all incarnations in bodies of matter. That description, of course, could only apply to the transcendent/non-dual Self. Bentov then gave a similarly networked visual depiction of his named "higher self" (i.e., Self), as the "Spirit within us," at the level "just below" the wholly unrippled, unmanifested Absolute, i.e., at the level of Chaos. Indeed, this idea of "multiple Selves"—i.e., one for each of us—is hardly new:

> Beyond [*Prakriti,* Nature] are the innumerable ... transcendental Selves *(Purusha),* which are pure awareness, forever witnessing the continuous motion of Nature....
>
> Yoga teaches that there is not merely a single transcendental Self *(Atman),* but countless such Selves *(Purusha).*
>
> —Georg Feuerstein, *Spirituality by the Numbers*

Given that, and the regard of yoga for the Self as being a pure white vibration, plus the "As above, so below" hope of finding a similar structure on the physical level, we are led to try to find a way to bring all of those together into a coherent view. Further, we would wish to reconcile them with the idea of the Witness being *formless*

In that regard, note that we began by considering all of creation, including the white-light aspect of the Self, to be ripples on the *surface* of the Absolute or Infinite Ocean. Thus, although we find the experience of the formless (but not structure-less) radiance of the "Clear Light of the Void/Self" at that chaotic surface level, we can also imagine sinking/ dissolving into the always-already existing, boundary-less depths of the Absolute. In those calm depths of what is literally a higher dimension of Non-Being than the surface of Becoming and Being, we will find no forms, not even white light. For there we have just a "transparency of awareness," at a deep level of witnessing Self without personal identity, at which one may truthfully say "this *Atman* is *Brahman.*" When mystical traditions or personal experiences refer to the "formless causal Witness" or to a "Void" at the highest causal level, they are referring to this transcendent deep Self *(Brahman/Paramatman).* That is, they are taking both the surface Self and deep Self as belonging to the causal level.

Of course, even the surface, chaotic nature of the Self, as the *Atman,* has a radically different structure than the rest of the causal level, being beyond *maya* or duality and its rhythmic process of creation, with all such surface Selves interpenetrating and being in constant communication with one another. That non-duality, indeed, is why we have been rightly regarding even the "Clear Light" surface facet of the Self as "transcendent" (i.e., as existing above the causal level), and will continue to do so herein. By any choice of terms, though, the structure is the same. Thus, although the truly formless deep Self, as Absolute Subject, cannot be taken as an object of perception on any level, the surface Self (which is of course not at all merely the "self," or ego) certainly can be, as Brennan's and Bentov's descriptions, along with the yogic history of multiple Selves, clearly show.

> People want to see the Self as something. They desire to see it as a blazing light, etc. But how could that be? The [deep] Self is not light, not darkness, not any observed thing. The Self is ever the Witness. It is eternal and remains the same all along.
> —Ramana Maharshi

The surface Self, however, is indeed both light and darkness, both Void and Chaos, and may be experienced as both ... or as neither ... with logic and mathematics being fully able to resolve all of those apparent paradoxes, and more.

Note further that Bentov again claimed experientially that the expansion of "spheres of information" occurred not only for human beings, but even for *atoms*. It would be very satisfying, then, if elementary particles did not merely "have" a sphere of consciousness, but were rather *formed from out of that sphere*. Those causal, astral and physical-level particles would then interact or exchange information simply via the spatial overlapping of the subjectively-feeling and objectively-vibrating spheres of consciousness/Spirit which each of them *is*. The type of sub-quantum, sub-quark, sub-superstring particle, and the level of reality to which it belonged, would then be determined by the resonant frequency of each such sphere. This is, of course, opposed to the earlier view of the interference of waves from multiple spheres of consciousness giving rise to "islands" in that Ocean, but nevertheless produces the same discontinuous, "process" nature of reality. That earlier view was given simply as a "motivating argument," for being easier to visualize from one's daily experience.

Each of those (even atomic or lower) spheres will then have its own point-contractions. We may allow, however, that it is only when an individualized Star-Self is "looking through" (i.e., is identified with or attuned to) a specific sphere of consciousness that *individualized* self-awareness will be associated with that particular sphere. (The same structure again produces the experience of the dilation of subjective time, which is a characteristic of the way in which the witnessing *subject* or Self "views" *mayic* reality.) Both Brennan and Bentov actually showed those star-like Selves as being connected/tied to their respective causal bodies via laser-like lines of light, so we do indeed have good reason to have confidence in this approach.

Now, in order for the process of manifestation to proceed beyond the Limitless Light of Chaos into duality, that One Being must polarize into a Second, forming the complementary pair of the Father and Mother of creation. From the Father and Mother are produced the Ten Thousand Things, or the multiplicity of objects in the sphere of manifestation. These then exist, motion picture-like, as relatively conserved and temporarily stable rhythmic oscillations "on top of" a randomly-fluctuating or chaotic cosmic ocean surface. Indeed, computer-generated fractal landscapes—of realistic mountains, waving oceans, etc.—are typically derived by applying appropriate filters to exactly such a random background to produce the desired forms.

Both the unruffled Infinite Ocean of Spirit and the Limitless Light of Chaos are again "unmanifested" *and transcendent* relative to the Cosmic Nature which condenses out of them. The Limitless Light of Chaos, further, is Ramakrishna's "limitless, infinite, *effulgent* Ocean of Consciousness," in which the delusory material cosmos is non-existent, or leaves "no trace whatsoever." This state existed not only at the beginning of the process of manifestation, but underlies all created forms *even at this moment,* as their Source and Ground, and can thus be realized by each one of us at the Star-Self level.

The realization of the Self via a climbing of the spine further provides an interpretation of the East Indian "rope trick" myth. There, the performer climbs a thread attached to the branch of a tree, is "sliced into [chaotic] pieces" when atop it, and is subsequently reborn intact after the pieces have been sprinkled with water. This, then, is just as the holy baptismal water of Om macrocosmically forms and re-forms the cosmos from Chaos. The "Sun which is ever sounding forth 'Om'" is thus also the Star-Self level; as usual, the idea applies in more than one way.

Now, the *Tao Te Ching* states that "the Tao [Non-Being] bore the One and the One bore the Two." There, the One corresponds to Being (as the root of Becoming) or "The Uncarved Block." The Two of T'ien and T'i then refer, not simply to Heaven and Earth, but to the Father and Mother of creation, corresponding to the Hindu Purusha and Prakriti. Equivalently, when Adam is split into Adam and Eve, this is exactly the differentiation of Chaos into Father and Mother: "And Adam called his wife's name Eve; because she was the *mother of all living*"—Genesis 3:20. (The ribs "vibrate" at the same rate as the breath—being pushed outward in inhalation, and returning inward to their rest position in exhalation. Thus, Eve being formed from Adam's rib indicates the derivation of Nature from Spirit via a cosmic "breathing" process.) The Light of Chaos, although it contains both the Father and Mother within itself in potential, is taken there as Masculine (e.g., the original Adam) simply because the Father remains as the original chaotic state, while the Mother is a further modification of that state.

Alternatively, because Eve was produced from Adam, it is often said that the latter must have been "hermaphroditic," or containing both male and female principles. That is, Adam was both the Father and the Mother, or the state of Being prior to the differentiation into Active and Passive Poles. Thus, the idea of creation being a Woman drawn from Man, and the alternative of manifest Nature being the offspring of an androgynous or hermaphroditic Masculine-Feminine figure, are equally correct, and not the least bit incompatible or contradictory. Also, consider that the Second Sephiroth Hokhmah—interpreted in some schools of Kabbalism as both the "One without a Second" (i.e., Being) and the Point—projects the Third Sephiroth Binah, who is called the Mother of the other Sephiroth and the rest of creation. Binah is thus comparable to *Maya,* worshipped as the Mother, which can be taken as equivalent to Prakriti or Nature.

If Being and Non-Being were simply two different descriptions of Spirit on the same level, with the attempt to categorize Spirit producing the paradoxical assertion that It is "both Being and Non-Being," the Kabbalists would never have associated Non-Being with the Ayn or No-Thing (Zero), and Being with the second Sephiroth. Rather, those differing assignments fully indicate that they were viewing Non-Being as a wholly different structural level than Being, not as an "opposite" to it. Even Lao Tzu affirms, after all, that "Being comes from Non-Being," while the *Tao Te Ching* again states that "the Tao [Non-Being] bore the One." Only when viewing spiritual structures through the theory of logical classes is one tempted to compress those differing levels of cosmic structure into a single level, and then call that a paradox.

The "copulation" of the "Primordial Couple"—of Positive and Negative, Male and Female, Adam and Eve—fertilizing the universal egg and giving birth to all children of matter, is repeated regularly in the world's mythologies. Thus: "Brahma began the process of creation. Dividing into man and woman, they made love. Together Brahma and Saraswati begat the whole race of mortals"—*Shiva Purana*. Similarly, many of the world's cultures have "order out of chaos" or "generation" (or regeneration, e.g., Flood) myths involving eggs. The Vedas, for example, record that "the cosmic egg, formed and incubated in the primal waters, gives birth to the first man called Prajapati," who "speaks" all things into existence. In others, the first Man is formed from out of a chaotic, amorphous "mass of meat."

Likewise, in China, wonton soup is ceremonially consumed in "regeneration" celebrations at the winter solstice. (Wonton dumplings are composed of very finely minced, indistinguishable, "chaotic" vegetables.) And one of the meanings of "huntun"—the personified Chinese name for the cosmic creative egg—is "dumpling"! "Wonton" is actually just a dialectical variation of huntun. The same idea is preserved in Christianity, in the decorating or patterning of hard-boiled eggs at Easter. That is, when the egg is boiled, the "watery, embryonic chaos" inside it is congealed into form. (In other contexts, the bright yellow yolk can be viewed as representing the sun.) We can hardly fail to note, not only the relation of all this to the golden egg-shape of our universe (according to Bentov), but also the association of eggs (fertility symbol, etc.) with the reproductive process, and so with the "womb of creation."

The mythological theme of the primal chaos time, condition or "thing" can be shown to embrace and support a whole cluster of homologous motifs—for example, the image of a watery, fluid, or embryonic state; a primordial whirlpool or abyss; the idea of the deluge; the symbolism of darkness, void, emptiness, and nothingness; the notion of [an uncarved] primal matter or "mass of flesh" ... [the] imagery of a feminine womblike condition [which, of course, has nothing to do with "cosmic sexual organs"!], the incestuous reunion of a primordial couple, or the idea of the hermaphroditic bisexuality of an animal ancestor or cosmic giant.

— N. J. Girardot, *Myth and Meaning in Early Taoism*

All of those ideas, again, are meant to be taken as referring to a cosmic *structure* which is fully independent of language, surrounding culture and sociology, and is in no way merely an "anthropomorphization" of God, or projection of human attributes onto Him.

CHAPTER XI

WHOLENESS AND
FRAGMENTATION — I

IT IS ONLY IN SPIRIT that all opposites, and time, are transcended. Nevertheless, one frequently encounters misled attempts to explain the transcendence of duality as being attained to when we simply stop naming our experiences. These attempts associate *maya* merely with human conceptualizations, where we abstract "distinct" and "separate" objects or measures from our "all-at-once" sensory experience or gestalt, relating them to previously-formed memory-classes: "a chair," "a cloud," etc. That is, "duality" or *maya* is often interpreted by Western scholars as referring only to the way in which the human "naming" or conceptualizing of sensory experiences—this being inherently based in memory—"creates" seemingly-distinct objects from the "unfragmented" sensory gestalt. In that view, all "things" are believed to be "created" by the words or concepts or names that we use to represent them, in speech and language.

Rightly understood, however, *maya*—the "measurer"—is that structural principle which extracts finite measures and forms from the formless Infinite of cosmic consciousness. It is not merely human conceptualizations of sensory experiences. Nature cannot exist without *maya,* for this measurer is not merely an "imperfection" in Nature, it is the very fabric and structure of all finite phenomena. *Maya* is the "ceaseless

183

Becoming of creation," whereby the positions of the Real and the unreal are inverted or interchanged. Thus, the Real becomes unreal, while the unreal seems real. That is, the "unreal" or transitory phenomena of Nature, formed of waves of subtle light in an Ocean of Light, appear to the person in delusion to be impenetrable, permanent matter, and to be all there is. The Real which has become all phenomena, and which alone exists, however, seems to be non-existent.

If this delusory force were removed from creation, the waves on the Ocean would all be tranquilled, and vibratory Nature would cease to exist. It, as its Biblical counterpart in the devil, is thus "from the beginning," or structurally inherent in the realm of finite vibratory creation. Eliminating the influence of *maya* from one's own being, in cosmic consciousness, does not eliminate it from the cosmos, for conceptual opposites are only one *instance* of the law of *maya* or duality, not the *basis* of it.

Thus, the problem of "the One and the Many" has not to do with the way in which we conceptualize our "unitary, one, unbroken" sensory gestalt into "many" abstract "fragmented" classes of objects. Rather, it is more properly addressed to the way in which the transcendent, chaotic Ocean appears as its many waves of manifestations. The "many" braille dots on a page are no *opposite* to the "one" paper from which they are formed. Likewise, the many waves of reality-in-itself, forming our bodies and minds and everything around us, are no "opposite" to the Ocean which has become them.

Space is filled with the structural symbols of the presence of God. These have inherent meaning, by virtue of their very shape and vibratory constitution as modifications of consciousness. That meaning then exists with or without our sensory perception and linear conceptualized interpretation in the lower mental production of meaning. ("Whatever is willed by the Source of Being comes spontaneously into Being and bears profound meaning"—the Koran, v. 24:41-5.) Compare Franklin Merrell-Wolff's description, again in *The Philosophy of Consciousness Without An Object,* of his own experience of a state in which

> in a sense, the words and that which they mean are interblended in a kind of identity. Abstract ideas cease to be artificial derivatives derived from a particularized experience, but are transformed into a sort of

universal substantiality. So "Satisfaction" and the *state* of satisfaction possess a substantial and largely inexpressible identity.

Of course, this experiential statement completely contradicts the accepted viewpoint, in which abstract ideas are indeed seen as merely and inherently artificial. Consider, however, that creation is again characterized by the yogis as God's "dream." We do not hesitate to allow that the elements in human dreams have meaning. If a pillar, for example, figures prominently in our nocturnal reveries, it might represent the *sushumna,* or a mere phallic symbol, or perhaps something else. Dreams, however, cannot only be interpreted or have meanings *attached* to them, but rather *arise from and contain* inherent meanings which the subconscious is attempting to communicate to the conscious mind. Given that, it would be highly odd if *God's* dream of creation had no meaning! that is, if the objects in it had meaning only insofar as human beings assign it to them.

> On earth, we use language that takes a long time to get ideas across. On a higher level, a symbol such as a tetrahedron is thrown at you and right away you know and understand all that it would take hours to explain.
> —Itzhak Bentov, *A Cosmic Book*

Evidently then, geometrical figures too, like colors, possess inherent meaning, even aside from that which may be arbitrarily assigned to them by human minds.

Just because the actual experience of such deeply developed intuition as Bentov described above transcends reason, does not mean that the mechanism by which intuition functions is indescribable in logical and mathematical terms. Itzhak himself, for one, proposed exactly such a logical explanation, essentially identical to the one shown herein, and consistent with his own experiences in higher states of consciousness. Those experiences are completely inexplicable within the boundaries of the wish to fully transcend duality merely by banishing all concepts, yet they exist, and are in no way merely low astral level phenomena.

Indeed, in order for intuition to supersede *but not contradict* reason, there must be a definite and traceable relation between these two faculties. For if there were no such traceable connection, contradictions would abound. That is, if mathematics and logic were creations only of the human intellect, and so were unrelated to the Way things are, contradictions between these two ways of seeing the universe—through the intellect and through intuition—would be frequent and inevitable.

One of the indications that one's intuition is developing is that when one hears truths stated about life and the cosmos, they seem familiar, as if one had heard them before. The development of intuition is also indicated by the feeling, when confronted with *wrong* interpretations of religion, that they don't "resonate." That is, those raise the feeling of something being missing, even if it may take years to develop the logical steps to prove what exactly that is. Comparably, the presence of biases in one's view of the world is equally indicated by one's railing against *correct* ideas.

Now, "fragmentation" in our thinking processes is typified by the inability to see the interrelationships in complex webs of ideas. It is held to result from "linear thinking" because the conceptualization of reality into "separate objects"—as opposed to "interconnected patterns"—appears to inherently result in such objects being considered to exist independent of their environments, as autonomous entities. And given that independent existence, such objects could be treated in whatever way we chose without that affecting the environment which surrounds them. This is believed to result eventually in problems such as the ecological crisis, for example.

The viewing of reality as "separate objects" also readily gives rise to reductionism, or the attempt to explain any relative whole as being merely the sum of its "fundamental" and independent parts. It is thus often regressively believed that any labeling or naming of our sensory experience of reality which divides it into segments that appear to occur sequentially, rather than all-at-once, reinforces linear thinking, and thus increases our level of "fragmentation." (That condemnation would include the act of reading and writing. Of course, speech is every bit as linear as is writing, although the oral transmission of ideas does indeed allow for nuances of expression and body language which cannot be conveyed in print. On the other hand, one would have no fun at all trying to develop or convey any precise scientific or mathematical ideas merely verbally.)

The existence of linearly-conceptualized "autonomous" objects is also said to lead easily to the ordering of such objects into a hierarchy of importance. In that ordering, then, the higher elements (e.g., human beings) may be seen as being "more important" than the lower. They may thus easily give in to the temptation to use, abuse or oppress the lower—in a "power-over" relationship—if the need should arise, i.e., if short-term selfish benefit would be had from this.

Further, human explanations of the logical or linear chain of causes and effects between conceptually-isolated objects are criticized as tending to ignore the interrelationships or feedback in the systems being studied. (Such feedback is created when the effect in the present cycle becomes part of the cause in the next round.) This shortcoming is not shared by mathematical models, however.

Note also that computer programs are simply a series of cause-effect logical steps, yet they are completely able to incorporate the notion of feedback. This is not simply because such programs have short time intervals in between their steps, for the iteration of equations could be done just as well without such time intervals, merely by following the series of logical steps through. (Such iteration involves feeding the "output" of the present stage back into the "input" of the equation, in a feedback loop.) This involves mathematical equations rather than "pure logic," of course. However, at a programming level, even equations are simply a series of logical steps.

The conceptualizing of reality into linear chains of cause and effect may indeed predispose us to viewing each effect as having been the product only of a single cause, rather than of a variety of "input variables," where a change in one seemingly-minor variable (e.g., the loss of one species in a food chain) might affect the whole system. Of course, the converse of this natural feedback is the ability of organisms and ecosystems to *compensate* for such a loss, without "grinding to a halt" in the manner of a machine which has lost an important working part. The very interdependence of Nature, if we think about it, implies a tremendous resiliency, which cannot be encompassed in the idea of a linear food chain.

Aside from the points we shall make later regarding linear thinking, ecological awareness and fragmentation, then, note first that in the traditional "ontological hierarchy of Being," or the manifestation of God successively as the causal, astral and physical levels of reality, the higher vibratory levels of reality pervade and sustain the lower, but also exist beyond them, and can indeed exist very well without the lower. (Need-less to say, spiritual hierarchies further differ from human ones in that no accomplished spiritual being need be "demoted" in order for each one of us to be "promoted" to a higher or highest state of consciousness.) Thus, it is not at all the alleged absence of hierarchy in Nature which results in it being "all One," and behooves us to treat even the physical level with respect, but rather the fact that, as Ramakrishna experienced, it is "all Pure Spirit."

We cannot validly "think backwards" from the traditional negative results of the view of human beings as "more important" than animals or Nature, to assert that because the *effects* were detrimental, therefore *the original idea must have been wrong and perhaps even calculated to yield those negative effects.* Indeed, the idea that one can "think backwards" in that way is actually a blatant example of linear thinking—consider how much it ignores, in reducing the effect to a single alleged cause. The same goes for the effect of hierarchies, whether human or spiritual/ontologi-cal, and for "Heavenly Father" metaphors. (Contrary to widespread belief, ontological hierarchy is not incompatible with Divine imma-nence. After all, the existence of waves of differing sizes or frequencies on the ocean in no way precludes the water of the ocean from being present in each wave, regardless of its size/frequency.)

Warnings against this tendency to "think backwards" apply doubly to any attempt to read mythology exoterically as merely a sociological indicator or provider of "role models"—such as when the myth of Narcissus is taken as merely a warning against vanity, i.e., against the danger of being too much fascinated with one's own "image in the mirror"! Sociological interpretations of myth invariably yield answers which are every bit as wrong as the fundamentalist readings. These two approaches may be poles apart from one another, but they are neverthe-less equally far from the truth.

Interestingly, the idea that the universe is a Giant Machine is a blatant anthropomorphic projection, much moreso than is any religion formed around belief in a personal God. For the Father, Mother and Son all existed well prior to the appearance of the first men and women on our planet, but *only humans build machines.* The "living process" rather than "mechanical" nature of creation, however, in no way precludes the valid application of mathematics to the description of the behaviors of the cosmos. On the contrary, the anti-rational belief that any mathematical description of matter or mind renders the universe "cold and sterile" is as wrong as is the view of it as a mere machine.

The disdain for the attempt to quantify the laws of Nature can come only from the confusion of ignorance with faith. That is, it derives from the idea that once we understand how something works, it loses its mystery and beauty, and need no longer be wondered at. The same disdain will also generally include a tacit acceptance of those laws of Nature as *a priori* existing, without asking Who put them there and sustains them; forgetting that "not a leaf turns but that God is behind it." A detailed understanding of the laws and perfect order by which seeds germinate and grow to become adult plants, to produce seeds again, for example, should never cause us to lose a sense of awe at these amazing processes, or to think that we have "got it all explained." The same obviously goes for the mathematical laws by which snowflakes are formed, or by which lightning and thunder or the Northern Lights or rainbows are generated.

Of course, the neglect of this point is present just as much among scientists as among persons who are distrustful, not merely of the *abuse* of science, but of rational thought in general, wrongly believing that it is irreconcilable with intuition—a trap into which no one who was either truly rational or genuinely intuitive could ever fall! But in any case, the order implicit in mathematical regularity is again the undeniable hallmark of a Universal Intelligence, not the reduction of Nature to a "mere machine, stripped of its aliveness and spontaneity."

The division between "living" and "non-living" systems is actually every bit as anthropomorphic and dualistic as are the mind/body split and the imagined separation between God and Nature. That is to say, as Bentov noted, we project our own attributes onto matter by saying that starting with electrons, atoms, minerals and metals there is no life. When the aggregates of molecules have reached a certain stage of complexity, however, "life" suddenly appears because we can recognize our own behavior in it. The fact is that the same Ocean of Consciousness which has become the "living organism of the earth" has become not only all minerals and metals but also *the machines made from them*. Indeed, the idea that "all living things are sacred" but that machines are in some way "separate" from God is a fine example of fragmented thinking! For it is not only "living things" that dance with the creative light of Spirit, but inanimate matter just as well.

Given all this, one cannot assert that sociological and environmental problems arise from "too much reasoning." For if unbiased reason agrees with intuition, *and especially if clear reasoning develops one's intuition,* it cannot be that the former is self-destructive, if the latter is not. Indeed, the fact that we indulge in self-destructive behaviors (demonstrated by ideas such as "I'd rather live a few years less than go without eating meat") even in full knowledge of their long-term harmful effects to *our own* bodies and minds—not only to *others*—*proves* that the mistreatment of Nature and of other human beings does not arise simply from us considering that we are of a higher grade than they, and can thus supposedly treat them however we want. Nor does it arise from feeling ourselves as separate from them, for we are harming ourselves just as much in the long term—whatever boundaries we may ascribe to "ourselves." That is to say, if we were merely causing harm *to others* in our pursuit of pleasure, one could argue that it resulted from us viewing ourselves as "higher" or more important than they. But since we are prepared to knowingly do harm even *to ourselves* in that pursuit, the willingness to cause such harm *cannot* be based simply in us viewing ourselves as more important than other creatures.

Similarly, whenever we buy commercial produce rather than the more expensive organic equivalent, we are knowingly harming not only the environment but our own health in the long run, in return for a few dollars saved. It is rare that we need this extra money to afford only the barest living accommodations, for one can, in a pinch, live quite comfortably in a bachelor apartment and eat lentils, potatoes and other inexpensive, if monotonous, foods. Indeed, yogis in the Himalayas live in caves—with the nearest fresh-water stream often being three or four miles away—while monks in Tibet subsist on tea and barley flour, and people in Ireland several centuries ago ate practically nothing but potatoes: an average of over eight pounds a day, per person, in peasant families! Gandhi likewise, while travelling across India via train in torrid, humid weather for seven months in 1921, ate nothing but modest amounts of toast, oranges, grapes and raisins, and goat's milk.

When we indulge in any restlessness-producing behavior which we simply "like," it is not from our thinking being "fragmented" or from being unable to see the long-term effects of our actions. Rather, it is again simply because we again *intentionally ignore* the eventual detrimental effects on ourselves, in favor of the short-term satisfaction of selfish desire. This obviously cannot be blamed on any of the common scape-goats.

As a final example of the pull of selfish desire, consider the indul-gence in unprotected sex, given the risk of contracting not only AIDS but also the many other relatively "minor" sexually-transmitted diseases, as well as the potential for unplanned pregnancy. Such careless indulgence again derives only from the blatant willingness to invite our own long-term suffering in return for the maximization of our own short-term pleasure. It has nothing whatsoever to do with hierarchy, fragmentation, or with "too much linear logic"!

There is even ample room here for allowing for inclusion of the wish to dissolve the habitual feeling of separation from others. That is, of love-making in general as being one possible expression, though by no means the highest, of the want for unity. Nevertheless, when we are willing to harm not only others but equally ourselves simply for maximizing our own pleasure in that already-secured intimacy, the idea that we are prepared to mistreat others only because we see them as separate from ourselves can hardly be rationally sustained.

Further, if sex were to cause us significant pain rather than pleasure, or if it were simply a bland and unexciting experience with the sole function and reward of propagating the species, we would gladly forego the intimacy associated with it. Thus, it is evident even here that the pursuit of pleasure is a much greater motivating factor in human behav-ior than is the wish to be "whole." Without wholeness being simulta-neously *pleasurable* in one way or another, we do not care for it. That is, not one of us would choose a painful wholism over a relatively pleasur-able feeling of separation from others.

Consider further that one well-known advocate of vegetarianism—a former cattle rancher, no less!—who speaks regularly on the subject, encourages his audiences to stop eating meat *simply for their own health benefit,* not for whatever effect that it may have on the environment or for concern over the ethical treatment of animals. This advice speaks of a very astute and important observation regarding human psychology. For, while it is good for us to consider all three of the above factors in our daily decisions, if we are not willing to do something for our own personal and selfish advantage, we will be most unlikely to do it for the benefit of others, particularly if that simultaneously inconveniences us or requires "too much effort."

In any case, the tenuous position that we mistreat others only because we see them as separate from ourselves—i.e., that we would never behave selfishly were we not steeped in hierarchal thinking and conceptual "fragmentation"—is simply a convenient and sanctioned way for us to blame the way that "society" has taught us to conceptualize others as separate from ourselves, for our own selfish behaviors. That is, we pretend that "if 'society' had only taught us differently, i.e., had not taught us to be so 'linear and fragmented,' we would be better people." As usual, it's "somebody else's fault," and we have done nothing, and could have done nothing differently, karmically or otherwise, to change the state we find ourselves in.

Again, none of the behaviors discussed above originate in hierarchy, fragmentation, or any drive to dominate Mother Nature. More specifically, they have nothing to do with the understandable wish to secure ourselves against the unpredictabilities of a varying food supply or extremes of weather. Rather, they arise simply from the decision (i.e., the *free choice*) to satisfy our immediate and selfish desires even to our own long-term detriment.

This dynamic, of course, is not limited to the examples above, in which it can be clearly shown to be operative as the primary motivator of human behavior. Rather, it plays a *dominating* role in nearly all of our daily lives, even if it is generally difficult to prove that this, rather than "fragmentation" or hierarchy, is the cause of the world's problems. For, as with the influence of subconscious biases on our behaviors, there are a hundred subtle instances for every blatant one.

The typical difficulty of proof here arises from the fact that in most cases our self-destructive actions are also destructive to others. And any actions in which the negative effect on others is greater than the effect on ourselves can easily be analyzed—in accord with the prevailing ideas of the "wholistic paradigm" in general—as being due simply to us feeling ourselves as separate from them and/or the environment, and thus either ignoring the effects that our actions have on them, or considering ourselves to be "more important" than they are. The fact that we regularly ignore the predictable and inevitable negative effects of our self-destructive actions on *our own* bodies, minds and states of consciousness, however, again proves that "fragmentation" from our environment cannot be the primary motivating factor in human behavior. A self-destructive person who pollutes the rivers of blood in his own human body, for example, even were he to consciously inhabit the whole earth, would simply slowly destroy that greater region—e.g., polluting the rivers in that larger body—even if it meant poisoning and destroying himself along with it in the long term.

The selfish nature of human behavior and motivations is underscored clearly by the following concrete example:

> During the Berkeley riots protesting the war in Vietnam, a team of researchers gave a representative sample of the students the Kohlberg test of moral development. The students, after all, claimed that their major objection to the war was that it was *immoral*....
>
> What the researchers found was that a small percentage of the students, something like 20%, were indeed operating from the *post*-conventional stages (or the "trans"-conventional stages). That is, their objections were based on universal principles of right and wrong, they were not based on any particular society's standards or on individual whim. Their beliefs about the war might have been right, they might have been wrong, but their moral reasoning was quite highly developed. On the other hand, the vast majority of the protesters—around 80%—were found to be *pre*conventional, which means their moral reasoning [in *all* aspects of their lives, not merely with regard to the war in question] was based on personal and rather selfish motives. They didn't want to fight, not because the war was immoral, not because they were actually concerned with the Vietnamese people, but because they didn't want anybody telling them what to do. Their motives weren't universal or even social, but purely selfish. And, as one would expect, there were almost no students at the conventional [i.e., conformist] level, the level of "my country right or wrong" (since these students would not have seen any reason to protest in the first place).
>
> —Ken Wilber, *Grace and Grit*

Other studies have shown that only around thirty percent of people ever grow psychologically to the postconventional stage of moral development. That is, grow to the point of being genuinely concerned with attempting to discern and enact universal moral principles in their own lives.

Given all this, human selfishness, the hunger for power and the exploitation of the environment cannot be blamed on any abstract Newtonian or Cartesian "mechanistic paradigm"—i.e., the reduction of Nature to an insentient Giant Machine. Nor can the application of "cold and unfeeling" mathematics to the description and control of Nature be regarded as at fault. That is to say, while war, ecological disaster, the subordination of women, slavery, racism and colonialism do indeed all involve "power-over" relationships, the idea that they can be blamed simply on hierarchal and patriarchal culture—rather than on human selfishness, pride and egocentricity in the established stages of psychological development, these leading to the *abuse* of power—is wholly incorrect. For again, so long as we are willing to kill ourselves slowly in satisfying our own short-term selfish desires, we will certainly be willing to endanger others also.

The idea that hierarchal thinking and power structures are the *cause* of human selfishness and unfairness is actually similar to the suggestion that "money is the root of all evil," in which case we would *inherently and necessarily* need to get rid of all money in order to eliminate evil from the world, after which purge we would all live "happily ever after"! Except that the *greed* which gave rise to the hoarding of money would remain, and would simply find a different means of expression.

Thus, while human views as to the value of Nature and of other human beings may indeed give us *license* to exploit them, such paradigms do not *create* the willingness to mistreat others. In the same way, *emotional* responses in general, although they may of course be shaped and even to a degree precipitated by a flawed intellectual or conceptual understanding of reality, are not *caused* simply by faulty intellectual paradigms.

The fact is that whenever we spend time, money or energy on satisfying our own desires for "unnecessary necessities," or even on unnecessarily extravagant actual *necessities,* it could always have been used instead to ease the suffering of others: how many Third World children could be fed for the cost of, say, one restaurant meal? If we do not take this into account in our daily lives, and comfortably close our eyes to the fact that every decision we make affects not only ourselves but impacts on others also—this latter point being the very essence of wholism, and its denial the core of fragmentation—it is not "society's fault" for teaching us to be "too logical."

Further, as long as we offer help to others only when it "suits us," or rationalize making them wait in distress until it is convenient for us to ease their suffering—effectively "causing" pain by failing to promptly do what we can to heal it—we have not yet understood what compassion is. Indeed, we are then in all likelihood offering help, when we do, more as an ego-project to make ourselves feel "generous," than as a spontaneous outpouring of the soul.

Now, it is interesting to note that chimpanzees are genetically closer to humans than are any other animal: more than ninety-eight percent of chimp genetic material is identical to ours. Examples of rudimentary toolmaking, planning, political coalitions, the adoption of orphans and the forming of brief monogamous relationships have indeed been observed in chimpanzee communities. And male chimps, "like neighborhood bosses, engage in much handshaking, backslapping, and hugging as they form shifting alliances." Yet, in spite of the fact that they live in close contact with Nature and do not "fragment" their experience of reality with abstract reasoning, Jane Goodall found that chimps can be "as bad as humans." Indeed, they are fully "capable of scheming, deceiving, and waging war" in which they "tore at their victims' flesh with their teeth as if they were common prey" (Peter Miller, "Jane Goodall," in *National Geographic,* December, 1995).

When we as human beings behave like animals toward one another, it is because we are using too much *jungle* logic, not too much *linear* logic! ("Human beings are really just beginning to develop the [third level] mental body and are **just beginning** to use their intellects in clear ways. For that reason we are very conscious of mental activity and consider ourselves an analytical society"—Barbara Ann Brennan, *Hands of Light.*) That is to say, such dismal behavior derives from our animalistic heritage—as do our lower emotions—and is in no way created merely by any limited intellectual paradigms.

Even animals such as chickens and horses have a "pecking order" or social hierarchy, as do wolves, bulls and birds. And that certainly cannot be blamed on them thinking "too linearly," or "fragmenting" their immediate sensory experience of reality by conceptualizing it into abstract ideas removed from experience. Nor can we accuse them of then arbitrarily setting up a "hierarchy of importance" among those "separate objects," after which the "more important" ones take precedence over the "less important." That is, we cannot assert that if chickens were not "so intellectual, and divorced from their bodies," those birds high in the pecking order would not treat the others so unfairly! Neither can we really ascribe that order to merely the human perception or *analysis* of the situation. That is, to assert, in effect, that "in reality the chickens are all interdependent and equal," whatever that might mean. We are thus forced to admit that *since such social hierarchies are present even among decidedly pre-rational animals, not only can they not be viewed as mere human creations, but they also cannot have anything to do with "linear logic" or "conceptual fragmentation."*

Interestingly, Jane Goodall notes that when adolescent female chimpanzees leave their community to join another, the males in the new community are predictably delighted, "but the females beat her up. They don't want the competition. One strategy the newcomer can use, however, is to attach herself to a high-ranking female, even if she is treated badly by that female. The others will eventually accept her." One young woman to whom this story was told remarked that it sounded "just like high school," as indeed it does. Thus, these ridiculous human behaviors, too, cannot have anything to do with abstract "linear thinking," *nor can they be blamed on human "patriarchal culture":* if either of those were relevant to the problem, pre-verbal chimpanzees would not, and could not, display the aforementioned behaviors.

In the same way, since the impulse for murder and war-making occurs not only at the human level but also in the sub-human chimpanzee mind, it cannot be argued to result merely from any psychological dynamic peculiar to humans. That is, it cannot be merely a "substitute sacrifice" of blood made in the hope of ensuring one's own lengthened life or immortality—unless we are willing to attribute the same motives to the pre-verbal chimps!

There may be little difference in response to stimuli between one protozoan and another, or one rose and another, or one ant and another. By the time we get to lab rats, however, these come in both "nervous" types who do not like being petted, and those who do enjoy it. And dogs and cats, as anyone who has had even casual contact with them knows, each have their own personalities, sometimes quite distinctly so. Indeed, it is easy to observe not only fear, happiness and depression, but obvious evidence of guilt, self-esteem and loyalty—all of which are quite abstract emotions—and even obsessive compulsive behaviors in domesticated animals. Such differentiation, of course, becomes even more regular and pronounced among the members of the human species.

As we move up the ladder of evolution and the "quality of consciousness" or variety of responses to stimuli of the species increases, so does the degree of differentiation or distinction of the members of each species from one another increase. And this naturally, unavoidably and rightly leads to both an increasing degree of specialization in the activities and talents of the members of the more highly evolved species, and to a greater degree of difference between the most proficient and least proficient members.

> One study found that in a wide variety of professions—writing, football, invention, police work, and aircraft piloting—the top 20 percent of the people produced about 50 percent of the output.
> —Steve McConnell, *Code Complete*

Further, these differences in proficiency cannot but give rise to envy and other negative emotions on the part of the less proficient, directed toward the more skillful. Even if there is no overt reward for that proficiency—e.g., if the results of the hunt or garden harvest are divided up completely equally among the tribal community—there will unquestionably be communal respect granted to the more gifted.

A cold and unfeeling Darwinian "survival of the fittest" might indeed exclude cooperation among the members of the species, as opposed to when birds allow a lame member of their flock to have its share of food, without "bullying" it. However, one does not need to appeal to any such principle in order to see that *no culture could maintain itself were it to draw no distinction between competence and incompetence in the fulfilling of its most basic food needs,* simply to avoid hurting anyone's feelings!

As anyone who has ever observed a mother cat push the runts of her litter out to die—even when these are repeatedly put back in by human hands—will agree, the idea of a survival of the fittest, though by no means the only factor governing animal and human evolution, is in no way merely a "human construct." That is not at all to say, of course, that human beings should emulate the behavior of the aforementioned mother cats! As a species, we are indeed poised halfway between the animals and the gods. The task, then, is to use our discrimination to emulate the gods in spite of our inherent animalistic tendencies, never mistakenly glorifying the latter. For it is unquestionably true that not every "return to Nature" is a step in the right direction.

With regard to the differences in proficiency between different members of a species, consider for instance the Hopi Indians, who are regularly presented as an example of a non-competitive culture:

> The classic type of Hopi education makes the economic specialist practically non-existent. Each child is thoroughly trained in all the conventional activities associated with its sex, though it is inevitable that some individuals for one reason or another stand out in the community as possessing greater skills than the average in such work as weaving, silver- or skin-working. These experts are called in when there is work to be done that requires an extra delicacy of treatment or perfection of finish. The employer usually provides the materials to be worked and feeds the expert while he is employed. When the job is finished compensation is paid in food, today occasionally in money.
> —Ernest Beaglehole, *Notes on Hopi Economic Life*

Further, at the very least the consistently less proficient members of the community will be advised to "practice more." This, indeed, would apply to those lacking great skill in weaving, to the hunters who miss the prey, to the gardeners with "brown thumbs," to the musicians whose performance in spiritual ceremonies was less than inspired, and to the shamans whose shamaning was a sham. Thus, while there may be no overt and open competition or rewards for the "top spots," the fact is that even when the less proficient members are advised to practice more by their elders or peers, *this is a covert and embarrassing acknowledgment of their failure.* And that designation of failure or *inferiority* will carry the same psychological weight among those "non-competitive" societies as it does in ours. That is, it will either actually spur the relevant individuals on to increased practice and proficiency or, more regularly, cause them to simply be envious of those more gifted than they are, without doing anything positive to bridge that gap.

Even when, as in certain primitive hunting groups, all you had to do to be a big hero was to catch more game than anyone else—*and then give it all away*—there can still be no question at the end of the day as to which people are "the heroes" and which are not, even if everyone in the group sleeps with their hunger for food equally satisfied. And what obvious environmental effect would the regular attempt to be a hero by "catching more game than anyone else" have, if applied on a large scale? Would it not obviously result in even a greater environmental destruction than we see in our own society?

Plus, if there is no proportional reward for skilled efforts—in money, or at least in prestige—the more proficient gardeners and hunters will inevitably come to resent the less proficient, and come to feel that they are "subsidizing" the latter. And, when mating time comes, unless the procedure entails an orgy where sexual partners are chosen completely at random with no lasting bond or commitment beyond that (as one indeed finds in some tribal communities), there are going to be preferences expressed by both the youths in question and their parents. That will apply whether the marriages are arranged by the parents or freely chosen by the youths, and will be related at least in some part to those varying degrees of proficiency, and the prestige which comes with marriage to the best hunter, etc. (Consider the contemporary tribal Achuar people of the Amazon, who have had, in recent generations, one of the highest murder rates on earth. Indeed, their traditional greeting translates as "Are you living?"! A 1993 poll of villagers revealed that fifty percent of their immediate male ancestors had died from shotgun blasts. In Achuar communities, warriorship accounts for up to three-fourths of a man's social status.)

All of that cannot help but give rise to "power games"—and to *the need to feel superior*—even among "non-competitive" or non-hierarchal societies. In any case, it is obvious that profound psychological factors are involved in the poor behaviors of contemporary primitive societies. After all, people who are genuinely "unencumbered by aggression, competition, or sexual repression" do not murder and rape one another.

> Some societies have hidden their angry urges behind apparently gentle, good-humored serenity. The Gebusi, living in the New Guinea rain forests, are an example. But behind their conviviality lurks a brutal paradox. The Gebusi murder each other at a rate that is among the highest ever reported—about four times the rate in the United States. Their pattern of peaceful living is punctuated by aggression which is unrestrained and frequently homicidal....
>
> Even the near-utopian Samoa, originally described by Margaret Mead as unencumbered by aggression, competition, or sexual repres-

sion, has since been found to be much more complex, and even violent. Rape is not an uncommon occurrence.

The Bushmen of the Kalahari Desert in Africa, dubbed "the harmless people" several decades ago because they were gregarious and peaceful, have recently been discovered to have a homicide rate nearly three times that in the United States.

Similar patterns of goodwill and self-effacement are combined with occasional flare-ups and even murders in Eskimo groups, in aboriginal Malaysians, and in the nomadic tribes of Tanzania.

—Valerie Hunt, *Infinite Mind*

The combination of envy, laziness and feelings of inferiority among young members of the community who are advised to "practice more" but do not, must further give rise to both a denigration of those in the community who learn quickly and excel in what they do—as "shaman's pets" rather than "teacher's pets," say. It will also produce attempts by the same failing students to feel superior on the basis of other differences between themselves and others, to compensate for that feeling of inferiority. And from this comes the need for others to "fit in" with the social norms and "not be too good" at their work in order to be accepted, i.e., to avoid the pain of rejection. Decisions affecting the village may be made communally and democratically, and the local religion may be without an "authoritative priesthood to dictate to the village people what God wants from them," but none of that skirts the unavoidable psychological realities of the situation. That is, none of it gets around the fact that gradations in proficiency must give rise to feelings of superiority and inferiority.

Consider also that whenever we acknowledge distinctions of right and wrong there are going to be differences from one person to the next as to the degree of "righteousness," and thus objective superiorities and inferiorities. This will be so even if "right" is to "flow with the Tao," and wrong is to go against that intuitive flow, as opposed to the usual ideas of right and wrong being related to rigid Commandments. And this automatically opens the door for one to envy those superior to oneself, or look down on those who are inferior, etc. The same is true of individual and societal standards of beauty, whatever they may be in particular, and even if they may vary from culture to culture.

Likewise, proponents of non-hierarchal cultures and spiritual paths necessarily feel that their ideas and theories are "better" than hierarchal ones, this leading to a hierarchy of correctness in which the non-hierarchal theories are seen as "superior" and the hierarchal ones "inferior." The naïve statement that "there is no 'best' in the truth of Oneness," for example, is obviously implicitly held to be *better* by its proponents than the alternative hierarchal orderings proposed by other viewpoints. Such categorizations of "better" and "worse," however, are in principle forbidden by such views, so that this gradation cannot be openly admitted to exist, but must rather be psychologically repressed instead. The obvious fact, however, is that if hierarchy were merely an arbitrary human construct, any attempt to regard non-hierarchal theories as being *better* than hierarchal ones would be inherently self-contradictory.

The skewed implicit hierarchy of correctness among "non-hierarchal" theories further produces the tacit demand that one endorse the non-hierarchal ideas if one is to "fit in" with that element of society. It conversely gives rise to the penalty of being viewed as "part of the problem" if one does not fall in line in that way. That is, predictably, the psychology and lack of tolerance for the questioning of authority (even if that authority is "non-hierarchal and democratic," here) is the same for both sides, only the criteria for acceptance is different. This dynamic is unavoidable in a world in which the vast majority of the population never grows psychologically beyond the conformist stage.

Further, in such a predominantly conformist world as ours, all that one needs in order to be discriminated against or picked on is to be *different*. Whether that difference is based on gender, race, religion, intelligence, appearance, social adeptness or any of a hundred other attributes is secondary, and does not alter the root psychological cause of the intolerance.

Differences exist—both in terms of advantages for evolutionary survival and in higher or spiritual development—and it is not wrong or detrimental for us to be aware of them, or even to categorize specific attributes as superior or inferior. For just as we can have differing amounts of money in the bank without feeling superior to those with less or inferior to those with more, it is quite all right for one person to be recognized as more athletic, artistic, beautiful, intelligent or wise than another, and even for the person in question to be *aware* of those objective superiorities. After all, there is a huge difference between being "humble in the face of Truth," and being unduly humble in the face of other people's ignorance! The fact that one's lacking of the latter attribute is often viewed as arrogance, disrespect or "ego," shows only how skewed our ideas regarding humility are.

> I cannot picture to myself a time when no man shall be richer than another. But I do picture to myself a time when the rich will spurn to enrich themselves at the expense of the poor and the poor will cease to envy the rich. Even in a most perfect world, we shall fail to avoid inequalities, but we can and must avoid strife and bitterness.
> —Mahatma Gandhi

In a world in which there were no differences, there would certainly be no hierarchies or categorizations of superior and inferior—nor would we be able to learn from one another. But the answer to the problem of power abuse in hierarchal relationships, for example, is certainly not to deny that differences exist. This is just as the fix to a discrimination against short people, for instance, would never be to assert that "in reality, height does not exist; it is only by 'fragmenting' our sensory gestalt into arbitrary measures that we perceive it as existing; therefore, the way to stop discrimination on the basis of height is by not fragmenting our view of reality into distinctions of tallness and shortness."

Note how that sort of argument parallels and is generally advanced along with the wrong idea that it is the "distinction-making intellect" that causes desires and attachment. Thus, the way to nonattachment would allegedly be to stop "fragmenting" reality into liked objects and disliked ones. In short, the idea is that we should stop *thinking,* not merely in meditation but in our daily lives! In reality, however, it is our *emotional* reactions to the likes and dislikes elaborated from our conceptualizations which are the real motivators of our behavior.

To merely intellectually distinguish between pleasurable sensations and painful ones not only does not produce attachment, but is essential to one's survival—we would not last very long if we did not heed the warning of physical pain, for example. Ideally, one would simply impartially witness such sensations, and take reasonable steps to avoid situations which produce inharmonious feelings. When we form likes and dislikes from those, however, and then react emotionally to the liked and disliked sensations and objects in question, that does indeed result in attachment and aversion.

Now, any literal sphere—of consciousness or otherwise—can be completely described by specifying its radius and the location of the point at its center. And the expansion of any such sphere then obviously corresponds simply to an increase in its radius. This mathematical description cannot be dismissed as "mechanistic," however, for although this is indeed the *mechanism* or *lawful basis* (or structure, or process) underlying intuition, it is no reductionistic *machine* composed of gears and pulleys, or even of physical atoms and molecules.

> The essential point of mechanism [i.e., of the mechanistic world view, not of physical or higher laws in general] is to have a set of fundamental elements that are *external to each other* and externally related.
> —David Bohm

Mathematically-describable structures, forces, laws and mechanisms are not at all synonymous with "machines," although these are all unfortunately regularly lumped and regressively dismissed together, as products/sources of "fragmentation."

It is not the admirable attempt to understand the laws of the cosmos that "de-sacralizes" Nature, but rather a lack of wonder in the face of the cosmic regularities and a failure to ask Who created and sustains them. Similarly, it is again not merely the "Gaia hypothesis"—the idea that the earth is a living society/organism, not a machine, of which we are a part—but rather the immanence of the Divine in all matter that behooves us to treat Nature with respect.

> Plotinus the Platonist proves by means of the blossoms and leaves that from the Supreme God, whose beauty is invisible and ineffable, Providence reaches down to the things of earth here below. He points out that these frail and mortal objects could not be endowed with a beauty so immaculate and so exquisitely wrought, did they not issue from the Divinity which endlessly pervades with its invisible and unchanging beauty all things.
> —St. Augustine, *The City of God*

Significantly, Itzhak Bentov made his living as a biomedical engineer, inventing tools for medical usage. (Bentov's degree of spiritual attainment was as high as it is rare, yet he never hesitated to attempt to formulate in quantitative terms the laws underlying that evolution and realization of the Self.) Barbara Ann Brennan, likewise—whom Elizabeth Kübler-Ross characterized as "probably one of the most gifted spiritual (not psychic) healers in the Western hemisphere"—earned a degree in Atmospheric Physics, and worked for a time for NASA. Rosalyn Bruyere was similarly trained as an engineer. Yogananda, too, not only fully supported and worked toward the reconciliation of science and religion, but took great delight in the technological innovations of his day, such as the garbage disposal.

Bentov and Brennan have together given by far the most detailed and veracious experiential expositions of macro- and microcosmic structure to be found in print today. Both of them explicitly compared their profound and precise experiences of macrocosmic and microcosmic structure with the testimony of others who had independently and repeatedly experienced the same structures, and found that their experiences meshed, not only in general terms, but down to many unexpected details.

The attempt to "return to the Ground of our Being" thus neither requires nor benefits from anti-technological or anti-rational sentiments, nor has it anything to do with simply "getting back to Nature." The Ground of Being is the Absolute, not the dust of the earth; and, although we are indeed all formed of that Ground, as ripples of Becoming, we do not in any way "reach" or gain conscious realization of that omnipresent state simply through having our sensory experiences be "unfragmented" by conceptualization or language.

Consider further, for a moment, how dependent we are on the inventive insights and collective labors of our ancestors in our daily lives. Even for us just to produce pencil and paper from scratch would take lifetimes. That is, to mine and refine the metals (lacking even pickaxes) to make the appropriate tools to harvest and process the wood, etc. Left "alone in the forest," without the technological fruits of human ingenuity, we would very soon be reduced to cavemen! using stones for tools, foraging for nuts and berries, and hoping to not be devoured during the night by some larger animal! The viewing of reason and technology—i.e., of machines in general—with suspicion is as far from truth as is the regard of Nature as nothing more than exploitable "raw materials."

> The spinning wheel is a machine; a little toothpick is a machine. What I object to is the craze for machinery, not machinery as such.
> —Mahatma Gandhi

Of course, criticisms of technological progress in general, in order to be self-consistent, should ideally be disseminated only orally—or at most by quill and parchment—never via books written under electric lights on computers whose internal workings are based in binary "Aristotelian logic"! This is especially true since the denigration of logic is frequently accompanied by an allergy to hierarchy. For, as computers become increasingly complex and powerful, the languages in which they are programmed are becoming more and more "object-oriented" or *modular and hierarchal.* Such hierarchy then allows for complex programming objects and data to be interacted with on a high programming level, without one's having to be concerned with "every little detail" of the structure inside them

In any case, there is probably no more succinct demonstration of the fact that technology and the power gained through knowledge of Nature's laws are only *benign* tools, to be used wisely or foolishly—just as a sharp knife can be used either as a scalpel or as a weapon—than that the instruments used to write, print and distribute books on spirituality and ecology, on recycled paper, are identical with those utilized in the production of military documents.

CHAPTER XII

WHOLENESS AND FRAGMENTATION — II

THE ABSOLUTE HAS LONG BEEN REGARDED as both the highest level of reality and the Source and Ground of all lower states. And the omnipresent nature of impulse-driven consciousness having an infinite resonant frequency further discloses that this correct but seemingly paradoxical characterization is not a real paradox. For these two characteristics are not mutually exclusive, but are rather merely two different ways of describing the single state of continuous omnipresence. That is, in order for something to be the Source and Ground of all matter and consciousness, it must be continuously present in all such vibratory manifestations. And the realization of this continuous omnipresence comes only via the "sphere of circumference nowhere," in the highest state of consciousness. Indeed, the easiest way to fulfill the requirement that the highest state of consciousness must also be the Ground of all lower states of consciousness is via a sphere of consciousness which literally expands into space as its level or resonant frequency is raised, becoming omnipresent when its filtering resonant frequency limitations are released into infinity.

We have already encountered the common belief that mathematics and logic are inherently dualistic creations only of the human mind, based only in abstractions from sensory data. Those sciences are thus believed to intrinsically have no necessary relation to reality-in-itself. They then allegedly cannot be "pushed too far," without exceeding their region of approximate validity. We have also seen, however, that this view is irreconcilable with the fact that sagely intuitive perceptions of supraintellectual cosmic structure are logically and mathematically self-consistent in their mechanism and content. Logic and mathematics, then, absolutely *should* be pushed to their farthest limits, even to infinity, in the attempt to (intellectually) understand the universe in these abstract terms.

The "law of the excluded middle" claims that there is no possible logical "middle" alternative to the duality of determinism and indeterminism, for example. This then produces the assertion that, to logic, everything is either black or white, never intermediate shades of gray. We know by now, however, that logic, via mathematics, can bend very naturally to circumvent this exclusion. Indeed, it can even be pressed to be amenable to the possibility of one's being only *partially* beyond duality. All of the necessary characteristics for the existence of free choice are thus completely logical, in addition to being in accord with the structure averred by the mystics, regarding the relation between the manifest and unmanifest states.

In any case, in this digital age, everyone should be aware that there is nothing inherently "black or white" to even binary logic. After all, any desired shade of gray can be achieved through an appropriate combination of microscopic black and white dots; and any color through miniscule stipplings of yellow, magenta and cyan (blue). Likewise, any intermediate position of compromise between the binary "yes" and "no" can be produced through the proper combination of more-detailed yes's and no's. In a similar way, even the most subtle and stirring music of compact disc digital audio consists, in its electronic form, of binary, uncompromising ones and zeros. The association of linear, Aristotelian-logic thinking with only "yes" or "no" answers, and an alleged consequent inherent inability to see shades of compromise between these binary poles, then, is fully untenable.

Reason is again transcended, not violated, in intuitive spiritual perceptions. There can be no justification for viewing it with suspicion, on the basis of the seeming "inherent limitations" of its binary nature. Sloppy thinking, short attention spans, disorganization and the fear of logic, after all, are *not* the same thing as intuition and its associated genuine non-linear thinking!

Neither should we then shrink from treating religion/mysticism quantitatively, for talking precisely about it—even in the most accurate language of mathematics—in no way subjects it to any detrimental "fragmentation"! Nor is the *mayic* "world of change" the *opposite* of transcendental Reality—it is rather simply a finite rippled region of that Infinite Ocean. Thus, it is not the *intellect* that causes us to regard the "world of change" as separate from transcendental Reality, but rather a lack of understanding/experience of the *structure* involved. Without knowledge of that structure, the "changing" and "changeless" aspects of reality do indeed *sound* like logically irreconcilable opposites, but they are not. For there, the waves change constantly, but it is always the same water.

In the same way, as with formlessness versus form, wholeness is not the opposite of fragmentation, but is rather the substratum from which any apparent fragmentation is drawn. Similarly, linear thinking is not the opposite of patterned-whole or metaphorical thinking—which itself is not in any way the same thing as intuition—but is simply the stringing-out of that whole into sequence. Likewise, the opposite of infinity is not *zero,* but rather *minus* infinity. This, indeed, is the very nature of "pairs of opposites," i.e., where $x + (-x) = 0$. After all, even in the duality of "increasing" and "decreasing," the latter does not stop at zero, but enters the realm of negative numbers, the *opposites* of positive numbers. Zero is thus, metaphysically, both a void and a plenum containing all possible numbers and their opposites.

Opposites annihilate one another to yield, not a vacuum of "nothing," but the unmanifested Void from which they came. This is just as when the crest of one wave and the trough of another meet, they cancel each other out. That then produces, not an empty vacuum, but rather a temporarily quiescent region in the ocean, which *appears,* for its absence of vibration, to be "empty."

"Every sheet of paper has two, opposite sides" ... but which side is which, in a Möbius strip? Between any two points on a number line there are an infinite number of other points. Yet that transfinite set is larger than the also-infinite set of "the number of numbers that can be counted." That is, some infinities are larger than others. And as to the nature of time, in attempting to account for the character of a big-bang universe some physicists have proposed that time, like the circumference of a circle, has neither beginning nor end, but is still finite in extent. That idea itself, regarding the nature of time, need not be valid in order for us to take from it the useful knowledge that mathematics can grant insight into the expandable limits of logic, which general semantics and the ready recourse to the "dualistic nature of all concepts" absolutely cannot. Even an idea as "self-evident" as that "a beginning in time implies an end" fails when confronted with the fact that an ever-expanding big-bang universe would not comply with that assertion.

The completely logical and mathematically-describable nature of the sagely intuitive perceptions of aspects of the cosmic structure well beyond that of the human intellect could cause us to question in more detail the possible relation of mathematics and logic to reality-in-itself. That is to say, although the idea of an apple would seem clearly to not *itself* be a miniature apple inside the head of the person conceiving it, this in no way precludes our concepts from having a mathematical relation to the structure of reality-in-itself. That is, it does not bar our concepts from having a relation to the underlying structure of the patterns of waves on the surface of the Ocean of Reality, constituting objective manifestation. By comparison, although the DNA in our cells is not itself a miniature human being, this does not mean that it has no relation to the "finished product." For it is, indeed, simply an efficiently condensed "seed" form of the body, each cell containing all the information necessary to create an entire organism.

Of course, clairvoyant perceptions of potatoes and spoons, etc., circling in the auras around the heads of persons thinking about them, would in any case call for a re-evaluation of the idea that "the idea of an apple is not itself a miniature apple." For clearly in some significant ways it is.

We find, further, that in terms of abstract ideas, one plus one equals two. Also, one apple plus one apple always equals two apples, even if these continuously re-created macroscopic spatial inhomogeneities interpenetrate at their basis in rippling consciousness. Such interpenetration is commonly presented as evidence of the inherent inability of boundary-drawing human concepts to describe reality-in-itself. For reality-in-itself is, according to the intuitive perceptions of the sages, an interpenetrating whole—with matter consisting of modifications or waves in the Universal Field of Existence, rather than of permanent, impenetrable particles "separated" by intervening space. Thus, conceptualizations which chop it into apparently autonomous and continuously-existing "apples" and "oranges" supposedly cannot accurately represent it.

The former interpenetration, however, is again no transcendence of the applicability of the concepts of mathematics, but rather points to a deeper level of mathematical law. This is so in Bohm's view, too, where mathematics is applied to physics, not as paint is applied to wood, but where mathematics and physics are rather viewed as having a common basis and natural interrelationship. "Patterns of movement," after all, are as mathematically expressible as are autonomous "things."

Anyone who holds to the idea, then, that mathematics is an invention only of the human mind, is obliged to explain how the most basic mechanism of creation, *experienceable at its basis only through intuition,* can form the basis of all activities of the cosmos, including those of little human intellects, and yet be fully consistent with the laws of mathematics valid in those intellects. Indeed, such intuitive perceptions are in accord in their mechanism and content with a mathematics and logic supposedly based on, and applicable to, only macroscopic "continuously existing" conceptualized "apples." That is, the mechanism of intuition, which transcends reason, can be described mathematically, and *intuitive perceptions are found to be mathematically self-consistent.* How then can mathematics be limited only to the sphere of human reason?

Consider further that the laws of probability by which gambling houses make their profits are every bit as much abstractions as are the same distributions applied to the subatomic realm in quantum physics. For, no one has ever sensorially observed a "probability," whether macroscopic or microscopic. And yet the mathematical laws apply without fail in both regions, notwithstanding the fact that any temporary failure of mathematics to account for a given range of phenomena will inevitably be touted, until the problem is solved, as arising from mathematics being "pushed too far beyond its macroscopic region of approximate validity." The same purely conceptual nature is true of the rules of manipulation of "imaginary numbers"—i.e., numbers containing the square roots of negative quantities—and multi-dimensional geometry.

It is true, then, that physics does not discover "laws of Nature." Rather, all experience gained through the senses and intellect is only "maps" of the territory of reality-in-itself; the territory and its laws can be experienced only through non-sensory intuition. The important point here, however, is that the laws of logic and mathematics valid in the sphere of human mental activity, by which the self-consistent maps of physics, for example, are constructed, are accurate reflections of higher cosmic archetypes, by which the undulation of the territory is governed.

God's book of Nature is written in the alphabet of mathematics.

—Galileo

God is a mathematician.

—Leibniz

Mathematics is the archetype of the beauty of the world.

—Kepler

Interestingly, Wolfgang Pauli showed that Kepler made use of occult images or archetypes as the basis for his thinking in formulating his laws of planetary motion.

In considering the applicability of mathematics to mental and spiritual levels of the cosmos, note that Valerie Hunt has done groundbreaking work relating clairvoyantly-perceived colors in the aura to particular frequencies simultaneously measured in the electromagnetic field surrounding the body—this being the one component of the aura which we can, at present, measure. That is, envy, sadness and other emotions will again show in the aura as specific clairvoyantly-visible colors which have, as Hunt's studies confirm, particular physically-measurable vibratory characteristics. (Hunt's work is detailed in *Infinite Mind,* as well as in Bruyere's *Wheels of Light.* Robert O. Becker's *The Body Electric* and *Cross Currents: The Promise of Electromedicine, the Perils of Electropollution* likewise provide unequalled contemporary scientific mappings, in the tradition of Harold S. Burr, of the physically measurable electromagnetic characteristics of the human body, and of the potential for the long-overdue use of this structure in future non-invasive medicine.)

Our thoughts and emotional energies are thus not only sensible to persons with developed clairvoyant faculties, but even in a sense mea-

surable by insentient machines, for having signature patterns of vibration. That is, no more of a "phenomenological hermeneutic" interpretation is needed to recognize that a particular shade of green in the aura
corresponds to "envy," for example, than would be required in collecting
and analyzing the data in a physics laboratory.

Further, since there is a transfer of emotional energies among
persons in close proximity to one another, a person sufficiently sensitive
to that would not even need to *interpret* the "meaning" of that color in
another's aura, but would rather be able to *feel* it empathically in his or
her own consciousness. In fact, we *all* do this to varying degrees. Indeed,
this occurs, for example, whenever we do not merely interpret other
people's facial expressions and actions to guess that they are angry, etc.,
but rather feel their auras and emotional energies directly, without the
intermediary of mental interpretation.

Given that entities such as pride and envy are internal mental
productions which thus cannot be empirically measured, it would seem
to be evident nonsense to ask, for example, "How much does envy
weigh?" However, even there, Brennan has noted that "blobs" of stagnant energy in the aura sometimes behave as if they have weight. That is,
the person will hold his or her body in such a way as to compensate for
the force *and inertia* of the subtle energy blobs. Given this, it is obvious
that the subtle vibrations of thoughts and emotions do exhibit a "weight"
whose effect is visible on the physical level, even though they would not
seem to be directly measurable in laboratory scales, or to be explicable
in terms of biochemistry or the laws of physics. Rather, these latter two
would be "special cases" of a more comprehensive, but nevertheless
equally mathematically-rigorous set of laws, governing not only physical phenomena but astral and causal ones as well.

It is sometimes said that human beings a thousand or a million years
ago never had the thought "I need to go to the corner store for groceries,"
for example. This is then presented as an indication as to how much one's
thoughts are tied to one's cultural surroundings. However, the thought "I
need to go into the bush to gather nuts and berries," which must have
been formed by our distant ancestors, is more or less structurally
identical to the contemporary idea of going to a corner store for food.

It is likewise sometimes claimed that contemporary EEG measurements of human brain waves can only tell us about the general state of

consciousness that a person is in, but not disclose the content of that state. This, however, does not mean that there are not subtler and even physically-measurable vibrations in the aura corresponding to specific forms and contents of those states of awareness. For, in all likelihood, there are indeed such measurable frequency patterns, perhaps even to the point of measurable dissonances when thoughts or words are spoken that one's higher self, or even one's subconscious, knows intuitively to be untrue. Indeed, in many ways it would be surprising if that *weren't* the case. Further, as far as EEGs go:

> Brain researchers have found that the overall pattern of the brain's electromagnetic field correlates with what the subject is thinking. In experiments performed by Robert Chapman and coworkers at the University of Rochester, subjects were shown words grouped into six categories—such as good words like "beautiful" and bad words like "crime." Each connotation gave rise to a distinctive pattern in time ... that a computer could use to guess what category of words the subject had seen.
>
> —Eric Lerner, *The Big Bang Never Happened*

The generally reductionistic quantification of reality sometimes leads to the objection that "seven is *bigger* than three, but it is not *better* than three." That is, it leads to the concern that the reduction of reality to numbers may seem to exclude assigning moral *values* to it. Here too, however, even if "seven is not morally better than three," a sphere of consciousness expanded to a radius of seven units is assuredly "morally better," and more intuitive and wholistic, than is one expanded to three units. The fact that neither of these spheres can be measured physically in no way detracts from the fact that any sphere assuredly has a definite and quantifiable radius and location.

Bentov has further suggested that when we feel an instant attraction to someone, the frequencies in our auric fields must have been beating together in harmony. Further, when instant aversions were felt, dissonances must have been produced. Indeed, the fact that thoughts and emotions are simply more subtle vibrations of the Ocean of Light than is physical matter necessitates not only that they have a rational order to them, but that there must be a mathematically-describable component to that order. That is true whether or not we can at present measure the electromagnetic components of these, or even if their higher components are likely in principle not measurable via physical instrumentation.

Any law of Nature, or apparent cause-effect influence in the universe (maintained only by the will of God, all things being kept in store by the word of Om) can be observed only over the passage of time. That is to say, any effect of the "law of gravity," or of any other force, acting between two particles, for example, is shown (i.e., made visible or evident or observable) only by the differences in the relative positions of these two particles as time passes. At any single point in time, there are no "forces" acting between particles, only the co-dependent origination of all things in the Mind of God, as the Drummer skillfully beats the Drum.

In a similar way, in computer-generated animation, the trajectory of a baseball moving across a video display terminal or a motion picture screen may appear to be inexorably governed by a gravitational force inverse to the square. In actuality, however, each successive frame of the picture bears lawful relation to previous frames only through the continuous coordinating influence of the immanent Cosmic Director, Editor and Projectionist.

The baseball here, further, is again no continuously-existing material object in motion, composed of impenetrable subatomic particles "separated" by intervening space. Rather, it consists of a series of "snapshots" or rhythmic re-creations of the light-formed "object" shown in quick succession, giving the illusion of governed motion and of continuity of existence. The character and motion of all matter as waves in the Ocean of Consciousness, and the regularity of all laws of Nature in the cosmic motion picture, are based on similar principles.

It would be wrong to assert that "since we never find a single water wave in Nature, but always only large regions of waving water, languages which lack a word for the singular 'wave' are closer to reality than is ours." Indeed, given the inherently modular and hierarchal nature of reality, plus the fact that higher states of consciousness are literally *spatially expanded* states of consciousness, and that highly abstract and synthesizing thought is a characteristic of the causal body, exactly the opposite is true. That is, languages having a low level of abstraction may indeed be closer to our *sensory* experience of the *physical* level of reality, but they are *not* closer to the *intuitive* experience of reality-in-itself.

Further, as anyone familiar with Fourier analysis and synthesis knows, any possible waveform can be created from a signal containing all possible frequencies, simply by placing appropriate filtering limitations on that signal. We can, indeed, use precisely that method to create a single, isolated wave in an otherwise calm body of water. In any case, tidal waves are very nearly exactly such single waves in otherwise relatively calm oceans; and seaside cultures most certainly have words for those, e.g., *tsunami!*

The abstract models we develop, in human minds, of the workings of reality, are not more real than reality itself, it is true. They are, however, more real than our nerve-electricity-conveyed *sensory experiences* of the physical level of reality—which have no *necessary* relation to reality-in-itself—in that they reflect the abstract principles upon which this, and all, levels of reality are structured. Again, if this were not so, how could intuitive perceptions be *mathematically self-consistent* in their mechanism and content?

We cannot tacitly substitute "reality" for "sensory experience of the physical level of reality" in our discussions, without fundamentally changing the meaning conveyed. Indeed, whenever we appeal to higher principles of morality and conscience, for example, we are petitioning something notably abstract. For morality is certainly not physically sensible; but is it then "less real" than are physical sensations, which the animals have just as well? an invention only of the human mind? If all that were "real" were our bodily sensory experiences of the physical level of reality, what a dreary world this would be! What point to existence, then?

The right answers to the fundamental questions of existence are simple, elegant and precise—there is no room for "fudging" on them; they are very "black and white"—and are no less than what the sages, speaking in metaphors, have long attempted to convey. They do not require, nor is their understanding aided by, a scholarly background in the subject. Philosophy made simple! as it should be. There is nothing new, of course, to the suggestion that the sages have spoken in metaphors. What is not widely appreciated, however, is that these metaphors are often in no way arbitrary or merely human-created, but rather contain profound "As above, so below" hints as to the nature of the micro/macrocosmic structure of creation. Further, it is not just that we must include God, the existence and nature of good and evil, and freedom of choice in our discussions of the nature of the universe, but much more that *when we have properly answered on any one of these basic points, we have solved the others also.*

Although enlightenment may occur spontaneously, never is this a product simply of having "let one's conceptual guard down," i.e., of being merely freed from habitual patterns of conceptualization. Conversely, meditation is not merely a "practice in non-conceptualization," this skill to then allegedly be applied to one's sensory experiences in daily life. Nor are "content" meditations or astral-level visualizations, etc., done merely so that our minds may get "bored" with even subtle phenomena! and thus that we may more easily "slip into" the witnessing Self. Rather, they are used to *attune oneself* to (i.e., to resonate with) the subtle and causal *structural* aspects of the cosmos and the microcosmos that constitute (and thus can be used to literally *expand)* one's mind and consciousness. It is true, of course, that it is only via the existence of the archetypal Self witnessing all of one's states of consciousness that self-awareness exists, and that the Goal consists in realizing oneself as the witnessing Self, not merely in experiencing various higher states of consciousness. However, this in no way negates the existence of a structure leading from normal awareness to Self-realization via such expanded states.

Again, although the experience of cosmic structure is only one of many ways in which the cosmos may reveal itself to the interested devotee, the emphasis on structure and mathematics is advantageous in that it leaves less open to interpretation. It thus entails less potential for misunderstanding and distortion than do less precise descriptions of reality—in terms of poetry, for example. Even there, however, note the wonderful precision in the poetry of Kabir, when this is properly understood.

Conversely, the disadvantage of emphases from which structure is absent is that they can readily degenerate, under the force of the accepted theory as to the "dualistic nature of all concepts," into the idea that it is only our habitual patterns of conceptualization that keep us from slipping from our normal awareness into union with the Self beyond duality. Indeed, it has long been believed that even inharmonious feelings and the like, so long as they were experienced "in their pristine, edenic nature" without categorizing them as "bad," would transcend time and duality.

The same would allegedly be true then for emotions experienced "as they are," i.e., before being labeled as "anger," etc. All of that, however, is simply confusing the absence of the psychological "sensation" of objective moral imperatives with the actual transcendence of good and evil.

A comparable problem with "devotional" paths is that they tend to elevate any minor experience of peace, bliss or light to the status of being an express and direct manifestation of God to the devotee. Those phenomena, however, rather arise much more often simply from the contact between waking consciousness and one's own astral or causal bodies. While playing this "psychological trick" on oneself may have some spiritual benefit—i.e., in terms of the practice of viewing everything in one's life as coming from God, as it indeed *ultimately* does—there is nevertheless a profound sense in which such a position plays false with the universe.

The misapplied emphasis on the "dualistic nature of all concepts" further fosters the idea that higher states of consciousness, being only witnessed by the Self, have no relation to realization of the Self. However, self-awareness—gained via the witnessing of the internal objects of one's mental milieu by the transcendent, archetypal Self—is not the only attribute common to all states of consciousness. For the proportional dilation of subjective time is, according to Bentov and to the reflections of the behavior of consciousness in special relativity, equally universal. Indeed, both of those sources indicate that a person's level of consciousness may be described by his-her ratio of subjective to objective time.

Again, our spheres of consciousness or subtle light are assuredly not composed of physical photons. Nor is consciousness bound by the macroscopic physical limitation of not being allowed to exceed the velocity of light in its expansion. Nevertheless, the same patterns or archetypal structures as are found in the elementary attributes of consciousness are reflected in the behavior of physical-level matter. This is so particularly in terms of the dilation of subjective time and the increase in "mass" in literally-expanded states of consciousness being embodied in the equations of special relativity.

The dilation of subjective time must then undeniably be inexorably associated with our self-awareness. For in this dilation we simply feel as though that subjective aspect of ourselves which *witnesses* our internal milieu has a greater amount of time, relative to the passage of objective time, to so witness. Indeed, what else does it mean for this time to be *subjective?* where we are not witnessing a greater number of mental objects per unit time, or even necessarily perceiving "subtler phenomena" in spite of that literal expansion of consciousness, but rather have an increased amount of personal time to witness the ones present.

Thus, it is, so to speak, our *self-awareness* that dilates in higher states of consciousness. The attainment of such higher states, then, does not merely present a subtler range of objects—of visions or of the experience of higher levels of reality—to an unchanged witnessing subject. Rather, it effects a necessary metamorphosis in that very subject. That is, the raising of consciousness affects the way in which the Self is able to view the objects via the increase in subjective time—the greater number of "frames" in the subjective motion picture—not a change in the transcendent Self itself.

At the very least, it is obvious that objective time, "narrative time," and time "stopping" in transcendent states of consciousness are *not* three different "types" of time! It would, after all, be an odd trick to assert first that "time doesn't exist," but is rather allegedly merely a human conceptual ordering imposed on seamless Reality. But then, having done that, to quote narrative time and time dilations as proof that "different types of time" *do* exist, thus supposedly proving that objective time *doesn't* exist!

For all of these reasons, not only is the expansion of consciousness (and so the recognition of good and evil, as we have discussed) not a hindrance to realization of the Self, it is absolutely *vital* to that realization. And moral proscriptions such as the Ten Commandments, although their rules must ultimately be transcended in the reception of intuitive guidance from the soul, are a valuable first step in considering others' welfare on a par with one's own, which is the beginning of the expansion of consciousness.

If other persons or other cultures express a greater degree of compassion than we do, then, it is because the fourth or higher levels of their auric fields are more developed than ours. It has nothing to do with them simply being taught to conceptualize their sensory gestalts into "less fragmented" pieces, or to see themselves as "less separate from others" on the level of linear mind. *And this development of the heart in no way excludes or interferes with a comparable development of the intellect.*

It may even be that the development of the heart and astral body tends to balance one's linear thinking with patterned-whole thinking and visualization, etc. Needless to say, however, such astral-level visualizations cannot be equated with the profoundly synthesizing thought of the causal level, whereby "very complex ideas are imprinted on the mind instantaneously." Patterned-whole thinking in visualization—which is regularly confused with intuition—may *sound* similar to that causal insight, but they actually have little in common. The expression of intuition in one's daily life, in any case, is certainly not dependent on one's thinking in visual terms, nor is its manifestation even particularly helped by that way of thinking.

Now, even were we to experience our sensory impressions without conceptualizing them, this would not be an experience of reality-as-it-is *in the present.* For first of all, those impressions are conveyed to the brain only via impulsive spikes of electricity in the nervous system. Therefore, we truly can never experience "things-in-themselves" through the senses, but instead have access only to indirect, coded representations of the external physical reality. And secondly, by the time these electrical impulses reach the brain and are decoded there, the objective physical reality which gave rise to them has receded into the past.

Thus, not only is there no such thing as a "direct experience of reality" through the senses, but we can experience only *the past* through our senses, never the present. That is true even though our microcosmic experience of the internal perceptions elaborated from our sensory impressions may be—indeed, can *only* be—"in the present." (Even memories of the past are *experienced* only "in the present.") The only way to directly experience reality-in-itself is to be consciously spread through it.

Consequently, there are at least two profound difficulties with the common idea that space and time exist only in human minds, as internal conceptual representations of sensory experiences, having no inherent relation to reality-in-itself. The first of these is that if there were not a *precise* correspondence between our internal perceptual elaborations of our physical sensations, and what is actually "out there," we would be completely unable to function in the external world. Even the "survival of the fittest" guarantees this. Second, meditators who have become identified with their own expanding spheres of consciousness have perceived, in that *non-sensory* state, the everyday objects of the physical world composed of subtle light—plus, of course, astral and causal objects without physical counterparts—*having precisely the same spatial extension and distribution, and temporal sequence, as when they are cognized through the physical senses.* The existence of this space and time *even on the causal level* is proof that time and space do not exist only in human astral-level (or lower, conscious) minds. Indeed, even the transcendent Star-Self level, as described by Brennan, again consists of separated centers of white light, existing in a space which overlaps that of the causal, astral and physical levels.

Of course, given Bohm's suggestion that the background of space-time may ultimately be such that every point enfolds every other point, the spatial separation which exists on *all* levels of reality would be somewhat less "real" than it seems. And yoga, interestingly, for all its precise and profound descriptions of the structure of the cosmos, states that ultimately "there is no space, no container, nor anything to be contained." Nevertheless, to the same extent to which space and matter exist even on the levels beyond the third-chakra rational and fifth-chakra mental, these differentiations of form and whatever laws they obey must be mathematically expressible.

The dilation of subjective relative to objective time is again present in altered and expanded states of consciousness—including hypnotic trance, some narcotic-induced experiences, astral-level dreaming, and more importantly in states transcending the third and fifth (i.e., linear and mental) levels. It further occurs with the same mathematical precision among persons who do not conceptualize their experience of this phenomenon—i.e., who do not note that it is happening—as among those who *do* take note of it. Likewise, the subjective time dilation in the dream state occurs constantly whether or not we realize it.

Our experience of subjective *time* is thus built into the very structure of consciousness, at all levels, including the causal—and *all levels of reality are states of consciousness.* It is thus evident that "time" is not merely a human measure superimposed on reality. Rather, it has a very objective, real and measurable existence. This is in no way mitigated by the fact that time may "fly" or "drag" in the psychological sensation of its passage, depending only on one's own attitude of interest or boredom—something which, in any case, is an entirely different phenomenon. So again, although our subjective experience of time may vary depending on our specific state of consciousness, or be suspended in one-pointed concentration (which is one type of *samadhi)*—and although clairvoyants can move consciously both backward and forward in time—this does *not* mean that "time doesn't exist."

Of course, this line of argument must ultimately be squared with statements such as Bentov's assertion that time is "just a measure of distance, a dimension overlapping one of the three dimensions of space.... Time is not flowing anywhere; it just *is*. It is *matter* that moves along, not time. As we move in space, we are also moving along the time axis." This idea is actually very close to Bohm's notion of the implicate order, in which "time" or temporal order is related to the "degree of implication" of material particles, with all time, space and matter thus existing simultaneously, separated only by their degree of implication/ enfoldment. ("Movement is fundamental and time is an order which we derive"—David Bohm, in Paul Buckley and F. David Peat's *A Question of Physics.*)

Further, clairvoyants who are able to astrally project themselves into the past or future to see the events occurring there, have noted that not only are they able to witness *themselves* (i.e., their "real," unprojected bodies) in their future actions at those times, but that when they actually go through those actions in the future in their "unprojected" body, *they are able to see their previously-projected astral self watching them.* A similar astral projection into the future—done either unconsciously or during half-remembered dreamful sleep—undoubtedly underlies the phenomenon of déjà vu. (That feeling, though, can also be triggered by physical sceneries in which we have spent extended amounts of time during previous lives, and which we thus recognize, on a certain level, when first presented with them in this life.) Significantly, studies have shown that over sixty percent of all precognitions occur during dreaming.

Nevertheless, to simply say on that basis that "time doesn't exist" offers no insight into why or how it *seems* to exist in our daily and nightly experience of sequential events. Nor does it distinguish between the actual transcendence of time on the level of the Self, and the clairvoyant ability to travel through time on higher levels of reality than the physical. The latter, of course, is no more a "transcendence" of time than the ability to travel through space could be viewed as a spatial "transcendence." That is, the ability to travel through time is not an experience of past, present and future *simultaneously*. It is, rather, simply a skill analogous to the common ability to move through space, without experiencing all of space at once. Similarly, even being consciously spread through all space (or time), or experiencing all of space (or time) at once, is different from the idea that space (or time) "doesn't exist."

Now, in tantra yoga philosophy the seat of the soul in every human being is again designated by a point or *Bindu* in the crown of the head. That is, that seat is placed in the pericarp of the thousand-petaled lotus, reached via the *sushumna*. It cannot be doubted, then, that the raising of kundalini relates directly to high spiritual realization. There can be no dispute, of course, that both the dormant kundalini energy, and this energy when awakened, are part of the same Ocean of Consciousness. The underlying question, however, not answered by this observation, is whether one can realize oneself as the Ocean of Consciousness, in Self-realization, without having the inner passage of the *sushumna* and its causal counterparts opened. That is to say, this observation does not settle the question as to whether the raising of kundalini is a *necessary* condition for enlightenment and/or its pinnacle of Self-realization, or merely a *sufficient* condition for enlightenment, with other means possible which did not involve this energy *even implicitly*. For there are certainly valid spiritual paths which do not make *explicit* use of it, but simple unawareness of the underlying structure of consciousness does not mean that one can so easily circumvent it.

There are records of Christian saints, for example, who had the ability to enter the breathless, ecstatic *samadhi* state simply through profound devotion—i.e., through *bhakti* yoga—without meditative practice in that life, and so entering the same state as is normally achieved through yogic practice, without being aware of the structure involved, particularly in terms of the kundalini energy. Ramana Maharshi likewise "slipped into the witnessing Self" simply through deeply contemplating "Who am I?" But this too is no proof that this was not achieved on the foundation of many previous lifetimes of deep meditation.

Significantly, in his youth Maharshi slept so soundly that it was impossible for others, even in physically beating him, to wake him up.

This is precisely an indication of the ability to withdraw the life energy from the body. And such abilities do not come simply "out of the blue," but rather have their basis in past lives of meditative practice. At any rate, whatever underlying mechanisms there are in consciousness, these are relevant even for a person who has realized the Self, for that Self is still generally "tied to the body." That is, sensory impressions still generally occur only through one particular set of eyes—the same ones as before Self-realization occurred—or even through one specific spiritual eye, or one sphere of consciousness.

Again, the description of non-conceptualized sensory awareness as an "unfragmented experience of reality as an interpenetrating whole, without (conceptualized) boundaries" *sounds* mystical. However, it is only on the non-sensory most basic level of expanded consciousness that the unfragmented nature of reality as an interpenetrating web of waves of light and shadow can be experienced. For, the events of the unconceptualized sensory gestalt do not "interpenetrate" simply for having no intellect-drawn boundaries. Likewise, only if the astral and causal bodies were mere "bodies of concepts," without objective existence or literal extension in space, would getting rid of all concepts forever "free" one from such "bodies," while still existing in the physical body! (The physical form, after all, is the *solidified outcome* of our thoughts and visualizations, not merely the *container* for those mental processes.)

Such conceptualization is said by scholars to form the basis for the psychological sensation of the passage of time, in the comparing of present conceptualized objects to past objects, held in memory. Thus, the removal of conceptualization from one's sensory experiences would allegedly free one from bondage to both time and duality, given the "dualistic nature of all concepts." Whether or not this validly accounts for the sensation of the varying speeds of time's mental passage/"flying," however, it can inherently offer no explanation for the origin of the dilation of subjective time.

Further, anything which radically interferes with one's short-term memory—e.g., narcotics or dementia, etc.—would have the effect of making time seem to "stop." For, if one cannot remember when one has last checked one's watch, for example, it will seem like a great deal of time has passed since the last check, even if only a few seconds have passed. That is, it will seem as if objective time—and one's watch—have "stopped." That kind of state, however, says absolutely nothing about the potential pliability of time and space. Similarly, the absence of perceived time in the removal of conceptualization can again in no way be taken as a full explanation of the nature and means toward the transcendence of duality. That is so even though, in the absence of conceptualization, both the internal milieu and the witnessing Self would then be "beyond," or at least without, concepts. Further,

> people have a sleep-wake cycle and also a body-temperature cycle, both non-linear oscillators that restore themselves after slight perturbations. In isolation, without a daily resetting stimulus, the temperature cycle seems to be about twenty-five hours, with the low occurring during sleep. But experiments by German researchers [involving subjects living for periods of time with no daylight, no temperature change, no clocks and no telephone] found that after some weeks the sleep-wake cycle would detach itself from the temperature cycle and become erratic. People would stay awake for twenty or thirty hours at a time, followed by ten or twenty hours of sleep. Not only would the subjects remain unaware that their day had lengthened, they would refuse to believe it when told.
> —James Gleick, *Chaos: Making a New Science*

There is an obvious "flying" of time there—in a thirty-hour period seeming like a normal one on the order of fifteen waking hours, for example. Yet there is no reason to believe that the conceptualizing ability (or short-term memory) of the experimental subjects was in any way altered. This therefore provides good reason to question whether gross conceptualization has anything to do even with the "flying" of subjective time.

Further, persons involved in cross-country walks in the absence of timepieces have noted that, with practice, they were able to tell the time to within an accuracy of five minutes, simply by noting the position of the sun. Conversely, people hiking on cloudy days near the earth's Poles have found that they very easily lost track of time. (At those Poles, the sun never sets during the summer months—and never rises over the winter. Thus, when cloud cover diffuses its light, there is a constant level of illumination, irrespective of the time of day or night.)

Undoubtedly there are many other subtle clues which we rely on without consciously knowing it, in deciding for ourselves "how fast time is passing." These influences range from external cycles to internal bodily rhythms (which are frequently tied, in practice, to external cycles in Nature), including our breath and heartbeat, to variations in the earth's magnetic field. When these clues (or short-term memory of them) are absent, we would thus very reasonably have difficulty in estimating how much time had passed. And such clues are indeed absent in deep concentration, in deep sleep, in living fully in the mystical Now, and in the artificial isolation from relevant natural external cycles, as in the experiment noted by Gleick above.

The advantage of mathematics, again, even as applied, and validly applicable, to supraphysical cosmic structure—including consideration of the dilation of subjective time—is that it provides inherent internal checks and balances, as it were, lending its admirable quantitativeness a unique predictive and eliminative value. We need not simply allow that creation is both a cosmic motion picture *and* arises from the beating of a cosmic drum, for example, without understanding how this could be (except in taking these as merely poetic descriptions). Nor need we split graying scholastic hairs about which description is correct, or attempt to trace their ideational development, "perhaps rooted in sun worship" or rhythm-induced trances, etc., to fragments of papyrus. Neither would we do that without bothering to wonder why rhythm and dancing could be not only sexually arousing but trance-inducing (via the stimulation of the kundalini). Rather, we can show, by considering their identical structures, that the truth of one of these descriptions straightforward implies the other. Further, these both imply the continuous God-sustained re-creation of matter as waves in the Ocean of Consciousness.

We have already seen that koans such as "What is the sound of one hand clapping?" are not real paradoxes, but are rather perfectly understandable on the basis of reason. The same is true of the genuine paradox of the sphere which both inflates and deflates simultaneously. That is, no breach of logic is involved; although the failed attempt to understand such statements without reference to cosmic structure may give the *appearance* that they cannot be explained logically, and so are "unsolvable paradoxes which can be understood only through intuition."

The same is true of other well-known koans. Thus, in the case of "A cow passes by a window. Its head, horns, and the four legs all pass by. Why did not the tail pass by?" Coomaraswamy notes that the symbolism

is the same as in the clashing rocks. That is, the tail represents the ego/
personality, left behind in mystical experience. Similarly with "A long
time ago a man kept a goose in a bottle. It grew larger and larger until it
could not get out of the bottle any more. He did not want to break the
bottle, nor did he wish to harm the goose. How would you get it out?" the
answer being simply, after a few moments of silence, "It's out!" The
goose (Sanskrit *hamsa,* "I am He") trapped in the bottle here corresponds
to the genie (or even to the Self), released from its entrapment without
either breaking the bodily bottle or harming the inner spirit.

> Yun Men showed his staff to the assembly and said, "The staff [spine]
> has changed into a dragon [kundalini] and swallowed the universe
> [expanded consciousness to infinity]. Mountains, rivers, the great
> earth—where are they to be found?"

The same structural nature is again true of form coexisting with
Formlessness, not as an opposite but rather as a subset; of Om being an
"Unstruck Sound"; of *samadhi* being "conscious sleep," and of numerous other seeming "contradictions" or paradoxes. For these are in fact
fully explicable in logical terms, but only with reference to the structure
of the macrocosm and the microcosm, never by too readily dismissing
them as mere products of the inability of the dualistic logic of the
intellect to describe supraintellectual reality.

Thus, in the koan "We were parted many thousands of *kalpas* [ages]
ago, yet we have not been separated even for a moment. We are facing
each other all day long, yet we have never met," we may reasonably take
the part of ourselves that "has never been separated" and which "faces
each other all day long" as the Self or soul, and the aspect which "was
parted many ages ago" as the ego. In any case, as far as the idea that
koans, whether seemingly paradoxical or not, are meant to take us
beyond the linear thinking process into intuitive knowledge—which
they are indeed meant to do—we can hardly fail to note that deep, one-
pointed concentration on *any* idea (i.e., any *concept),* whether it relates
to cosmic structure or not, will take us beyond the thinking process.
There is nothing special about koans and/or paradoxes in this regard.

We must further understand that when sages "see no difference"
between earth, water and sky, that occurs most deeply not from a
"freedom from conceptualization," but rather because of their direct

knowledge of these as varied expressions of the single creative Light of God.

> A yogi who through perfect meditation has merged his consciousness with the Creator perceives the cosmical essence as light [vibrations of life energy]; to him there is no difference between the light rays composing water and the light rays composing land.
>
> —Paramahansa Yogananda,
> *Autobiography of a Yogi*

There is a Zen koan expressing the same idea: "If you can swallow all the water in the Pacific Ocean in one gulp [a metaphor for the expansion of consciousness], you will know that to walk on land is the same as to walk on water, and to walk on water is the same as to walk on land," for in both cases we are walking on light rays (and witnessing that from the same transcendent Self). Indeed, nearly every spiritual phenomenon for which a "freedom from habitual patterns of conceptualization" explanation is commonly given, can be eminently more reasonably explained in terms of the flow of life energy or subtle light.

This is particularly true in the case of Vimalananda, a twentieth-century master of tantra yoga, who disgustingly consumed raw human flesh in the hope of obtaining the life energy from it, *not* to shock everyone else out of their (very reasonable) moral judgments regarding cannibalism! Indeed, there are contemporary spiritual paths which will consume only animal flesh that has been preserved (i.e., smoked) in a certain way. This, too, has to do with imbibing the life energy from it, not with merely "breaking arbitrary patterns of conceptualization" to see reality "as it is"!

Consider also the story of Swami Nityananda, who ate the food given him with such disinterest that one of his disciples one day wondered out loud to another, in private, if the master would eat human excrement, were it put on his plate. Whereupon, several days later, having divined the elements of this conversation, the saint was found covered in excrement, smilingly offering handfuls of it to his disciples as "treats" to eat. Again, this was not for the simple shock value, but was rather indicative both of his sense of humor and his inner perception of all things as varied manifestations of God's Light. And perhaps of a lack of personal hygiene as well, since one should never rule out the human aspect of the story, or dangerously assume that just because a "sage" is doing something out of the ordinary, that it therefore makes sense. In any case, a similar story is told of Yogananda, who was dared to eat a handful of rotting rice, did so with relish, and then forced a comparable handful into his daring companion's mouth, to complete the bet.

As further example, consider the case of traditions for whom the normal rules of asceticism, vegetarianism and celibacy are periodically suspended in religious feasts of meat and the proverbial "wine, women and song." Any spiritual benefit accruing from such occasions can be reasonably taken to be due simply to the many normally-suppressed desires and emotions in the participating disciples being simultaneously satisfied, this fulfillment temporarily releasing the energies associated with that suppression. Indeed, how could one *not* vault temporarily into higher states of consciousness, with those blockages being released? For while nonindulgence in desires is never itself unhealthy, to "clamp down on them" or deny their existence altogether, in the belief that to have them at all makes one a failure on the spiritual path—so that their presence evokes this negative self-judgment—is neither healthy nor the way to be free of them.

Consider also that when the spine is properly aligned we literally feel centered in our inner divinity, i.e., in our Star-Self. And indeed, in some Zen traditions (in particular the *rinzai* or "sudden enlightenment" school), this alignment of the spine is accomplished by the *roshi* or guru striking his students appropriately on the back with a stick, to correct for their improper postures and the resulting clairvoyantly-visible energy restrictions. The resulting free flow of important spiritual energies then aids in the attainment of higher states of consciousness.

> Many students are not free from the entanglement of objective things. I treat them right at the spot. If their trouble is due to grasping hands, I strike them there. If their trouble comes from their mouths, it is there I strike.
>
> —Rinzai

Such "troubles," of course, are going to be visible in the aura at exactly the level of hands and mouths, i.e., at the specific physical locations where they manifest as energy imbalances or blockages in daily lives. Any valid claims of spiritual benefit arising from chiropractic spinal adjustment must have a similar basis. Of course, as with the aforementioned Zen enlightenment practice, one would have to be on the verge of that state beforehand in order to experience any "miraculous" results. Indeed, this is a principle which probably applies to all forms of alternative healing.

Obviously, then, any states of *satori* (i.e., *samadhi)* or enlightenment experienced by such stricken disciples are unlikely to have anything to do with those persons simply having been "shocked out of their normal patterns of conceptualization" (to "see reality 'as it is,' without superimposed conceptualizations") by suddenly being hit! Rather, the positive effects of this act are again completely explicable in terms of the flow of life energy.

Probably even some of the spiritual benefits of something like *vipassana* meditation can be explained in those terms. In *vipassana* meditation, one's attention is expanded to focus on all of the objects in one's internal mental milieu, including physical bodily sensations. This is in contrast to forms of "content" meditation, in which one's attention is restricted to a single object of concentration.

Directing one's attention toward whatever sensations or thoughts may be momentarily present in one's mental milieu is obviously going to result in the psychologically-beneficial effect of making one's hitherto unconscious/subconscious thoughts and sensory impressions conscious. That impartial direction of attention is also going to effect an equilibration of energy throughout the body-mind. And that, in turn, will encourage both the release of stagnant (i.e., suppressed/repressed) energy blockages, and the proper spinning/functioning of the chakras, which "content" forms of meditation and healing generally work explicitly, not merely implicitly, to effect.

Much has been made in contemporary theorizing of the apparent association of the "linear, analytic" activities of the left hemisphere with reason, and of the "patterned-whole" thinking of the right hemisphere with "intuition." And it is indeed probably true that a balancing of the cerebral activities of the left and right hemispheres is a prerequisite for the attainment of high states of consciousness. (That balancing would correspond to an equilibration of the masculine and feminine energies in the right and left halves of the body, which are controlled by the left and right hemispheres, respectively.) Measurements of persons in deep meditation have in any case indicated equal electromagnetic activity in both halves of the brain. This measurable activity is of course simply one *indicator* of the processes of consciousness, or one aspect of the aura which fortunately happens to be detectable via today's physical instruments, but is not itself the source of consciousness.

That balance, however, simply provides one more indication that the "patterned-whole" or "artistic" thinking of the right hemisphere cannot in any way be equated with "intuition." For, if the linear mind were a function simply of the left hemisphere, and genuine intuition a product only of the right, the left cerebral hemisphere would have to be *inactive* in high (i.e., intuitive) states of consciousness, not *balanced* in its electrical activities with the right. Further, near-death experiences in which chunks of intuitive knowledge are frequently imprinted on the consciousness of the individual—though largely forgotten when the subject returns to the body—occur with *flat* EEG traces. That is, they occur with no activity in *either* cerebral hemisphere. Thus, these experiences can be neither hallucinations nor dreams, for both of the latter are accompanied by brainwave activity.

Interestingly, persons hypnotically regressed to the between-life realm have been found to enter a state of consciousness in which they were *acutely self-aware and had a heightened moral and ethical sense.* The aforementioned near-death experiences and between-life regressions further demonstrate that none of us have rushed to incarnate on the physical plane simply to "be creative" on this level, for the creativity of the astral realms is a thousand times greater and easier to indulge in. Further, given that intuition is the source of all creativity, the increase in creativity produced by long-term meditation can in no way be presented as arising merely from a regular practice of, and thus an improvement in, our ability to concentrate.

> My various scientific studies originated from the wisdom obtained by concentration on the ajna [chakra]. I began to perceive that one of my tasks in this life is to help make this knowledge as clear as possible through scientific means, and to attempt to explain it in a way that others will understand. In this way my approach differs from that which employs the ordinary inductive methods of scientific research which were devised to examine physical phenomena in the effort to establish

a synthetic scientific truth. I, rather, am attempting to manifest in the physical dimension, using deductive and scientific methods, the wisdom granted me while concentrating on the ajna chakra.

—Hiroshi Motoyama, *Theories of the Chakras*

Compare Gopi Krishna's experience of being "in occasional contact with an inexpressible fount of all knowledge" in the form of waves of conscious, knowledge-carrying electricity felt passing through him. This actually lead him to compose inspired poetry—in which he hitherto had little interest or skill—in no less than ten different languages, only some of which were prior known to him. (One may reasonably guess, however, that he did know and use those languages in *previous* lives.) Compare this further with the Biblical day of Pentecost, wherein "tongues of fire" appeared on the heads of the apostles: "And they were all filled with the Holy Ghost, and began to speak with other tongues, as the Spirit gave them utterance"—Acts 2:4.

A marked increase in quality of writing following illumination experiences is similarly well-known in the case of Balzac—regarded as "perhaps the greatest name in the post-Revolutionary literature of France." Likewise for Walt Whitman; in Whitman's instance, there being even no intermediate practice of the art. And why should this not be so? when, even only in astral-body-identified dreamful sleep, each one of us demonstrates a creativity and depth of visualization and audibilization which, could it but be brought into our waking lives, would make of each one of us an artistic genius.

Interestingly, the German biologist Friedrich Kekulé hit upon the idea of the benzene ring—the structure which forms the basis for all organic chemistry—during a period of spontaneous imagery when he was half-asleep. As he described it in his diary:

I turned my chair to the fire and dozed. Again the atoms were gamboling before my eyes. This time the smaller groups kept mostly in the background. My mental eye, rendered more acute by repeated visions of this kind, could now distinguish larger structures, of manifold conformation; long rows, sometimes more closely fitted together; all twining and twisting in snakelike motion. But look! What was that? One of the snakes had seized hold of its own tail, and the form whirled mockingly before my eyes. As if by a flash of lightning I awoke.

Likewise,

> the story goes that Otto Loewi had wrestled with the problem of the synapse for a long time without result, when one night he had a dream in which the entire frog-heart experiment was revealed to him. [This classic biology experiment provided the first proof that nerve transmissions across synapses have a chemical nature, i.e., are not merely electrical. The first such "neurotransmitter" thus discovered was acetylcholine, for which discovery Loewi received the Nobel Prize in 1936.] When he awoke, he knew he'd had the dream, but he'd forgotten the details. The next night he had the same dream. This time he remembered the procedure, went to his lab in the morning, did the experiment, and solved the problem.
> —Robert O. Becker and Gary Selden,
> *The Body Electric*

Even more impressively, the recognized East Indian mathematical genius Srinivasa Ramanujan—discoverer of the "modular functions" which play an essential role in today's attempts by physicists to unify the known physical forces via "superstring theory"—claimed, in all seriousness, to have received many of his discovered formulae in dreams.

> [The brilliant Cambridge mathematician Godfrey H. Hardy] tried to estimate the mathematical skill that Ramanujan possessed. He rated David Hilbert, universally recognized as one of the greatest Western mathematicians of the nineteenth century, an 80. To Ramanujan, he assigned a 100. (Hardy rated himself a 25.)
> —Michio Kaku, *Hyperspace*

Or consider the testimony of W. Thomas Wolfe, an American computer programmer, who at age twelve experienced a curious phenomenon that, in retrospect, amounted to a first kundalini energy awakening:

> At the time, he was participating in a rapid calculation contest. As the teacher was reading the first question, Wolfe felt a strange excitement and his body started to vibrate "with some inner energy." Then "I noticed a brightness through and about me—a light that had never been so bright before. In a way the feeling was similar to, but stronger than, the activity one feels in his midsection just before throwing up. But now it was noticeable throughout the whole body, and was a good feeling, an 'alive' feeling, rather than a sensation of sickness."
> —Lee Sannella, *The Kundalini Experience*

No sooner had his teacher finished the arithmetical question than Wolfe blurted out the correct answer: "The answer was literally *thrown* out of my mouth by some forceful inner impulse. I couldn't have stopped it if I wanted to!" He had never before evidenced any especial propensity for rapid calculation; nevertheless, he continued to produce the correct solutions, and won that contest and several others over the next few years. "I never knew how I got the answers!" Wolfe recounts in *And the Sun Is Up: Kundalini Rises in the West.* "I could feel them being worked out, or at least I could feel some kind of super fast activity going on within me, but I couldn't begin to track it consciously."

At the very least, phenomena such as these demonstrate that the subconscious is "smarter" than the conscious mind. So the question then becomes (a) How/Why is it more gifted, and (b) if the subconscious is so gifted, what of the superconscious?

> Tesla was [said to be] able to receive the plans and designs for his inventions in a very direct way, right into his imagination. Even the originals of the complicated electrical machines he was later to invent appear to have been received in a flash. A device, in all its detail, would miraculously appear in his mind and he would then begin to construct the working apparatus simply by copying the design from his imagination.
>
> —F. David Peat, *In Search of Nikola Tesla*

The probability of that means of invention being more than a latter-day exaggeration of Tesla's abilities is increased by the fact that transformers similar to the ones which Tesla utilized in his attempts at wireless power transmission are today designed to withstand lightning strikes. Again from Peat's book: "The design is pretty complicated and the whole thing has to be done on a computer. There are a lot of equations to be solved.... If you get the distance between the coils right and your geometry correct, then such a transformer can stand up to a power surge. But this was exactly what Tesla did in the 1890s. He built a transformer which actually resonated under a continuous power surge and he didn't even have a computer to help him."

> Confucius said to a pupil, "Do you think I have come to know many things by studying them?"
> The pupil said, "Yes. Isn't it so?"
> Confucius said, "No. I penetrate them by their underlying unity."

Now, to the "conceptualization is the root of all good and evil" viewpoint, mythological symbolisms and archetypes arise only as outward projections of the psychological state of their originators, having no objective or universal validity: "Patterns of matter reflect patterns of mind, and what we see depends on our concepts." Needless to say, the ensuing reading of esoteric, *structural* symbolisms as if they merely reflected the psychological and sociological attitude of individuals and their surrounding culture invariably grossly misses the mark, to put it mildly.

Of course, the idea that "what we see in the world depends on our concepts"—i.e., on what we *expect* to see—certainly has a range of validity. The same is true of the suggestion that any of us—not only mystics—must put our experiences into an agreed-upon language in order to explicitly convey anything, however limited, about them, to other persons around us. Ironically, however, when these paradigms are applied to the understanding of religion, they find there, *in accord with their expectations,* nothing more than commentaries on the "dualistic nature of all concepts," even in the myriad often-quoted verses concerning the Word and Name of God which in reality have nothing at all to do with that idea.

Contemporary scholarly understandings of Eastern religion again ignore the dilation of subjective time as a marker of one's state of consciousness. They are further unaware of the existence of any subtle mechanism by which reality can be experienced without sensory intermediary. Thus, they have little choice, in attempting to develop a theoretical basis for mystical experience, but to believe that sensory experiences without superimposed conceptualization "transcend duality," and constitute the sagely-described experience of reality-as-it-is. It is likewise inevitable that they then further wrongly regard any bodily immobility (e.g., in the identification with one's sphere of consciousness) in *samadhi* as mere withdrawal into a cataleptic trance or visionary state, supposedly markedly inferior to the (sensory) experience of reality-in-itself. And yet, simultaneous with that derision, they unknowingly celebrate the same level as the home of the "point-like and yet [potentially] infinite" transcendence of duality!

In that regard, compare Coomaraswamy's observation that "D. T. Suzuki entirely misses the point when he renders *Lankavatara Sutra*

II.115 [The mind being 'in its own pasture, beholds all things at once, as if in a mirror'; similar to Chuang Tzu's 'The mind of the sage being brought to rest becomes the mirror of the universe'], *sva-gocare,* by 'in its own sense-fields'; the meaning really being 'in its own pasture'—i.e., when *not* directed toward sense objects."

This view further reduces scriptural accounts of "single eyes" to nothing more than not seeing the world through the "two eyes" of duality—i.e., experiencing it sensorially, as before, but simply not conceptualizing it into "good" and "bad." Again, until one recognizes the existence of subtler, literal "eyes" and senses than the physical, the continuous field of the unconceptualized sensory gestalt will seem to be "unfragmented," and scriptural interpretations will be bent to fit that expectation. And in this same absence of understanding of subtle structure, the only plausible explanation for the near-identity of spiritual symbols and themes throughout the diverse cultures of the world is in them having "borrowed" the ideas from one another.

These misunderstandings amply illustrate the danger of demanding that reality fit into one's limited and changing intellectual understanding of it. The same applies to the general semantics-based idea that scriptural "words" and "names" refer only to the way in which human conceptualizations of sensory gestalts "create" objects in our minds. If this mistaken approach cannot account for Biblical verses such as "And it came to pass the same night, that the Word of God came to Nathan, saying ...," these are *not* "ambiguities in the Bible," or places in which it has not been properly thought through. Rather, they are ways in which reality does not fit into the accepted theory! For words and names cannot be both "the only thing that bind us to duality" *and* the conveyors of divine revelation. We should not blame *reality* for discrepancies like that, or for that fact that Merrell-Wolff's experiences, for example, do not accord with the expectations of today's theory—notwithstanding his experience of the widely-misunderstood state of being simultaneously point-like and unbounded in consciousness. Indeed, with that discord, his name (as with Bentov's and Yogananda's and Brennan's) is rarely mentioned in contemporary "serious" transpersonal or integral literature, being perhaps something of an embarrassment.

Conversely, Ramana Maharshi is regarded by many scholars as "perhaps the greatest sage of the twentieth century" largely because his expounded philosophy of asking "Who am I?" is almost wholly bereft of an exposition/understanding of the detailed structure underlying higher states of awareness. It is likewise without techniques of content meditation, and can thus be easily made to "fit in to" the phenomenological position. (Cf. "To a child with a hammer, everything looks like a nail." And anything which can't be thus nailed must be unimportant or "not related to transcendence.")

Of course, the same persons who view Maharshi so highly—to take nothing away from the sage himself—would uniformly regard koans as mere "nonsense riddles," not bothering themselves as to how each one of those contemplative riddles can then have a unique solution. Nor do they even generally concern themselves with the *basic question* as to how a Self unburdened by conceptual boundaries could still see the world only through its own set of eyes, without there being an underlying (and perhaps even *conceptually-expressible) structure* governing that.

By contrast to that forced and overextended application of phenomenology, consider how easily, seamlessly and beautifully everything from mythology to psychology to science fits together when one begins instead from valid and deep principles of "structural metaphysics." This is not surprising, for mythology expounds, via well-chosen metaphors, the differentiated laws and structures underlying spiritual evolution and higher states of reality/consciousness, while physical science deals with the "As above, so below" reflections of those same laws and structures. Of course, to get to that context of understanding, one must first acknowledge that mathematics and logic can validly describe the structure of levels of reality beyond the human mind. Conversely, regardless of how sincerely one may insist that one's ideas are not "the last word," so long as one clings to the belief that seemingly-paradoxical (e.g., "point/infinity") descriptions of trans-mental states in general arise only from the "dualistic nature of all concepts," etc., there can be no precise understanding of what transcendence is, how freedom of choice works, or even of what the "sound of One Hand clapping" is.

The point/infinity pairing is not actually paradoxical, since both one's transcendent Self and one's causal-level sphere of consciousness are potentially infinite, and are linked by that Point even when the latter sphere is finite. That is, the description of the soul/Self as being both point-like and infinite is not paradoxical, in spite of the fact that it is exactly the filtering of the impulse which results in both our experience of that point, and our conscious expansion into space, even to infinity.

The psychological sensation of the passage of time is again believed by scholars to originate in the comparing of present conceptualized objects to past objects, held in memory. Conversely, the removal of conceptualization from one's sensory experiences would allegedly free one from bondage to both time and duality, given the "dualistic nature of all concepts." This explanation derives from a branch of philosophy founded by Husserl and continued by Heidegger. Known as phenomenology, this system of thought proudly concerns itself only with a description of the phenomena in one's internal mental milieu, without inquiring as to the form of the laws (whether biochemical or otherwise) underlying these phenomena, or concerning itself with the nature of existence in general.

In its practice of the introspective observation of the phenomena in one's mental milieu, Husserl's phenomenology has been favorably compared by contemporary transpersonal psychologists to Buddhist *vipassana* or "mindfulness" meditation—a comparison which is probably valid. It is obvious, however, that phenomenology cannot encompass any deep consideration of cosmic structure, for it treats only (some of) the *symptoms* of transcendence, not the underlying mathematical laws and causes. Nor can phenomenology provide a meaningful understanding of what intuition is, beyond associating it vaguely with transcendence and a nebulously-conceived freedom from rigid conceptualization.

Being thus steeped in such a comfortably narrow view of reality, the phenomenological approach is in practice wholly unable to provide an understanding of the structure emphasized by Christ, the Old Testament sages and yoga. Nor can it address the same features in the Zen/Buddhist and Taoist paths, in terms of Chuang Tzu's Pivot, and Zen's admitted "sphere of center everywhere, circumference nowhere" and "sound of one hand clapping." Indeed, the last of those can in no way be reduced to being simply a fusion of the metaphorical clash between the "two hands" of subject and object, in ordinarily dualistic experience. Neither can phenomenology distinguish between a mind which is "without concepts" for being either in the coma state or for simply being "blank," versus one which transcends thought via one-pointed concentration.

(Yoga warns against the former state as being susceptible to the influence of possession by "tramp souls," or low astral-level disembodied
entities.) Likewise, how could the concept-less mind of the infant be
distinguished from that of the sage, without presupposing some other
structure underlying those perceptions in, for example, grafting stages of
psychological development onto that phenomenological indistinguish-
ability?

And yet, in spite of these drastic and fundamental shortcomings, the
phenomenological analysis of mystical states forms the theoretical basis
for the scholarly understanding of what transcendence is. That is, this
paradigm is responsible for the transcendence of space, time and duality
being viewed as merely "the transcendence of all dualistic concepts." It
is further responsible for "chaos" and "primal or virgin matter" being
taken as referring only to the "undifferentiated" state of the unconceptualized sensory gestalt, prior to the application of conceptual "words"
and "names" to it. This statement is then compared with scriptural
accounts of how the Word of God creates material forms from the
primordial Chaos, and believed to be identical with it, when in fact the
two positions have nothing at all in common.

Of course, it may even be that the action of "words" in "creating"
objects in one's internal mental milieu is a valid, albeit lower, reflection
of the archetypal cosmic processes operating at the root of the creation of
subtle and gross matter. In the end, however, the fact is that general
semantics and phenomenology have *no valid application whatsoever* to
the interpretation of scriptural "Words" and "Names." Rather, they can
at best yield an unintentional discovery of reflections of archetypal
cosmic processes, which are then unfortunately prone to being mistaken
for the archetypal processes themselves.

Exactly the same problem occurs in attempting to distinguish "sun
worship" from "Son worship." Further, the latter transcendent religion
will quite naturally degenerate into the former primitive approach, if the
esoteric meaning of the symbols is withheld from the uninitiated, or if the
understanding of that meaning simply fades with the passage of time
even among the initiated. Thus, not only can Son-worship and sun-
worship co-exist in the same culture, making use of exactly the same
symbols and rituals, but the former can degenerate into the latter at least
as reasonably as the latter could evolve into the former, and will so

degenerate whenever its symbols are interpreted only literally or poetically instead of structurally.

The literal or fundamentalist interpretation of scripture is generally regarded as "exoteric" or dealing only with the superficial or outer meaning of scripture, with the poetic/figurative reading taken as "esoteric," or penetrating to the inner and hidden meaning. In actuality, however, the structural interpretation is the esoterically intended one, for only it can be related to the techniques of meditation which are taught along with the esoteric knowledge.

Thus, there are two important things to note about poetic or figurative interpretations of mythology. First, even if they provide valid and intended meanings, these are by no means the most interesting or profound ones contained in the scriptural allegories. Second, such figurative interpretations are proposed only when one lacks an adequate knowledge of the esoteric structure to which such myths positively refer. This latter point, especially, demands that any figurative interpretations of myth which go contrary to the structural interpretations of the same allegories must be approached with great caution, with the tenuous nature of the former being fully appreciated.

On the other hand, it is encouraging that very often the scholarly, figurative interpretations of mythology, if executed properly, can be reconciled with the structural interpretations, as a "subset" of the latter. This is thankfully the case with, for example the scholarly reading of the various symbols of the *axis mundi,* which is by and large correct, but which is generally not seen to refer esoterically and structurally to the spine.

CHAPTER XIII

PSYCHOLOGY AND TRANSCENDENCE

IT IS AGAIN NOT THE SIMPLE ACT of *conceptualization* that results in energy blockages and repression, nor even the impartial recognition of harmonious sensations as being beneficial to the welfare of the body, and inharmonious ones being detrimental to it. Rather, those blockages or stresses come from our attempts to stop the flow of disliked physical or mental sensations, in the wish to avoid the associated feelings of pain, as opposed to "relaxing into it," or impartially witnessing it. Note, then, Itzhak Bentov's observation that when the cycle of raising the kundalini energy is completed, stresses in the body are eliminated as soon as they are accumulated. Indeed, he characterized kundalini as "the ultimate stress-release mechanism."

It is precisely because of this release of stress or suppressed energy that persons undergoing rapid spiritual awakenings will sometimes have involuntary thrashing movements, or spontaneously assume hatha yoga postures, particularly during meditation and sleep. Presumably, the postures assumed are exactly those recognized by yoga as promoting the specific energy flows pertaining to the particular release in each case. It would certainly be surprising if they weren't.

Kundalini yoga and similar spiritual disciplines involving the spinal energies, in opening not only the higher chakras but the lower ones also, further work implicitly to effect the "grounding" of our energies into the earth, through the legs. Yogananda, for example, describes his first experience in cosmic consciousness as involving his body becoming "immovably rooted" to the ground. If that is not a profound demonstration of good "grounding," what is?! By the same token, however, in tasting an orange after a particularly high and extended spiritual experience, he found even the innocent sensation of its sweetness to be unspeakably and intolerably gross.

Unfortunately, in spite of the potential for meditation to effect transformations not only in one's state of consciousness during meditation, but in one's everyday psychology as well—via the release of energy blockages—it is, in practice, sadly true that neurotics who begin meditating tend to become merely "more relaxed neurotics." Further, meditating monks intent on "killing the ego" will nevertheless use their renunciation of the world as a means of feeling superior to non-monastic others who are obviously "less serious about finding God" than they are, and will not hesitate to set themselves up as "teachers" for anyone who can be coerced or cornered into being a "student" to their wisdom.

Indeed, one finds that even people who have meditated deeply for half a century or more, or who can go into *samadhi* at will, cannot be relied upon to have the humility, honesty or integrity to admit that they do not have all of the answers, or that they might be able to learn from others. Nor can they be trusted to have the discernment necessary to avoid the subtle lie of concealing aspects of their religious organization which they believe would harm the "image" of it which they prefer to present to the public.

The sad fact is that if someone does not possess intelligence, compassion, causal-level intuition or integrity when he begins meditating, he or she probably won't have those qualities after a lifetime of meditation, even if that lifetime has produced an actual kundalini raising or other bliss-filled "enlightenment."

Conversely, simply because a "sage" radiates profound vibrations of Peace or Bliss, or has even attained to the witnessing Self, does not mean that he or she will be in any way free of the neuroses and power issues which existed prior to that enlightenment. One is unlikely to find any comprehension of that, however, in a typical ashram/monastic setting.

Indeed, such an understanding would rather be actively resisted, all in the name of obedience to some ossified authority's idea of what constitutes "God's will."

The net result of all that is the sad fact that one is probably more statistically likely to be profoundly psychologically abused in our world's "spiritual" environments than in the "real world." For one may reasonably regard the attempt to rob one of one's independence and intellect as psychological abuse, accompanied as that is by the consistent voicing of the notion that those are "bad things" which interfere with one's spiritual advancement. Indeed, in suitably depraved "Crazy Zen" or Gurdjieff-like settings, one is likely even to be seduced/raped ... "in the Name of God" and for ostensibly "killing one's ego" in allowing oneself to be so abused.

In reading accounts of the ubiquitous (and especially sexual) indis-cretions on the part of spiritual authority figures (many of whom, such as Krishnamurti, hypocritically taught "the importance of celibacy" to their disciples), one's jaw drops to see the extent to which disciples will rationalize the inexcusable behaviors of their guru-figures. A husband and wife are forcibly stripped naked before the "guru," as humiliating punishment for a minor offense at a spiritual retreat ... and come back for class the next day, not wanting to miss the instruction! Another man allows his wife to be raped by the Crazy Zen "Master," in the bizarre belief that the latter is thereby simply teaching him to "not be attached" to her.

At the same time, the "sage" himself believes and teaches that so long as he is merely "witnessing" whatever sensations may present themselves to his consciousness, he is unbound by moral laws, and guided by profound intuition. (None of that situation is helped by the pervasive allergy to the "more concepts" of cosmic structure. For that aversion precludes any intelligent, much less insightful, discussion as to the nature of free choice and the existence of good and evil, etc.) And so on, so miserably on.

Indeed, a 1985 survey done by psychologist and meditation teacher Jack Kornfield reported that, of fifty-three Buddhist and Hindu teachers surveyed in the United States, thirty-four of those teachers admitted to having had sex with their students. One can only guess how pathetically high the figure really was, above that sixty-four percent, since one cannot assume that every "No" answer given by those "holy teachers, committed to the unbiased perception of truth," was an honest one. (A good source of disillusionment in this regard is Wilber, Anthony and Ecker's *Spiritual Choices: The Problems of Recognizing Authentic Paths to Inner Transformation;* not to mention www.yogananda-dif.org, www.anandainfo.com, www.anandaanswers.com, and www.rickross.com.)

> Of one hundred persons who take up the spiritual life, eighty turn out to be charlatans, fifteen insane, and only five, maybe, get a glimpse of the real truth. Therefore beware.
>
> —Swami Vivekananda

The situation is actually worse than that, since most of the fifty-three meditation teachers surveyed above would probably qualify as having gotten "a glimpse of the real truth."

> Ashrams, in my experience, are lunatic asylums filled with jealous and needy people.... Most of the ashrams I have known and visited are *not* sacred environments where people progress; they're places in which people regress—to blind adoration, spiritual vanity, sibling rivalry, mirroring and parroting of the so-called master—and in my experience, I have to say, sadly, that I have seen very little real spiritual progress made in them.
>
> —Andrew Harvey, *The Return of the Mother*

My own experience, of nine wholly regrettable months—in what became the worst period of my life, by far—spent in one of Yogananda's approved southern California ashrams, has led me to the same conclusions. Nor was that experience isolated, as is demonstrated by the postings at www.angelfire.com/blues/srfwalrus from other persons who have suffered through comparably disillusioning experiences in that environment.

One learns the hard way that the "behind the scenes" behaviors of ochre-robed monastics are not only no better than those of the average person, but are frequently actually worse than those of the average smut peddler. Indeed, Buddhist monks in Thailand have been known to proudly exhibit expensive collections of antique cars, and to don disguises, sneak out to local karoake bars, and be caught with pornography, alcohol, sexual paraphernalia, and *more than one woman* at a time!

"Everyone makes mistakes," of course. But the problem is not simply that such monastic dalliances are often not merely isolated and regretted events, nor that such trysts are of the same psychological status as incest, being between revered father-figures and their naïvely trusting followers. Rather, as if that weren't enough as far as problems go, the same behaviors evoke the pathological need of the persons involved to hide such indiscretions, so as to maintain a public appearance of holiness.

Indeed, even in a recent scandal involving the alleged sexual activities of a highly-placed male monastic minister at Yogananda's Self-Realization Fellowship organization, who was ultimately forced to leave the Order, persons familiar with the details have expressed dismay at the church's handling of it. That handling included a reported one-third of a million dollars in compensation paid to the unfortunate woman involved, but that's not the disillusioning part. After all, one can understand the wish to keep the details of such a three-month-long relationship out of the public eye, even though doing so involved a fair chunk of their members' money (including some of my own), donated *in good faith* to further the spread of Yogananda's teachings, not to cover up the indiscretions of his "spiritually advanced monks." No, the disillusion, disgust, indignation and outrage come from what follows:

> [Persons familiar with the details] contend that several top SRF leaders—including [lifetime President] Daya Mata—not only turned a deaf ear to [the woman in question] after she sought help while still involved with the monk, but that those leaders attempted to ruin her reputation within the church even as they sought to preserve [the monk's] monastic career.... "They [the church leadership] pretty much destroyed [the involved woman's] faith and ruined her life"....
> —Ron Russell, "Return of the Swami,"
> *New Times Los Angeles,* July 1-7, 1999

The fact that yoga teaches that "God is Bliss" certainly doesn't help any of this situation, producing as it does the fallacy that so long as one is blissed-out from meditation (i.e., is a "bliss bunny"), one is in tune with God, with one's actions and intuition thereby allegedly being in effortless accord with the will of God. For with that, even the most despicable and uncaring behavior, and dearth of integrity (e.g., in the covering-up of various "indiscretions") can be excused, as if God

Himself, in the form of Bliss—or "for the good of The Work"—sanctioned it.

> Man at the apex of his being, is divine, one with God. To contact that Self is the goal, the aim, and end of all yoga practices. To contact this Self in deep meditation is Bliss, and is also the source of all truth. To contact it intuitionally gives inspiration, wisdom, genius. Self-realization means all of these things.
>
> —Gyanamata, *God Alone*

Thus, Bliss = Self = Intuition = Truth = Wisdom = Genius. And on the causal and transcendent levels themselves, that equation is even *relatively* valid, give or take. But in bringing that down into one's daily life, it's just too painfully obvious that blissed-out or even Self-realized meditators are not, generally speaking, geniuses, or even particularly wise or keenly perceptive of truth. (That is, they are not even close to being "spiritual geniuses.") Much less are they *ever* all-knowing, infallible, or with no further progress to make in their own psychological, moral and spiritual development. Nor are they generally honorable enough in their own psychologies to admit to that.

Of course, one encounters the same subtle dishonesty among contemporary healers, who are rarely able to do deeply meaningful work, and yet will excuse that inability on the grounds that "it's not their style" to work that way. What they really mean, however, is that they *can't* do work at the same level as their revered teachers. After all, anyone who *could* do healing work at that high level, *would.* The exorbitant hourly rate charged to their clients, though, is the same either way, thus effectively restricting the access to such "compassionate healing" only to the wealthy. It's quite the leap, after all, to go from validly saying that "a healer shouldn't feel obliged to do healings for free," to feeling justified in charging indefensible fees, comparable to those in the equally-overpaid psychological profession, even if one can't do meaningful work.

My own search for healing has included multiple sessions with two different $45/hour (Cdn.) well-experienced Reiki Masters, and two $90/hour graduates of Brennan's school—one of whom, grossly guilty of blindly guessing and "playing psychologist" during our session, now acts as a dean there. This was followed by a wholly ineffective $50/hour healer, touting the virtues of Neuro-Linguistic Programming, and intent on imposing its suspect view of psychological healing on every aspect of human behavior, who claimed to have healed herself of multiple sclerosis and to have literally "made the crippled walk." Plus a Native American healer who turned a deaf ear to my pleas for help. Not to mention a "pressure-point" chiropractor, unable to do in seven sessions what a traditional chiropractor could do in one, who was yet ready to take credit for my deepened breathing during his sessions. (The gentleman evidently could not see that, in laying face-down for half an hour with only intermittent attention from him, there was simply nothing else for me to focus on but that!) Plus, a $50/hour "sound therapist," whose cassette recordings of "healing sound," carefully tuned to the nearest one-hundredth of a semitone, could easily have had exactly the opposite effect as intended, were they to have any significant effect at all. (Cassette tape transport speed varies significantly from machine to machine. Thus, when the recordings were played at home, if the machine's speed were a few percent too slow relative to the machine on which the tapes were recorded, they could just as easily have retarded one's healing as expedited it.) Indeed, that therapist's catch-all explanation as to why I wasn't experiencing the transforming effects that other of her clients experienced was simply that perhaps I didn't *want* to let go of the relevant emotional pain!

There may indeed be healers on this planet for whom a single session of work can produce the same breakthrough results as "half a year of psychoanalysis," as some of their clients have claimed. Ironically, though, the non-dean graduate of Brennan's school mentioned above admitted to me, after payment had been received, that her clients often required literally "half a year" of her services before experiencing a breakthrough. That is, that even with her four years of training and half a decade of experience giving healings, there was *no difference* between the fruits of her healing efforts and the effects of psychological counselling. In the latter, of course, the patient ultimately simply *gives himself permission* to feel suppressed/repressed emotional pain, etc., without any explicit assistance from the counselor in moving those blocked energies.

Astrology, homeopathy, ear candling, iridology, dowsing, thought transmission, remote viewing, Egyptian curses, crystals and Therapeutic Touch laying-on-of-hands have all been prone to failing to show their purported effects when they have been subjected to appropriately stringent experimental controls and/or statistical analysis. (Martin Gardner's *The New Age,* as well as his *Science: Good, Bad and Bogus* and *Fads and Fallacies in the Name of Science* are, in general, reasonable sources of disillusionment in this regard. The same is true of Milbourne Christopher's *Mediums, Mystics & the Occult,* and the archived exposés at www.skeptic.com and www.csicop.org.)

On the other hand, however, the same skeptics who perform or report those negative results have their own set of issues. As one interesting example: there is currently a large monetary prize being offered to anyone who can demonstrate parapsychological phenomena under laboratory conditions. When I attempted to interest the gentleman offering that prize in the claimed abilities of Barbara Ann Brennan and Ken Wilber, and suggested that he approach them in that regard, he first responded that he had "never even heard of either of them." When I wrote back a week later, informing him that Wilber was well-known to another transpersonal psychologist with whom the gentleman regularly worked, he responded with words to the effect that "these people (a) know about the challenge, and (b) simply refuse to apply," and expressed his disdain for the thought of having to do the work of "chasing after" them. (This was said while he was simultaneously very willingly expending significant energy chasing after persons who were *obvious* frauds, but who had made the mistake of provoking him.) As to how the skeptic in question could go from not having heard of these forefront-of-their-fields people one week, to be certain a mere seven days later that they were both guilty of *refusing* (his word) to put their claims to the test ... well, one could presumably at least rule out clairvoyance on his part!

The same man's web site states plainly that there is no evidence whatsoever that low frequency, low magnitude electromagnetic radiation can have negative effects on human beings, or that direct-current magnets may have beneficial effects. He is himself, however, completely unaware of Robert O. Becker's research, which proves those effects; and indeed dismissed that, when informed of it, as having "no parapsychological claim." (Becker has twice been nominated for the Nobel Prize in Medicine for his work with bioelectricity. No one who is unfamiliar with his work can claim to be properly informed about the effect of magnets and electromagnetism on living cells.) Appendix B in Rupert Sheldrake's *The Sense of Being Stared At* offers additional insight into the not-unbiased approach of affirmed skeptics to parapsychological phenomena.

Things do, however, get much worse than that:

> I was taught to lie and to get around the petty rules of the "unenlightened" in order to get favorable reports into the media.... We thought we weren't doing anything wrong because we were told it was often necessary to deceive the unenlightened to advance our guru's plan to save the world.
>
> —an ex-mantra meditator

One will, sadly, find this propensity for deceit in *every one* of the world's religions and spiritual organizations, simply because the typical psychology of the individuals involved, as leaders and followers, is essentially a constant. For the same reason, any enclave of devout followers/disciples is a cult—intolerant of competing ideas—waiting to happen. Whether these are followers of a great sage, great scientist, or great psychologist, makes no difference at all.

> At least a third of the population is what Eric Hoffer calls "true believers." They are joiners and followers, people who want to give away their power.
>
> —Dick Sutphen

One can hardly help but take the view, then, that for the overwhelmingly vast majority of the guru-figures in this world it is only the ignorance, gullibility and conformity of the disciples that makes the guru-figure look wise or deeply intuitive by comparison. It is equally clear that the percentage-wise understanding of detailed points of scripture and metaphysics, even among "advanced disciples" of contemporary sages, is no greater now than it was a century or a millennium ago. The only difference in esoteric understanding between now and then is that a number of contemporary sages, mediums and clairvoyants have given highly detailed and sensible expositions of the meaning of scripture and the structure of subtler levels of reality, which their disciples and readers have been able to learn from. Beyond that, the dearth of insight and corresponding degree of blundering is the same as it ever was, even among persons who can go into *samadhi* at will.

What then can one salvage from such situations, other than the reminder that "disillusion" means getting rid of one's illusions and seeing truth more clearly? Plus, a courage stemming from the knowledge that no job or relationship could possibly be worse than the lasting effects of following the world's abusive spiritual leaders. For one would simply walk away from it if it were even remotely as bad, without being accused of "letting God and Guru down."

And as to the problem that an "omniscient, Christ-conscious guru," even a departed one such as Jesus or Yogananda, would stand idly and irresponsibly by, while his "most advanced disciples" heap not merely "beneficial discipline" but *profound psychological abuse* on others, one can only conclude that God and Guru keep less of a keenly watchful and interventive eye on the day-to-day activities done "in their name" than one might hope. Of course, it is not the case that every business or organization which one has set in motion in this life need generally be watched over even after one's death. But when one has founded a spiritual organization filled with persons prayerfully and meditatively beseeching the Guru for intuitive and visionary guidance even after his death, what good excuse can there be for his not making that small effort? Particularly when it would be so *easy* to offer well-chosen words of advice or disapproval, in such visions, to prevent those "advanced" disciples from making gross mistakes "in his name." For those mistakes end up misleading, hurting, betraying and absolutely ruining the lives of others.

Indeed, such a master could easily convey those words of advice in prayer-beseeched vision *without infringing on the supplicant's free will;* a point which sets this fundamentally apart from the question as to why God allows suffering and evil to exist without stopping them, etc. Conversely, in the face of self-appointed "perfected beings," clergy sexual abuse and lies told "for God and Guru," the idea that any Ascended Master could be smilingly watching the sins committed in his name with amusement, ready to intervene "if necessary"—as some have unbelievably suggested—is at best foolishly naïve, and at worst a cruel joke.

With all of this, one can hardly avoid concluding that the bulk of the "guidance"—one could say well over ninety percent of *valid* guidance, never mind the ubiquitous, childish attempts to regard every green traffic light in rush hour as being an explicit and manifest answer to prayer—typically attributed to external Divine Beings rather comes from one's own higher self. Consider, for example, that the disciples of every charlatan who has ever paraded as a sage will have sworn that they were receiving boundless blessings, joy and guidance in their meditations and daily life, from that guru. That is, they could actually *"feel his blessings,"* even if he was in reality totally unequipped to so bless. (Cf. Bhagwan Shree Rajneesh, who reportedly once admitted, while sniffing laughing gas to get high, that he was "so relieved to not have to pretend to be enlightened any more.")

Given that, how much of even a genuine "guru's blessings" and spiritual experiences in general—or of the believed effect of prayers and thoughts on others, or of spiritual *and psychological* healings—must then be either purely imagined, or at best the product of people simply psychologically allowing themselves to feel in certain ways? In all likelihood, the overwhelmingly vast majority. It is not unlike the characters in *The Wizard of Oz,* who gained their courage, heart and intelligence *only through their own efforts,* not from any "blessings" on the part of the Wizard. On the "spiritual path," however, the credit for those transformations would all be unthinkingly given to the Wizard/Guru.

In any case, if merely appealing prayerfully and humbly to God and Guru were sufficient to guide one's intuition aright, whatever truth is contained in this book would have been put into print aeons ago. Conversely, if that were a prerequisite to a proper understanding of what is going on in the cosmos—or if intelligence, intellect or independence stood in the way of spiritual advancement, i.e., of developing one's intuition—or if the widespread misunderstandings about the nature of ego-death and its relation to spiritual progress were valid, my own attempts to understand and convey any high degree of truth in this book would have been doomed from the start. The task, indeed, should then have been left to persons without "big heads," who can go into bliss-filled *samadhi* or Self-level witnessing at will, where allegedly/laughably/dangerously Bliss = Wisdom = Genius = Intuition = Truth = God = No Ego.

As Ken Wilber notes in his *One Taste* journals, the point of transcending the psychologically defined ego is not to destroy it or the associated individuality in one's daily life—e.g., in meekly following where one is told to go, without thinking for oneself. No good can come out of killing one's independence or intellect, in spite of the criminal insistence, by spiritual authority figures of all stripes—having no small vested interest in their followers' unthinking obedience—that this is not only beneficial but allegedly absolutely *necessary* for spiritual advancement. *It is not!* Rather, we want to inhabit our waking egos *fully*, enthusiastically, with self-confidence and gusto, as manifestations of Spirit and necessary vehicles through which our own unique perceptions and experiences of higher truths can be shared with others.

Wilber himself is not only widely regarded as being the foremost theoretician in transpersonal/integral psychology, but claims to have realized a semi-permanent witnessing consciousness, including the measurable and measured ability to enter the breathless and brainwave-less state—that is, the state with no alpha, beta or theta-waves, but maximum delta activity. That realization has come in spite of the fact that he has been neither celibate nor a teetotaler throughout his life, and has not minced profanities in at least a few of his books, or avoided popular music in his daily life. Nor has he "killed his ego" in the dangerously simplistic way that Eastern religion is generally taken as dictating is supposedly necessary for Self-realization—for example, in humbly/ meekly "knowing one's place," and leaving the "important" work for those "more spiritually advanced" and "God-inspired" than oneself. Neither was that significant spiritual progress made by meditating "sixteen hours a day"—as some yogis (e.g., Sivananda) baselessly claim is necessary in order for one to realize God—or gotten via the "blessings of a guru." All of that makes it almost painfully obvious that none of those forms of abstinence or obeisance, much less the confusion of a low self-image with the killing of one's ego, can be regarded as beneficial, much less necessary, for high spiritual realization.

Putting all of those glaring problems aside, however, the aforementioned (potential) effect of meditation working to produce positive transformations in one's daily psychology is true even if the technique in question seems on the surface to be simply an attempt to absorb one's mind in one-pointed concentration on a particular and seemingly-arbitrary mental concept in visualization or inner audibilization. Indeed, if the chakric seals control energy exchange between the layers of the auric field, their opening must allow a less restricted exchange of energy or *information* between these levels, amounting to a conscious integration of one's lower (i.e., personality) and higher (trans-personal) natures. One aspect of that, then, would certainly be a radically increased intuition and abiding Joy in one's daily life. (The fact is that, whenever we bring the peaceful effects of meditation into our daily lives, we are "grounding" those energies.) These seven seals are the "seven veils" keeping us ignorant of our true spiritual nature, which must be removed to denude the soul hidden behind them.

It is easy to find case histories of repressed childhood pain being cathartically released through the practice only of one-pointed "content" meditations and techniques of life-force control. For the fact is that any increase in the intensity or frequency of energy flowing in one's subtle bodies will knock loose psychic energy blockages which were too threatening to be consciously felt at the time they were formed. And these increases in energy flow occur particularly in conjunction with the opening of the chakras. Thus, techniques of meditation which work with the chakras and the energies flowing in the spine again work not only to elevate one's state of consciousness, but also to integrate the subconscious into conscious awareness, and thus transform one's daily personality.

That transformation in one's daily consciousness of course again comes, not only through the significant integration of one's higher and lower selves, but also (and earlier) through the encouraging of the proper spinning of the chakras and the associated undoing of one's psychological projecting. It comes further through the effect, via the increase in frequency and intensity of the energies flowing in the subtle bodies, of moving the stagnant energy blockages that constitute the repressed unconscious. (Just as in our previous discussion of good and evil, the opening of the chakras in spiritual awakening is the time-reversal of their closing, and "clamping down" on energy flows is the time-reversal of releasing them.)

The deficiency of energy in various parts of the physical, emotional and mental bodies in the suppression of healthy energy flows *sounds* similar to the withdrawal of life energy into the spine in deep meditation, but it is fundamentally different. (That withdrawal occurs in *all* deep content meditation, not only when techniques of life-force control are being utilized.) If one were to assert that the latter control of the life force was unhealthy, he would need to concurrently contend that *sleep* was similarly detrimental to one's psychological balance. In the same way, if spending eight hours every night in sleep is not condemned as an "unbalanced" unawareness of the body, how could one assert without prejudice that it might be selfish, "unhealthy" or conducive to imbalance for one to spend a comparable amount of time in *samadhi,* obviating the need for sleep?

All techniques of meditation used toward realizing the soul necessarily work with the subtle structure and attributes of the astral and causal bodies, whether implicitly or explicitly. The explicit use of this structure, then, is to be commended, not denigrated, for it is both more efficient, and produces more predictable and reproducible results, than do the implicit techniques. Indeed, the Buddhists, too, speak of the depth of the "space experience" as an indication of one's spiritual advancement. (That is, a depth where space is not merely experienced visually, but is felt in one's own consciousness.) Thus, expanded states of consciousness again cannot be denigrated as "only" altered states, for expansion has no limit other than infinity. Only in "confined" views of the nature of mind and consciousness could a non-literal "expansion" have nothing to do with intuition and higher realization.

In case histories presented in Sannella's *The Kundalini Experience,* we find reports of "a sense of being in touch with an unshakable core, a center, that is unaffected by all the ups and downs of everyday life," which "gives a sense of oneness with all life, and from that comes a love and a joy of existence" and a feeling of being in touch with "the Source of all things." We also find records there of a "dramatic strengthening of personality structure, character, and ways of dealing with the world"; of withdrawn and reserved persons blossoming into "secure, intact and fun-loving" ones; and of "emotional problems and unfinished incidents seeming to find solutions very rapidly and at great depth" in meditation.

Those positive changes, of course, are due simply to the increase and balancing of energy flows, on many layers of the aura, effected by the awakened kundalini energy. Thus, while in most practical cases it is indeed true that "neurotics who begin meditating will simply become more relaxed neurotics," that does *not* mean that meditation is inherently incapable of solving one's psychological problems.

Now, the denigration of logic which one frequently encounters in contemporary spirituality is every bit as much a psychological defense as is the avoidance of emotion. That is, the psychological dynamic is the same, only being applied on a slightly different level. For it is obviously much easier to go through life behaving selfishly, and justifying these actions as being the product of "following one's feelings"—where these are equated with intuition—than it is to trace the detailed long-term effects of one's actions on oneself and others, and to modify one's behavior accordingly. The latter course would indeed demand that one consciously *accept responsibility* for the effects of one's actions, this inevitably resulting in a certain amount of "unpleasant" restricting of the satisfaction of one's personal desires, in the hope of effecting a greater good.

Conversely, it is obvious that merely "following one's feelings" demands no such discrimination or conscious acceptance of responsibility in the tracing of the detailed effects which one's actions have on others. For there the feeling itself is sufficient as both justification and reward for one's actions. Indeed, each one of us regularly *behaves* selfishly, without *feeling* selfish. Or, if we feel selfish at all, it is usually from bringing some amount of *reasoning* to bear on the situation.

Further, each one of us has *irrational* fears and oversensitivities, which are completely "valid" and "inarguable" as a basis for action if taken only as *feelings,* without being subjected to rational analysis. But needless to say, just because we are behaving illogically, in "following our [irrational] feelings" or otherwise, does *not* mean that we have "transcended linear thinking," much less that we are "following our intuition"! How reliable are those feelings, then, as a guide to right behavior?

Of course, the following of *genuine and deep* intuition, even without the conscious tracing of the relevant causes and effects, would result in exactly the same unselfish behavior as is dictated by the clear and informed use of reason. But rarely are one's feelings sufficiently unclouded by personal desires and psychological quirks to qualify as being impartially guided by intuition, even when the causal body is adequately refined for this intuition to be *deep.* Plus, even if one's intuition is highly developed, it is still fully possible for those subtle feelings to be overwhelmed and misled by the widely-accepted proclamations of "experts." That, indeed, is particularly a problem when one is considering ideas which are not in one's field of professional expertise (so that one assumes too readily that those experts *can't all be wrong!).*

Any suppression on the lower levels of our auric fields will act to prevent our higher, spiritual energies from being grounded—e.g., from manifesting in our daily lives. Thus, the fear of reason (and the abdication of responsibility for the effects of one's actions which commonly accompanies this) will result in a lack of grounding just as surely as will the avoidance of emotion. Indeed, one cannot help but wonder if the emphasis in New Age circles on the grounding of one's energies via sexuality and emotionalism is not perhaps an overcompensation for the avoidance of rational thought. That is, just as others "hide in the intellect" to avoid emotional pain and sexuality, it is equally possible to avoid the responsibility of the intellectual level by hiding in the emotional and physical bodily levels, which again demand no accountability at all. If one then loses touch with one's body via the former hiding-in-the-intellect, however, that loss of feeling comes from the dynamic of avoidance, not from the use of the intellect itself!

Note further that yogic texts speak of the presence of chakras below the coccygeal—i.e., existing in the legs. Thus, just as one can have an active intellect without these energies automatically grounding through the second and first spinal chakras, it seems completely reasonable that one could be emotionally and sexually energetic—which is often taken as evidence of being "grounded"—without this producing an actual grounding of one's energies down through the minor chakras in the legs, into the earth. In this case, bringing particular energies into one's waking awareness would not be strictly synonymous with grounding them, for one can have the former presence (as in the condition of having an active rational mind in one's daily life) without necessarily having the latter grounding.

Of course, it does seem likely that increased activity in the lower two major spinal chakras would be more likely to have *some* actual grounding effect—simply for being closer to the legs and their minor chakras—than would activity on the level of the linear mental-rational third chakra. This, however, would still be consistent with the proposal that if one were not psychologically/subconsciously resisting the grounding of energies through one's legs—particularly in terms of not wanting to psychologically "stand on one's own two feet"—one would not need to overcompensate for this with such a high level of emotional and sexual energy in order to *feel* grounded. That is, in order to have those latter energies *overwhelm* the simultaneous resistance.

If the relation between abdicating responsibility and the lack of independence in not standing on one's own two feet is not obvious, consider that the blaming of others for our problems entails a deep psychological dependence on them. For if the enemy were not readily at hand, the view of oneself as being an innocent bystander in the world could not be sustained.

Of course, the alternative common pole of human behavior is likely the confusing of the activities of the first and second chakras in one's daily life, which is said by some contemporary healers to lead to the equating of power with sexuality, and to the defining of one's self-image on the basis of external accomplishments. If this is accurate, it would presumably be related to the production of "strong fields in the legs and thighs, with uneven energy in the body," as observed by Valerie Hunt.

It is further not surprising that persons who denigrate rational thought, mathematics and technology have usually felt somewhat intimidated by these. That is, they have been caused psychological pain by their presence, and so have naturally searched for ways to avoid that pain, from childhood onward. Thus, they have grown to be certain of the limitations of reason, without having mastered it; blaming this tool, rather than the workman, for a job poorly done. Not coincidentally, this tactic allows them to feel *superior* to others who "think too linearly," and are thus supposedly "more fragmented" (i.e., less spiritual or wholistic) than they are. Such a view, of course, cannot be argued with, if for no reason other than that it takes any attempt at logical argument to be "part of the problem."

In the end, the belief that rational thought and intuition are mutually exclusive is a tremendously *fragmented* and dualistic point of view, which again derives from a *lack* of reason—and of intuition—not from "too much" of it. The idea that "you are either part of the problem or part of the solution" to the ecological crisis is another fine example of such fragmented thinking. For we all contribute, to varying degrees, to *both* the problems and the solutions in this world.

CHAPTER XIV

SUMMARY

THE PHRASE "THE CONSCIOUSNESS OF LIGHT" encapsulates the truism that velocities approaching the velocity of light reflect the behavior of levels of consciousness advancing toward the highest state of God-Light, of infinite subjective time and mass, and so omnipresent. Just as Tao-Truth descends to become absolutely distinguishable *yin* and *yang,* light can differentiate into matter and anti-matter. Conversely, the resolution of all possible dualities (cf. the meeting of matter/anti-matter pairs of all possible energies) produces a sphere of white light. The simplest truly white signal is the impulse, disclosing that omnipresence and the sphere of truly white Light imply each other. Further, in this Ocean we have free choice in proportion to the degree to which we unfold/raise/attune our consciousness to the Divine to manifest the limitless perfection of God already within us. The rhythmic nature of consciousness and matter then follows from

(i) Om as arising from the "beating of a Cosmic Drum";

(ii) Om as deriving ultimately from the impulsive "knocking" at the door between Spirit and creation;

(iii) Om as the sound of One Hand clapping;

(iv) the vocal vowel incantation of "o" and subsequent "mmm" closing of this aperture, modulating a sound of a certain pitch or rate of oscillation, in chanting "Om"; this implying a similar behavior in the most basic mechanism of consciousness;

(v) the "electrical spike" character of the nervous system (and the relation of the subtle nervous system and its chakras to spiritual evolution or the expansion of consciousness, plus "As above, so below");

(vi) the averred motion picture basis of creation;

(vii) the cosmos being a living, *breathing*-as-an-act-of-energy-distribution entity: all matter is consciousness in varying degrees of spiritual evolution (so that light, too, is consciousness);

(viii) this cosmic entity having a heartbeat: when the breath is calmed, the amplitudes of the time-varying pressure waves produced by blood leaving the heart assume a shape nearly identical to the "bouncing" oscillation of the bandpass-filtered impulse. Thus, such rhythmically re-initiated decaying impulsive oscillation is implicitly associated with body and blood in all manner of living creatures. The brain sends a rhythmic series of electric pulses to the heart. Each such spike causes the heart's muscles to contract, forcing pressure waves of blood out through elastic arteries and so producing an oscillating and decaying-in-amplitude-with-the-passage-of-time response to this semi-impulse. The Universal Breathing is thus also a Cosmic Heartbeat; and

(ix) Om as arising from the "swinging of a Cosmic Pendulum." In the words of Kabir: "Held by the cords of love, the swing of the Ocean of Joy sways to and fro; and a mighty sound breaks forth in song." Further, in an "Ocean of Joy," this Bliss cannot be the product merely of any internal self-stimulation of one's pleasure centers, or temporary suspension of conflicting drives. Likewise, Shankara's designation of God as beginningless and endless Existence-Consciousness-Bliss, and the idea that the causal body is woven of wisdom and Bliss, would not be valid if this Bliss were explicable in terms of synaptic functioning. Indeed, if the experience of Bliss were so explicable, it would be a fairly selfish pursuit, certainly not ever-existent or "beginningless and endless," and having no obvious relation to the realization of one's unity with the Ocean of Consciousness. Nor would this Bliss be ever-new or free from growing stale, or be experienced via intuition. Thus, there *must* be more to it than that.

> From joy does spring all this creation, by joy it is maintained, towards joy does it progress and into joy does it enter.
>
> —Rabindranath Tagore

> Brahman is Life, Brahman is Joy,
> Brahman is the Void.
> Joy, verily that is the same as the Void,
> The Void, verily that is the same as Joy.
>
> —Chandogya Upanishad

> Perceive the undivided, eternal, blissful Self everywhere! Perceive the entire universe in the Self, like an image in a mirror.
>
> —Hemalekha

> On the vast canvas of the Self the picture of the manifold worlds is painted by the Self itself. And that Supreme Self [i.e., Spirit], seeing but itself, enjoys great delight.
>
> —Shankara

> He whose self is unattached to external contacts and findeth joy in the Self, having the self harmonized with the Eternal by yoga, enjoys imperishable Bliss.
>
> —Bhagavad Gita

Om as the "noise of many waters" implies that this sound is also responsible for the "birth," maintenance, and "death"—or rising and falling—of all the transitory oceanic wave-forms of creation. Further, as God is, in Cusa's terms, "the coincidence of opposites," consciousness united with infinite God must exemplify the reconciliation of oppositional states. That is, it must, for one, be both immanent and transcendent—being all creation's waves, and transcending relative space and time through full union with transcendent God. (Again, that which is transcendent, or "formless and without quality," fills all space—as water "fills," or *is,* all the ocean. But that Transcendent only becomes manifest and visible as immanent creation, taking on qualities and form, when it vibrates, as waves, in the sound of Om. Being "formless" thus does *not* mean simply that it lacks human conceptualizations of boundaries, in its supraintellectual true nature.) This highest state of consciousness, being one with infinite continuous Reality, must further attain to the "sphere of circumference nowhere." It must likewise move with infinite velocity, and so be present everywhere at once in a state of complete rest; and must implicitly contain within itself all possible frequencies of vibration, or a true whiteness.

If any "bouncing" sphere of consciousness is to pass or "fit snugly" through the door between creation and transcendent Spirit, this door too must be spherical; and points are spheres of zero radius. Alternatively, in order for the planar wavefronts "entering" creation in the primordial impulses to be "diffracted" into perfect spheres, the apertures, or doors, through which they squeeze must be ideal points, at the centers of the resulting spheres; this follows from elementary mathematical laws of wave behavior. We must further be able to speak of rippling spheres of consciousness as "light," in order to invoke the hologram and special relativity analogies. Also, the progressive dilation of subjective time in higher states of consciousness, in accord with its lower reflection in the time dilations of special relativity, must occur on the same level on which our conscious "mass" increases and becomes infinite. In that state, one is travelling at the infinite "velocity of Light," for one's sphere of consciousness having an infinite resonant frequency. (Dilated subjective time, by itself, would still be *linear*. But that dilation and experience of higher levels of reality evidently opens up access to a non-linear experience of "time.") And the attainment of such "infinite mass" in omnipresence implies movement at infinite velocities: you cannot get to infinity at any finite rate of expansion.

Scholars are quick to point out that there is actually no word in the Sanskrit language for "soul," and that *Atman* should thus always be translated as Spirit or Self. However, the yogic use of "Soul/soul" again refers to the Self as an *"individualized* spark of Spirit," in which case Self is not strictly synonymous with (Supreme) Spirit.

It has further been noted, with some justification, that *Atman*/Self/Spirit are precise terms, while "soul is a word which means everything, and hence nothing, to English-speakers." The same, however, can certainly be said of "spirit" (referring variously to astral-level ghosts or "disembodied souls," causal-level consciousness, transcendent Self as individualized Spirit, or transcendent Spirit even prior to individualization) and "self" (lower, higher, or transcendent?). Further, *"Atman"* too means very little to most English-speakers, so that, until we are clear on the structure involved, no amount of haggling over definitions will clarify the issue.

To unambiguously categorize the levels of physical body, mind, consciousness and self-awareness requires four distinct terms (and a fifth to indicate Reality prior to the individualization of self-awareness), referring to the physical, astral, causal and transcendent, respectively. Thus, even the common nomenclature of "body, mind and spirit" will not suffice, even were we regularly clear on what these terms refer to.

Given all this, any precise and tenable explanation of the basic nature of creation, purporting to be in accord with the intuitive perceptions of the sages and so to give a valid explanation of the nature of higher states of consciousness, must be able to explain, or provide naturally for

(i) a meaningful and deep application of the widely-expounded nature of creation as waves on/of the Infinite Ocean of Consciousness;

(ii) why the "sphere of circumference nowhere" should be associated with the highest state of consciousness, of infinite resonant frequency;

(iii) the nature of Om as arising from the beating of a Cosmic Drum, in the Dance of Shiva;

(iv) the cosmic motion picture (in the sky) nature of creation (with its implicit continuous re-creation of matter of all degrees of subtlety);

(v) *maya* as a cosmic structural "measuring" principle, rather than being related merely to human conceptualization;

(vi) the mechanism by which God "creates by the power of speech," i.e., of how creation is "kept in store" by the Word of God (or of how "God said..." or "hath declared");

(vii) why the ideal point should deserve scriptural mention, as the meeting ground of the manifest and unmanifest states;

(viii) the progressive dilation of subjective time and free choice, in higher states of consciousness;

(ix) the meaningful transcendence of time and all dualities in literal omnipresence, and of higher states of consciousness being, literally, *expanded* states;

(x) the mechanism of intuition's ability to experience reality-in-itself;

(xi) the precise and meaningful manners in which the behaviors of consciousness and mind are reflected in the behavior of physical matter, as measurable in the physicists' laboratories, and the related condensation of physical out of astral out of causal levels of reality, in a way eminently more meaningful than that in which human conceptualizations may cause "objects" to "precipitate" out of the sensory gestalt;

(xii) the fact that the Absolute is both the highest level of consciousness, and the Source and Ground of all lower states; and

(xiii) good and evil being absolutely distinguishable "reflections of the same Light," and no mere subjective products of human conceptualization. Just because good and evil are transcended in a state which is pure awareness, without conceptual content, does not mean that good and evil are *only* concepts, existing solely in the human mind. The same is true of time and space. Of course, we certainly do not want to confuse our conceptual representations of reality with reality-in-itself, but should rather always keep in mind that whenever we speak of "space" or of any other attribute on any level of reality, we really mean "the attribute/ emanation of God which we conceptualize as 'space.'" But neither should we blindly assume that our concepts, particularly as they relate to mathematics, are merely arbitrary, precluding consideration of them being accurate reflections of Nature.

The bandpass-filtered impulsive structure of human and all lower consciousness as the basis of intuition is again explicitly advocated by Itzhak Bentov, on the grounds of his own meditative experiences. And the "bouncing" (in proportion to its resonant frequency) nature of consciousness, in this application of the "cosmic motion picture" structure, follows inexorably and inarguably from a properly detailed consideration of Bentov's proposed process. Thus, the only question in this context is whether the conjoining of this characteristic with the sagely-averred nature of the ideal point as the doorway between the manifest and transcendent unmanifest states is valid.

In either case, however, there can be absolutely no question that the idea of an expandable "sphere of consciousness" is meant to be taken fully literally, whether or not it "bounces." Further, if the association of that point with transcendence were not valid, then how to account for the transcendence of duality or freedom of choice in other than an "all or nothing" way? And what significance to ascribe to the points in time when Bentov's "observer"—which he again shows graphically as being spherical and centered in the brain, and which again *must* "bounce," from the mathematics of the situation—switches from contraction to expansion, and so is momentarily at absolute rest?

The possibility of expanding the boundaries of the individualized wave to realize its unity with the Infinite Ocean in the state of literal conscious omnipresence further implies a voluminous nature of consciousness. That is to say, if one acknowledges that the Consciousness of God is omnipresent and infinite, and that it is possible for us to realize our unity with this Consciousness, no inexorably "confined" nature of mind or consciousness can be reasonably asserted. Likewise, the basis of all matter in the sound of Om as the beating of a cosmic drum, the nature of creation as a cosmic motion picture and the aforementioned God's-Will-sustained nature of this matter as waves on/of the Ocean of Consciousness are not open to argument, having been directly perceived by genuine sages, and expounded *in these specific terms*.

Thus, only the particular structural interpretation proposed herein, not the wording of these descriptions, can be opened to debate: these specific phrased descriptions are no mere invention of this humble author's imagination! but are rather part of the established vocabulary of mysticism. There is neither need nor license to allow that they be "bent" to fit into narrower views of the cosmos. Accordingly, no explanation of the most basic nature of creation and consciousness which does not inherently and naturally include these attributes can be correct even to a generous approximation, much less reasonably claim to be in accord with the mystics' vision of creation. That is, given these detailed sagely perceptions, any attempt to provide a sensible, meaningful and precise reconciliation of the principles of physical science with those of meditation-based religion must begin with the recognition that all phenomena are waves in the Ocean of Consciousness, making ample allowance for the possibility of conscious omnipresence.

Having said all this with regard to the structure of the cosmos, however, and recognized that every aspect of relative creation, interpenetrating or not, must ultimately have a mathematically-describable component, we nevertheless find that, ironically, the same "As above, so below" reflection of patterns of structure that allows us to guess about the basic nature of creation by "playing on words" or metaphors, also opens the door for confusion. For, when similar structures exist on different levels of creation, it can be difficult to discern which of those levels, exactly, a specific reference to structure is intended to designate. That, of course, is even aside from the more common reductionism of taking similarities in structure or language on different levels as referring to one and the same level, usually that addressed by quantum physics.

In any case, it is undeniable that the underlying unity of science and religion goes inestimably deeper than could ever be expressed in terms of vague ideas regarding interpenetration or interdependence. Indeed, that unity goes deeper even than a shared reliance on the reproducibility of experience, to common patterns of structure—which is what "As above, so below" *means*. Thus, Galileo's statement that "philosophy is written in this grand book—I mean the universe" is very true: religion is not separable from the structure of the cosmos, reflected in the structure of human consciousness.

According to Posidonius, physics and theology are two aspects of one knowledge, since God is immanent throughout Nature as well as infinitely transcendent. Science, therefore, deals with the material body of which God is the living spirit.

—Joseph Campbell,
The Masks of God: Occidental Mythology

The scientist does not study Nature because it is useful; he studies it because he delights in it, and he delights in it because it is beautiful. If Nature were not beautiful, it would not be worth knowing, and if Nature were not worth knowing, life would not be worth living.

—Henri Poincaré

It is my inner conviction that the development of science seeks in the main to satisfy the longing for pure knowledge.

—Albert Einstein

Happy is he who bears a god within, and who obeys it. The ideals of art, of science, are lighted by reflection from the infinite.

—Louis Pasteur

Hence, also, the physical sciences, which now are held in so much repute, and everywhere draw to themselves a singular admiration, because of the wonderful discoveries made in them, would not only take no harm from a restoration of the philosophy of the ancients, but would derive great protection from it. For the fruitful exercise and increase of these sciences it is not enough that we consider facts and contemplate Nature. When the facts are well known we must rise higher, and give our thoughts with great care to understanding the nature of corporeal things, as well as to the investigation of the laws which they obey, and of the principles from which spring their order, their unity in variety, and their common likeness in diversity. It is marvelous what power and light and help are given to these investigations by Scholastic philosophy, if it be wisely used ... there is no contradiction, truly so called, between the certain and proved conclusions of recent physics, and the philosophical principles of the Schools.

—Pope Leo XIII (1879)

If at any time we feel that there is a conflict [between religion and science], we may well be sure that either we have misread our scriptures or misunderstood the Nature around us or blundered in both. We cannot possibly have understood both aright and yet found unreconcilable antagonism between the two.

—Jagadguru Shankaracharya Bharati Krishna Tirtha

Galileo, too, considered that since the Bible and the laws of physics were both true, there could be no actual contradiction between them—that any errors must lie in our *understanding* of their truths.

> Next to us the grandest laws are continually being executed. Next to us is, not the workman whom we have hired, with whom we love to talk, but the Workman whose work we are.
>
> —H. D. Thoreau

> 'Tis not the place but the state which makes heaven and happiness. For God is alike in all places, He is substantially omnipresent, and as much present in the lowest Hell as in the highest heaven, but the enjoyment of his blessings may be various according to the variety of places, and according to this variety he is said to be more in one place and less in another, and where he is most enjoyed and most obeyed, there is heaven and his Tabernacle and Kingdom in the language of the Prophets.
>
> —Isaac Newton

> All this is immutable Brahman. Brahman is before, behind, to the right, to the left, above, and below all. This whole universe is an **expansion** of that highest Brahman.
>
> —Mundaka Upanishad

CHAPTER XV

CONCLUSIONS

THE CONSONANCE OF UNIVERSAL BEHAVIOR with the inner perceptions of the mystics is not merely coincidental. And the inescapable conclusion of their harmony is this: deep meditation opens the door to a level of consciousness inclusive of but transcending all finite states.

Theories regarding the nature of the physical world are testable through physical experiments. The "theories" of consciousness expounded by the mystics of all ages are also verifiable, but not through external experiments. Rather, the nature and behavior of consciousness can be known only through the performance of the appropriate experiments in the expansion of consciousness. That is, through concentration used to know God, which is meditation.

Meditation has sometimes been reasonably spoken of as "scientific." This, however, is not meant to imply that a knowledge of higher mathematics is required in its practice! Rather, what is meant is that, just as physical experiments performed with careful attention to the requisite techniques of experimentation will always produce the same results, independent of the preconceived beliefs of the experimenter, so also the meditative experiments in the expansion of consciousness, when performed with due attention and devotion, will produce the same results (in the expansion of consciousness) regardless of one's system of beliefs. The capacity for the conscious realization of Infinity is built into the most basic nature of each one of us, and needs nothing more for its cultivation than that we *be still,* in mind and body.

We can again derive numerous "conclusions" of the sages from fundamental philosophical principles outlined by the same individuals, with reference to basic mathematical principles. This fact must, at the very least, establish the philosophies of the East, with their assertion that consciousness is the fundamental reality at the basis of all creation, as a tenable and logical alternative to Western philosophical materialism. Further, the fact that we can develop explanations of observed physical phenomena from the elemental and archetypal principles of the Oriental systems of thought is strong and essentially undeniable indication that the Eastern tenets have their origin in a means of knowledge acquisition transcendent of the methods of physical science. That is, they must have their basis in the direct conscious experience of Reality. For those Eastern principles were enunciated well before the Western scientific discovery of their physical manifestations.

Were it not for the true meditative origin of these precepts, there would be no necessary relation between the conclusions drawn logically/ mathematically from them, and the behavior of the physical world. And, given the demonstrated correspondences between the structure and behavior of the material level of reality, and the mystical perceptions, it can hardly be disputed that such a relationship does exist, and is not the product of mere "picking and choosing." Of course, until one can explain *everything,* there must be some implicit picking and choosing, from both directions, in purporting correspondences between physical science and mystical perceptions. But still, there are varying *degrees* of this, in inverse proportion to one's understanding of cosmic structure.

These mathematical correspondences must also render absolutely untenable and illogical the suggestion that meditation is nothing more than a form of self-hypnosis—that its revelations are merely "what you want them to be." Of course, visions and the like *are* frequently little more than the product of one's own imagination; but they are not *inherently* nothing more than that.

Lacking the precise language of mathematics, it would be very difficult to objectively and forcefully demonstrate that creation can be both a "cosmic motion picture" and arise from the "beating of a Cosmic Drum." For, to the casual eye, what similarities exist between motion pictures and drumming? Further, one could not convincingly argue that this structure or body of God has anything to do with the lower reflected human nervous and circulatory systems; as well as with knocking, with breath, with mouths and words, with true cloud-whiteness, clockwork-like pendulums, and divine Hands clapping. But, given a simple application of the quantitative language of mathematics, the equivalence of these various structural descriptions becomes obvious.

Therefore, the principles of Eastern philosophy and the yogic science cannot be regarded as merely "arbitrarily assumed doctrines." Consequently, the truly objective person, committed to an unbiased appraisal of both Eastern and Western philosophies, cannot dismiss untested the claims made by the mystics regarding the nature of reality. It is not reasonable to reject the Oriental philosophies on the supposed basis that "the best evidence of science indicates that they are not true." Not only is this bias rooted in the preconceived philosophical materialism of physical science, it is in any case quite ridiculously false. For, as we have seen, the "best evidence of science" corroborates/reflects wonderfully (to a necessarily limited degree) the inner perceptions of the mystics.

Further, no scripture is "so vague that it could be taken to mean almost anything." Religious texts are always founded on the highest precision, with well-intended, specific (though often multiple) meanings intended to be conveyed—"multiple," in the sense that all scriptures support valid physical, mental and spiritual interpretations. This must not, however, be freely taken as indicating that any particular symbol may actually give rise to diverse but authentic interpretations on any one of those levels. When a variety of interpretations of a given scriptural allegory occurs, this typically derives from a lack of consideration of the precise structure involved. That is, such diversity generally arises from ignoring, as unimportant "filler," everything which does not mesh with one's preferred reading. ("If there are many treatments for a disease, it is because no one knows much about that disease"—medical aphorism.)

Scriptural references to "sleep," for example, may mean either being held in sway by the *maya*-trance of delusion, or the awakening from this delusion in the "conscious sleep" of *samadhi*. Exactly the same thing is true of "death." In the same way, the Bhagavad Gita's Kamadeva—"Desire; the god of love"—although popularly equated with the Roman Cupid and the Greek goddess Eros, represents "the first awakening desire of the One Spirit to become many." Thus, without considering *every detail* of the context involved, one could easily give exactly the opposite interpretation to that which was intended.

Now, puns involve plays on words, or the "working" of an idea on more than one level. This working of an idea on more than one level is again a very metaphorical ("above/below" or "self-similar") characteristic. That is, "As above, so below" correspondences, as has been previously noted, generally take the form of metaphors (e.g., "creation is waves on the surface of the Infinite Ocean"). And Nature is built on "As above, so below," or the self-similar reflection of archetypal structure on many different levels of creation, from highest causal to lowest physical. Thus, puns are (potentially, at least) the highest, not the lowest, form of humor: they have the greatest capacity to express the intelligence of God enfolded in the self-similar universal structure.

Metaphors, which are again the language of Nature, establish non-logical connections across levels of creation. The "getting" of any pun, as with the understanding of scriptural metaphors, requires a re-establishment of the non-logical connections enfolded in the pun or metaphor. It should in any case be clear that puns cannot be the lowest form of humor, in that vaudevillian pies-in-the-face, or physical humor with no context, are obviously a less intelligent form of comedy than one which requires some mental acuity to "get."

Additionally, the alternative comedy of dramatic irony, sarcasm, satire and parody most often involves implicit criticism—laughing *at* childlike naïveté rather than *with* it—a characteristic decidedly in discord with seeing the world "through the eyes of a child." (The attributes admirable in children—as in Mark 10:15, "Whosoever shall not receive the kingdom of God as a little child, he shall not enter therein"—are their trust, sense of wonder, curiosity, absence of guile and cynicism, and their optimism and focus on the good in the world, not their pre-rational, non-conceptual "freedom from language.") And significantly, W. Thomas Wolfe notes, in *And the Sun is Up,* that "around the time of the kundalini awakening, the subject will begin to notice a feeling a buoyancy, lightness of attitude, lightness of mind and body. This can cause him to develop giggling spells or to **pun incessantly.** It is as though a part of his being has been banished from the basic being, thereby making him 'lighter.'"

When you are clearing a chakra, with your left hand over it, you may feel "bumps" in the energy flow, or feel as if little energy-things are popping against the palm of your left hand. Often, you feel as if something has been physically relaxed under your hand, or you may sense emotional feelings being released, or you may sense a "smile" coming out of the chakra—clear energy always has a smile in it.
—Ric A. Weinman, *Your Hands Can Heal*

Now, it is not the long life that is worth living, but the one rich in the gathering of wisdom. What is tragic is when old men die suffocated in the delusion that there is nothing more to the universe than that which is perceptible through the five senses, and that the interpretations of science and philosophy which deny the potential divinity of humankind are in any way noble pursuits worth devoting one's life to. In the words of Albert Einstein,

Science without religion is lame, and religion without science is blind.

I maintain that cosmic religious feeling is the strongest and noblest incitement to scientific research.

You will hardly find one among the profounder sort of scientific minds without a peculiar religious feeling of his own.

Of course, this pairing occurs exactly because "physicists' intuition" and thoughts of genius come from the same causal level as does one's subtle, inner intuitive "religious feeling" as to the existence of a greater Intelligence and purpose to the universe.

I want to know how God created this world. I am not interested in this or that phenomenon, in the spectrum of this or that element. I want to know His thoughts; the rest are details.

Einstein was of course greatly influenced by Gandhi's philosophy of non-violence, considering the Mahatma to be "the greatest man of our age." Albert and the Nobel Prize-winning Bengali poet Rabindranath Tagore also had a well-publicized dialogue concerning their respective views of reality. He was familiar with Buddhism through the writings of Schopenhauer, and devoutly believed in a central order to the cosmos.

In addition to Einstein, many of the founders of the quantum theory of physics—developed in the 1920s and 30s—had active interests in Eastern philosophy; among them,

- Erwin Schrödinger (Nobel Prize in Physics—NPP—1933)—developer, of course, of the Schrödinger equation, and the first person to suggest that genes could be viewed as concrete physical information carriers whose physical structure corresponds to a succession of elements in a hereditary code script—had read the Upanishads.

- Werner Heisenberg (NPP 1932)—known for his formulation of the Heisenberg Uncertainty Principle—was aware of and interested in the apparent similarities between quantum mechanics and the Eastern religions. He also met with Tibet's Lama Govinda on one occasion, and spent some time in India as a guest of Rabindranath Tagore.

- Wolfgang Pauli (NPP 1945, 1989)—who originated the Pauli Exclusion Principle, which determines the arrangement of electrons in atoms, and who collaborated with Carl Jung in the development of the theory of synchronicity—stated that

  contrary to the strict division of the activity of the human spirit into separate departments—a division prevailing since the nineteenth century—I consider the ambition of overcoming opposites, including also a synthesis embracing both rational understanding and the mystical experience of unity, to be the mythos, spoken or unspoken, of our present day and age.

- Niels Bohr (NPP 1922)—developer of the classical quantum theory of atomic structure, or the first application of the idea that electrons move in specific discrete orbits around the nucleus; an idea which laid the foundation for modern atomic and nuclear physics—when knighted, chose to include on his coat of arms the Taoist *yin/yang* symbol, representing the "dynamic unity of polar opposites." Prior to World War II, Bohr's Institute in Copenhagen had become the world center for atomic physics.

These four, along with Einstein, are absolute "giants" in the history of physics—not a textbook is published at any level in the field without drawing explicitly on their work. And, although they are probably the "biggest names" in science to have voiced genuine appreciations for Eastern philosophy, this by no means exhausts the list:

- Nikolai Tesla, the inventor of the alternating-current electrical generator among his 700 patents, is said to have had an interest in the Vedas.

- J. Robert Oppenheimer—leader of the Manhattan Project, in the development of the atom bomb during World War II, whose fame after the war approached Einstein's—learned Sanskrit in order to study the Bhagavad Gita and other East Indian works in their original text.

- The physicist and astronomer Sir Arthur Stanley Eddington likewise found no antagonism between religion and science:

  The idea of a universal Mind or Logos would be, I think, a fairly plausible inference from the present state of scientific theory; at least it is in harmony with it.

Neither Eddington nor any of the above physicists considered physics to have *proved* the validity of mystical perceptions. Nor did any of them recognize the applicability of "As above, so below" beyond the idea of "unbroken wholeness" both in the physical and supraphysical realms. They simply found nothing irreconcilable between science and religion.

- Max Planck (NPP 1918)—the man who first proposed the existence of discrete "quanta" of energy, and the originator of the idea that when electrons in an atom change energy states, they do so via an instantaneous "quantum leap" from one orbit to another, without passing through the intervening space—asserted:

  Religion and natural science are fighting a joint battle in a second, never-ending crusade against skepticism and dogmatism, and against superstition. The rallying cry for this crusade has always been and always will be "On to God!"

- Robert Milliken (NPP 1923)—the physicist credited with experimentally demonstrating the quantized nature of electric charge, who also discovered cosmic rays, performed important experiments verifying the predictions of Einstein's explanation of the photoelectric effect (thus establishing the existence of the postulated light quanta or photons), and was instrumental in bringing Einstein to the United States—was deeply interested in Theosophy. As was the astronomer Edwin Hubble, known for his studies of spiral nebulae and classification of galaxies, and remembered in "Hubble's constant," which determines the rate of expansion of the big bang universe.

- David Bohm was greatly influenced in his philosophical outlook by the contemporary pundit Krishnamurti (whose own philosophy was heavily swayed by misplaced phenomenological considerations, i.e., by the idea that "conceptualization is the root of all duality"). Interestingly, in his youth Krishnamurti—a close friend of Aldous Huxley—was groomed as a prophesied "World Teacher" of the Theosophical Society, a position which he later fully repudiated.

Both Bohm and Krishnamurti were vegetarians; as were Newton, Leonardo da Vinci, Socrates, Plotinus, Tesla and the mathematician Srinivasa Ramanujan.

> Nothing will benefit human health and increase the chances for survival of life on earth as much as the evolution to a vegetarian diet.
> —Albert Einstein

- Sir J. J. Thompson (NPP 1906) (the discoverer of the electron) and Lord Rayleigh (NPP 1904) (co-discoverer of the noble gas argon) were both first officers of the Society for Psychical Research in Britain.

Isaac Newton, too—who framed the laws of gravity and optics, discovered the general binomial theorem, and invented the calculus, all within a two-year period in his early twenties—devoted much time to metaphysical matters, including alchemy and Kabbalistic studies (his personal library contained at least 138 books on alchemy). As did the physicist and chemist Robert Boyle (developer of Boyle's Law, or the fact that, at a constant temperature, the pressure of a gas varies inversely with its volume). Among influential scientists and poets having genuine mystical experiences, we may number at least

- Blaise Pascal—the brilliant seventeenth-century French mathematician and philosopher, whose name is remembered in "Pascal's Triangle"—who experienced a vision of a flaming cross. After his death, a sketch of this vision was found sewn up in his doublet—so as to be always kept with him—along with the following words:

  FIRE. God of Abraham, God of Isaac, God of Jacob, not of the philosophers nor of the Wise. Assurance, joy, assurance, feeling, joy, peace.

- Dante likewise testifies in his "Divine Comedy" that

  I have been in that heaven the most illumined
  By light from Him, and seen things which to utter
  He who returns hath neither skill nor knowledge;
  For as it nears the object of its yearning
  Our intellect is overwhelmed so deeply
  It never can retrace the path it followed.

- And Henry David Thoreau, whose years spent at Walden Pond are well known:

  I hearing get who had but ears,
  And sight who had but eyes before,
  I moments live who lived but years,
  And truth discern who knew but learning's lore.

  I hear beyond the range of sound,
  I see beyond the range of sight,
  New earths, and skies and seas around,
  And in my day the sun doth pale his light.

- Alfred Lord Tennyson further wrote, in his memoirs, of

a kind of waking trance I have frequently had, quite up from my
boyhood, when I have been all alone. This has generally come upon me
through repeating my own name two or three times to myself silently, til
all at once, as it were out of the intensity of the consciousness of
individuality, the individuality itself seemed to dissolve and fade away
into boundless being; and this is not a confused state, but the clearest of
the clearest ... utterly beyond words, where death was an almost
laughable impossibility, the loss of personality (if it were so) seeming
no extinction, but the only true life.

• And the American poet Walt Whitman recorded that

As in a swoon, one instant,
Another sun, ineffable full-dazzles me,
And all the orbs I knew—and brighter, unknown orbs;
One instant of the future land, Heaven's land.

The ocean filled with joy—the atmosphere all joy! Joy, joy in freedom,
worship, love! Joy in the ecstasy of life: Enough to merely be! Enough
to breathe! Joy, Joy! All over joy.

Divine am I, inside and out.

• Honorè de Balzac adopted the main tenets of the theosophy of
Emanuel Swedenborg, holding that the cosmos is one as it proceeds
from, and ultimately will revert to, the singleness of God; that
everything created is the product of an "ethereal substance" which
we designate in turn by the names of electricity, heat, light, etc.

• Jacob Behmen (Böhme/Boehme), the "Teutonic Theosopher," recorded of his third illumination experience that

the gate was opened to me that in one quarter of an hour I saw and knew
more than if I had been many years together at a university.... For I saw
and knew the being of all beings, the byss and abyss and the eternal
generation of the Holy Trinity, the descent and original of the world and
of all creatures through the divine wisdom.

• The ancient Roman philosopher Plotinus—founder of Neoplato-
nism—likewise informs us:

Each being contains in itself the whole intelligible world. Therefore All is everywhere. Each is there All, and All is each. Man as he now is has ceased to be the All. But when he ceases to be an individual, he raises himself again and penetrates the whole world.

You can only apprehend the Infinite by a faculty superior to reason, by entering into a state in which you are your finite self no longer—in which the divine essence is communicated to you. This is ecstasy. It is the liberation of your mind from its finite consciousness.... In the reduction of your soul to its simplest self, its divine essence, you realize this union—this identity.

Plotinus experienced this state on at least seven different occasions.

- Further, William Wordsworth:

There was a time when meadow, grove and stream,
The earth and every common sight,
To me did seem
Appareled in celestial light.

I have felt
A presence that disturbs me with the joy
Of elevated thought; a sense sublime
Of something far more deeply interfused,
Whose dwelling is the light of setting suns,
And the round ocean, and the living air,
And the blue sky, and in the mind of man—
A motion and a spirit, that impels
All thinking things, all objects of all thought,
And rolls through all things.

- The brilliant quantum physicist Richard Feynman (NPP 1965) had several out-of-the-body experiences, although he regarded them as mere products of the imagination, i.e., as unreal. (Aldous Huxley and Goethe, too, both reported having OBEs. Roughly nine-tenths of the world's societies have at least some tradition regarding these; approximately one in ten persons has such an experience in his or her lifetime.)

We find, further, many explicit endorsements of the mystical viewpoint from other well-known poets, scientists and philosophers:

- William Butler Yeats—awarded the Nobel Prize in Literature in 1923—prepared a translation of ten of the principal Upanishads, and had an abiding interest in alchemy.

- T. S. Eliot spent two years studying Sanskrit, and a year applying this toward understanding Patanjali's *Yoga Sutras*. He received Literature's Nobel Prize in 1948.

- Emily Brontë (author of *Wuthering Heights*) penned the following lines in her poem "No Coward Soul":

With wide-embracing love
Thy spirit animates eternal years
Pervades and broods above,
Changes, sustains, dissolves, creates, and rears.

Though Earth and moon were gone
And suns and universes ceased to be
And thou wert left alone
Every Existence would exist in thee.

There is not room for Death
Nor atom that his might could render void
Since thou art Being and Breath
And what thou art may never be destroyed.

- William Blake declared that "Jesus Christ is the only God, and so am I and so are you," and claimed to have written his poem "The Jerusalem"

from immediate dictation, twelve or sometimes twenty or thirty lines at a time, without premeditation, and even against my will.

And elsewhere pronounced,

To see a World in a Grain of Sand
And a Heaven in a Wild Flower
Hold Infinity in the palm of your hand
And Eternity in an hour.

Both Blake and Newton gave intensive study to Jacob Behmen's writings, with Blake having read Swedenborg as well. He further claimed to have seen and conversed with his own late brother Robert on a regular basis; Blake's later poetry collections were printed using an engraving process which Robert had described during one of these post-mortem conversations. Actually, Blake not only purported to channel the spirit of John Milton, but drew portraits of famous dead persons—including Sir William Wallace and Edward I—who would, he claimed, come and "sit" for him.

- Thomas Traherne, an English clergyman and writer, in his "Centuries of Meditations," similarly affirms:

    You will never enjoy the world aright till the sea itself floweth in your veins, till you are clothed with the heavens, and crowned with the stars, and perceive yourself to be the sole heir of the whole world, and more than so, because men are in it who are every one sole heirs as well as you.

- Ralph Waldo Emerson likewise writes, in "Compensation":

    The universe is represented in every one of its particles. Everything is made of one hidden stuff. The world globes itself in a drop of dew.... The true doctrine of omnipresence is that God appears with all His parts in every moss and cobweb.

And in "Brahma":

    They reckon ill who leave me out
    When me they fly, I am the wings
    I am the doubter and the doubt
    I am the hymn the Brahmin sings.

Both Emerson and his friend Thoreau had studied the Bhagavad Gita and some of the Upanishads. Further, Emerson, Walt Whitman, Thomas Edison, Rudyard Kipling, Oscar Wilde, Charles Dickens, Sir Walter Scott, W.B. Yeats and Francis Bacon all accepted the doctrine of reincarnation.

- William James, the "father of American psychology," and author of the classic *The Varieties of Religious Experience,* co-founded the American Society for Psychical Research, and asserted that

  our normal waking consciousness is but one special type of conscious-ness, while all about it, parted from it by the filmiest of screens, there lie potential forms of consciousness entirely different.... No account of the universe can be final which leaves these other forms of consciousness quite disregarded.

Niels Bohr's Copenhagen Interpretation of quantum theory was actually influenced by James' notion of the "stream of consciousness."

- The Swiss psychologist Carl Jung, referring to hatha yoga, stated:

  Yoga is ... the perfect and appropriate method of fusing body and mind together so that they form a unity which is scarcely to be questioned. This unity creates a psychological disposition which makes possible intuitions that transcend consciousness.

Interestingly, F. David Peat notes, in *Lighting the Seventh Fire,* that

  Jung made his most far-reaching breakthroughs following a personal crisis that, to outsiders, had all the appearance of a psychotic episode. Jung had the sensation of literally falling into madness and of walking and conversing with different beings. In the midst of one of these episodes a voice dictated an important piece of writing, *VII Sermones ad Mortuos* [*Seven Sermons to the Dead*].

Jung also had a near-death experience, the beauty of which freed him from all fear of dying.

- The historian Arnold Toynbee participated in a discussion on world peace with the late Jagadguru Shankaracharya Bharati Krishna Tirtha, in the latter's tour of America in 1958. On several occasions in his life, again according to F. David Peat, Toynbee found himself

  projected across time and space to become a participator in another historical era. One time he found himself in the Italy of 80 B.C. witnessing a suicide. Another time, while walking near Victoria Station in London he had the experience of being plunged not into a particular historical period but into the entire passage of history and time.

- The English writers Arthur Koestler and Aldous Huxley (whose book *The Perennial Philosophy* is a celebrated anthology of passages from Eastern and Western mystics) and the architect Frank Lloyd Wright were members of an esoteric school run by Gurdjieff. This school was established in France during the Russian Revolution, under the protection of the esteemed French mathematician Jules Henri Poincaré—the scientist who first gave clues into the way in which non-linearity and chaos work on the cosmic scale, through his discovery, in the late 1800s, of unstable orbits in the classical many-body problem. Koestler also travelled to India to see Ananda Moyi Ma—Bengal's "Joy-Permeated Mother."

- Frank L. Baum, who wrote the original story for *The Wizard of Oz*, was a devoted student of the yogic science.

- Vincent van Gogh experienced a vision of the resurrected Christ.

- Sir Arthur Conan Doyle, regarded as the author of the "Sherlock Holmes" mysteries, produced a two-volume work entitled *The History of Spiritualism*.

- The British naturalist Alfred Russel Wallace—independent co-developer, with Darwin, of the theory of evolution—obtained several alleged spirit-photographs of his mother through the agency of a medium, and published a book *On Miracles and Modern Spiritualism*.

- The English physicist Sir William Barrett—known for his work on magnetism and radiant heat in the latter part of the nineteenth century—was one of the founders of the Society for Psychical Research. In 1876, he brought the subject of Spiritualism before the British Association for the Advancement of Science, with a paper dealing with mesmerism and Spiritualistic phenomena.

- Sir William Crookes—the British physicist who discovered the element thallium, produced diamonds artificially, discovered the sodium amalgamation process for separating gold and silver from their ores, and whose experimental work on radiant matter in the late 1800s changed the conception of it in both physics and chemistry— was author of *Researches in the Phenomena of Spiritualism.*

• Camille Flammarion, founder of the French Astronomical Society, was affiliated with the Society for Psychical Research, and summarized the results of his investigations in *Mysterious Psychic Forces.*

• The physicist Sir Oliver Lodge—knighted for his work with lightning, electromagnetic waves and wireless telegraphy a century ago—believed unequivocally in the possibility of communication between the living and the dead, and authored a book on the mediumed communications between himself and his deceased son.

The Nobel Prizes were instituted in 1901; had the honor been available earlier, it is fair to say that each of the knighted "Sirs" mentioned here would have received it.

• Charles Robert Richet, Nobel Prize-winner in Medicine, known for his research into the phenomenon of anaphylaxis—the hypersensitive reaction to allergens—coined the term "ectoplasm," authored *Thirty Years of Psychic Research,* and wrote in *The Sixth Sense* that

metaphysics is not yet officially a science, recognized as such. But it is going to be.... At Edinburgh, I was able to affirm before 100 physiologists that our five senses are not our only means of knowledge and that a fragment of reality sometimes reaches the intelligence in other ways.

• The Electrical Engineer Charles Steinmetz—regarded as one of the "greatest scholars and scientists in the electrical field" in the early part of the twentieth century, and holder of over 200 patents—stated:

I think the greatest discovery [in the next fifty years] will be made along spiritual lines. Here is a force which history clearly teaches has been the greatest power in the development of men. Yet we have merely been playing with it and have never seriously studied it as we have the physical forces. Some day people will learn that material things do not bring happiness and are of little use in making men and women creative and powerful. Then the scientists of the world will turn their laboratories over to the study of God and prayer and the spiritual forces which as yet have hardly been scratched. When this day comes, the world will see more advancement in one generation than it has seen in the past four.

• The British statesman and philosopher Douglas Grant Duff Ainslie was a disciple of Paramahansa Yogananda, and wrote the Preface for Yogananda's *The Science of Religion.* George Eastman—inventor of the Kodak camera—was another of the same sage's American admirers.

• The Nobel Prize-winning (1930) physicist Sir C. V. Raman (discoverer of the "Raman Effect," regarded as one of the greatest breakthroughs in experimental physics, revealing the molecular structure of solids, liquids and gaseous substances) had contact with Yogananda in India, as did the East Indian physicist Jagadis C. Bose (whose investigations branched from physics into the boundary separating physics and plant physiology, or inanimate and animate matter).

• Cambridge's Brian Josephson—winner of the 1973 Nobel Prize in Physics for his discovery of the superconducting "Josephson junction," which has applications in future computers—is a longtime meditator, and supports the inclusion of God or Mind within the framework of science. He has stated (in *The Reach of the Mind: Nobel Prize Conversations*) that "Vedanta and Sankhya hold the key to the laws of mind and thought process, which are correlated to [but not a reductionistic outcome of] the quantum field, i.e., the operation and distribution of particles at atomic and molecular levels." He further holds that "mystical experience by self-development through meditation, etc., is not only the key to one's own development but also the key ... to putting [the] attempt to synthesize science and religion on a solid foundation."

Strong mystical leanings can also be found in many of the world's great philosophers:

- Spinoza—considered to be the founder of modern philosophy—believed that the different forms of existence are unified in one all-embracing whole or Substance: one absolutely independent Being, which includes all things and determines itself and all things through the necessity of its own nature. He regarded God as being exactly this underlying nature or Ground, from whose essence all things proceed in a regular and uniform order:

  I do not know why matter should be unworthy of the divine nature, since outside God no substance can exist from which the divine nature could suffer.... Therefore in no way whatever can it be asserted that [substance extended] is unworthy of the divine nature, provided only that it is eternal and infinite.

- Leibniz was familiar with Chinese thought through translations he received from Jesuit monks, so that it is likely that his "monadic" philosophy was influenced by the Neo-Confucian school of Chu Hsi, which in turn has roots in Mahayana Buddhism. (Leibniz independently invented calculus twenty years after Newton's own unpublished discovery of the same.) He was in any case also versed in the Hua-yen (i.e., Avatamsaka Sutra) school of Buddhist thought, which was founded in the seventh century by Fa-Tsang. This particular system of thought likened the universe to a network of jewels in which each one reflects all of the others—like a candle in a room full of mirrors, from which Leibniz could well have borrowed his idea of "monads," each of which contains a reflection of the whole universe—and taught that every point in the cosmos was its center.

- Heidegger praised Zen scholar D. T. Suzuki's books as being exactly "what I have been trying to say in all my writings."

- Schopenhauer considered that "access to the Vedas is, in my eyes, the greatest privilege this century may claim over all previous centuries," and held the Upanishads to be "the solace of one's life" and "the most rewarding and elevating reading possible in the world."

- Schlegel recognized that "even the loftiest philosophy of the Europeans, the idealism of reason as set forth by the Greek philosophers, appears—in comparison with the abundant life and vigor of Oriental idealism—like a feeble Promethean spark against a full flood of sunlight."

• Immanuel Kant—who wrote an entire book on Swedenborg—himself felt, along with his fellow philosopher Henri Bergson, that there was sufficient evidence to allow for the existence of parapsychological phenomena.

• And Bertrand Russell—recipient of the 1950 Nobel Prize in Literature; Bergson received the award twenty-three years earlier—while not himself endorsing the mystical viewpoint, nevertheless was rightly impressed by the calibre of many of the persons who did subscribe to it, stating in particular:

For my part, I am convinced that [William] James was right on this matter [of the union of subject and object in the act of knowing], and would on this ground alone, deserve a high place among philosophers.

And of the ancients:

• Socrates believed himself to be inspired by a divine voice or *daimon,* and entered trance on occasion. (Plutarch described the *daimon* of a person as a being floating in a higher world but connected by a cord to the person below. That is, of course, very much in accord with the idea of it relating either to an astral or higher self, or at least to a literal guardian angel or spirit guide.) Socrates' chief disciple, Plato, postulated a world of Becoming, in constant transition from Non-Being to Being. He taught that the world is a living, organic whole, and held that our highest goal is to become, as far as we can, like God, the Absolute Good. He further considered the universe (i.e., cosmos) to be spherical in shape, composed of the elements earth, air, water and fire. Aristotle, then, was one of Plato's disciples. In spite of that noble and mystical pedigree, however, Aristotle is of course regularly *blamed* for giving us "binary, fragmenting, yes-or-no Aristotelian logic," when he should rather be *praised* for the same.

- Pythagoras taught the transmigration of souls—the idea that, at death, the human soul migrates to inhabit another, perhaps animal, form—and held that "all things are numbers." He was further said to remember his previous lives; to have subdued animals, even wild beasts, merely through a powerful mesmeric gaze; and to be able to hear the "music of the spheres."

> It is written of Socrates that he heard within him a peculiar sound which pulled him irresistibly into higher spiritual realms. Pythagoras also talked of *Shabd* [i.e., Om], for he described God as "Supreme Music of the nature of Harmonies." God was to him, "Absolute Truth, clothed in light." When he commanded an eagle to fly down to him and a bear to stop ravaging [the city of] Apulia, the wondering multitude inquired of him the source from where such powers came to him. He replied that he owed it all to the "Science of Light."
> —Kirpal Singh, *The Crown of Life*

The Pythagoreans (c. 500 B.C.) were aware of the existence of subtler bodies than the physical, holding that the light of these luminous bodies could produce a variety of effects on the human organism, including the cure of illness. (In *Future Science,* John White lists ninety-seven different cultures throughout the world, each of which has its own name for the healing or life energy fields.)

- Porphyry distinguished four grades of human evolution, in the highest of which we become "the father of the gods."

- Heraclitus believed in a world of eternal Becoming—of constant flow and change—designating by "Logos" the Unity which contains and transcends all opposites and passing forms.

- We should also not neglect to mention the Milesian school of early Greek philosophy—"those who think matter is alive." Of those, Anaximander saw creation as an organism supported by the cosmic breath, "pneuma"—holding the first principle or cause of all things to be "the infinite or boundless," i.e., a substance different from all, which is infinite and from which arises all the heavens and the worlds within them—while Thales believed that water was the first principle, and that "all things are full of gods."

Is this not perhaps significant? that so many of the prominent persons whose work has shaped scientific/artistic/philosophical thought—including no less than a dozen Nobel Prize winners—have allowed for the possible/probable validity of points of view regarding the basic nature of the universe that deviate markedly from the established train of Western thought and its prevailing philosophical materialism? (In that materialism, of course, consciousness is viewed as a by-product of chemical reactions in the brain, rather than as the basis of all life and matter.)

Considering all this, what is surprising is not that the world is undergoing a spiritual renaissance, but only that it has taken this long for us to begin to realize how much we once knew but have forgotten, and how many of the world's finest minds (i.e., most highly developed *intellects,* for whom reason in no way interfered with intuition) have been there before us.

The Vedantic ideal, too, is for the rational mind and intuition to work together. That is, the intellect is never viewed as an inherent hindrance on the spiritual path. Thus, when the mind is regarded as a "tool of the devil," this is *not* because it forces a dynamic and flowing reality into fixed, static concepts. Rather, that regard comes only from the fact that, when swayed by emotional biases, the intellect will tend to provide rationalizations for whatever one most *wants* to do, rather than to impartially dictate, in accord with one's intuition, what one *should* do.

The intellect, and higher education in particular, are sometimes cursed as being sources of a feeling of superiority to others, and of "having it all explained." However, it is obvious from experience that the political, religious, scientific and superstitious convictions of uneducated or even illiterate persons are as firmly held as are the reasoned conclusions of the educated, or the intuitive insights of the wise. The ignorant person will *know* that the sun goes around the earth once a day, for example, and will not hesitate to persecute anyone who dares to suggest otherwise. Galileo was actually sentenced to death by the Inquisition in the sixteenth century—a punishment mercifully commuted to simple banishment—for disproving that idea *through his right use of reason.*

The detrimental feeling of "having it all explained" is again a problem/outcome of individual psychology, not a product of the intellect as such. That feeling may be surrounded and supported by intellectual rationalizations, but it is not *caused* by the use of the intellect. Conversely, to denigrate or renounce the intellect simply because of its complicity with that hubris is a comparable fallacy to the fearing of reason, or the refusal to think rationally or to trace the causes and effects of one's actions on others, simply because that logical tracing demands the acceptance of responsibility, and may thus easily result in feelings of guilt at the negative effects of one's actions.

Further, as to the value of reason and scientific knowledge, consider the experience of an individual who served at one time in the Peace Corps in India. When disclosing to the people there that he was from America, the usual response from local villagers would be "Oh—how far away is that by train?" Or this, from the *San Diego Tribune,* October 30, 1998: "The forecasts [by scientists, of upcoming solar ionic storms are] likely to come in handy for police dispatchers and sheriff's deputies, who fielded numerous calls when Northern Lights lit up skies over Florida, Alabama and Texas. 'People worry,' said [a scientist at the Space Environment Center in Boulder, Colorado]. 'They think it's Martians.'" When misled individuals wish for a return to the days before the Age of Reason, or the curse of "linear, rational thought" and the grossly overrated, unreasonably villainized Cartesian split, they are effectively arguing in favor of a flat Earth—orbited by the sun, once a day—in constant danger of a Martian invasion!

Being "rational" entails far more than simply being able to use the tools of logical reasoning proficiently. For, not only can those be executed equally well by computers, but they can again be called on to provide rationalizations for whatever position one *a priori* prefers to hold. A person who places mundane concerns ahead of his own spiritual growth is not behaving "rationally." Nor are self-destructive persons behaving so, regardless of the intellectual gymnastics which they may be able to perform in their professional lives: there is no necessary correlation between intelligence and wisdom. In any case, with rare exception, advanced mystics, while fully recognizing the limitations of the intellect, distrust neither reason nor science as such. Of course, the same people are easily fooled by the purported "new-paradigm correspondences between mysticism and the New Physics," but that is a separate issue.

Note further that if it were only concepts or linear reasoning that prevented us from intuitively experiencing reality-as-it-is, no amount of "clear reasoning" could ever develop one's intuition: they would be mutually exclusive. Linear thinking would likewise inherently work contrary to the expression of compassion purported to be engendered by the (intellectual) recognition of the wholistic interdependence of all things. That intellectual recognition, however, could at best tell us why we *ought* to feel compassion, but never produce the actual *feeling* of empathy. In any case, it has been very astutely observed that no one has ever escaped from delusion without the discriminative use of the intellect, since without that use, we could never have realized that we were in delusion in the first place!

> Our Scriptures categorically [lay] down the wholesome dictum [that] whatever is consistent with **right** reasoning should be accepted, even though it comes from a boy or a parrot; and whatever is inconsistent therewith ought to be rejected, although emanating from an old man or even from the great sage Sri Shuka himself.
> —Bharati Krishna Tirtha

> One can assuredly prove every truth.
> —Frithjof Schuon

> Believe not because some old manuscripts are produced,
> Believe not because it is your national belief,
> Believe not because you have been made to believe from your childhood,
> But reason truth out and after you have analyzed it,
> Then if you find it will be good to one and all,
> Believe it, live up to it, and help others live up to it.
> —the Buddha

> Even as wisdom often comes from the mouths of babes, so does it often come from the mouths of old people. The golden rule is to test everything in the light of reason and experience, no matter from where it comes.
> —Mahatma Gandhi

> I do not feel obliged to believe that the same God who has endowed us with sense, reason, and intellect has intended us to forgo their use.
> —Galileo Galilei

Now, when Jesus' faith faltered on the cross—i.e., when he cried out "Father, why hast thou forsaken me?"—it was his *realization* of the non-dual *samadhi* state, not his *confidence* in the "unseen" Lord, which temporarily waned as he became momentarily conscious of delusion, i.e., of the painful state of his own one body. That cannot be interpreted merely in psychological terms, i.e., of him simply being totally honest with himself as to the existence of doubt in his consciousness at that point—e.g., the question as to whether God was still "taking care of him" in allowing him to suffer, etc.—or of him "not repressing his doubts." Even in more common cases, the idea of faith as belief in the presence of doubt, although widespread and often encouraged, is not valid. "Faith is the substance of things hoped for; the evidence of things not seen.... Through faith we understand that the worlds were framed by the word of God" (Hebrews 11:1-3); "So then faith cometh by hearing, and hearing by the word of God" (Romans 10:17).

The potential for confusion, in taking metaphors too literally and failing to discern their relevant structural applications, is a danger in any use of analogy. If, for example, we misunderstand the applicability of the idea that creation is a "cosmic motion picture show"—several possible levels of applicability (there may well be others) of which have been presented herein—we may begin to ask where the extra-large cosmic pails of popcorn are, and how much this movie cost to produce. Absurd as this example may seem, distortions of comparable magnitude are abundantly present in the common too-literal interpretations of the incredibly profound structural symbolisms of the Books of Genesis and Revelation, for example.

The metaphorical images present in any scripture have been carefully and wisely chosen, and should never be taken as in any way arbitrary. If it is a serpent that tempts Adam and Eve, rather than a yak or a ferret, or if the Wise Men followed a star of the East, this is no mere "filler," but is all of great structural significance. The same is again invariably true of trees (of the human body's nerve-branches, growing from the trunk of the spine), staffs (of the spinal column) and rivers (of life energy). When metaphors are understood, they are the most succinct way of communicating spiritual/structural truths; when misunderstood, however, a hornet's nest of troubles ensues!

Evidently, then, the Bible and other scriptures gain nothing from human attempts to rewrite them to circumvent any sociologically detrimental readings. It is only our understanding of the Bible, not the

Biblical symbolisms themselves, that requires revision. Ignorance, after all, should be fought with wisdom, not with more ignorance.

> Most important and of universal application is the proposition that "the parabolical [i.e., spiritual or mystical] meaning is contained in the literal." For this reason it is very necessary not only to have understood the precise meaning of the ... symbols, but also to translate them literally.
> —A. K. Coomaraswamy, "Some Pali Words"

> A parabolical or magical phrase or dialect is the best and plainest habit or dress that mysteries can have to travel in up and down this wicked world.
> —Jacob Behmen

The proper understanding of the "key" to the meaning of scriptural symbolisms does not bias us in our interpretation of religion and mythology—i.e., in viewing them only through that particular paradigm or model. Rather, as with all "secret codes," this is the only way in which their intended meaning can possibly be deciphered. The attempt to decode it with any key other than that with which it was written can yield only predictable nonsense.

The search for the non-exclusionary fundamental postulates having the widest region of explanatory power must be the goal of any theorizing endeavor, as an attempt to understand the universe, meriting the name "scientific," even in the area of religion and consciousness. This theoretical approach must nevertheless be conjoined with, and superseded by, the "experimental" nature of the reproducible experience of higher states of consciousness, in comparison with which any intellectual understanding of theory or scripture is pale and worthless. And "economy of hypothesis," again, is as central to the theoretical application of the scientific method—even as this pertains to religion and spirituality—as reproducibility is to its experimental half. That is to say, although experimental results stand with or without an intellectual understanding of theory, the "scientific approach" validly utilized in physics, for example, is no less applicable to theory than to experiment.

It would, however, be a mistake for "experimental" meditators to feel superior to religious "believers," on the basis of the dubious assertion that the latter approach inherently engenders a rigid system of psychological defenses against considering the possibility that such beliefs may be ultimately incorrect, while the former is supposedly free of this, for being based in the eventuality of proof via personal experience. A confirmation at the passage of death of the existence of a heavenly afterlife obtained through Jesus Christ alone, for example, would constitute experiential proof to exactly the same degree as would any hoped-for future realizations of the meditator. The timing of the proof—at death, versus while still living—in no way by itself inherently renders the latter superior to the former: they are equally "provable," in this sense.

We are all mere "believers" until we have experienced for ourselves *every* aspect of reality expounded in our respective spiritual paths. For theory without personal experience *is belief,* independent of whether that theory is right or wrong, logical or illogical. And if the theory underlying meditation were fundamentally wrong—e.g., if its revelations were in principle merely hallucinations—we would be wasting our lives every bit as much as any other "believers," in accepting and living according to it. The fear of "hellfire and brimstone," and any particular rigidity deriving from this (e.g., in "staying on the right side of the line" between meriting a heavenly afterlife and suffering eternal damnation), is an outcome only of the *specific* beliefs of the exoteric Christian religion, not of unproved belief in general.

Anyone who believes that he has found the truth is morally obligated to attempt to share those ideas with others, i.e., to proselytize at least to some degree. This proselytizing cannot be dismissed, as it is in the common psychological interpretation, as being merely an attempt to quell one's own doubts—although it certainly does not exclude that dynamic as well. For, particularly if we believe that we may be saving others from eternal damnation, or even from lesser sufferings, attempting to "convert" them is simply the *logical* thing to do, independent of whether or not we are allaying our own doubts in the process. To fail to make that attempt would be selfish in the extreme, and would indeed be readily condemned as such by the same persons who dismiss any proselytizing as the product only of psychological unhealth.

Now, intentions may indeed be more important than actions, but nevertheless, as the saying goes, the road to hell is paved with good intentions. People's lives get ruined, absolutely *ruined,* by being seduced, raped and/or psychologically abused by "spiritual Masters" (including but not limited to the "Crazy Zen" variety), in particular when the latter have been recommended to them by persons whose opinion they value. To offer spiritual advice from one's respected position, and feel that it is enough to merely be *trying* to speak the truth, is highly irresponsible indeed.

By contrast, consider the attitude of one such as David Bohm, who discovered near the end of his life that a certain aspect of the ontological formulation of quantum theory might have been in error. (The point in question concerned the quantum wavefunction in the first instants of the hypothesized big bang creation, which presents outstanding difficulties in orthodox quantum theory as well.) For a time, and until that problem was resolved with the help of his colleague Basil Hiley, Bohm regarded that as being a major defect in his work. Indeed, that concern progressed to the point where he felt that *The Undivided Universe* (the summary of his life's work in physics) should not even be published. In that state of extreme agitation, he further considered that he had deceived (however unintentionally) his colleagues and students, and that his life's work was worthless.

Of course, Bohm's reaction occurred in the midst of a severe depression and other difficulties, not the least of which was the discovery of inexcusable inconsistencies and hypocrisies in the life of his spiritual teacher and father-figure, Krishnamurti, and the corresponding feeling that everyone whom he had ever deeply trusted in his life had betrayed him. (Bohm at one point admitted to having "almost no feeling" between his chest and legs. That chronic suppression of energy flow—as with Bohm's noticeable cringing whenever anyone tried to show affection to him—comes only from an equally chronic guarding against being hurt by others. And all of that comes simply from feeling psychological pain so keenly, and taking desperate steps to avoid that hurt.) Nevertheless, the basic principles of integrity and responsibility that he displayed are immensely admirable, and sorely lacking in a world where people "would rather be president or pope than admit to being wrong," and not worry about ruining other people's lives by erring when giving unsolicited, or even requested, spiritual advice.

Further, one does not have to spend any amount of time at all around scholars, psychologists and meditators, to realize that they exhibit exactly the same rigid defenses and willingness to persecute others at variance with themselves, as can religious "believers," when their respective cherished ideas and emotional investments are called into question. Along with that, they will equally exhibit obvious feelings of superiority to those who are "so much more ignorant" than they, as to see things in a different way. Consider the experience of a certain contemporary scholar who, when he chose to abandon his vocation to live in a spiritual community, suffered insults from his academic peers. Then, half a decade later, when he decided to return to his former scholarly pursuits, he received the same verbal abuse from the members of the spiritual community he was leaving!

Such intolerance, again, is a sad but basic attribute of human psychology, and discloses a lack of resolve to face and accept the truth, whatever that may be, and however it may grate against what one at present finds comfortable. It is only the presence of biases and vested emotional interests that produces that discomfort. As soon as these are gone and the willingness to see things as they are begins to blossom, Truth becomes the most natural and comfortable thing, in all its facets, whether complimentary or uncomplimentary to one's present state of development.

In any case, our intellectual beliefs, even those concerning spiritual matters and the nature of creation, karma, or life after death, are not what matter in our lives, nor is it supremely important whether one meditates or not. A compassionate and considerate person living a good and honest life, with simultaneous tolerance for others' opinions and a deep concern for keeping his promises, for example, is unquestionably a more spiritual individual than is someone who meditates regularly—even deeply—but who yet lacks those positive qualities. Nevertheless, all other things being equal, and keeping in mind that bliss and other meditative experiences are a poor substitute for reliability, intelligence and integrity in one's daily life, there are many good reasons why one should practice regular meditation, even if it were to have no effect other than on increasing one's own peace. This is so particularly since meditation has been statistically shown to measurably advance one through the proven stages of psychological development.

Less than 2% of the adult population have realized Jane Loevinger's highest two stages of self development (called "autonomous" and "integrated"). *No practice has been shown to substantially increase that percentage.* With one exception: studies have shown that consistent meditation practice over a several-year period increases that percentage from 2% to an astonishing 38%.

—www.integralinstitute.org

One's understanding of metaphor-based scriptures, their philosophy rooted in the intuitive experience of the "As above, so below" nature of creation, can easily be most flawed in the places where it seems most inarguably correct, for being based in simple and literal interpretations. Sometimes a snake is only a snake, and a candle only a candle, it is true— but sometimes they are much more. The belief that one could grasp any amount of the deep profundities of any inspired scripture, then, simply by reading it superficially but "without bias" or "with an open mind," is misguided, to say the least: Truth is simple, but not simplistic. (Such superficial readings fall easily into one's trusting the mere literalist "first impressions" generated, with "open mindedness" being shown by one's understanding falling naturally in line with the accepted and "obvious" literalism, there being no attempt to penetrate beyond it.)

Conversely, even an "impeccable, ultimate and unsurpassable" translation of the Bible, for example, would do nothing to further the intended understanding of its symbolisms. It is the ignorance of readers, not flaws in translation, that accounts for all but rare misunderstandings of scriptural meaning; penetrating insight can easily see through errors in translation, to find the intended message.

None of those messages or symbols of mythology, however, can be comprehended even partially without an understanding, necessarily indistinguishable from yoga, of the theoretical basis forming the cosmic foundation of the meditative experience-based origin of all genuine religions. (Of course, even the higher forms of yoga tend to neglect the witnessing aspect of the Self almost as much as contemporary understandings of Zen Buddhism neglect the astral and causal structure leading to that Self. Neither side gives a balanced approach, even though everything neglected is still implied, if one looks closely enough.) This underlying "theory," though, differs from the theories of physical science, in that it is not merely an intellectual construct invented by humans to describe experimentally observed behaviors in Nature, but has rather been directly seen and experienced by sages in meditation. The astral structure—of the chakras on that level, etc.—in fact, can be seen even by clairvoyants. The mathematics underlying the full (chakric, etc.) mechanism by which meditation works must then necessarily be more complex than even that found in the known laws of physics, for the latter are merely a subset of a more comprehensive set of laws embracing the entire range of levels of reality.

In the end, it takes either great wisdom or great ignorance to believe that one understands the world's scriptures at anything approaching their intended depth. For it is easy to think that one has all the answers, if one has simply not yet asked the right properly-detailed questions. It takes only a slight skewing of perspective, further, for one to become overly confident in the correctness of one's own thoughts and interpretations of scripture, thinking them to be more guided by intuition than they actually are.

Fortunately, however, techniques of meditation work with the same efficiency regardless of one's incomplete and potentially-flawed understanding of the theory underlying them. Indeed, it is not unusual to find rather glaring errors in understanding even among highly respected and spiritually advanced persons. There is an astounding difference between the calibre and veracity of the properly-understood teachings of personages such as Christ and Krishna, and the ideas of other persons, both contemporary and past, having experienced genuine enlightenments and kundalini raisings; not all "sagely teachings" are created even remotely equal.

Further, the plethora of irresponsibilities, deliberate lies and psychological and sexual abuses perpetrated by persons of both genders who could go into *samadhi* at will, or who have even realized the witnessing Self, makes it embarrassingly clear that none of those indications of "spiritual advancement" have any correlation with integrity, truthfulness, or even with otherwise being a basically decent and caring person. Development on the causal level will indeed tend to produce those latter valuable qualities—*whether or not one meditates*. But it is, sadly, fully possible to contact the causal and transcendent Self levels regularly in meditation, and yet bring none of that integrity into one's daily life. Or, worse, to retain that witnessing consciousness in daily life, and use that "God-realized" witnessing or one's lower experience of "God as Bliss" as license to rape and deceive. There are just too many "sagely" examples of that problem to deny it.

Nor does "spiritual advancement" even necessarily grant one any meaningful "how to live" wisdom—never mind detailed insight into how the cosmos works, such as Bentov gleaned. Unless, of course, one wants to consider the "obedience good/independence bad" idea—which countless "enlightened" individuals have endorsed and not been shy in enforcing with the help of their henchmen/disciples—as a "wise" notion. At any rate, what good is "holy calmness and forgiveness" in one's daily life, if one simultaneously twists/suppresses Truth "for the glory of God and Guru"? Or lacks compassion and integrity—and thus needs all the forgiveness one can get, for deliberately deceiving, or turning one's back on other people's suffering?

Consider, further, that not only does the influx of mere imagination too often inform astral-level visions, but that saints have sometimes experienced visitations of Jesus, for example, but claimed to be able to feel that "it wasn't really him"—i.e., that it was "Satan in disguise"—by the vibrations given off. (Of course, well-known experiments have been done in which persons who believed that they were receiving psilocybin were fed a placebo instead. Some of those subjects, however, still reported experiencing comparable trips on that placebo as were detailed by persons taking the real thing. Thus, one should never underestimate the human capacity for self-delusion in any capacity, least of all when it is applied to religion/mysticism/spirituality.) And added to that, we have the problem that the world's religious organizations are invariably populated with Judases and Doubting Thomases. Consequently, the version of truth which makes it past their guardianship into the public eye will inevitably have been distorted according to their own ubiquitous wishes for power and blind respect. Such selective editing will further be coupled with the covering-up of their own indiscretions and deliberate sanitizing of the "holy Master's" life for presentation to the world.

All in all, my own conclusion, after having been on the receiving end of all of that cruel nonsense myself, is that it is *extremely* rare for guru-disciple relationships to not do far more harm than good. (Of course, every disciple thinks that his or her "all-knowing and all-loving" guru is the exception to that concern. Once upon a time, I foolishly did too.) Rarely do such relationships produce significant spiritual advancement on the part of the disciple. They do, however, very successfully kill the independence, intelligence, intuition and creativity of the naïvely trusting followers.

As one relatively benign attempted instance of that sickness, consider that, while spending time in Yogananda's ashrams, the author of this very book was advised that when he had "meditated more" he wouldn't feel the need to write or be creative. Rather, he would just humbly and anonymously "serve the Guru's work," without attempting to do anything original in the world. Put another way: according to the unduly respected individual giving that unsolicited advice, if the present author had been more spiritually advanced, this book itself would never have been written! When surrounded by other "believers," in a closed environment cut off from the rest of the world, it can take years for one to realize how wrong such widespread pressures to "spiritually conform" are. Yet advice such as the above is, sadly, what consistently passes for "wisdom" in the world's ashram environments.

Now, Jesus himself taught and practiced structural techniques of life-force control, such as can be used to enter the *samadhi* state at will— as did Shankara, Patanjali, Elijah, Kabir and Krishna—as is evidenced by St. Paul's ability to "die daily," as well as by John 7:38: "He that believeth on me ... out of his belly shall flow rivers of living water." "When the yogi in ecstatic meditation withdraws his life force from the body's trillions of cells and from the nerves, he beholds the life-force currents like little streams trickling back from the shores of the flesh through innumerable small channels into the large channel of the spinal cord"—Paramahansa Yogananda, *God Talks With Arjuna.*

The more one understands yoga, the more one realizes that not only does it have its origin in the same cosmic consciousness that enlivens Christianity and all true religions, but that it offers exactly the same emphasis on cosmic structure and life-force control as did Jesus and the other sagely originators of the Bible: Christianity, properly understood and practiced, is simply yoga by a different name. That, however, is equally true of every great religion or technique of introspection: they all work, whether knowingly or unknowingly, with microcosmic bodily structure as a means to the realization of the Self.

Taoist sages, too, have again elaborated techniques for opening the "Golden Flower" or crown chakra and obtaining the "Elixir of Immortality" by directing the flow of an inner light of life energy. (The literal translation of that "elixir"—from the original Chinese—is "golden ball [i.e. sphere].") Indeed, the *Hui Ming Ching* and *Secret of the Golden*

Flower together state that when "the thousand-petaled lotus flower opens, transformed through breath-energy," "one is aware of effulgence and infinity.... The pulse stands still and breathing stops.... The heavenly heart rises to the summit of the Creative [i.e., the thousand-petaled lotus in the brain], where it expands in complete freedom."

Chuang Tzu likewise narrates the story of a sage "old in years, but with the complexion as of a child." The sage practiced a "method" or technique, with the result that

> after three days [i.e., periods or levels of spiritual development] he could get beyond our world [to the "fourth" or astral level]; after seven days he could get beyond created things [i.e., beyond the seventh chakra]. After nine days he could get beyond life [in stopping the breath in *samadhi*]. After that he could be Morning Light [i.e., the transcendent white light of the Sun seen in the East, as gateway to the Self], then Solitariness [the "paradoxical isolation of omnipresence," in trance], then free from time [at the chaotic Self level, beyond relative time and space]. Then he entered into neither-death-nor-birth, where the destroyer of life does not die, and the producer of birth is not born [cf. the zero-average level of Chaos underlies the creation and destruction of all *mayic* matter, but is itself unaffected by all of that continual "birth" and "death" of consciousness, mind and matter]. As governor of things, he escorted and greeted them all [as witnessing Self-awareness in daily life], destroyed and perfected them all [as the chaotic transcendent Self itself, at which level the material cosmos is destroyed and perfected, or "leaves no trace whatsoever"]. The name is Active Tranquility. It means to achieve after action [cf. the yogic "fruits of action without action," or Zen's "choiceless awareness"].

Any technique which both retards the aging process of the body and provides the ability to "get beyond life," can only be based in control of the life force. (Compare the idea of a *"Fountain* of Youth.") The ability of sages to "transmit" spiritual experiences to their followers likewise exists only because of subtle, consciousness-raising energy flows from one person to another. That is, in any such explicit transmission, the phenomenon can in no way be wisely explained simply in terms of one's mind "shutting up" in response to particular words/koans or inspired actions on the part of the sage.

Consider also Ramakrishna's statement that "a man's spiritual consciousness is not awakened unless his kundalini is aroused," and the fact that the yogic system taught by Aurobindo was based in tantra yoga, as such inherently and explicitly incorporating the raising of this subtle spiritual evolutionary force. Further, according to Mahayana Buddhism, the Buddha's enlightenment is associated with him raising his eyes to the sky and perceiving the morning star—where the "morning" star rises in the East. One is, however, enjoined to not merely see this inner astral star, but pass consciously through it (simply because its central white radiance is claimed to be formed from the actual light flowing in the causal spine, as a gateway to the Self).

Compare this with the reference to Jesus as "the bright and morning star" (Revelation 22:16), and with the fact that this star is again seen in the blue sky-like sphere of the spiritual eye or Christ consciousness center. The white light of this star is again one of the manifestations of the "Clear Light" of the Self on which Tibetan Buddhists are admonished to fix their attention during the death process. Additionally, "the Buddha himself described certain yoga-exercises, which show clearly that he was not only conversant with, but for a time actively practicing, what may be called *nadi*-yoga, [through which he] was said to have stopped the ordinary breathing process"—Lama Govinda, *Foundations of Tibetan Mysticism*.

All of those techniques, however, are only steps toward the realization of the Self. For transcendent spirituality boils down to the radically perceptive observation—which Descartes, unlike his contemporary detractors, was so close to understanding—that self-awareness, in addition to being a constant through all of our states of consciousness, is the one thing that we cannot doubt exists. Even if all visions were hallucinations, even if all of one's memories were internal fabrications, even if all of one's daily reality were just a dream, present through all of those experiences—including in deep sleep, for persons who have progressed to be conscious of that state—is the awareness of the witnessing Self. And how could that continuous self-awareness *of the present moment*— the only moment that we ever actually have access to, whether we're conceptualizing its phenomena or not—through all experiences end at the experience called death?

"Because I think, and am able to witness my own thoughts, I must exist ... and I must be, at my core essence, more than any witnessed thoughts or experiences. I must be *That which witnesses.*"

There is, however, a *structure* by which that self-awareness is individualized and tied to the mind and body of each one of us. And that same structure is what is validly made use of explicitly in techniques of content meditation, and described poetically/symbolically throughout the world's mythologies and scriptures.

There is a land where no doubt nor sorrow have rule: where the terror of Death is no more.

There the woods of spring are a-bloom, and the fragrant scent "He is I" is borne on the wind:

There the bee of the heart is deeply immersed, and desires no other joy.

Behold how the thirst of the five senses is quenched there! and the three forms of misery are no more!

There the streams of light flow in all directions.

There falls the rhythmic beat of life and death:

Rapture wells forth, and all space is radiant with light.

There the Unstruck Music is sounded; it is the music of the love of the three worlds.

There millions of lamps of sun and of moon are burning;

There the drum beats, and the lover swings in play.

There love-songs resound, and the light rains in showers; and the worshipper is entranced in the taste of the heavenly nectar.

Look upon life and death; there is no separation between them,

The right hand and the left hand are one and the same.

There the wise man is speechless; for this truth may never be found in Vedas or in books.

I have stilled my restless mind, and my heart is radiant: for in That-ness I have seen beyond That-ness, in company I have seen the Companion Himself.

Living in bondage, I have set myself free: I have broken away from the clutch of all narrowness.

Kabir says: "I have attained the unattainable, and my heart is colored with the color of love."

Or, to paraphrase Ramana Maharshi: The waves are illusory; the Ocean alone is real; the Ocean has become all the waves.

It's as simple and logical as that.

BIBLIOGRAPHY

ACHAD, F., *The Anatomy of the Body of God*. New York: Samuel Weiser, 1973.

AJAYA, SW., *Psychotherapy East and West: A Unifying Paradigm*. Honesdale, PA: Himalayan International Institute, 1983.

ALLEGRO, J. M., *The Sacred Mushroom and the Cross: Fertility Cults and the Origins of Judaism and Christianity*. New York: Doubleday & Co., 1970.

ARMOUR, R. A., *Gods and Myths of Ancient Egypt*. Cairo: The American University in Cairo Press, 1986.

BAHADUR, K. P., *Upanisads (Five Verse)*. New Delhi: New Light Publishers, 1972.

BATESON, G. (DONALDSON, R. E., Ed.), *A Sacred Unity: Further Steps to an Ecology of Mind*. New York: HarperCollins, 1991.

BATESON, G., *Mind and Nature: A Necessary Unity*. New York: E. P. Dutton, 1979.

BATESON, G., *Steps to an Ecology of Mind*. New York: Ballantine, 1972.

BEAGLEHOLE, E., *Notes on Hopi Economic Life*. New Haven: Yale University Press, 1937.

BECKER, R. O. & SELDEN, G., *The Body Electric: Electromagnetism and the Foundation of Life*. New York: William Morrow & Company, Inc., 1985.

304 THE SCIENCE OF THE SOUL

BECKER, R. O., *Cross Currents: The Promise of Electromedicine, the Perils of Electropollution.* Los Angeles: Jeremy P. Tarcher, Inc., 1990.

BENTOV, I. with M., *A Cosmic Book.* Rochester, VT: Destiny Books, 1988.

BENTOV, I., *Stalking the Wild Pendulum.* Rochester, VT: Destiny Books, 1988 (1976).

BHALLA, S., *Quotes From Gandhi.* New Delhi: U B S Publishers' Distributors Ltd., 1995.

BOHM, D., & PEAT, F. D., *Science, Order, and Creativity.* New York: Bantam Books, 1987.

BOHM, D. & HILEY, B., *The Undivided Universe: An Ontological Interpretation of Quantum Theory.* New York: Routledge, 1993.

BOHM, D., *Wholeness and the Implicate Order.* London: Ark Paperbacks, 1980.

BOHM, D., *Unfolding Meaning: A Weekend of Dialogue with David Bohm.* London: Ark Paperbacks, 1985.

BOHM, D., "Hidden Variables and the Implicate Order," in *Zygon: Journal of Religion & Science.* 20/2. Osford: Blackwell Publishing, 1985.

BOYD, D., *Swami: Encounters with Modern Mystics.* Honesdale, PA: Himalayan International Institute, 1995 (1976).

BRENNAN, B., *Hands of Light: A Guide to Healing Through the Human Energy Field.* Toronto: Bantam Books, 1987.

BRENNAN, B., *Light Emerging.* Toronto: Bantam Books, 1993.

BRIGGS, J. & PEAT, F. D., *Looking Glass Universe: The Emerging Science of Wholeness.* New York: Simon & Schuster, Inc., 1984.

BRIGGS, J. & PEAT, F. D., *Turbulent Mirror: An Illustrated Guide to Chaos Theory and the Science of Wholeness.* New York: Harper & Row, 1989.

BRUYERE, R., *Wheels of Light.* New York: Simon & Schuster, 1994 (1989).

BUCKE, R. M., *Cosmic Consciousness.* Secaucus, NJ: The Citadel Press, 1961.

BUCKLEY, P. & PEAT, F. D., *A Question of Physics: Conversations in Physics and Biology.* Toronto: University of Toronto Press, 1979.

BUDGE, E. A. W., *The Egyptian Book of the Dead: (The Papyrus of Ani) Egyptian Text Transliteration and Translation.* New York: Dover Publications, Inc., 1967 (1895).

BURTON, R. F., *The Arabian Nights' Entertainments.* New York: The Modern Library, 1932.

BUTLER, W. E., *How to Read the Aura, Practice Psychometry, Telepathy and Clairvoyance.* New York: Warner/Destiny Books, 1978.

CAMPBELL, J., *The Masks of God: Occidental Mythology.* Markham, Ontario: Penguin Books, Inc., 1976 (1964).

CAMPBELL, J., *The Masks of God: Primitive Mythology.* Markham, Ontario: Penguin Books, Inc., 1976 (1959).

CAMPBELL, J., *Myths to Live By.* Toronto: Bantam Books, Inc., 1972.

CAPRA, F. & STEINDL-RAST, D., with MATUS, T., *Belonging to the Universe: New Thinking About God and Nature.* New York: Penguin Books, 1992.

CAPRA, F., *The Tao of Physics.* Bungay, Suffolk: Fontana/Collins, 1977 (1976).

CAPRA, F., *The Turning Point.* New York: Bantam Books, 1982.

CAPRA, F., *The Web of Life: A New Scientific Understanding of Living Systems.* New York: Anchor Books/Doubleday, 1996.

CASTANEDA, C., *Journey to Ixtlan.* New York: Simon & Schuster, 1972.

CASTANEDA, C., *A Separate Reality.* New York: Simon & Schuster, 1971.

CASTANEDA, C., *The Teachings of Don Juan.* New York: Ballantine Books, 1969.

CLEARY, T., *The Essential Confucius.* San Francisco: HarperSanFrancisco, 1991.

COOK, A. B., *Zeus: A Study in Ancient Religion.* Vol. 1-4. New York: Biblo and Tannen, 1964 (1914).

COOMARASWAMY, A. K., *Buddha and the Gospel of Buddhism.* New York: Harper Torchbooks, 1969.

COOMARASWAMY, A. K. (LIPSEY, R., Ed.), *Coomaraswamy,* Vol. 1-3. Princeton: Princeton University Press, 1977.

COOPER, J. C., *Yin and Yang: The Taoist Harmony of Opposites.* Wellingborough: The Aquarian Press, Ltd., 1981.

COURTOIS, F., *An Experience of Enlightenment.* Tokyo: Shunju-Sha, 1970.

CREMO, M. & THOMPSON, R., *Forbidden Archeology: The Hidden History of the Human Race.* Los Angeles: Bhaktivedanta Book Publishers, Inc., 1993.

DASS, R., *Be Here Now.* San Cristobal, NM: Lama Foundation, 1971.

DASS, R. & LEVINE, S., *Grist For the Mill.* New York: Bantam Books, 1979 (1977).

DAVID-NEEL, A. & YONGDEN, L., *The Secret Oral Teachings in Tibetan Buddhist Sects.* San Francisco: City Lights Books, 1967.

DAVIES, P. C. W., *Superforce: The Search For a Grand Unified Theory of Nature.* New York: Simon and Schuster, 1984.

DAVIES, P. C. W. & BROWN, J. R., *The Ghost in the Atom.* New York: Cambridge University Press, 1986.

DOSSEY, L., *Recovering the Soul: A Scientific and Spiritual Search.* New York: Bantam Books, 1989.

DOYLE, A. C., *The History of Spiritualism.* New York: Arno Press, 1975.

DUFTY, W., *Sugar Blues.* New York: Warner Books, Inc., 1975.

EINSTEIN, A., *Autobiographical Notes. A Centennial edition.* Chicago: Open Court Publishing Co., 1979.

EINSTEIN, A., (CALAPRICE, A., Ed.), *The Quotable Einstein.* Princeton: Princeton University Press, 1996.

EINSTEIN, A., *The World As I See It.* New York: The Philosophical Library, Inc., 1949.

ELIADE, M., *A History of Religious Ideas.* Chicago: University of Chicago Press, 1978.

ELIADE, M. (BEANE, W. C. & DOTY, W. G., Eds.), *Myths, Rites, Symbols: A Mircea Eliade Reader.* San Francisco: Harper & Row, Publishers, 1975.

EVANS-WENTZ, W. Y., *Tibet's Great Yogi Milarepa: A Biography From the Tibetan.* Second edition. New York: Oxford University Press, 1969 (1928).

FEUERSTEIN, G., *Holy Madness.* Toronto: Penguin Books Canada Ltd., 1992.

FEYNMAN, R., *Surely You're Joking, Mr. Feynman!* Toronto: Bantam Books, 1986.

FISCHER, L., *Gandhi: His Life and Message for the World*. New York: New American Library, 1954.

FOHR, S. D., *Adam and Eve: Spiritual Symbolism in Genesis and Exodus*. Second edition. Ghent, NY: Sophia Perennis Et Universalis, 1994 (1986).

FOHR, S. D., *Cinderella's Gold Slipper: Spiritual Symbolism in the Grimm's tales*. Wheaton, IL: The Theosophical Publishing House, 1991.

FRANCK, A., *The Kabbalah*. New York: Bell Publishing Co, 1940.

FREMANTLE, F. & TRUNGPA, C., *The Tibetan Book of the Dead: The Great Liberation Through Hearing in the Bardo*. Berkeley: Shambhala, 1975.

GARDNER, M., *Fads & Fallacies in the Name of Science*. New York: Dover Publications, Inc., 1957.

GERBER, R., *Vibrational Medicine: New Choices For Healing Ourselves*. Santa Fe: Bear & Co., 1987.

GIRARDOT, N. J., *Myth and Meaning in Early Taoism*. Berkeley: University of California Press, 1983.

GLEICK, J., *Chaos: Making a New Science*. New York: Viking Penguin Inc., 1987.

GODWIN, J., *Harmonies of Heaven and Earth: The Spiritual Dimensions of Music*. Rochester, VT: Inner Traditions International, Ltd., 1987.

GODWIN, J., *Music, Mysticism and Magic: A Sourcebook*. New York: Routledge & Kegan Paul, 1987.

GODWIN, J., *Mystery Religions in the Ancient World*. San Francisco: Harper & Row Publishers, 1981.

GOSWAMI, A. with REED, R. & GOSWAMI, M., *The Self-Aware Universe: How Consciousness Creates the Material World*. Jeremy P. Tarcher, 1993.

GOVINDA, L., *Foundations of Tibetan Mysticism*. New York: Samuel Weiser, 1974.

GOVINDA, L., *Psycho-cosmic Symbolism of the Buddhist Stupa*. Emeryville, CA: Dharma Publishing, 1976.

GOVINDA, L., *The Psychological Attitude of Early Buddhist Philosophy*. London: Rider & Company, 1961.

GROF, S., *Books of the Dead: Manuals For Living and Dying*. London: Thames and Hudson, 1994.

GYANAMATA, S., *God Alone: The Life and Letters of a Saint.* Los Angeles: Self-Realization Fellowship, 1984.

HARVEY, E. H., Ed., *Reader's Digest Book of Facts.* Pleasantville, NY: The Reader's Digest Association, Inc., 1987.

HAY, L., *You Can Heal Your Life.* Carlsbad, CA: Hay House, 1984.

HERBERT, N., *Quantum Reality: Beyond the New Physics.* Garden City, NY: Anchor Press/Doubleday, 1987.

HIGHFIELD, R. & CARTER, P., *The Private Lives of Albert Einstein.* Boston: Faber and Faber, 1993.

HILEY, B. & PEAT, F. D., Ed., *Quantum Implications: Essays in Honour of David Bohm.* New York: Routledge, 1987.

HIXON, L., *Coming Home: The Experience of Enlightenment in Sacred Traditions.* New York: Larson Publications, 1995 (1978).

HIXON, L., *Heart of the Koran.* Wheaton, IL: The Theosophical Publishing House, 1988.

HUME, R.E., *Thirteen Principal Upanishads.* London: Oxford University Press, 1877.

HUNT, V., *Infinite Mind: Science of the Human Vibrations of Consciousness.* Malibu, CA: Malibu Publishing, 1996.

HUXLEY, A., *The Perennial Philosophy.* New York: Harper & Row, 1970.

JAMES, W., *The Varieties of Religious Experience.* New York: Collier Books, 1961.

JOY, W. B., M.D., *Joy's Way: A Map for the Transformational Journey.* Los Angeles: Jeremy P. Tarcher, Inc., 1979.

JUNG, C. G., *Man and His Symbols.* New York: Dell Publishing, 1964.

JUNG, C. G., *The Secret of the Golden Flower: A Chinese Book of Life.* London: Routledge & Kegan Paul, 1962.

KAKU, M., *Hyperspace: A Scientific Odyssey Through Parallel Universes, Time Warps, and the 10th Dimension.* New York: Random House, 1995 (1994).

KAUR, S. P., *Peace Lagoon: The Songs of Guru Nanak.* Albuquerque: Brotherhood of Life Books, 1971.

KOCK, W., *Lasers and Holography.* New York: Doubleday-Anchor, 1969.

KRISHNA, G., *Kundalini: The Evolutionary Energy in Man.* Boston: Shambhala, 1971.

KRISHNA, G., *Secrets of Kundalini in Panchastavi.* New Delhi: Kundalini Research and Publication Trust, 1978.

LEGGE, J., *Chuang Tzu.* New York: Ace Books, 1971.

LERNER, A. B., *Einstein & Newton: A Comparison of the Two Greatest Scientists.* Minneapolis: Lerner Publications Company, 1973.

LERNER, E., *The Big Bang Never Happened: A Startling Refutation of the Dominant Theory of the Origin of the Universe.* New York: Times Books, 1991.

LISIEUX, ST. T., *Thoughts of St. Therese: The Little Flower of Jesus Carmelite of the Monastery of Lisieux, 1873-1897.* Rockford, IL: T A N Books & Publishers, Inc., 1988.

LONG, M. F., *The Secret Science Behind Miracles.* Marina Del Rey, CA: DeVorss, 1954 (1948).

MAGNUSSON, M., *BC: The Archaeology of the Bible Lands.* London: BCA, 1977.

MAHARSHI, R., *Talks with Sri Ramana Maharshi.* Tiruvannamalai: Sri Ramanasraman, 1984.

MANUEL, F., *The Religion of Isaac Newton.* Oxford: The Clarendon Press, 1974.

MATA, D., *A Paramhansa Yogananda Trilogy of Divine Love.* Beverly Hills, CA: Joan Wight Publications, 1992.

MATA, T., *A Forerunner of the New Race.* Los Angeles: Self-Realization Fellowship, 1981 (1971).

McCONNELL, S., *Code Complete.* Redmond, WA: Microsoft Press, 1993.

MERRELL-WOLFF, F., *Pathways Through to Space.* New York: The Julian Press, Inc., 1973.

MERRELL-WOLFF, F., *The Philosophy of Consciousness Without An Object.* New York: The Julian Press, Inc., 1973.

MILLER, P., "Jane Goodall," in *National Geographic,* December, 1995 (Vol. 188, No. 6).

MOTOYAMA, H., *Karma and Reincarnation: The Key to Spiritual Evolution and Enlightenment.* London: Piatkus Publishers Ltd., 1992.

MOTOYAMA, H., *Theories of the Chakras: Bridges to Higher Consciousness.* Wheaton, IL: The Theosophical Publishing House, 1981.

MOTOYAMA, H., *Toward a Superconsciousness: Meditational Theory and Practice*. Berkeley: Asian Humanities Press, 1990.

MURPHY, M., *The Future of the Body: Explorations Into the Further Evolution of Human Nature*. Los Angeles: Jeremy P. Tarcher, Inc., 1992.

PAGELS, H., *The Cosmic Code*. New York: Bantam Books, 1982.

PEITGEN, H-O. & SAUPE, D., Ed., *The Science of Fractal Images*. New York: Springer-Verlag, 1988.

PEAT, F. D., *In Search of Nikola Tesla*. Bath, England: Ashgrove Press Ltd., 1983.

PEAT, F. D., *Infinite Potential: The Life and Times of David Bohm*. Don Mills, Ontario: Addison-Wesley Publishing Company, Ltd., 1997.

PEAT, F. D., *Lighting the Seventh Fire: The Spiritual Ways, Healing, and Science of the Native American*. New York: Birch Lane Press, 1994.

PIERRAKOS, E. & THESENGA, D., *Fear No Evil: The Pathwork Method of Transforming the Lower Self*. Madison: Pathwork Press, 1993.

PIERRAKOS, E., *The Pathwork of Self-transformation*. New York: Bantam Books, 1990.

PIERRAKOS, J., *Core Energetics*. Mendocino, CA: LifeRhythm Publication, 1990.

PLANCK, M., *Scientific Autobiography*. (F. Gaynon, Trans.) New York: Philosophical Library, 1949.

RAMA, SW. & AJAYA, SW., *Creative Use of Emotion*. Honesdale, PA: Himalayan International Institute, 1976.

RAMA, SW., *Living With The Himalayan Masters*. Honesdale, PA: Himalayan International Institute, 1978.

RAMA, SW., *Nitnem: Spiritual Practices of Sikhism*. Honesdale, PA: Himalayan International Institute, 1989.

RAMPA, T. L., *The Cave of the Ancients*. New York: Ballantine Books, 1963.

RAMPA, T. L., *Chapters of Life*. London: Transworld Publishers, Ltd., 1967.

RAMPA, T. L., *The Rampa Story*. Second edition. London: Transworld Publishers, Ltd., 1965 (1960).

RIFKIN, J., *Biosphere Politics*. New York: Crown Publishers, Inc., 1991.

RING, K., *Heading Toward Omega*. New York: William Morrow, 1985.

ROBBINS, J., *Diet for A New America*. Walpole, NH: Stillpoint Publishing, 1987.

ROBBINS, J., *May All Be Fed: Diet for A New World*. New York: William Morrow and Company, Inc., 1992.

SANNELLA, L., *The Kundalini Experience*. Lower Lake, CA: Integral Publishing, 1992 (1976).

SAYBROOK PUBLISHING COMPANY, *The Reach of the Mind: Nobel Prize Conversations*. Dallas, TX: Saybrook Publishing Co., 1985.

SAYEN, J., *Einstein in America*. New York: Crown Publishers, Inc., 1985.

SCHINDLER, D., Ed., *Beyond Mechanism: The Universe in Recent Physics and Catholic Thought*. Lanham, MD: The University Press of America, Inc., 1986.

SCHUON, F., *Dimensions of Islam*. London: George Allen and Unwin Ltd., 1970.

SCHUON, F., *The Transcendent Unity of Religions*. New York: Harper & Row, 1975.

SCHWARZ, J., *Human Energy Systems*. New York: E. P. Dutton, 1980.

SCHWARZ, J., *Voluntary Controls*. New York: E. P. Dutton, 1978.

SCOTT, M., *Kundalini in the Physical World*. Boston: Routledge & Kegan Paul, 1983.

SHARMA, Y. S., *Kundalini Sakthi—Serpent Power*. Bangalore, India, 1971.

SINGH, K., *The Crown of Life*. Delhi: Ruhani Satsang, 1973.

SINGH, K., *Naam or Word*. Delhi: Ruhani Satsang, 1970 (1960).

SIVANANDA, SW., *Raja Yoga*. Fremantle: Divine Life Society, 1986.

SMITH, H., *Forgotten Truth: The Primordial Tradition*. New York: Harper & Row, 1976.

SMITH, H., *The World's Religions*. San Francisco: HarperSanFrancisco, 1991.

SPRETNAK, C., *The Politics of Women's Spirituality: Essays on the Rise of Power Within the Feminist Movement*. Garden City, NY: Anchor Press/Doubleday, 1982.

STEINEM, G., *Revolution From Within: A Book of Self-Esteem*. Boston: Little, Brown & Co., 1992.

SUZUKI, D. T., *Studies in Zen.* New York: Dell Publishing Co., 1955.

TAGORE, R., *Songs of Kabir.* New York: The Macmillan Company, 1915.

TALBOT, M., *Beyond the Quantum.* New York: Bantam Books, 1988.

TALBOT, M., *The Holographic Universe.* New York: HarperCollins Publishers, 1991.

TALBOT, M., *Mysticism and the New Physics.* New York: Arkana, 1993 (1980).

TAYLOR, A., *Healing Hands: A Practical Guide to Exploring the Powers of Healing.* London: Random House, 1992.

TIRTHA, SW., *Vedic Mathematics.* Delhi: Motilal Banarsidass Publishers Private Ltd., 1992 (1965).

TRUNDY, Z. P., *Buddha and Christ: Nativity Stories and Indian Traditions.* New York: E. J. Brill, 1993.

WALEY, A., *The Way and Its Power.* London: George Allen & Unwin Ltd., 1934.

WARE, J., *The Sayings of Chuang Chou.* Toronto: New American Library of Canada Ltd., 1963.

WATTS, A., *This Is It and Other Essays on Zen.* New York: Pantheon Books, 1960.

WEBER, R., *Dialogues With Scientists and Sages: The Search for Unity.* New York: Routledge and Kegan Paul, 1986.

WEINMAN, R., *Your Hands Can Heal: Learn To Channel Healing Energy.* Toronto: Penguin Books Canada Ltd., 1992 (1988).

WHITE, J., *The Meeting of Science & Spirit: Guidelines For a New Age.* New York: Paragon House Publishers, 1990.

WHITE, J., *What is Enlightenment? Exploring the Goal of the Spiritual Path.* New York: Paragon House, 1995 (1985).

WHITTON, J. L. & FISHER, J., *Life Between Life.* Garden City, NY: Doubleday & Company, Inc., 1986.

WILBER, K., *A Brief History of Everything.* Boston, MA: Shambhala, 1996.

WILBER, K., *Eye to Eye: The Quest for the New Paradigm.* New York: Doubleday, 1983.

WILBER, K., *The Eye of Spirit: An Integral Vision for a World Gone Slightly Mad.* Boston, MA: Shambhala, 1998.

WILBER, K., *Grace and Grit: Spirituality & Healing in the Life & Death of Treya Killam Wilber.* Boulder, CO: Shambhala, 1993.

WILBER, K., Ed., *The Holographic Paradigm and Other Paradoxes.* Boulder, CO: Shambhala, 1982.

WILBER, K., *The Marriage of Sense and Soul.* New York: Random House, 1998.

WILBER, K., *One Taste: The Journals of Ken Wilber.* Boston: Shambhala, 2000.

WILBER, K., *Quantum Questions.* Boulder, CO: Shambhala, 1984.

WILBER, K., *Up From Eden: A Transpersonal View of Human Evolution.* Boulder, CO: Shambhala Publications, 1983 (1981).

WILBER, K., ANTHONY, D. & ECKER, B., Ed., *Spiritual Choices: The Problems of Recognizing Authentic Paths to Inner Transformation.* New York: Paragon House, 1987.

WOLF, F. A., *Taking the Quantum Leap.* New York: Harper & Row, 1981.

WOLFE, W. T., *And the Sun Is Up: Kundalini Rises in the West.* Red Hook, NY: Academy Hill Press, 1978.

WOLFF, J. & COX, K., *Successful Scriptwriting.* Cincinnati: Writer's Digest Books, 1988.

WOODROFFE, J., *Principles of Tantra, Part I.* Fourth edition. Madras, India: Ganesh & Co., 1969 (1914).

WOODROFFE, J., *The Serpent Power.* Third edition. Madras, India: Ganesh & Co., 1928 (1918).

WOODROFFE, J., *Wave of Bliss.* Fifth edition. Madras, India: Ganesh & Co., 1961 (1916).

YEATS, W. B. & SWAMI, S. P., *The Ten Principal Upanishads.* London: Faber and Faber, Ltd., 1937.

YOGANANDA, P., *Autobiography of a Yogi.* Twelfth edition. Los Angeles: Self-Realization Fellowship, 1981 (1946).

YOGANANDA, P., *Beholding the One in All.* Cassette recording. Los Angeles: Self-Realization Fellowship, 1985 (1949).

YOGANANDA, P., *Cosmic Chants.* Sixth edition. Los Angeles: Self-Realization Fellowship, 1974 (1938).

YOGANANDA, P., *The Divine Romance.* Los Angeles: Self-Realization Fellowship, 1986.

YOGANANDA, P., *God Talks With Arjuna (The Bhagavad Gita: Royal Science of God-Realization)*. Los Angeles: Self-Realization Fellowship, 1995.

YOGANANDA, P., *Journey to Self-Realization: Discovering the Gifts of the Soul*. Los Angeles: Self-Realization Fellowship, 1997.

YOGANANDA, P., *Man's Eternal Quest*. Los Angeles: Self-Realization Fellowship, 1982.

YOGANANDA, P., *The Sayings of Paramahansa Yogananda*. Fourth edition. Los Angeles: Self-Realization Fellowship, 1986 (1952).

YOGANANDA, P., *The Science of Religion*. Los Angeles: Self-Realization Fellowship, 1982 (1953).

YOGANANDA, P., *Wine of the Mystic (The Rubaiyat of Omar Khayyam: A Spiritual Interpretation)*. Los Angeles: Self-Realization Fellowship, 1994.

ZIMMER, H., *Myths and Symbols in Indian Art and Civilization*. New York: Harper and Brothers, 1946.

ZIMMER, H., *Philosophies of India*. Princeton: Princeton University Press, 1951.

PERMISSIONS

THE AUTHOR GRATEFULLY ACKNOWLEDGES permission to quote from the following publications:

Quotation on page 176 reprinted with permission from *Coming Home: The Experience of Enlightenment in Sacred Traditions,* copyright 1978, 1989, 1995 by Lex Hixon.

Quotations on pages 52, 233–4 and 253 reprinted with permission from *The Kundalini Experience* by Lee Sannella. Copyright © 2002 Yoga Research and Education Center, www.yrec.org.

Quotation on page 73 reprinted with permission from *Science, Order, and Creativity* by David Bohm and F. David Peat. Copyright © 1987 Bantam Books, New York, p. 180.

Upanishadic verses taken from Robert E. Hume's *The Thirteen Principal Upanishads,* London: Oxford University Press, 1877; W. B. Yeats and S. P. Swami's *The Ten Principal Upanishads,* London: Faber and Faber, Ltd., 1937; and K. P. Bahadur's *Upanisads (Five Verse),* New Delhi: New Light Publishers, 1972.

Chuang Tzu quotations taken from J. Legge's *Chuang Tzu,* New York: Ace Books, 1971; and J. Ware's *The Sayings of Chuang Chou,* Toronto: New American Library of Canada Ltd., 1963.

Kabir quotations are taken from Rabindranath Tagore's *Songs of Kabir,* New York: The Macmillan Company, 1915.

INDEX

Aboriginals, 200
Absolute, 10, 15, 27, 30, 33, 57, 59, 69, 74, 119, 177.-8, 204, 206, 262, 285-6
Achad, F., 174
Achuar, 199
Acupuncture, 81, 84
Adam, 109, 180-1, 290
Agape, 166
Agriculture, 150
Ahimsa, 90
AIDS, 191
Ainslie, D., 283
Aladdin, 130, 132-3, 140-1, 143
Alchemy, 70, 161, 275, 278
Allegro, J., 162
Amazon, 199
Amphibian, 136, 146
Amrita, 109, 115, 152
Anaximander, 286
Anti-matter, 3-4, 30, 257
Anvil, 50
Apala, 151
Apana, 14, 103-4
Apples, 124, 209-10
Arabian Nights, 130, 132
Archery, 151
Archetypes, 27, 48, 53-4
  and human patterns of thought, 234
  reflected on lower levels, 2-3, 6, 10, 62-3, 211

Aristotle, 93, 285
Arrow; *see* Archery
"As above, so below", vii, 2, 8, 62, 93-4, 165, 177, 215, 236, 258, 264, 270, 273, 295
Ashrams, 100, 241, 243, 298
Astral body, 13-4, 21-2, 31, 80, 82-3, 85-6, 91, 98, 103-6, 112, 116-7, 119-23 , 125-6, 128, 130-2, 134, 142, 152, 157-8, 164, 217, 219, 221, 223, 231, 253, 261
Astral travel, 38, 116, 118, 120, 122, 128-9, 133, 158
Astrology, 246
Atman, 173, 177, 260-1
Athena, 110, 160
Atoms, 2, 20-1, 34, 74, 93, 178, 189, 203, 214, 231, 272-3, 278, 283
Attachment, 8, 77-9, 91, 96, 202
Augustine, 37, 203
Aum, 59; *see also* Om
Aura, 70, 81, 83, 86, 91-4, 97, 108, 127, 129, 151, 154, 156, 209, 211-3, 230, 253
Aurobindo, 30, 105, 300
Avatamsaka Sutra, 69, 175, 284
Axis, 107, 144, 146-8, 151, 221
  of spine, 103, 145, 150, 152-3
  World/*mundi*, 16, 111, 129, 142-3, 154, 158, 167, 239
Axle, 150-2

Ayn Sof, 27, 134, 174, 180

Bacchus, 106, 112, 161
Bacon, F., 279
Ball, golden, 70, 136, 298
Balloon, 13-4, 24, 28, 38, 118, 132
Balzac, H., 231, 276
Bandpass filtering, 12-3, 17, 24, 59,
    258, 263
Bandwidth, 12, 18, 24, 60
Baptism, 116, 163-4, 179
Barrett, W., 281
Bateson, G., 2, 88-90
Baum, F. L., 281
Beaglehole, E., 198
Beam, see Cosmic Beam
Beans, 160-1
Beauty, 9, 39-44, 77, 92, 123, 166, 200,
    203, 211
Becker, R. O., 211, 232, 247
Becoming, 59, 74-6, 177, 180, 184, 204,
    285-6
Bees, 116, 162
Behmen (Böhme/Boehme), J., 276, 279,
    291
Being, 42-3, 70, 75-6, 107, 174, 177,
    179-80, 184, 187, 204, 278, 284-5
Bells, 92, 116, 142, 149
Bell curve, 170-1
Belly, 91-2, 117, 119, 298
Bentov, I., 20-1, 23-4, 27, 69, 93, 116,
    118-9, 128, 132, 177-9, 181, 185,
    189, 203-4, 213, 217, 221, 235,
    240, 263, 297
Bergson, H., 285
Berkeley riots, 193
Bhagavad Gita, 57, 259, 269, 273, 279
Bible, 54, 56, 108-9, 132, 142, 163, 235,
    266, 290, 295, 298
Big bang, 20, 213, 274, 293
Billiard balls, 73
Binah, 180; see also Sephiroth
Binary, 205, 207, 285
Bindu, 53, 106, 222; see also Point
Birds, 109, 113-5, 132, 143-5, 150, 155,
    159, 195-7
    and pecking orders, 195-6
    Great, 141
    of Paradise, 143
Blake, W., 278-9
Bliss, 34-5, 37, 50, 80, 85-7, 99, 106,
    110, 114, 161, 167, 175, 217, 241,
    244-5, 250, 258-9, 294, 296

Bliss (continued)
    bunny, 244
Blood, 62, 103-4, 152, 193, 196, 258
Blueprint (astral), 80
Bochco, S., 90
Bohm, D., 38, 73-4, 100, 203, 210,
    220-1, 274, 293
Bohr, N., 272, 280
Bonaventure, 25
Book of the Dead, 58, 156
Bose, J. C., 283
Bottle, 130-3, 226
Bouncing, 13-4, 17-8, 24, 26, 48, 60,
    178, 258, 260, 263
Boyle, R., 275
Bracelet, 141
Brahma, 102, 105, 113, 157, 181, 279
Brahman, 1, 52, 58, 61, 72, 119, 172,
    177, 259, 266
Brahmanadi, 105, 109, 157-8
Brahmarandhra, 105, 157, 175
Braille, 184
Brainwaves, 230, 169, 251
Branches, 103, 159, 169, 179, 290
    of Menorah, 156
Branstock, 143
Breath, 23, 50, 57-8, 60-2, 85, 111,
    122, 167, 169, 180, 222, 225,
    246, 251, 258, 269, 276, 278, 286,
    299-300; see also Universal
    Breathing
    currents, 14, 103-4, 110, 118
Brennan, B., 27, 61, 70, 80, 84, 92,
    118-20, 126, 128-9, 138, 140, 157,
    172, 176, 178-9, 195, 203-4, 212,
    220, 235, 245-7
Brönte, E., 278
Broomstick, 158
Bruyere, 109, 125, 204, 211
Bubbles, 20, 34
    of consciousness, 62
    of thought, 94
Buckley, P., 221
Buddha, 2, 51, 75, 113-4, 148, 158, 289,
    300
Buddha-nature, 33, 156
Bulb, see Cosmic Bulb
Bull, 151, 195
Bull's eye, 151
Burr, H. S., 211
Bush, 212
    burning, 114, 143, 148
Bushmen, 200

Caduceus, 103, 105, 131, 148, 155-6
Cage, 143
Calculus, 274, 284
Campbell, J., 265
Carpet, 133
Cartesian, 194, 288
Castle, 91, 109, 117, 136, 140, 153, 168
Causal body, 13, 21, 31, 80-3, 85-7,
    97-101, 105, 112, 117-20, 123,
    126-8, 130-2, 139, 152, 157-8, 164,
    175, 179, 214, 216-7, 222-3, 253-4,
    258, 300
Celibacy, 98, 228, 242, 251
Chakras, 49, 53, 62, 70, 80-1, 83, 86,
    91-3, 98, 102-5, 108, 111-7, 120-2,
    125-6, 128-9, 133-8, 141-4, 146-7,
    150-60, 162, 167, 175, 220,
    229-31, 240, 252, 255-6, 258,
    271, 296, 298-9
Chaos, 54, 163-4, 172, 174, 176-81,
    238, 281, 299
Chariot, 2, 150-1
Cherub(im), 109, 151
Chimney, 115, 149
Chimpanzees, 195-6
Chitra/Chitrini, 104-5, 109, 157-8
Chocolate, 160-1
Christ, Jesus, 2, 50-1, 55, 162-3, 249,
    278, 289, 292, 297-8, 300
Christmas, 149-50
Chuang Tzu, 16, 56-7, 150, 152, 167,
    235, 237, 299
Church, 135, 149, 155, 163, 244
Cinderella, 107, 115, 129
Clairvoyance, 38, 83, 91-2, 94, 97-8,
    108, 118, 121, 127, 129, 131,
    151-2, 154-5, 165, 167, 209, 211,
    221, 228, 247-8, 296
Clapping; *see* Om
Clashing rocks; *see* Rocks, clashing
Clear Light (of the Void), 156, 175-8, 300
Clitoris, 164-5
Clouds, 91, 143, 145, 147, 183, 269
Comic strips, 94
Commandments, 200, 218
Compassion, 9, 38, 79, 96, 98, 100, 128,
    195, 218, 241, 245, 289, 297
Conceptualization, 44, 61, 78, 80, 98,
    111, 137, 154, 157, 183-4, 186-7,
    192, 194-6, 202, 204, 210, 216,
    218-20, 223-4, 226-7, 229, 234-8,
    240, 260-2, 270, 274, 300
Conch, 60, 142, 147

Cone, 112, 141, 144, 161
Conformity, 39, 193, 201, 248, 298
Confucius, 233
Conscience, 99-101, 215
Coomaraswamy, A., 15, 75, 110, 113,
    115, 141-2, 225, 234, 291
Cooper, J. C., 137
Cord, silver; *see* Silver cord
Cork, 131-2
Cornucopia, 25, 27, 159
Cosmic
    consciousness, 1, 12, 29-31, 34, 49-
        51, 56, 71, 84, 118, 143, 154, 158,
        175, 183-4, 241, 298
    Beam, 18, 25
    Bulb, 17-8
    Drum, 58, 60-1, 225, 257, 261, 263,
        268
    Pendulum, 24, 69, 258
    Projector, 18, 72
    Watch, 25
    Watchmaker, 48
Courtois, 26
Cow, 151, 160, 225
Crookes, W., 281
Cross, 16, 93, 162, 275, 289
Crown
    of kings, 155-6
    chakra; *see* Chakras
    Kabbalistic, 27, 175
Cupid, 151, 269
Cusa, N., 259
Cyclops, 105-6, 160

Da Vinci, L., 155, 274
Dagon, 164
Daimon, 285
Dance, 29, 175, 190
    of Shiva, 9, 58-9, 261
Dante, 275
Darwin, 197, 281; *see also* Evolution
David-Neel, A., 75
Death, 15, 27, 31-2, 75, 82, 90-1, 98,
    117, 120-4, 128-9, 153, 156,
    165-6, 230, 249-50, 269, 275-6,
    278, 280, 286, 292, 294, 299-301
    conscious, 104-5, 115, 131, 135, 157,
        168-9
Déjà vu, 221
Descartes, R., 70-1, 300
Desires, 9, 40, 46, 63, 77-80, 121, 124-
    6, 130, 132-3, 191-2, 194, 202,
    228, 254, 269

Devi, I., 94-5
Devil, 38, 138, 184, 287
Dharmata, 156
Dice, 170-1
Diffraction, 67-8, 154-5, 260
Dionysus, 105, 166
Discus, 106
Disk, 106, 156
Disney, 129
DNA, 41, 209
Dome, 113, 141-2
Door(way), 15-6, 24, 61-2, 98, 107, 110,
    143, 153, 156, 162, 257, 260, 263
Dot, see Point
Doves, 113-5, 151
Doyle, A. C., 281
Dragons, 113, 135, 226
Dreams, 13, 59, 82, 85, 121-4, 129, 142,
    169, 185, 221, 230-2, 300
    dilation of subjective time in, 5, 7,
    22-3, 220
Drop (of consciousness), 33-4, 56
Drum, Cosmic; see Cosmic Drum
Duality; see Conceptualization and
    duality
Dwarfs, 102, 108
Dynamic balance, 139-40

Eagle, 113-4, 143, 286
Earth, 9, 26, 111, 113-5, 134-6, 143,
    145-50, 153, 159, 164, 167, 180,
    226, 241, 255
    as astral element, 112, 116, 285
    as organism, 189, 203
    Mother, 29, 52
    planet, 42, 50, 54, 56, 63, 70, 131,
    144, 193, 204, 224-5, 287-8
Easter, 161, 181
Eastman, G., 283
Eckhart, M., 37, 49, 168
Ecology, 205
Ecosystems, 187
Ecstasy, 34, 43, 80, 276-7; see also Bliss
Ectoplasm, 282
Eddington, A., 273
Eden, 109
Edison, T., 279
EEG, 169, 212-3, 230
Egg, 54, 145
    in Aladdin tale, 141
    cosmic, 144, 181
    in aura, 81, 108, 143, 147-8, 150, 155

Ego, 1, 30, 37, 71, 78, 86, 89-90, 99,
    108, 110, 126, 129, 131, 134, 153,
    168, 176, 178, 194-5, 202, 226,
    241-2, 250-1
Egyptians, 34, 145, 156, 161, 163, 166,
    246
Einstein, A., 5, 9, 23, 36, 38, 43, 100,
    108, 265, 271-4
Electrons, 3, 189, 272-4
Elijah, 150, 298
Eliot, T. S., 107, 278
Elixir of Immortality, 298; see also
    Amrita; see also Nectar
Ellipses, 87
Emerson, R. W., 279
Emotion(s), 13, 33, 41, 77-84, 86, 89,
    91, 93-4, 100, 122-3, 127, 129,
    137, 154, 166, 194-7, 202, 211-3,
    217, 228, 246, 252-6, 271, 287,
    294
Empedocles, 25
Energy blockages, 82-7, 157, 228-9,
    240-1, 246, 252
Envy
    as feeling, 78, 197, 200, 202
    as color in aura, 91, 211-2
Epiphany, 51
Erechtheion, 142
Eros, 166, 269
Eskimo, 110, 200
Ether(ic), 33, 80, 112, 116, 128
Eve, 180
Evil; see Good
Evolution, 20, 37, 42, 87, 126-8, 146,
    160, 197, 201, 203, 236, 258, 281,
    286, 300
Excalibur, 113
Explicate order; see Order, explicate
Eyes, 21, 26, 29, 34, 66, 92, 105, 108,
    112, 115, 151-2, 160, 167, 223,
    231, 235-6, 268, 270, 275, 300;
    see also Spiritual eye

Faith, 189, 289-90
Farid, B., 168
Father, 50-1, 53-5, 106, 136, 143, 145,
    159-60, 164, 179-80, 188; see also
    Masculine
Feedback, 187
Feeling, 9, 40-1, 71, 77-80, 82-3, 96,
    100, 123, 139, 216, 254-5, 271,
    289, 293; see also Reason

Feminine, 52-5, 84, 93, 102, 105-6, 113, 135-8, 144-5, 150-1, 157, 160, 164, 180-1, 229
Fertility, 160-2, 164, 166, 181
Feynman, R., 277
Filtering, 18, 28, 60, 127, 179, 206, 215, 237; see also Bandpass filtering
Fire, 104, 112, 114-6, 132, 150, 159, 161, 167, 231, 275, 285
Fish, 136, 163-4
Fishing, 141
Flammarion, C., 282
Fleece; see Golden Fleece
Flood, 181
Flower, golden, 80, 167, 298; see also Chakra, crown
Flute, 116
Flying, 5, 22-3, 113, 116, 133, 149, 151, 158, 223-4; see also Samadhi; see also Astral travel; see also Time
Fohr, S. D., 107-8
Forces, 20, 34, 50, 74, 109, 203, 212, 214, 232, 282
Formlessness, 9, 30-1, 34, 53, 164, 173-4, 177-8, 183, 208, 226, 259-60
Fountain, 34, 121, 152, 299
Fourier analysis/synthesis, 171, 215
Fractals, 179
Fragmentation, 38, 183-4, 186-7, 189-96, 202-4, 208, 218, 223, 235, 256, 285
Free will, viii, 62, 249
Freedom of choice, viii, 45-7, 84, 236, 263
Freemasons, 143
Freud, 85, 115, 160, 165
Frog Prince, The, 136
Frontal personality, 86, 128; see also Personality
Fundamentalist, 188, 239

Gaia, 203
Galileo, 211, 264, 266, 287, 289
Gandhi, M., 43, 90, 190, 204, 271, 289
Ganges, 104
Garments, 2, 107, 117-8, 155, 159
Gateway, 16, 107, 114, 153, 156, 162, 299-300
Gebusi, 199
Gem; see Jewel
General semantics, 209, 235, 238

Genetics, 74, 195
Genie, 130-3, 140-1, 153, 226
Genius, 97-8, 130, 231-2, 245, 250, 271
Gerber, R., 81, 112, 155
Gestalt, sensory, 75, 78, 183-4, 202, 218, 223, 235, 238, 262
Gifts, 87, 105, 123, 125, 197-8, 204, 233
Girardot, N. J., 144, 181
Gleick, J., 224-5
Gnosis, 134
Godhead, 131
Godmother, 129
Godwin, J., 166
Goethe, J., 168, 277
Gold, 27, 49, 51, 56, 70, 80-1, 91, 102, 104-11, 113-4, 116, 121, 129, 132-3, 136, 140-1, 143-4, 146, 148, 150, 152, 154-5, 159-62, 167, 176, 181, 282, 289, 298
Golden Fleece, 110, 159-60
Gong, 116, 142
Good, 32, 36-40, 42-5, 48, 86, 111, 138-40, 145, 152, 162, 215, 217-8, 234-5, 242, 252, 254, 262, 285, 289
Goodall, J., 195-6
Gourd, 106
Govinda, L., 20, 150, 272, 300
Gnostic(s), 3, 144
gospels, 34, 51, 55-6, 166
Goose, 150, 225
Grapefruit, 41
Grapes, 161, 190
Gravity, 214, 274
Great Bird, 141
Grimm, 131, 136
Groceries, 212
Ground (of Being), 42, 70, 179, 204, 206, 262, 284
Grounding, 101, 131, 241, 252, 255
Guénévere, 140
Gurdjieff, 242, 281
Guru, 94-5, 120, 228, 242, 248-51, 265, 297-8

Hair, 27, 75, 94, 103, 160, 225
Hall, 94, 161-2
Hallucinations, 230, 292, 300
Ham, 150
Hamsa, 150, 226
Hammering
and phenomenology, 236
anvil, 50

Harmony, 39-40, 42, 213, 273
Harvey, A., 243
Healing, 229, 250, 286
  caduceus as symbol of, 103
  laying-on-of-hands, 70, 120-1, 138,
    245-6
  silver cloth, 131
Hearing, 29, 116, 157, 275, 290
Heartstrings, 91
Heaven(s), 9, 34, 45, 57, 92, 107, 111,
    113-5, 129, 134-6, 139, 142-8,
    150-1, 153, 164, 166-7, 180, 188,
    266, 275-6, 278-9, 286, 292, 299,
    301
Heidegger, 237, 284
Heisenberg, W., viii, 272
Hemalekha, 259
Hemispheres
  of brain, 169, 229-30
  of earth, 145, 204
Heraclitus, 3, 286
Hermaphroditic, 180-1
Hermeneutics, 212
Hermes, 105, 155
Hermetic, 2-3, 155
Hierarchy
  in conceptualization, 186, 191-2, 194,
    201, 202, 205
  ontological, 187-8, 214
  social/cultural, 195-6, 199-201
Hiley, B., 293
Himalayas, 190
Hixon, L., 109, 176
Hole, smoke; see Smoke hole
Holograms, vii-viii, 64-73, 260
Holomovement, 73
Holy Ghost, 50-1, 53, 151, 231; see also
  Om
Holy Grail, 140
Holy of Holies, 83, 140-1, 162
Homer, 105, 111, 143
Honeymoon, 162
Hopi Indians, 198
Horus, 155
House, 77, 108, 142-3, 167-8
Hubble, 274
Huei, Y., 33
Humility, 202, 241
Hunt, V., 129, 200, 211, 256
Huntun, 181
Hurakan, 104
Husserl, 237
Hut, 149; see also House

Huxley, A., 274, 277, 281
Hymen, 161-2
Hypnosis, 220, 230, 268
Hysteria, 85

"I Am", 27, 71, 175; see also Self-
  awareness; see also Witness(ing)
"I am He", 150, 173, 226
I Ching, 139
Ida, 103-6, 113, 137, 142, 164, 167
Imaginary numbers, 210
Implicate order; see Order, implicate
Impulses, 11, 13-5, 17-8, 24, 46, 48, 54,
    59-60, 72, 75, 171, 206, 237,
    257-8, 260
  in nervous system, 14, 219; see also
    Nervous system, spikes in
  and paradox, 28
Indra, 151
Inertia, 212
Infrared, 12
Inner child, 85-6
Instinct, 79, 92
Intellect, 23, 61, 78, 82-3, 100, 111,
    157, 186, 194-6, 202, 207-11, 218,
    223, 226, 235, 242, 250-1, 255,
    260, 275, 287-9, 291, 294-5
Intentionality line, 83, 92, 131, 137
Interference patterns, 19, 67, 69, 178
Interpenetration, 29, 32, 173, 177,
    209-10, 223, 264
Intuition, vii-viii, 26, 40, 46-7, 59-60,
    71, 78-81, 86, 95-100, 105,
    111-2, 115, 119, 123-4, 127,
    129-30, 134, 139, 155, 165, 175,
    185-6, 189-90, 200, 203, 207-11,
    213-5, 218-9, 225-6, 229-30, 237,
    241-2, 244-5, 248-50, 252-4, 256,
    259, 261-3, 271, 280, 287-9, 295-7
Islands, 19, 71, 74, 144, 178
Itch, 95

Jack and the Beanstalk, 150, 160
Jaiminiya Upanisad Brahmana, 129,
    133, 146
James, W., 280, 285
Janus, 16, 56
Jar, 130-2
Jesus; see Christ, Jesus
Jewel(ry), 132, 148, 167, 284
Jordan, 104
Joseph, 166
Josephson, B., 283

Joy, W. B., 23, 166
Jung, C., 85, 272, 280

Kabbala, 15, 27, 102, 105, 107, 174-5, 180, 275
Kabir, 1, 27, 30, 32, 34-5, 57, 59, 175, 216, 258, 298, 301
Kaku, M., 232
Kali, 53, 58, 163
Kamadeva, 269
Kamasutra, 125
Kant, I., 285
Karma, 100, 107, 120, 122-3, 125, 294
Keats, 42
Kekulé, F., 231
Kepler, 211
Kether(ic), 27, 81, 143, 160, 174-5
Khan, I., 34
Khu, 156
King(dom), 113, 117, 132-3, 143, 153, 155, 168, 266, 270
  of Soul, 152-3
Kipling, R., 279
Kiss, 134, 136
Knocking, 61-2, 257, 269
Knot, 87, 141
Koans, 61, 157, 174, 225-7, 236, 299
Koestler, A., 281
Kohlberg test, 193
Koran, 174, 184
Kornfield, J., 242
Krishna, 2, 50, 296, 298
  Gopi, 25, 106, 113-4, 118, 161, 231
Krishnamurti, 242, 274, 293
Kundalini, 25, 52, 99, 102-6, 108, 110, 112-4, 118, 125-6, 134-5, 143, 145-6, 151, 158, 160-2, 164-5, 167, 222, 225-6, 232-3, 240-1, 253, 270, 296, 299
K'un-lun, 144
Kübler-Ross, 204

Lao Tzu, 152, 174, 180
Ladder, 107-8, 132, 142, 156, 159
Lalleshwari, 33
Lamp, 98, 101, 132-3, 140
Lance, 151
Lancelot, 140
Language, 2, 10, 71, 93, 121, 169, 183, 185, 204, 214, 234, 270; *see also* Conceptualization; *see also* Fragmentation
Lasers, 131, 179

Lasers (*continued*)
  in holography, 64-5, 68
Lassooing, 115, 141
Left hand, 38, 84, 105, 137-8, 144, 162, 229-30, 266, 271
Leibniz, 211, 284
Lerner, E., 213
Levi-Strauss, C., 93
Leo, Pope, 265
Liege Lady, 141
Life current/energy/force, 13-4, 30, 92, 103-6, 109-11, 114-16, 119, 121-2, 126, 132, 137-8, 145, 152, 160, 162, 167-9, 223, 227, 229, 252-3, 286, 290, 298-9; *see also* Prana; *see also* Apana; *see also* Ida; *see also* Pingala
Lightning, 104, 113-4, 135, 143, 189, 231, 233, 282
Limitless Light of Chaos; *see* Chaos
Linear thinking; *see* Thinking
Lingam, 134-5
Lions, 109, 140-1
Lodge, O., 282
Loewi, O., 232
Logos, 62, 273, 286
Lotus, thousand-petaled; *see* Chakras
LSD, 297
Lunar; *see* Moon

Ma, Ananda Moyi, 37, 281
Machine, 71, 187-9, 203-4
  Giant, 188, 194
Magician, 132, 140
Magnet(ic), 70, 104, 145-6, 225, 247, 281
Magnusson, M., 109
Maharshi, R., 1, 119, 169, 178, 222, 235-6, 301
Manyness, 184
Maps, 211
Marriage, 133-6, 140, 143-5, 147-9, 199
Masculine, 52, 54-5, 84, 102, 105-6, 113, 135-8, 144-5, 150, 157, 159, 180, 229
Mata, T., 110
Matter, as condensed consciousness, vii, 1, 18-20, 29-31, 40, 47, 51, 56, 71, 123, 170, 172-3, 179, 206, 210, 258, 263, 299
Maya, 29-30, 33, 51-2, 54-5, 102, 104, 106, 111-3, 132-3, 136, 138-40, 142, 155, 162, 177, 180, 183-4, 261, 269

Mayan, 104, 113
McConnell, S., 197
Mead, M., 199
Meaning, 154, 184-5, 212, 291
Mechanistic, 94, 203
Meditation, vii, 3, 22, 35, 46-7, 49, 87,
    93-4, 98-100, 104, 106, 108, 110,
    116, 124, 127, 131, 148-9, 151,
    155, 158, 161, 169, 202, 216, 219,
    222-3, 227, 229-30, 236-7, 239-45,
    248-53, 263-4, 267-8, 278-9, 283,
    291-6, 298, 301
Memory, 22, 67, 74, 84, 92, 96, 111, 120,
    128, 183, 219, 223-5, 237, 300
Menorah, 156
Mermaid, 136, 164
Merrell-Wolff, F., 26, 43, 111, 184, 235
Meru, 143-4, 146-8
Metaphor, 2, 10, 43, 62-3, 70, 92-3, 109,
    121, 132, 147, 152, 156, 175, 188,
    208, 215, 227, 236-7, 264, 270,
    290, 295
Milieu, 22, 75, 217-8, 224, 229, 237-8
Miller, P., 195
Milliken, R., 274
Milton, J., 279
Mind, 5, 13, 18-9, 21-3, 31, 33, 37, 62,
    66, 72, 74, 77-8, 80-5, 87, 98, 101,
    112, 119, 122-3, 128-9, 139, 156-7,
    159, 168, 184-5, 189-90, 193, 196,
    206, 210, 215-6, 218-20, 230,
    233-8, 251, 253, 255, 261-3, 267,
    273, 280, 283, 287, 299, 301
  -body split, 30, 189
  of God, 214
Mirror, 50, 106, 108, 188, 235, 259, 284
Mithra, 149
Möbius strip, 208
Monad, 55, 284
Moore, C., 149
Morality, 43, 47, 56, 100-1, 108, 138,
    193, 213, 215, 217-8, 227, 230,
    242, 245, 292
Morning star; see Star, five-pointed
Morse code, 14
Mother, 50-1, 53-5, 136, 139, 143, 145,
    151, 163-5, 179-80, 188; see also
    Feminine; see also Nature
Motion pictures, 17, 22, 24, 38, 170, 179,
    214, 218, 225, 258, 261, 263, 268,
    290; see also Cosmic Projector
Motoyama, H., 118, 123, 231

Mount Kaf, 141, 143
Mount Olympus, 143
Mountains, 109-10, 141, 143-8, 159,
    179, 226
Mouth, 60, 91, 132, 164, 228, 269, 289
  of God, 57, 62, 134; see also Chakras
Mozart, 91
Murphy, M., 7
Music, 39-40, 44, 155, 198, 207, 251
  and human voice, 60
  of the spheres, 154, 286
  Unstruck, 301

Nada, 53
Nadis, 103, 105, 109, 157-8, 300; see
    also Ida; see also Pingala; see also
    Brahmanadi
Name, 27
  as concept, 183
  of God, 57-9, 234-5, 242
Nanak, Guru, 58
Narcissus, 166, 188
Nature, 2, 3, 10, 29-30, 37, 47, 52, 54,
    58, 60, 73, 93, 97, 155, 177 ,
    179-80, 183-4, 187-90, 192, 194-5,
    198, 203-5, 211, 214, 225, 263-5,
    270, 295
Navel, 119, 151-2
NDE (Near-death experiences), 115,
    128, 230, 280
Necklace, 141
Nectar, 109, 113, 115, 301
Needles, 115
Negative, 39, 52, 104-5, 136-7, 139,
    145-6, 181
  numbers, 208, 210
Nervous system, 103-4, 141, 150, 161,
    269
  spikes in, 14, 219, 258
Neuroses, 85-6, 99, 241, 253
Neuro-Linguistic Programming, 246
Newton, I., 155, 266, 274, 279, 284
  laws of, 19, 74
Nityananda, 227
Nirvana, 144
Nobel Prize, 232, 247, 271-2, 274, 278,
    282-3, 285, 287
Non-Being, 75-6, 174, 177, 179-80, 285
Non-competition, 198-9
Non-linearity, 208, 224
  in physics, 281
  of time, 260

North
  Pole, 146-7, 149
  Star; *see* Pole Star
Nuptial chamber, 136, 144, 149; *see also*
  Marriage

OBE (Out-of-the-body experiences), 277
Odin, 105
Odysseus, 105, 111, 160
Olympus, Mount; *see* Mount Olympus
Om, 50-1, 55, 57-61, 112-3, 116, 135,
  141, 143, 157, 164, 175, 179, 214,
  226, 257-61, 263, 286; *see also*
  Word of God; *see also* Holy Ghost
Omkar, 57
Oneness, 40, 61, 119, 126, 172, 201,
  253
One Hand, 61, 116, 136, 157, 225,
  236-7, 257
One Taste, 169, 250
Oppenheimer, J., 273
Order
  explicate, 73
  implicate, 73, 221
Organic produce, 190
Organism, creation as, x; *see also* Gaia
Orgasm, 125-6
Original wound, 84

Pagan, 63, 136, 150, 163
Pair production, 3, 6
Palace, 15, 51, 107, 109, 143, 152, 167
Pantheism, 32, 52, 72
Paradigm, 192, 194-5, 234, 238, 291
Paradise, 107, 109, 143
Paradox, 28, 157, 169, 173, 178, 180-1,
  199, 206, 225-6, 236, 299
Parapsychology, 247-8, 285
Pascal, B., 275
Pasteur, L., 265
Patanjali, 77, 278, 298
Patriarchy, 52, 194, 196
Pauli, W., 211, 272
Peace pipe, 104
Pearl, 163, 166
Pearly gate, 114
Peat, F. D., 73, 159, 221, 233, 280
Pentecost, 231
Persephone, 161, 166
Personality, 71, 80-2, 86-7, 89-90, 96,
  99, 110-1, 126, 128-31, 226, 252-3,
  276; *see also* Frontal personality

Phallic, 134-5, 161, 164-5, 185
Pharaoh, 145, 156, 161
Phenomenology, 212, 236-8, 274
Photoelectric effect, 274
Photons, 3-4, 12, 28-9, 217, 274
Pierrakos, J., 129
Pillar, 107, 114, 134, 141-2, 148, 159,
  164, 185
Pineal, 70, 112, 141, 161
Pingala, 103-6, 113, 137, 142, 164, 167
Pituitary, 70
Planck, M., 273
Plato, 3, 43, 166, 203, 276, 285
Plenum, 172, 208
Plotinus, 39, 43, 203, 274, 276-7
Plutarch, 285
Poetry, 40, 44, 105, 216, 231, 279
Poincaré, H., 265, 281
Point, 6, 25-8, 70, 75, 106-7, 116, 119,
  129, 135, 141, 143, 146, 150, 152,
  159, 175, 203, 222, 237, 260, 284
  and infinity, 111, 118, 234-6
  archetypal, 53, 76, 84, 174, 180, 236
  as meeting of manifest and unmani-
  fest, 15-6, 24, 27, 46, 53, 262-3
  contractions, 13-4, 17, 22, 46, 178
  of the turning world, still, 147, 149, 153
Pole Star, 143-7, 153
Popul Vuh, 104
Porch, 161-2
Porphyry, 286
Poseidon, 142
Positive, 52, 86-7, 104-5, 136-9, 144-6,
  181
  numbers, 208
Post, 156
Potatoes, 94, 190, 209
Power, 30, 62, 233
  archetypal, 52-4, 141, 262
  human, 90, 99, 187, 194, 199, 202,
  241, 248, 256
Prajapati, 58, 181
Prakriti, 177, 180
Prana, 14, 103-4, 152
Precognition, 221
Pribram, K., vii
Prince, 103, 133, 136, 150, 160, 166
Projection
  anthropomorphic, 54, 182, 188
  astral; *see* Astral travel
  psychological, 91, 93, 234
Projector, *see* Cosmic Projector

Prometheus, 167
Psyche, 23, 82, 84, 132, 166
Psychological development, stages of, 40, 42, 86, 94, 101, 128-9, 193-4, 201, 238, 294
Psychology, 7, 84, 138, 157, 191, 201, 235-6, 241, 248, 251, 280, 287, 294
    transpersonal, 237, 247
    integral, 295
Psychotics, 280
Puns, 270
Purusha, 177, 180
Pyramid, 141, 143, 145, 147
Pythagoras, 3, 39, 286

Quantization, 274
Quantum
    foam, 20
    mechanics, 73-4, 100, 210, 264, 272-3, 277, 280, 283, 293
Queen, 51, 102, 106

Ra, 156
Rabbits, 161
Rajneesh, B., 250
Raman, C. V., 283
Ramanujan, S., 232, 274
Rams, 159-60
Rainbow, 154, 189
Ramakrishna, 33, 37, 41, 179, 188, 299
Rampa, T. L., 158
Randomness, 45, 70, 73-4, 170-3, 179, 199
Rapunzel, 160
Rayleigh, L., 274
Razor, 146
R.E.M. periods, 7
Reason, 33, 47, 77, 79-80, 82, 97; see also Feeling
Reductionism, 186, 203, 213, 264, 283
Reincarnation, 89-90, 123-4, 279
Reiki, 245
Relativity, 5, 8-9, 217, 260
Repression, 82-6, 122-3, 127, 129, 199, 201, 229, 240, 246, 252, 290
Resonant frequency, 12-4, 17-8, 22, 24, 37, 60, 81, 123, 178, 206, 260-1, 263
Responsibility, 92, 100, 254-6, 288, 293, 296
Ribs, 180
Richet, C. R., 282

Ring
    golden; see Spiritual eye
    wedding, 116, 133, 138
Rivers, 58, 140, 193, 226
    of life energy, 104, 109, 116, 290, 298
Rinzai, 228
Rocks, clashing, 109-111, 160, 226
Rod, 109-10, 129, 141, 155
Rolfing, 84, 138
Rope trick, 179
Roshi, 228
Rosary, 141
Rumi, M., 168
Russell, B., 285
Russell, R., 244

Sah, 150
Salt, 33, 138
Samadhi, 104-5, 110-1, 114, 116, 118, 131, 133, 135, 145, 157, 158, 168-9, 221-2, 226, 229, 234, 241, 248, 250, 253, 269, 290, 296, 298-9
Samaya, 113
Samoa, 199
Sandalwood, 152
Sannella, L., 52, 232, 253
Sanskrit, 52, 103, 113, 134-5, 151, 160, 226, 260, 273, 278
Santa Claus, 149
Sap, 162
Saraswati, 104, 181
Sarfatti, J., 20
Satan, 297
Satori, 229
Scepter, 113, 153, 155
Schlegel, 284
Schopenhauer, 271, 284
Schrödinger, E., viii, 272
Schuon, F., 38, 59, 93, 289
Science fiction, 71
Scott, W., 279
Seamless, 32, 218
Seeds, 60, 189
Selden, G., 232
Self-awareness, 33, 71, 83, 175, 178, 216-8, 261, 299-301
Self-realization, 118, 216, 222-3, 245, 251
    Fellowship; see SRF
Semantics; see General semantics
Semen, 162

Sephiroth, 174, 180
  First, 15, 27, 175
Serpent, 102-3, 107, 113-5, 118, 135,
  146, 151, 156, 159, 290
  feathered, 145
Sexuality, 53, 94, 107, 124-6, 134-5,
  138, 144, 160-3, 165-6, 181, 191,
  198-9, 225, 242-5, 249, 296
  and aura, 80, 91, 154
  and emotionalism, 255-6
Shaft(ed), 92
Shakti, 52-4, 58, 102, 106, 134-7, 141-2,
  144, 146-7, 149-50, 152, 173-4
Shamanism, 97-8, 100, 142-3, 149,
  158-9, 198, 200
Shankara, 2, 175, 258-9, 265, 280, 298
Shava, 52
Sheep; see Rams
Ship; see Athena
Shiva, 52-4, 58, 102, 106, 112, 134-5,
  137, 141-4, 146-7, 149-51, 159,
  163, 173-4; see also Dance of
  Shiva
Silver, 198, 282
  cord, 119, 121
  cloth, 131
  spoons, 94
Singh, K., 115, 142, 149, 286
Sivananda, 34, 251
Sky, 28, 56, 62, 113-4, 143, 145-6, 151,
  153-4, 159, 165, 226, 261, 277,
  300
Sleep, 7, 13, 52, 59, 86, 120, 126, 128,
  221, 224-5, 231, 240, 253, 300
  and samadhi, 169, 226, 269
Smith, H., 15
Smoke hole, 149
Snake; see Serpent
Snow White, 102, 106, 108
Sociology, 44, 53, 182, 188, 190, 234,
  290
Socrates, 274, 285-6
Solomon's seal; see Star, of David
Solstice, 144, 149-50, 181
Soma, 109, 112-3, 148
Son, 50-1, 53-6, 106, 164, 188, 238,
Source, 3, 17, 28, 37, 57, 59, 72, 174,
  179, 184, 206, 253, 262
Spectrum, 12, 31-2, 41, 154, 271
Speech, 55, 58, 60-1, 121, 183, 186,
  262, 301
Sphinx, 93, 109, 140

Spikes, 14, 21, 24, 66, 219, 258; see
  also Impulses
Spinoza, 284
Spirit in the Bottle, The, 131
Spiritual eye, 49, 56, 62, 92, 103-6, 109,
  112, 114-6, 133, 143, 146, 152-6,
  163, 175, 223, 300; see also Star,
  five-pointed
SRF, 243-4
Staff, 103, 107, 149-50, 155, 161, 226,
  290
Star
  five-pointed, 49, 146, 150, 169, 175
  of David, 93, 133, 141, 162
  of the East; see Star, five-pointed;
    see Spiritual eye
  Pole; see Pole Star
  revolving, 153
Star-Self, 83, 92, 117, 119, 122, 143,
  172-3, 175, 178-9, 220, 228
Steeple, 134, 142
Steinmetz, C., 282
Stick, 103, 105-6, 160
  in Zen, 228
Stonehenge, 164
Stones
  in process of manifestation, 10-1,
    19-20
  as clitoris, 164
Subconscious, 21, 63, 82, 93-4, 100-1,
  121-3, 127-9, 185, 192, 213, 229,
  233, 252, 255
Superconscious, 101, 122-3, 129, 233
Suffering, 33, 96, 125, 191, 194-5, 249,
  292, 297
Sufis, 3
Sun, 20, 111, 153-4, 164-5, 224-5, 238,
  275-8, 287-8, 301
  as spiritual symbol, 98, 105-9, 112,
    114-5, 117, 129, 135-6, 141, 143-7,
    149-52, 155-7, 159, 167, 179, 181,
    299; see also Lions; see also Rams;
    see also Sundoor
Sundoor, 107, 110-2, 115, 148, 156
Superstition, 63, 93, 138, 141, 274
Superstring theory, 232
Sushumna, 103-4, 106-7, 109-13, 116,
  129, 132, 135, 141-3, 145-6, 148,
  150-1, 153-9, 162, 164, 167, 185,
  222
Sutphen, D., 248
Suzuki, D. T., 27, 234, 284

Swan, 150
Swedenborg, I., 276, 279, 285
Sword, 113, 140, 146
Synapses, 232
Synchronicity, 120, 272

Tagore, R., 259, 271-2
Ta-shih, Y., 174
Talbot, M., 20, 94, 166
Tantra, 26, 52, 106, 112-3, 138, 222, 227, 300
Tao, 16, 31, 57, 91, 105, 113, 136-7, 139-40, 144, 167-8, 179-81, 200, 237, 257, 272, 298
Taylor, A., 110
Temple, 33, 94, 142-3, 145, 156, 161-2
Tennyson, A., 275
Tesla, 233, 273-4
Testicles, 160-1
Tetrahedron, 185
Thales, 286
Theosophy, 274, 276
Thinking, 79, 83, 186-90, 192, 194-6, 202, 207-9, 213, 219, 226, 229-30, 254, 256, 289
  and self-awareness, 71
  non-linear, 21, 119
Third eye; see Spiritual eye
Thompson, J. J., 274
Thoreau, H. D., 266, 275, 279
Thought bubbles; see Bubbles of thought
Threads, 113, 115, 141, 148, 154-5, 159-60, 179
Throne, 117, 132, 143, 153
Thunder, 113, 135, 143, 154, 156, 189 -bird, 143
Thyrsus, 112, 161
Time, 5-9, 11, 13-5, 17, 20, 22-4, 26, 34, 38-9, 46, 54, 56, 60, 124-5, 173, 176, 179, 183, 209, 214, 216-25, 234, 237-8, 252, 257, 259-60, 262, 280, 299
Tiresias, 105, 135
Tirtha, B. K., 265, 280, 289
Tolstoy, A. K., 95
Toynbee, A., 280
Traherne, T., 279
Tramp souls, 238
Trance, 104, 116, 125, 158, 168, 220, 225, 234, 269, 276, 285, 299

Transmigration, 286
Tree, 102-3, 105-8, 111, 113-5, 117-8, 129, 131-3, 141-3, 145-52, 156, 158-9, 162, 167-9, 179, 290
Triangle, 93, 141-2, 144
Trident, 142
Trumpet, 114, 175
Trunk, 103, 169, 290
Tsunami, 215
Tunnel, 115-6
Turiya, 59
Turret, 134, 160

Umbilical, 121, 151
Ultraviolet, 12, 31
Unconscious, 82, 85, 120-1, 123, 127-9, 167, 221, 229, 252
  collective, 167
Underworld, 105, 159, 161, 166-7
Universal Breathing, 14-5, 25, 38, 72, 258
Universal Field of Existence, 168, 210
Universal Mind, 81, 129, 273
Upanishads, 2, 27, 57, 59, 75, 102, 112-3, 156, 259, 266, 272, 278-9, 284
Uroboros, 114
Uterus, 162

Vacuum, 19, 74, 92, 208
Vagina, 161, 163
Vajra, 104-5, 109, 113, 157-8
Valentine's heart, 151
Van Gogh, V., 281
Vedas, 2, 58, 110, 114, 151, 181, 273, 283-4, 287, 301
Vegetarianism, 191, 228, 274
Veil(s), 98, 161-2
  of maya, 30, 133, 155
  seven, 252
Vimalananda, 227
Vipassana, 229, 237
Virgin, 105, 135-6
  Mary, 50-1; see also Holy Ghost
  matter, 238
  princess, 133
Visions, 39, 53, 98, 117, 218, 234, 249, 268, 275, 281, 297, 300
Visualization, 21-2, 78, 118, 122-3, 148, 216, 219, 223, 231, 251
Vivekananda, 243

Void, 16, 20, 27, 33, 54, 56, 60, 116, 119, 156, 164, 172, 175, 177-8, 181, 208, 259, 278; *see also* Clear Light (of the Void)
Volsung, King, 143
Vortices, 83, 93, 102, 112, 155
Vulcan, 106

Wallace, A. R., 281
Wallace, W., 279
Wand, 112, 129
Water
  as astral element, 112
  as metaphor for life energy, 109
  of Immortality, 153
  of Life, 109, 112, 115, 121
Waterfall, 113, 116
Wedding, 126, 133, 138, 149, 162; *see also* Marriage
Weekdays, 46-7, 154
Weinman, R., 91, 108, 271
Well, 115, 136
Wheels; *see* Chakras
Wheeler, J., 20
White
  Head, 27, 175; *see also* Sephiroth
  light, 4, 11-3, 17-8, 60, 83, 117, 141, 143, 146, 154, 171, 173, 175, 177, 220, 257, 299-300; *see also* Chaos noise, 171
White, J., 171, 176, 286
Whitman, W., 231, 276, 279
Wholeness, 38-9, 100, 191, 208, 273
Wholistic paradigm, 192
Wick, 132
Wilber, K., 126, 169, 193, 243, 247, 250-1
Wilde, O., 279
Wind, 10-1, 19, 30, 52, 58, 110-1, 167
Wine, 105-6, 124, 161, 228
Wings, 103, 109-10, 113, 145-6, 151, 155-6, 160
Witchcraft, 51, 158
Witness(ing), 22, 26, 31, 61, 83, 85, 119, 141, 164, 169, 176-9, 202, 216-8, 222, 224, 227, 240-2, 250-1, 295-6, 299-300
Wizard of Oz, The, 250, 281
Wolfe, W. T., 70, 134, 232-4, 270
Womb, 50-1, 54, 84, 135, 161-3, 165, 181

Wonton, 181
Woodroffe, J., 26, 53, 162
Wool, 159-60
Word, 235, 238
  as concept, 128, 183
  of God (Om), 9, 55, 57-9, 62, 73, 214, 234, 262, 290; *see also* Name, of God
Wordsworth, W., 277
World Axis; *see* Axis, World
Wright, F. L., 281

X-ray, 12, 31, 41
  vision, 106, 112

Yakut, 159
Yeats, W. B., 278-9
Yin/yang, 113, 136-40, 144-5, 257, 272
Yoga, 23, 49-50, 84, 97, 107, 112-4, 117, 119, 124-5, 133, 151-2, 177, 220, 222, 237-8, 240, 244-5, 259, 280, 295, 298, 300; see also *Tantra*
Yogananda, P., 8, 17, 26, 39, 50, 153, 158, 204, 227-8, 235, 241, 243-4, 249, 283, 298
Yongden, L., 75
Yoni, 135
Yule, 150

Zen, 27, 174, 227-9, 237, 242, 284, 293, 295, 299
Zeus, 106, 113, 143, 145, 159,
Ziggurat, 143, 145, 147, 153
Zimmer, H., 58, 61
Zohar, 107
Zunis, 104

ABOUT THE AUTHOR

GEOFFREY D. FALK has studied Electrical Engineering and Physics at the University of Manitoba, and done research into the design of computer microchips under the auspices of the Natural Sciences and Engineering Council of Canada. He currently divides his time between computer programming and music composition.

Printed in the United States
26083LVS00005B/43-48

9 781577 331315